GRIMMY™: KING OF THE HEAP!

BY MIKE PETERS

TOR

A TOM DOHERTY ASSOCIATES BOOK
NEW YORK

GRIMMY: KING OF THE HEAP!

A Tor Book
Published by Tom Doherty Associates, Inc.
175 Fifth Avenue
New York, NY 10010

Tor Books on the World Wide Web:
http://www.tor.com

Tor® is a registered trademark of Tom Doherty Associates, Inc.

Library of Congress Cataloging-in-Publication Data

Peters, Mike.
[Mother Goose & Grimm. Selections]
Grimmy : king of the heap / by Mike Peters.
p.   cm.
"A Tom Doherty Associates book."
An all new collection of the best "Grimmy" cartoons.
ISBN 0-312-86069-2
I. Title.
PN6728.M67P4744   1997
741.5'973—dc20   96-44783
                                        CIP

First Edition: February 1997

Printed in the United States of America

0 9 8 7 6 5 4 3

to David Williams . . . a dog's best friend

YUCK, GRIMM... YOU SMELL LIKE GARBAGE!
IT'S MY NEW COLOGNE... "EVENING IN THE TRASH"

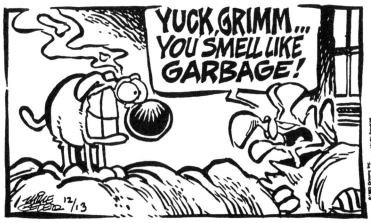

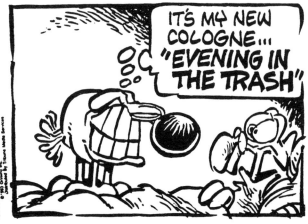

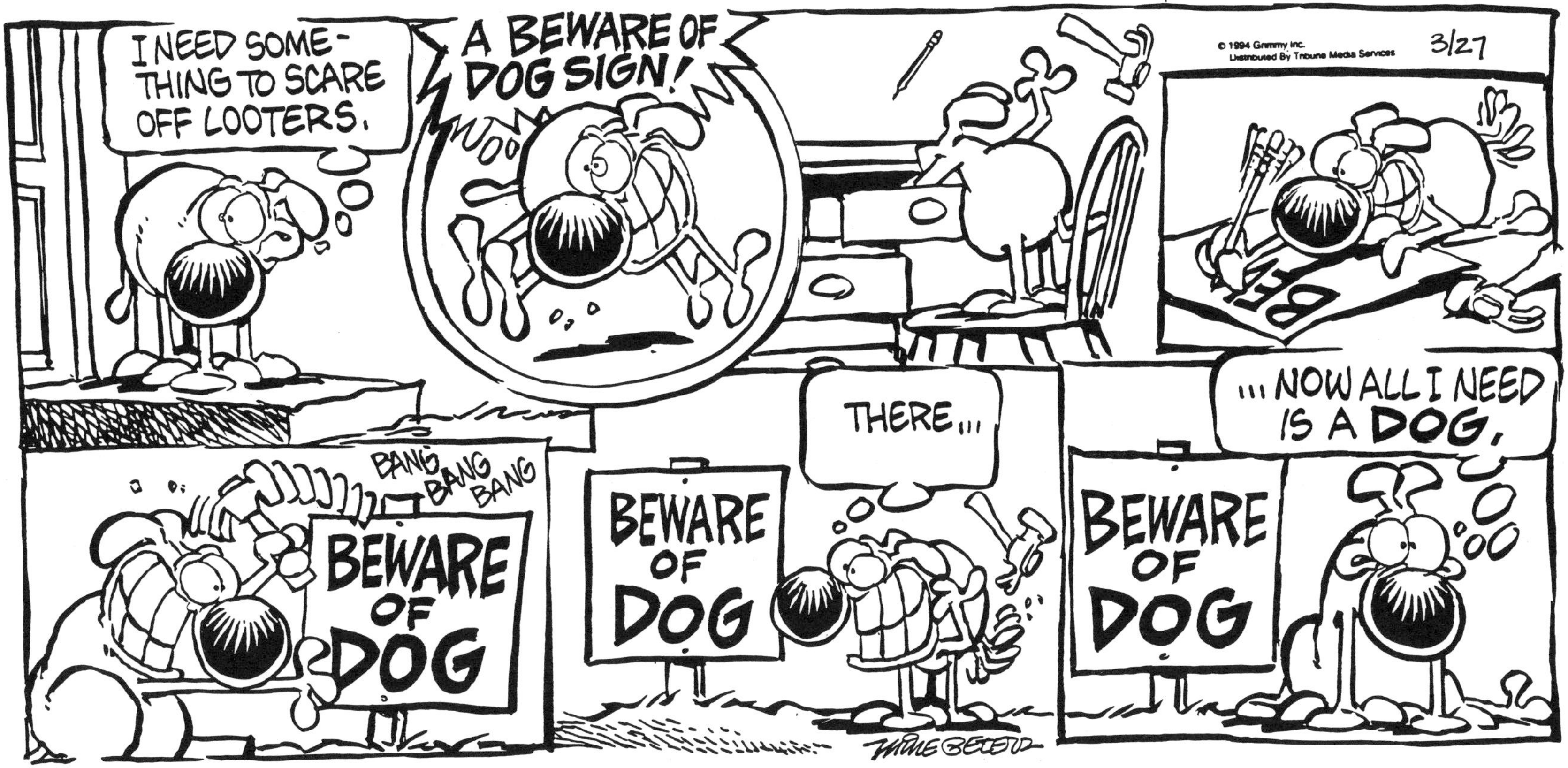

I NEED SOME-THING TO SCARE OFF LOOTERS.
A BEWARE OF DOG SIGN!
© 1994 Grimmy Inc.
Distributed By Tribune Media Services
3/27
BANG BANG BANG
BEWARE OF DOG
BEWARE OF DOG
THERE...
... NOW ALL I NEED IS A DOG.
BEWARE OF DOG

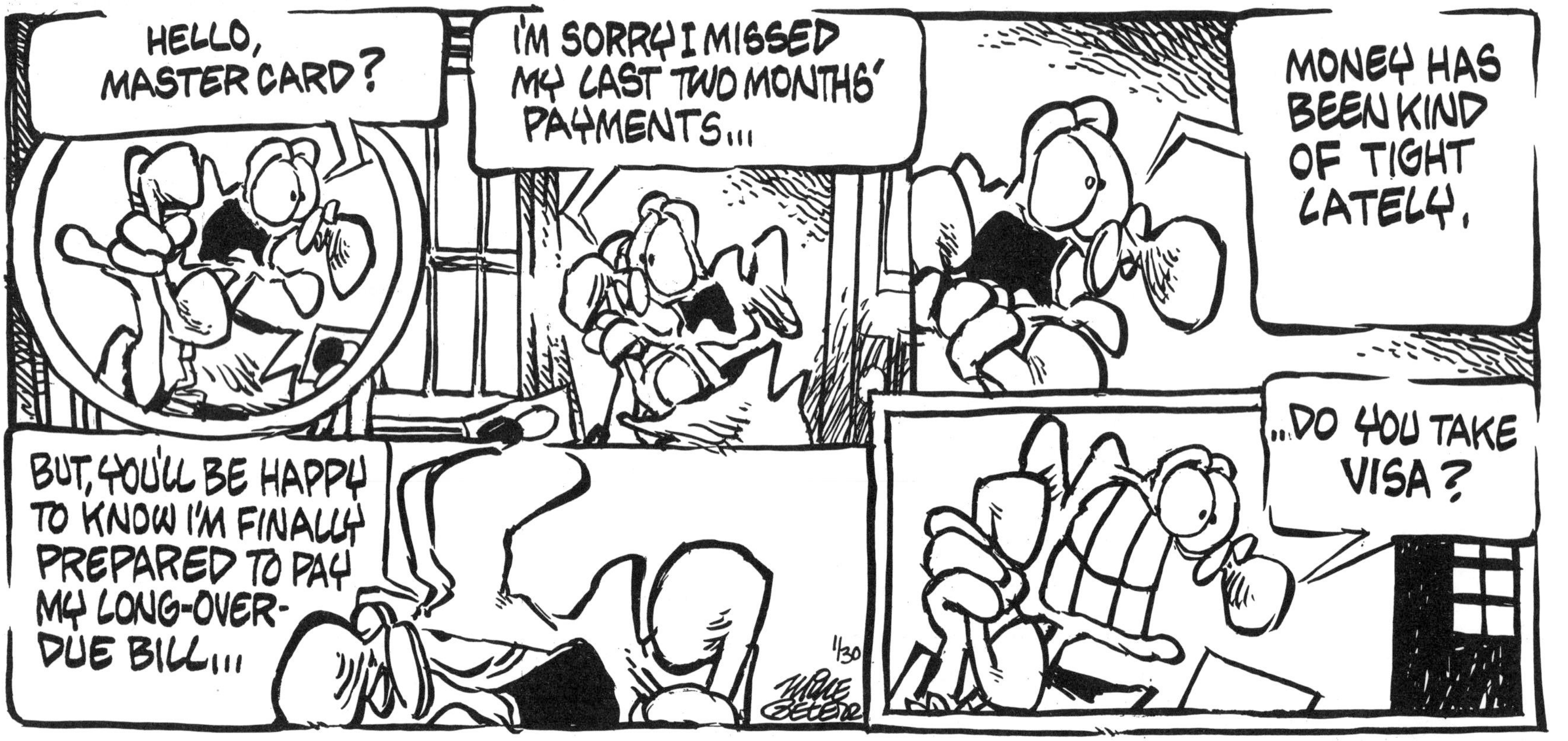
HELLO, MASTER CARD?
I'M SORRY I MISSED MY LAST TWO MONTHS' PAYMENTS...
MONEY HAS BEEN KIND OF TIGHT LATELY.
BUT, YOU'LL BE HAPPY TO KNOW I'M FINALLY PREPARED TO PAY MY LONG-OVER-DUE BILL...
...DO YOU TAKE VISA?
1/30

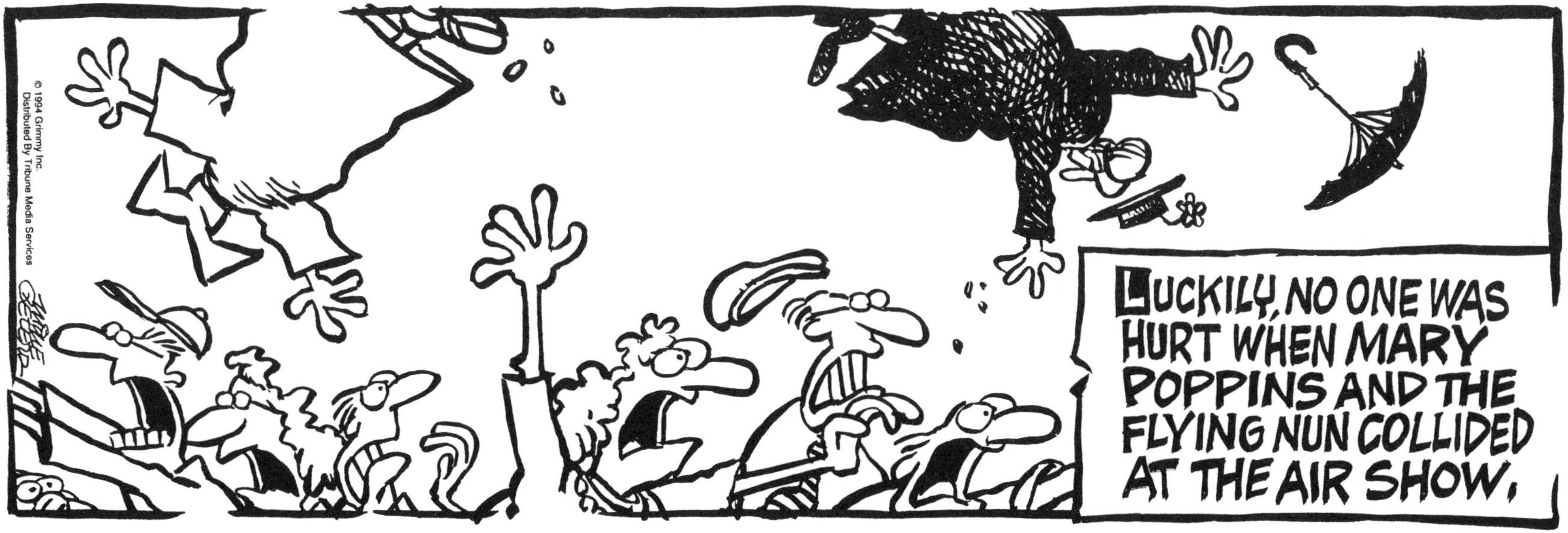
© 1994 Grimmy Inc. Distributed By Tribune Media Services
LUCKILY, NO ONE WAS HURT WHEN MARY POPPINS AND THE FLYING NUN COLLIDED AT THE AIR SHOW.

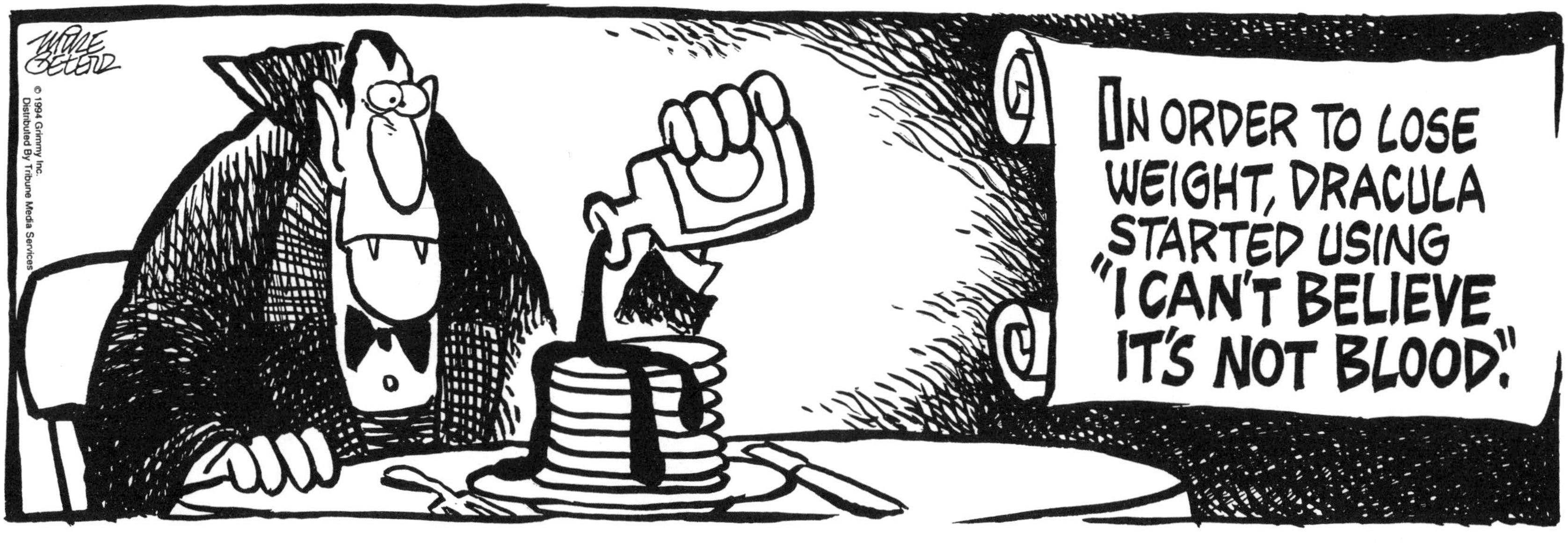
© 1994 Grimmy Inc. Distributed By Tribune Media Services
IN ORDER TO LOSE WEIGHT, DRACULA STARTED USING "I CAN'T BELIEVE IT'S NOT BLOOD."

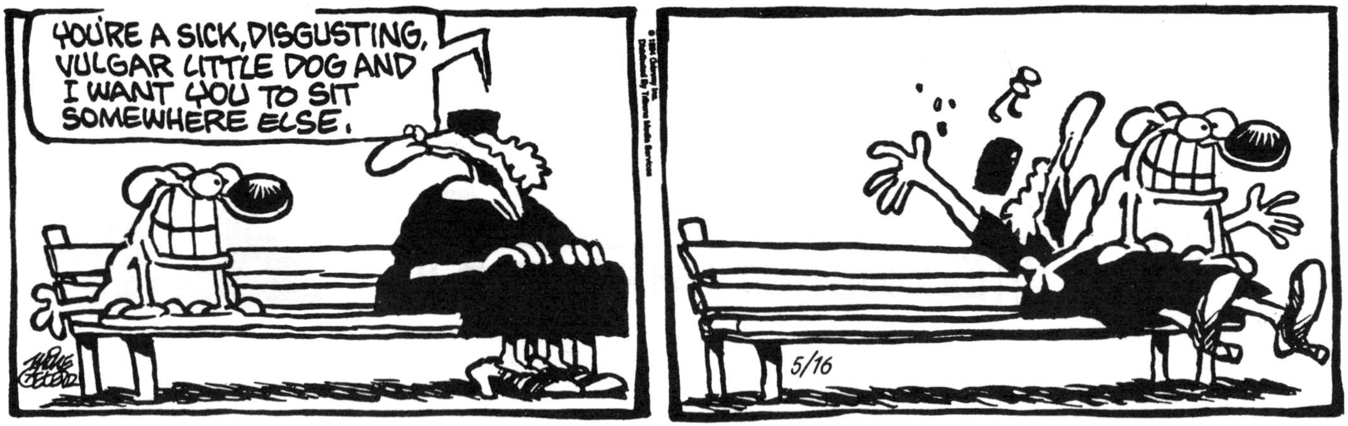
YOU'RE A SICK, DISGUSTING, VULGAR LITTLE DOG AND I WANT YOU TO SIT SOMEWHERE ELSE.
© 1994 Grimmy Inc. Distributed By Tribune Media Services
5/16

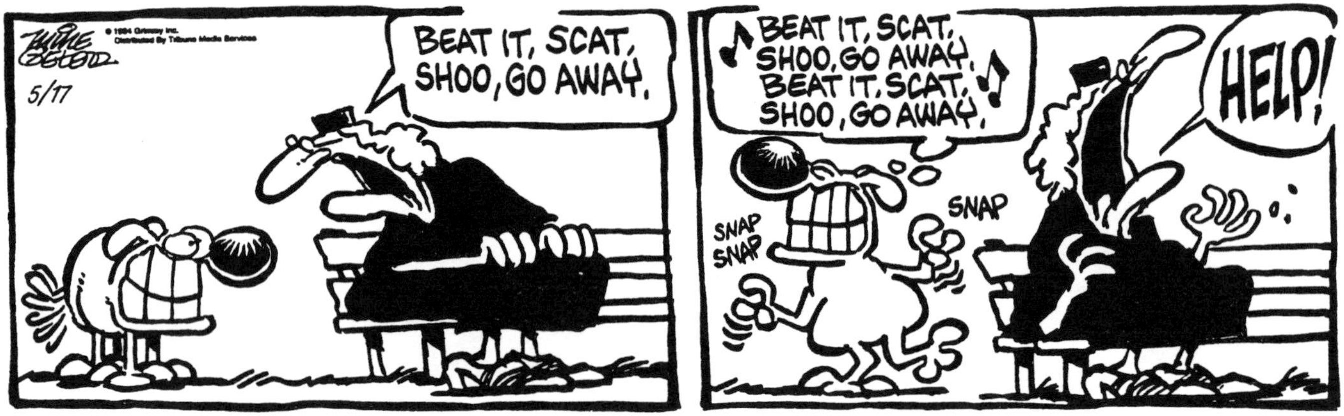
© 1994 Grimmy Inc. Distributed By Tribune Media Services
5/17
BEAT IT, SCAT, SHOO, GO AWAY.
BEAT IT, SCAT, SHOO, GO AWAY. BEAT IT, SCAT, SHOO, GO AWAY.
SNAP SNAP
SNAP
HELP!

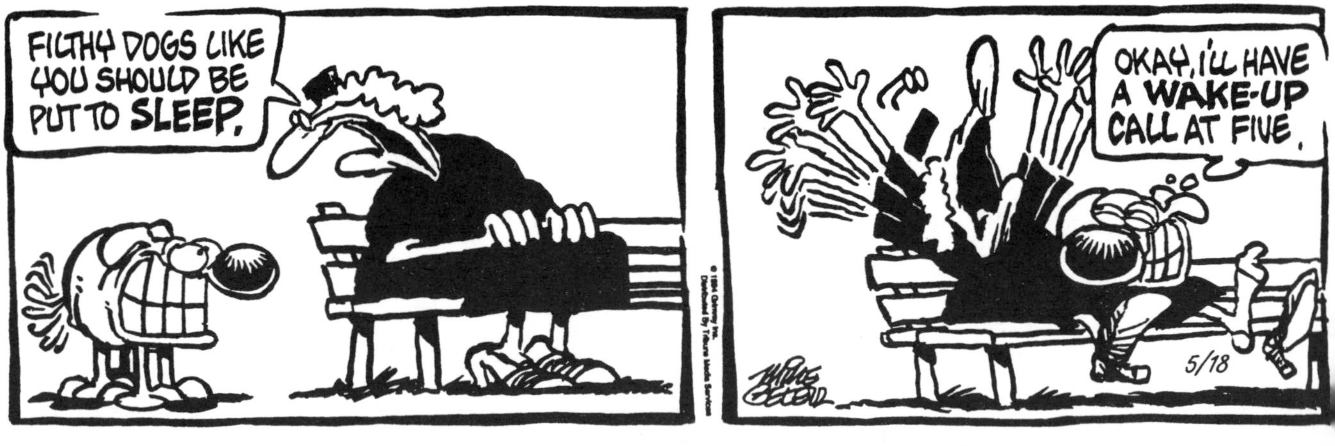
FILTHY DOGS LIKE YOU SHOULD BE PUT TO **SLEEP**.
© 1994 Grimmy Inc. Distributed By Tribune Media Services
OKAY, I'LL HAVE A **WAKE-UP** CALL AT FIVE.
5/18

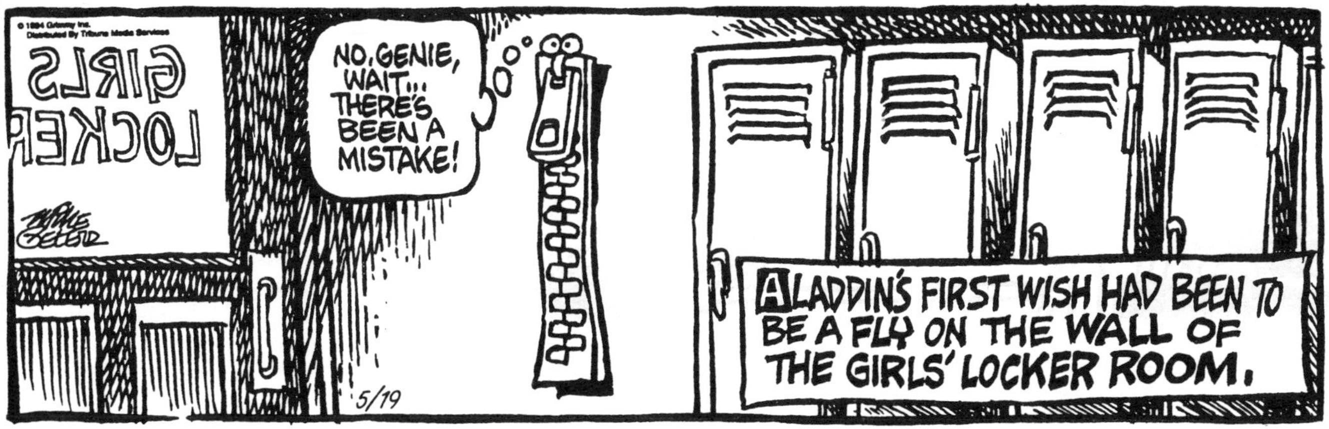
© 1994 Grimmy Inc.
Distributed By Tribune Media Services
GIRLS LOCKER
NO, GENIE, WAIT... THERE'S BEEN A MISTAKE!
5/19
ALADDIN'S FIRST WISH HAD BEEN TO BE A FLY ON THE WALL OF THE GIRLS' LOCKER ROOM.

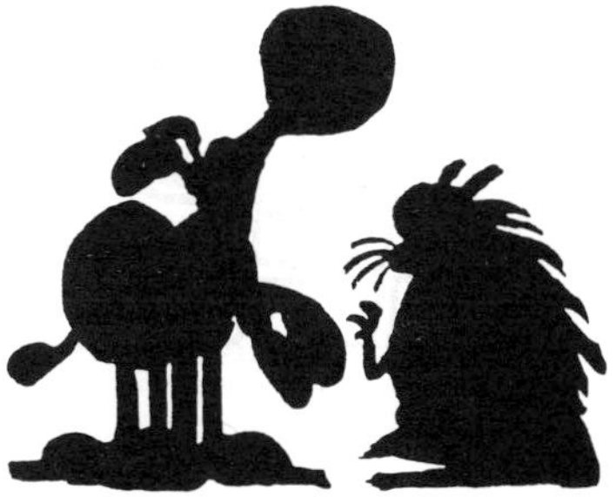

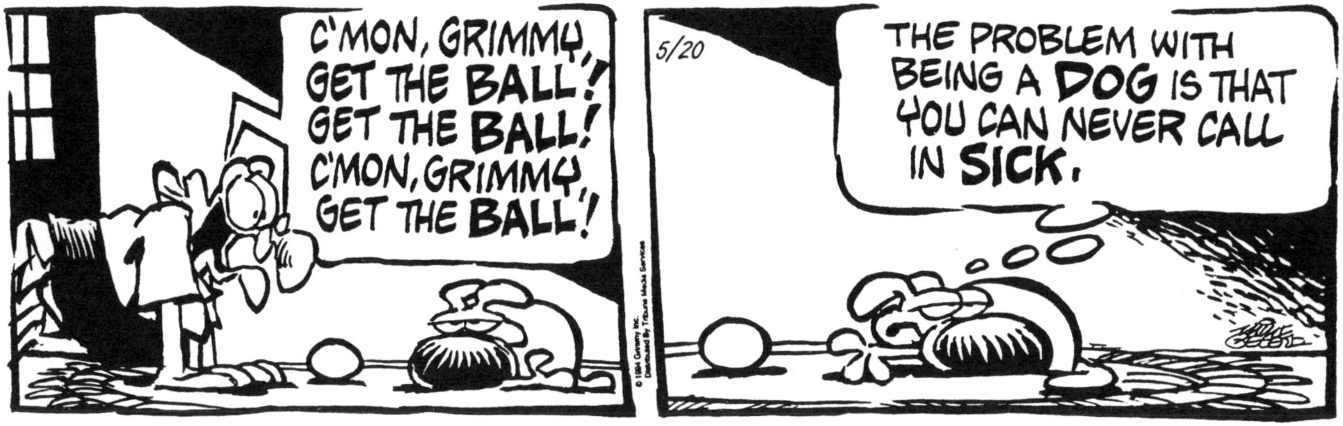
C'MON, GRIMMY, GET THE BALL! GET THE BALL! C'MON, GRIMMY, GET THE BALL!
5/20
THE PROBLEM WITH BEING A DOG IS THAT YOU CAN NEVER CALL IN SICK.

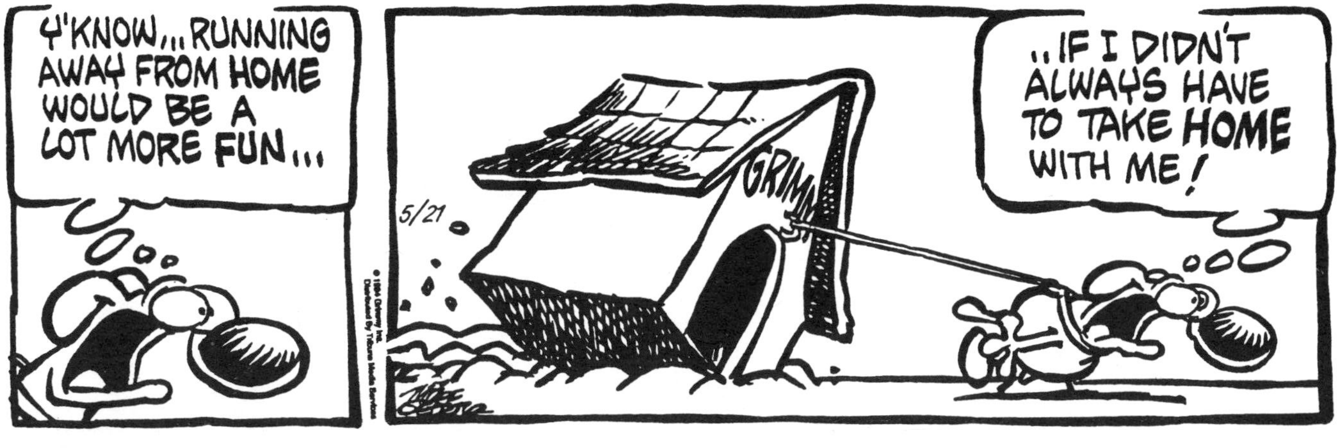
Y'KNOW... RUNNING AWAY FROM HOME WOULD BE A LOT MORE FUN...
5/21
GRIM
..IF I DIDN'T ALWAYS HAVE TO TAKE HOME WITH ME!

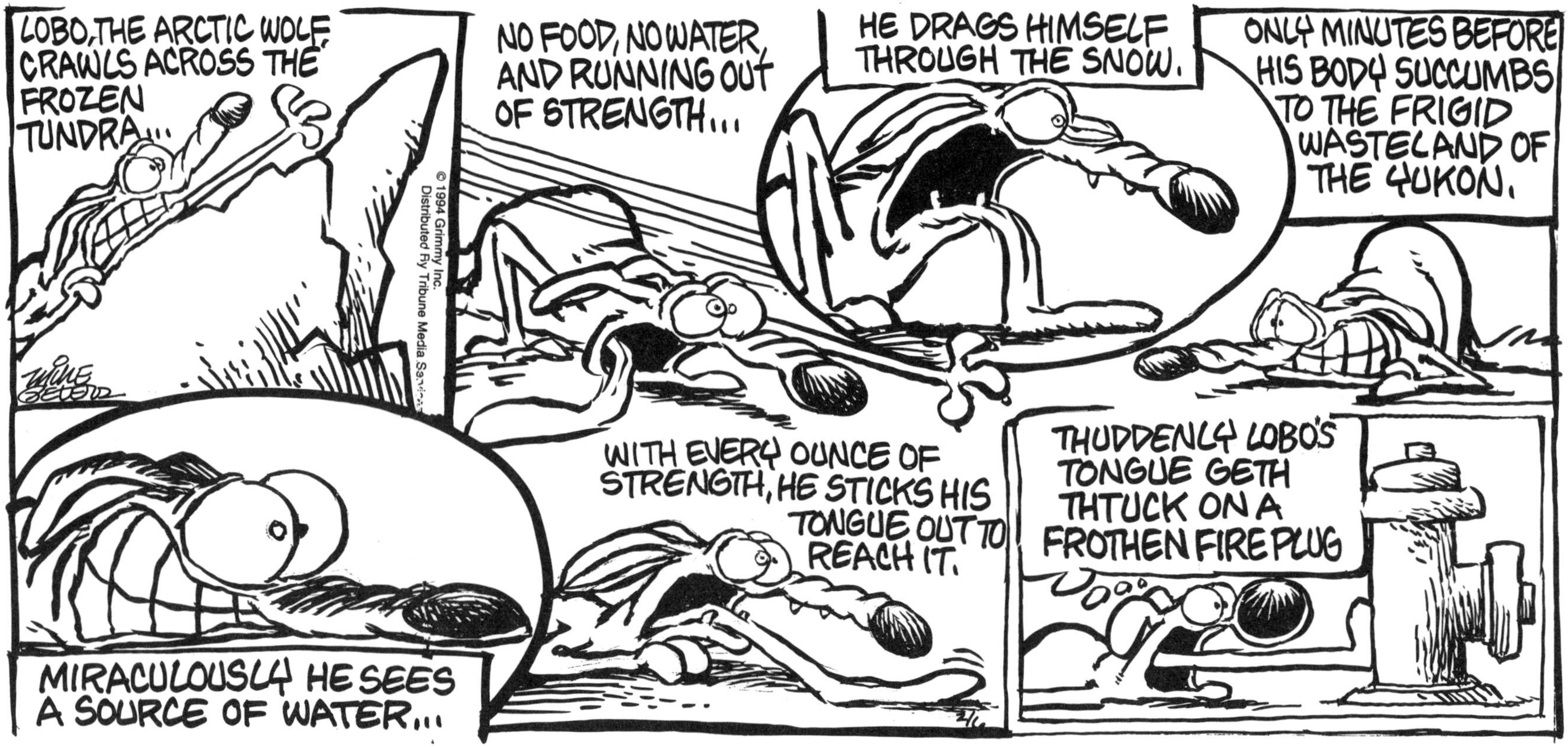
LOBO, THE ARCTIC WOLF, CRAWLS ACROSS THE FROZEN TUNDRA...
© 1994 Grimmy Inc. Distributed by Tribune Media Services
NO FOOD, NO WATER, AND RUNNING OUT OF STRENGTH...
HE DRAGS HIMSELF THROUGH THE SNOW.
ONLY MINUTES BEFORE HIS BODY SUCCUMBS TO THE FRIGID WASTELAND OF THE YUKON.
MIRACULOUSLY HE SEES A SOURCE OF WATER...
WITH EVERY OUNCE OF STRENGTH, HE STICKS HIS TONGUE OUT TO REACH IT.
THUDDENLY LOBO'S TONGUE GETH THTUCK ON A FROTHEN FIRE PLUG

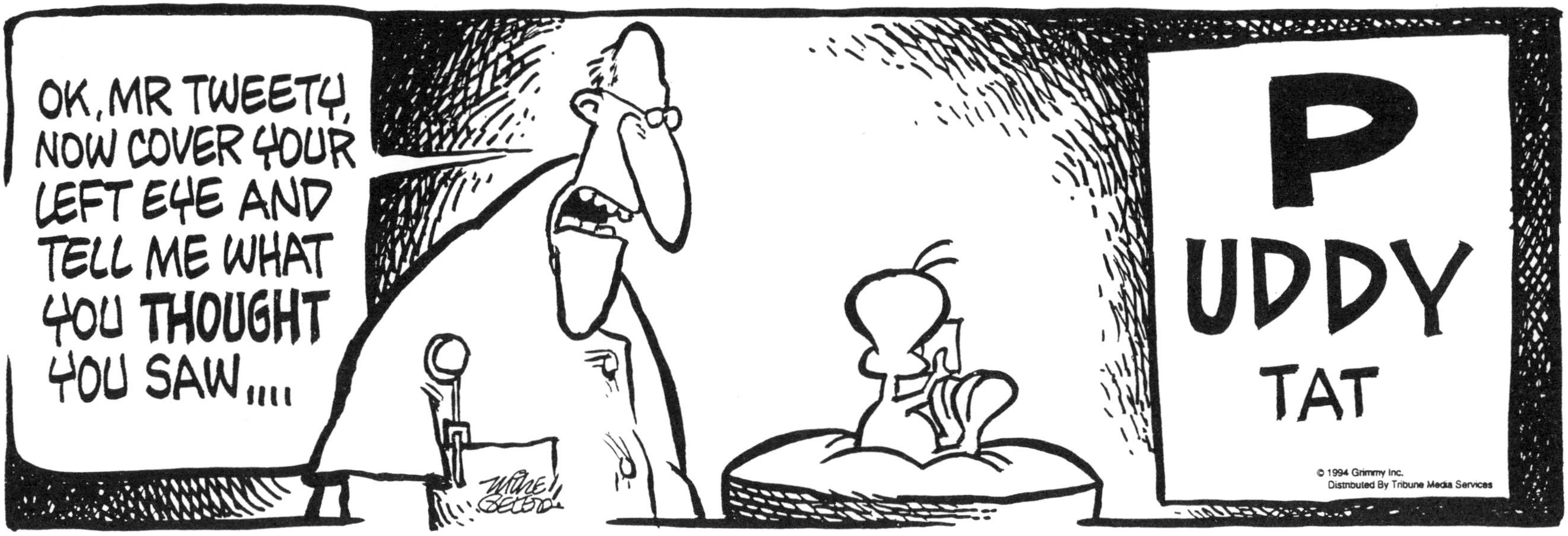
OK, MR TWEETY, NOW COVER YOUR LEFT EYE AND TELL ME WHAT YOU THOUGHT YOU SAW....
P
UDDY
TAT
© 1994 Grimmy Inc.
Distributed By Tribune Media Services

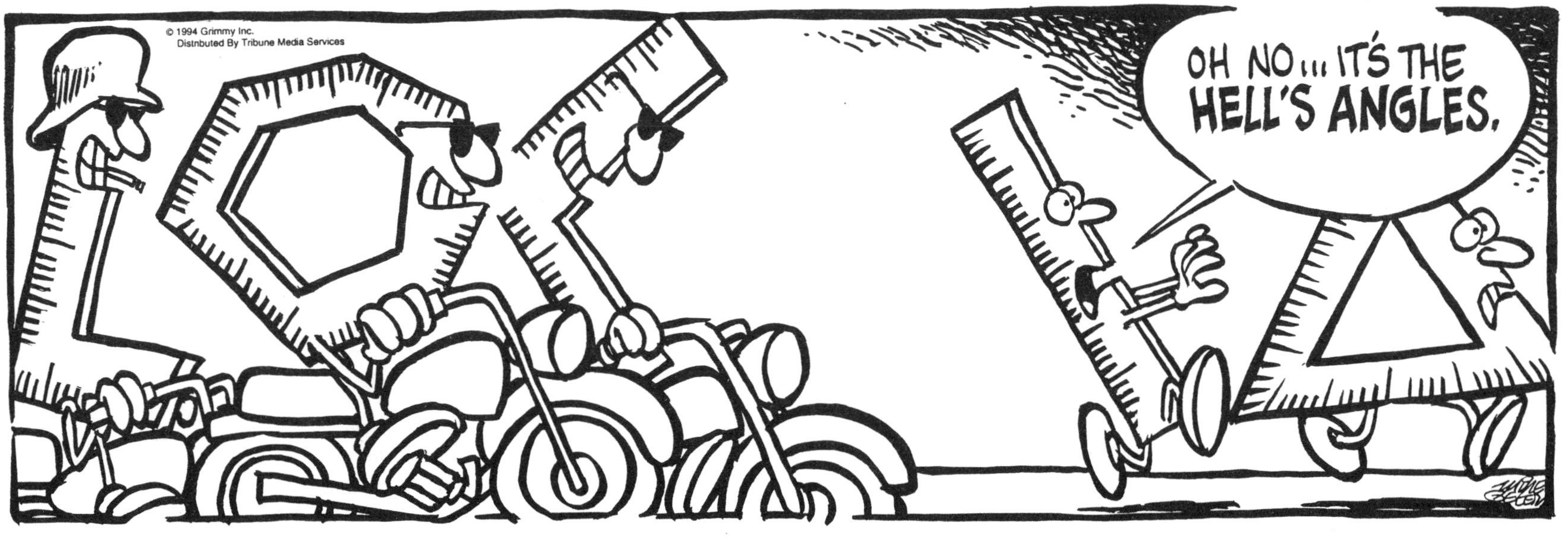
© 1994 Grimmy Inc.
Distributed By Tribune Media Services
OH NO... IT'S THE HELL'S ANGLES.

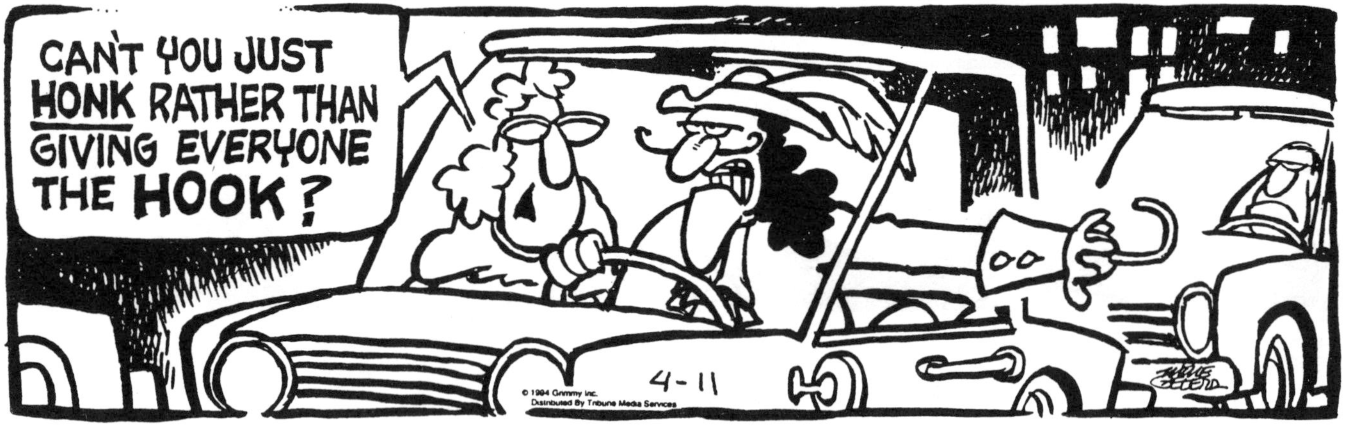
CAN'T YOU JUST HONK RATHER THAN GIVING EVERYONE THE HOOK?
4-11
© 1994 Grimmy Inc.
Distributed By Tribune Media Services

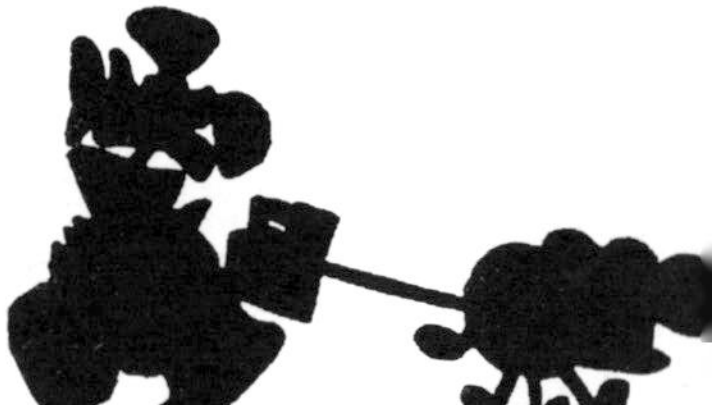

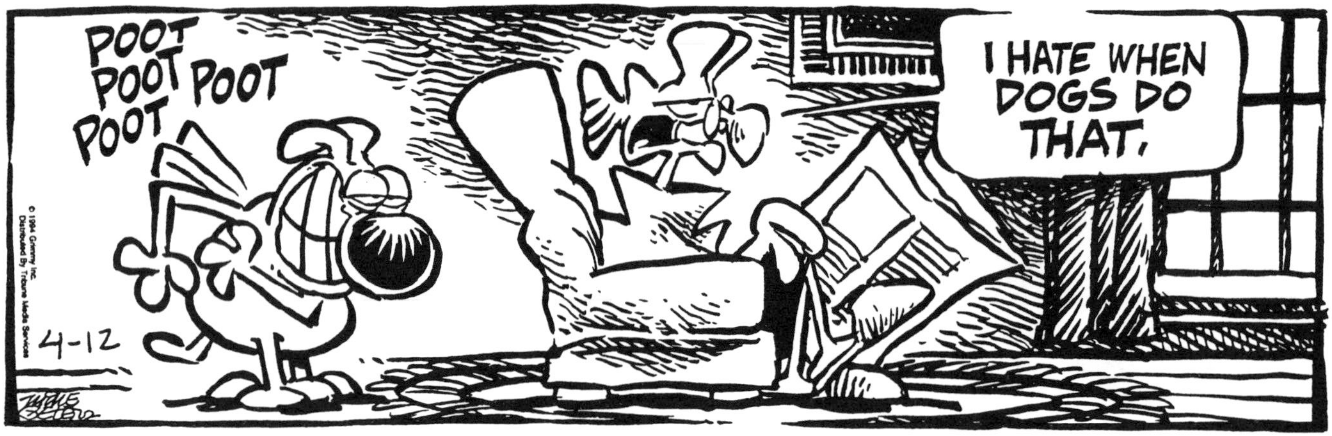
POOT POOT POOT POOT
I HATE WHEN DOGS DO THAT.
4-12
© 1994 Grimmy Inc.
Distributed By Tribune Media Services

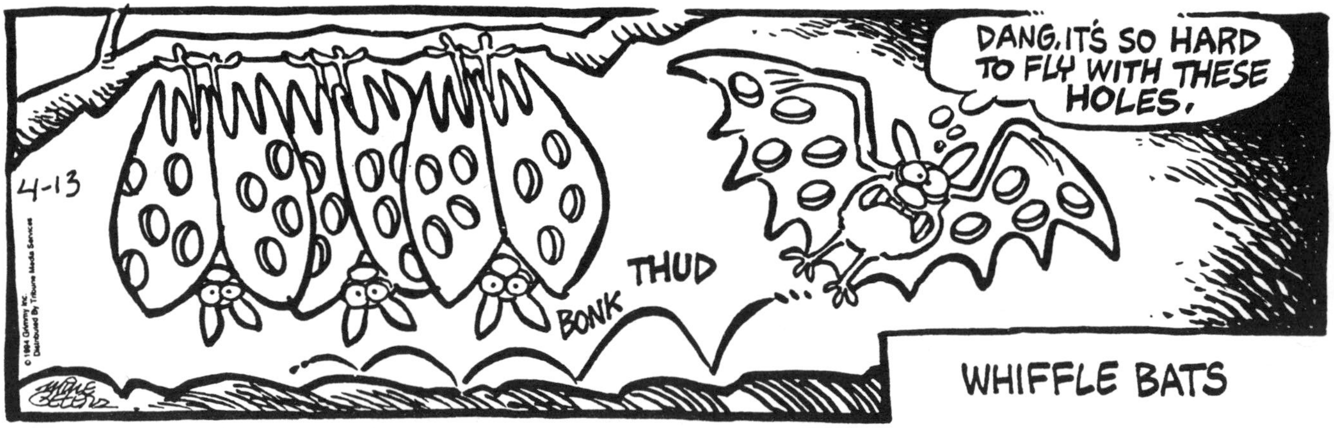
DANG, IT'S SO HARD TO FLY WITH THESE HOLES.
4-13
BONK
THUD
© 1994 Grimmy Inc.
Distributed By Tribune Media Services

WHIFFLE BATS

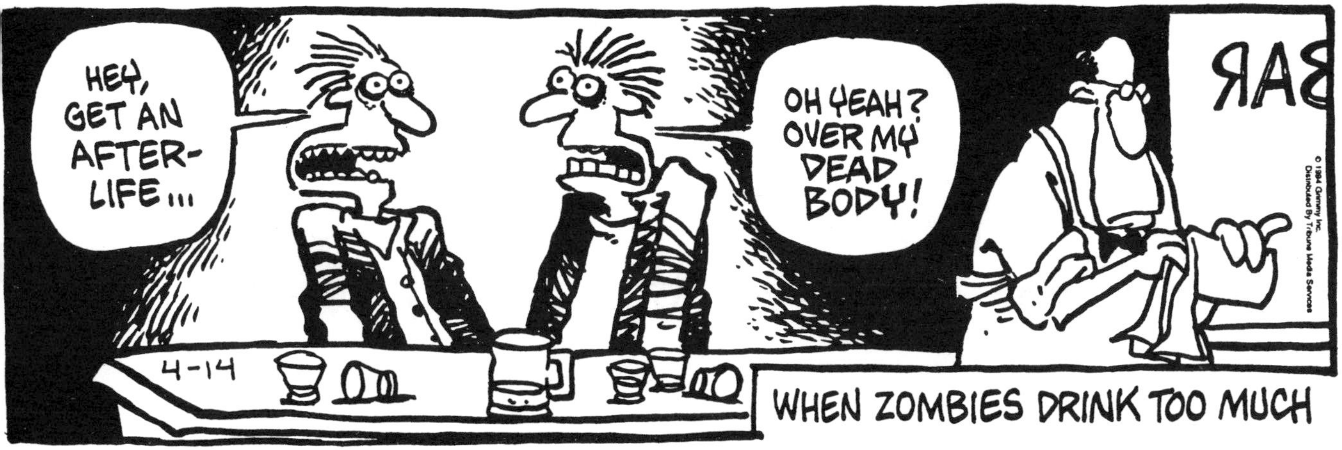
HEY, GET AN AFTER-LIFE...
OH YEAH? OVER MY DEAD BODY!
BAR
© 1994 Grimmy Inc. Distributed By Tribune Media Services
4-14
WHEN ZOMBIES DRINK TOO MUCH

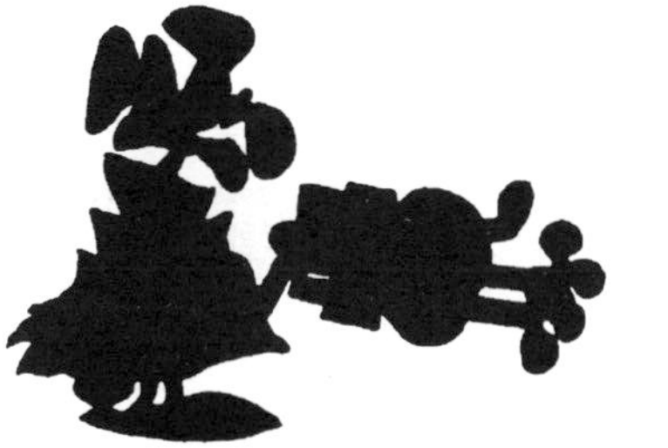

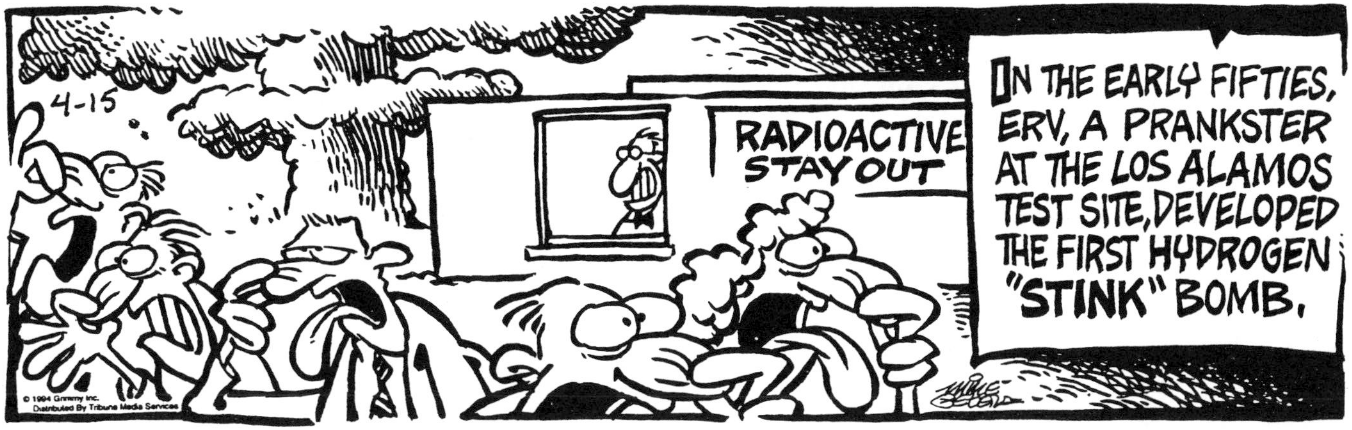
4-15
RADIOACTIVE STAY OUT
IN THE EARLY FIFTIES, ERV, A PRANKSTER AT THE LOS ALAMOS TEST SITE, DEVELOPED THE FIRST HYDROGEN "STINK" BOMB.
© 1994 Grimmy Inc. Distributed By Tribune Media Services

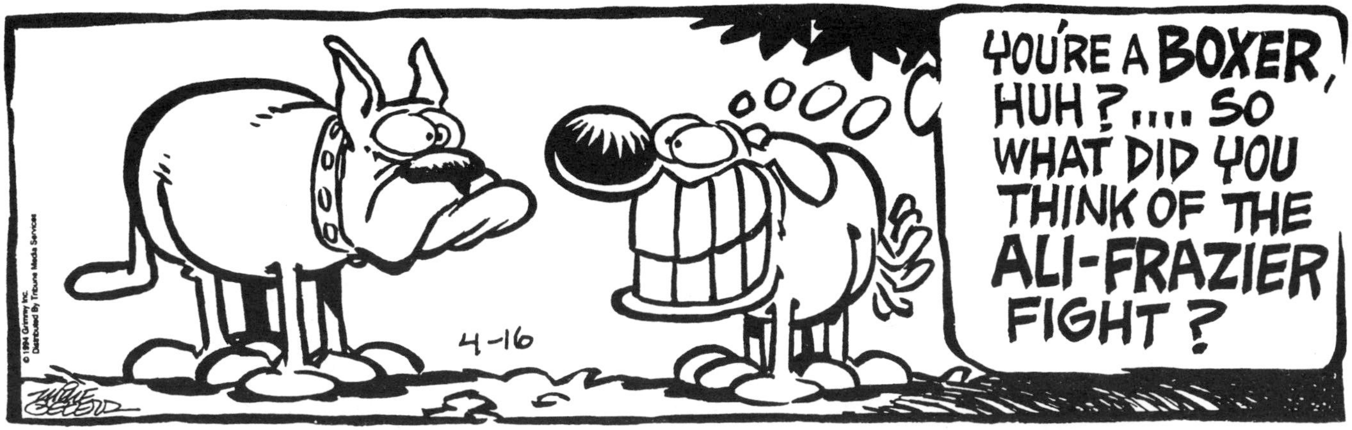
YOU'RE A BOXER, HUH?.... SO WHAT DID YOU THINK OF THE ALI-FRAZIER FIGHT?
4-16
© 1994 Grimmy Inc. Distributed By Tribune Media Services

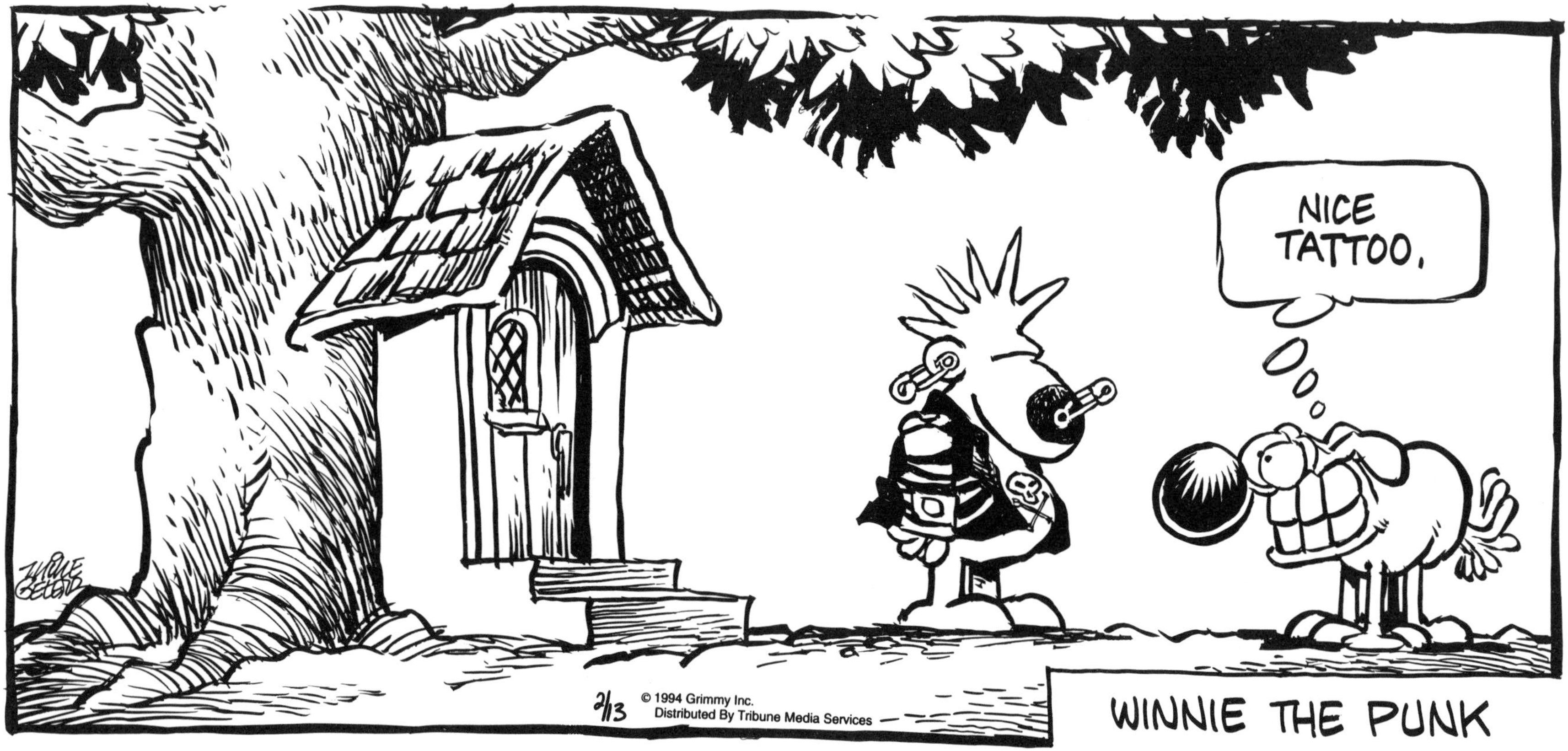
NICE TATTOO.
© 1994 Grimmy Inc.
Distributed By Tribune Media Services
2/13

WINNIE THE PUNK

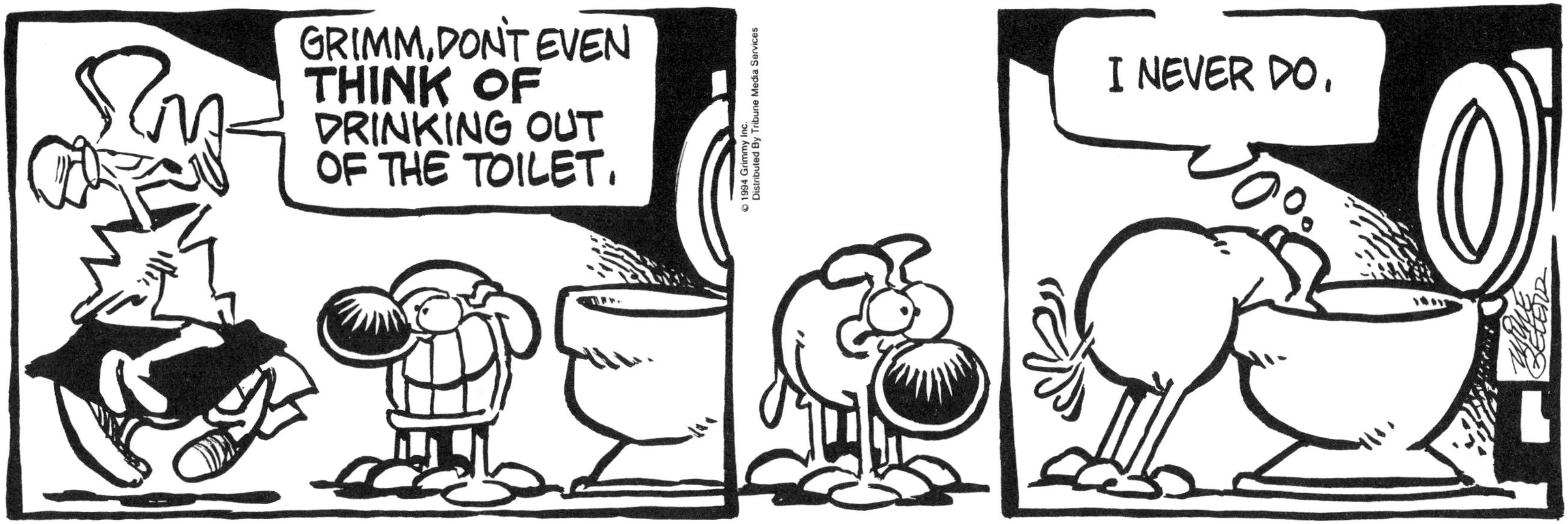
GRIMM, DON'T EVEN **THINK OF** DRINKING OUT OF THE TOILET.
© 1994 Grimmy Inc. Distributed By Tribune Media Services
I NEVER DO.

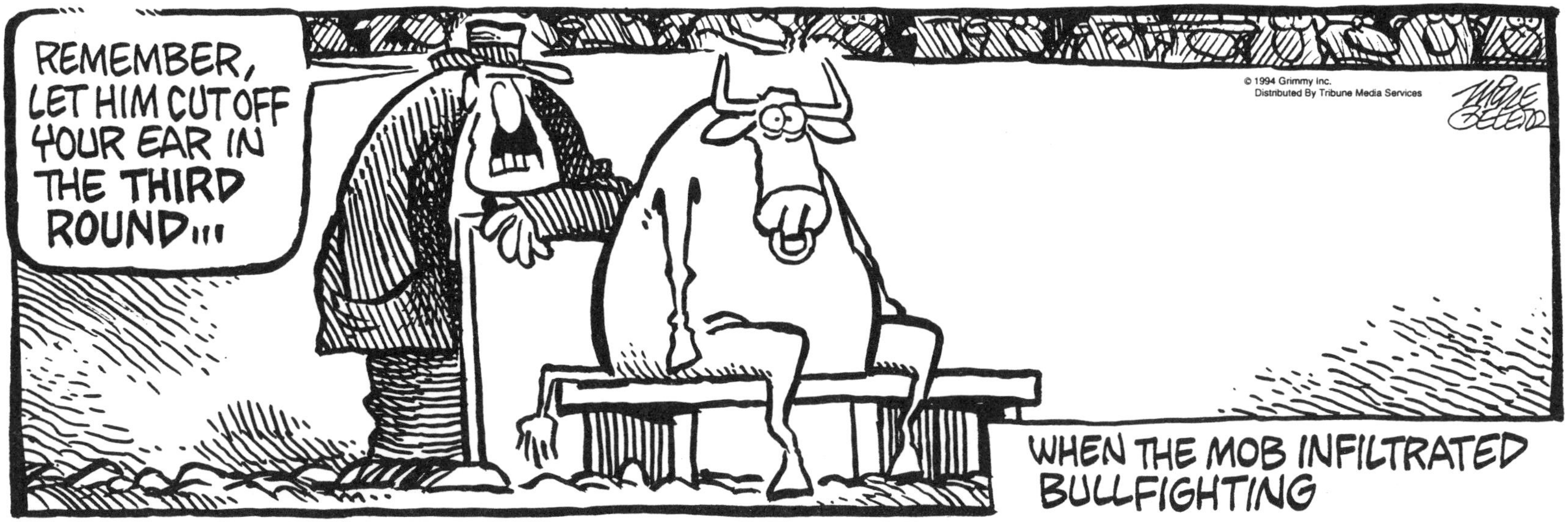
REMEMBER, LET HIM CUT OFF YOUR EAR IN THE **THIRD ROUND**...
© 1994 Grimmy Inc. Distributed By Tribune Media Services

WHEN THE MOB INFILTRATED BULLFIGHTING

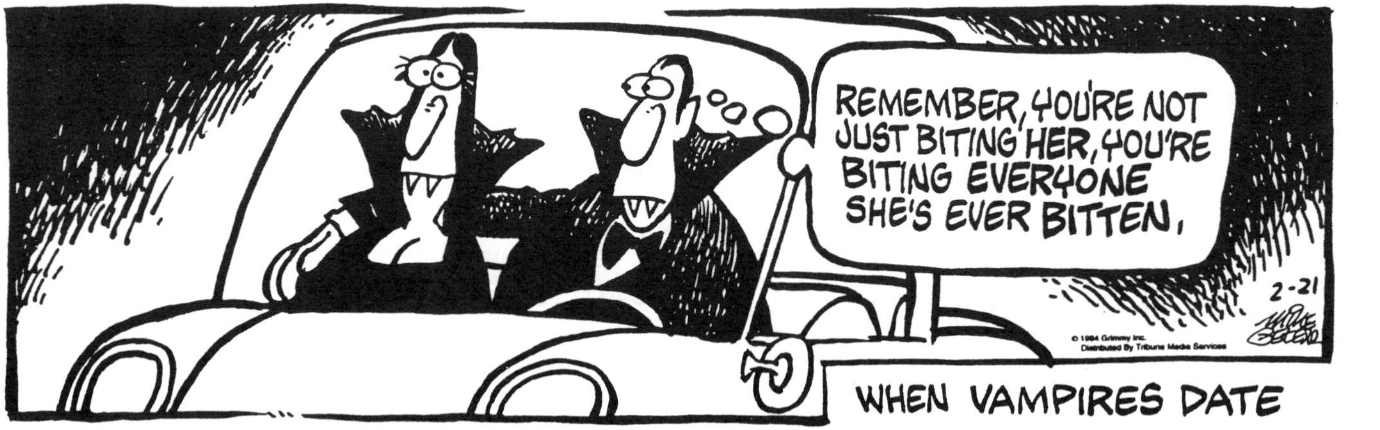
REMEMBER, YOU'RE NOT JUST BITING HER, YOU'RE BITING EVERYONE SHE'S EVER BITTEN,
2-21
© 1984 Grimmy Inc. Distributed By Tribune Media Services
WHEN VAMPIRES DATE

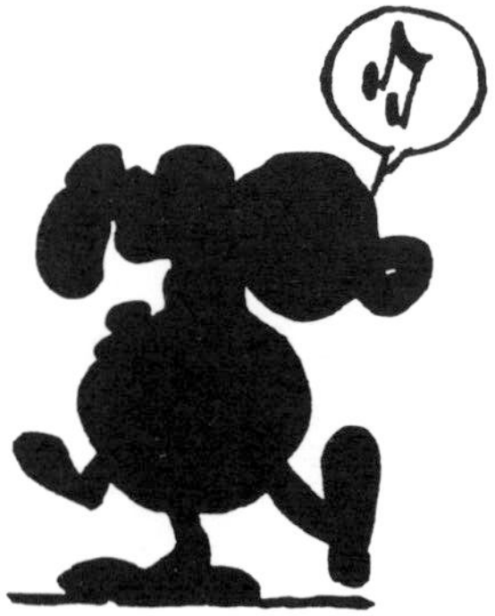

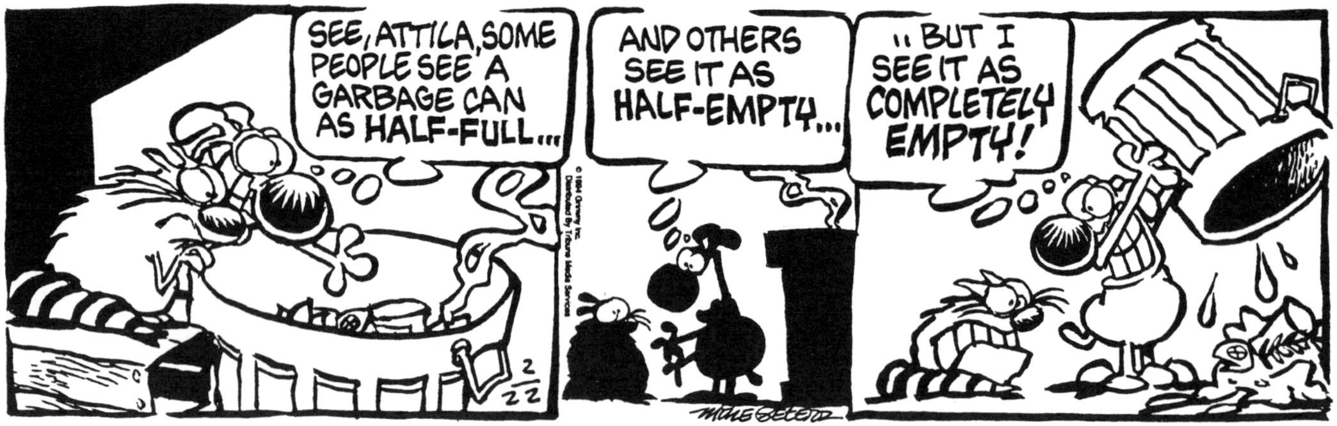
SEE, ATTILA, SOME PEOPLE SEE A GARBAGE CAN AS HALF-FULL...
© 1984 Grimmy Inc. Distributed By Tribune Media Services
2/22
AND OTHERS SEE IT AS HALF-EMPTY...
.. BUT I SEE IT AS COMPLETELY EMPTY!

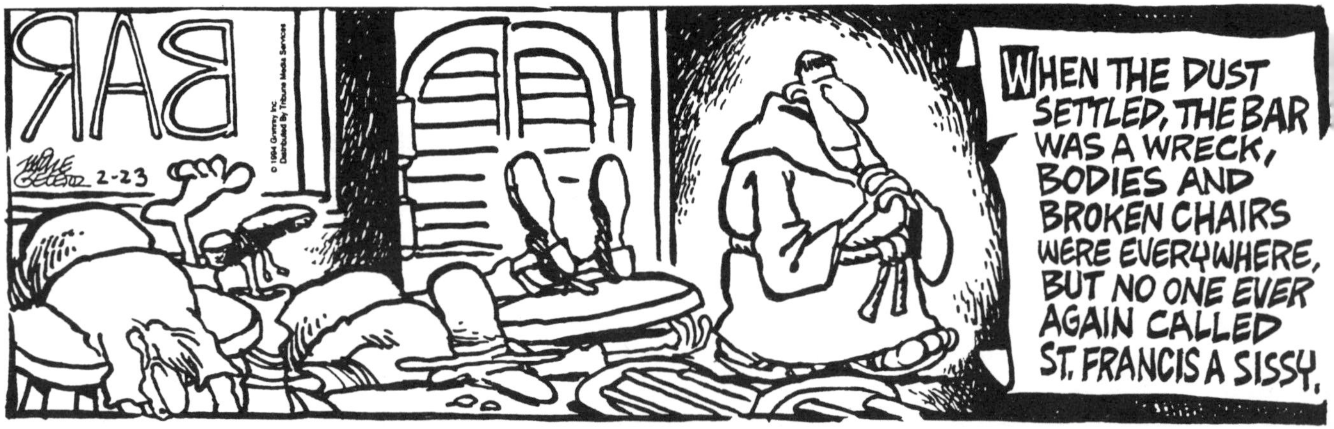
BAR
2-23
© 1984 Grimmy Inc. Distributed By Tribune Media Services
WHEN THE DUST SETTLED, THE BAR WAS A WRECK, BODIES AND BROKEN CHAIRS WERE EVERYWHERE, BUT NO ONE EVER AGAIN CALLED ST. FRANCIS A SISSY.

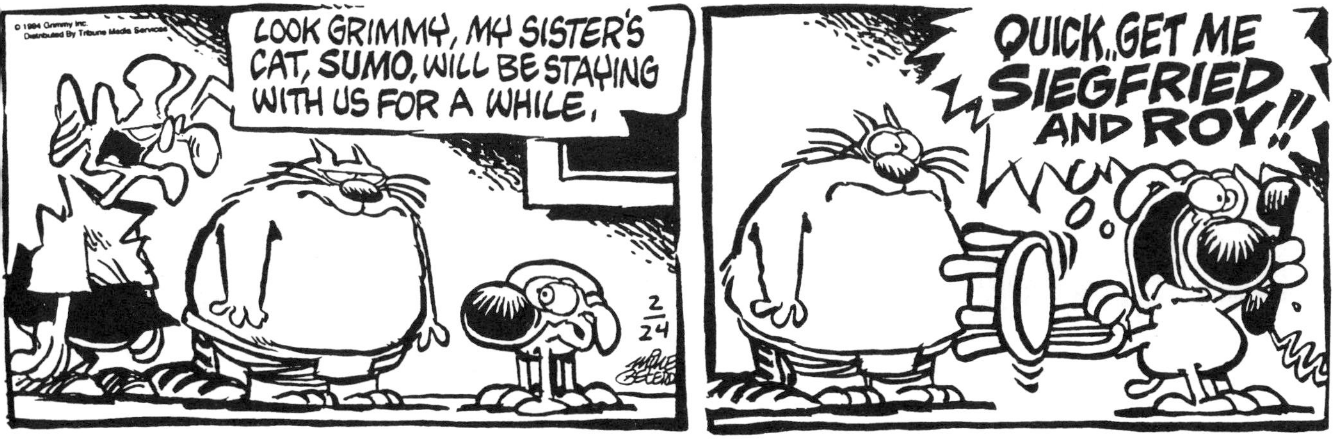
© 1994 Grimmy Inc.
Distributed By Tribune Media Services
LOOK GRIMMY, MY SISTER'S CAT, SUMO, WILL BE STAYING WITH US FOR A WHILE.
2/24
QUICK..GET ME SIEGFRIED AND ROY!!

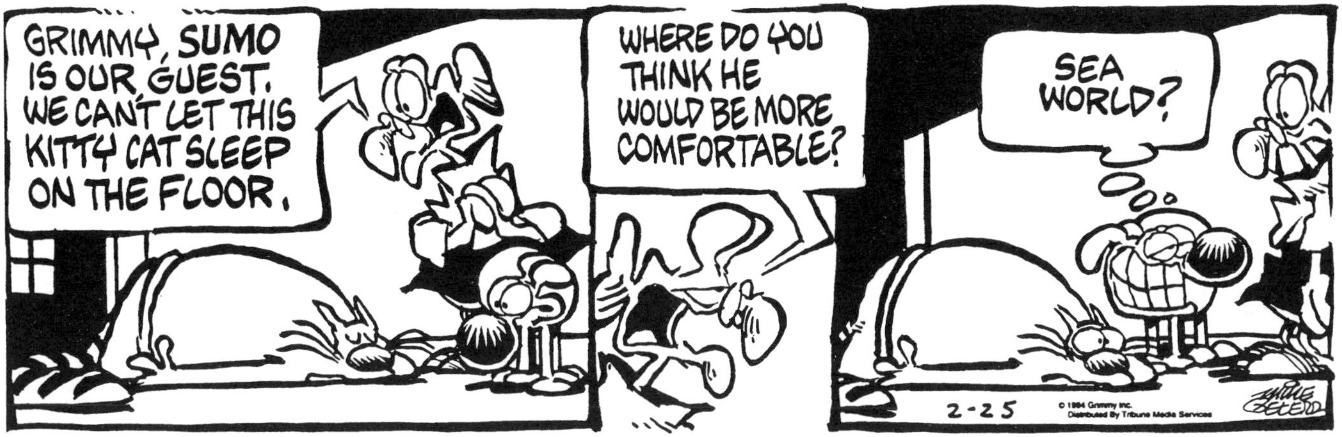
GRIMMY, SUMO IS OUR GUEST. WE CAN'T LET THIS KITTY CAT SLEEP ON THE FLOOR.
WHERE DO YOU THINK HE WOULD BE MORE COMFORTABLE?
SEA WORLD?
2-25
© 1994 Grimmy Inc.
Distributed By Tribune Media Services

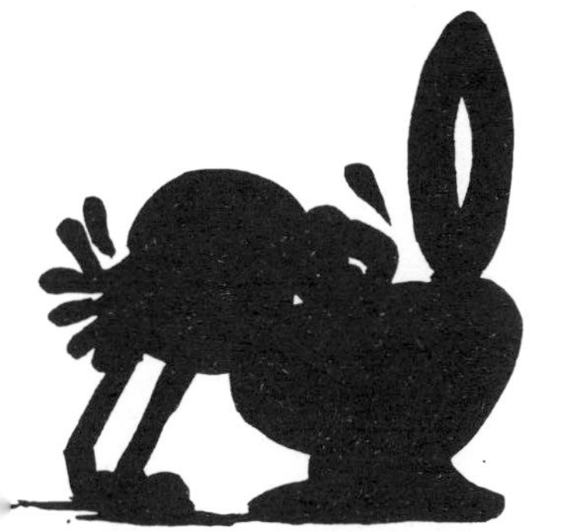

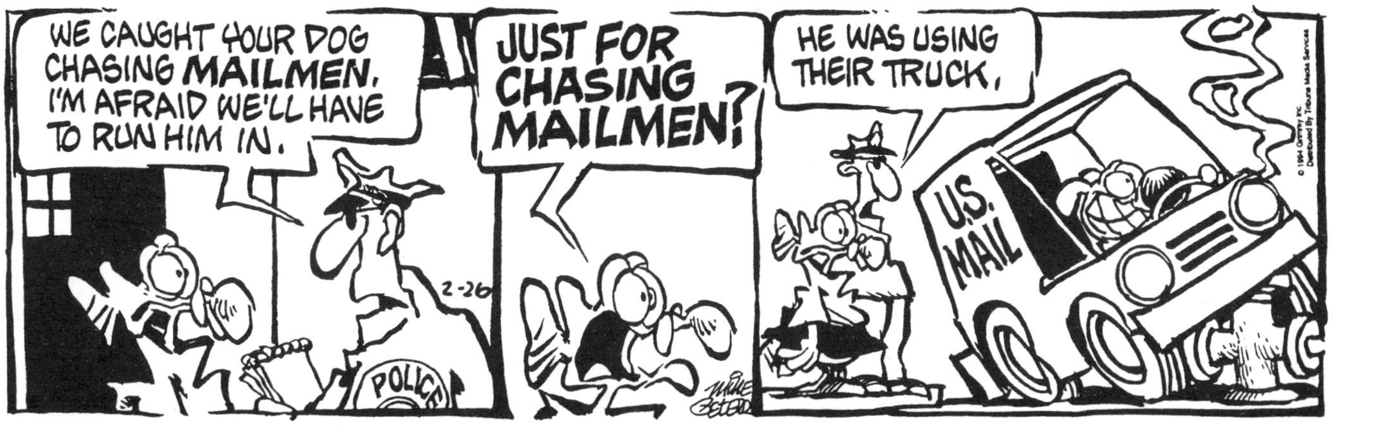
WE CAUGHT YOUR DOG CHASING MAILMEN. I'M AFRAID WE'LL HAVE TO RUN HIM IN.
POLICE
2-26
JUST FOR CHASING MAILMEN?
HE WAS USING THEIR TRUCK.
U.S. MAIL
© 1994 Grimmy Inc.
Distributed By Tribune Media Services

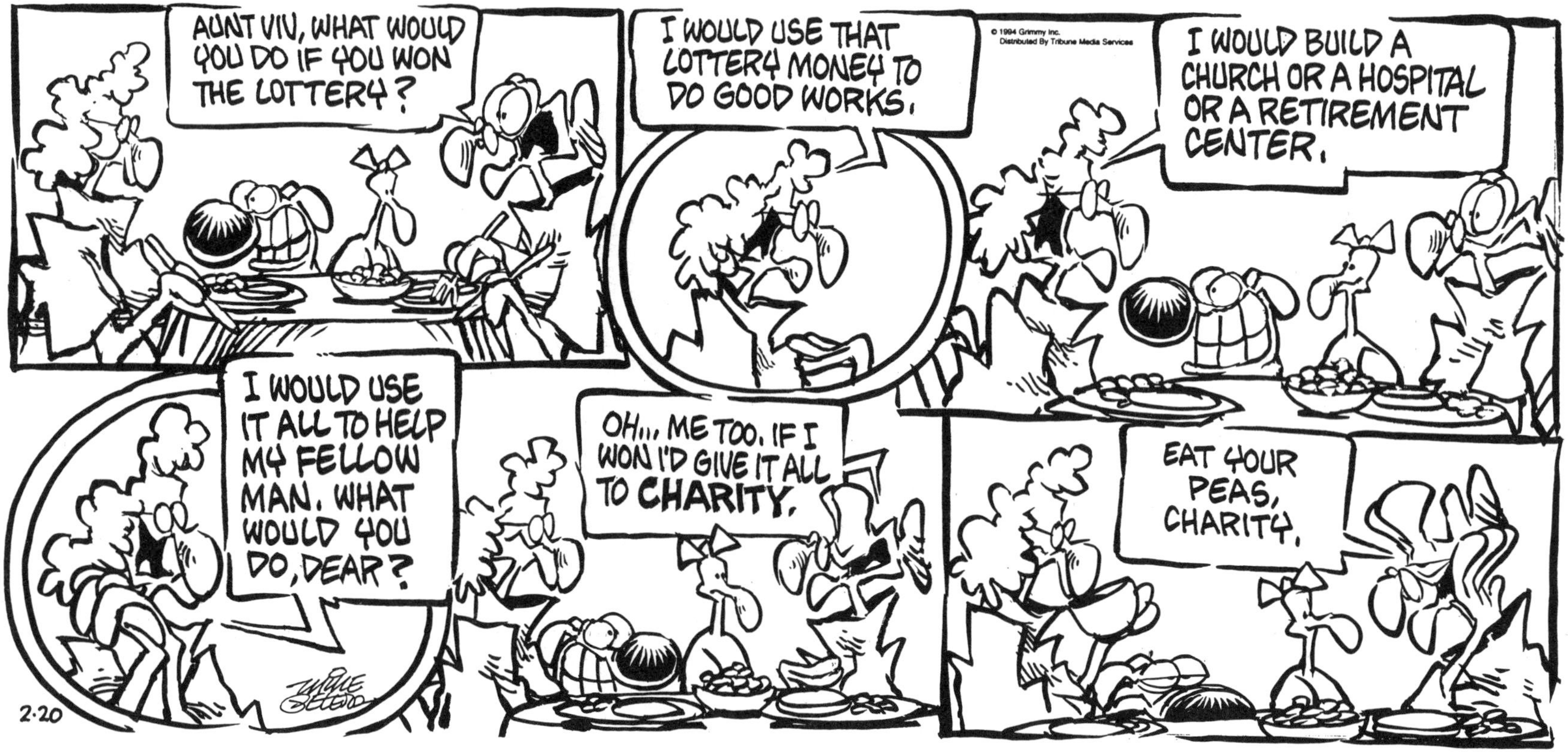
AUNT VIV, WHAT WOULD YOU DO IF YOU WON THE LOTTERY?
I WOULD USE THAT LOTTERY MONEY TO DO GOOD WORKS.
© 1994 Grimmy Inc. Distributed By Tribune Media Services
I WOULD BUILD A CHURCH OR A HOSPITAL OR A RETIREMENT CENTER.
I WOULD USE IT ALL TO HELP MY FELLOW MAN. WHAT WOULD YOU DO, DEAR?
2·20
OH... ME TOO. IF I WON I'D GIVE IT ALL TO CHARITY.
EAT YOUR PEAS, CHARITY.

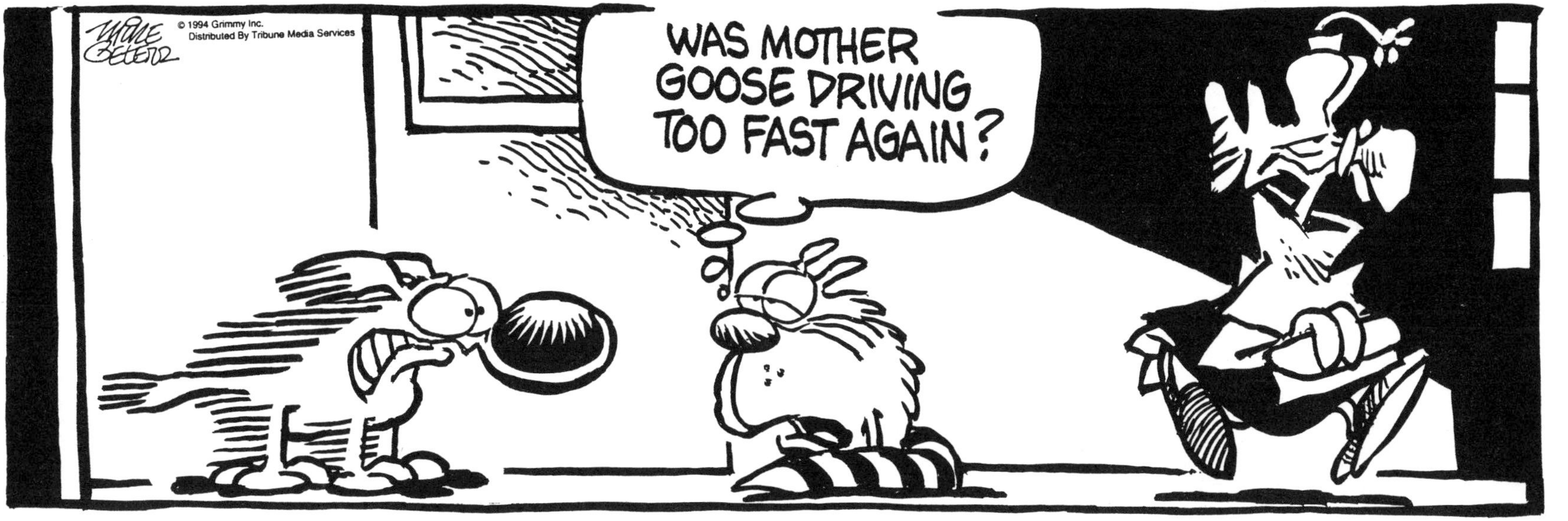
© 1994 Grimmy Inc.
Distributed By Tribune Media Services
WAS MOTHER GOOSE DRIVING TOO FAST AGAIN?

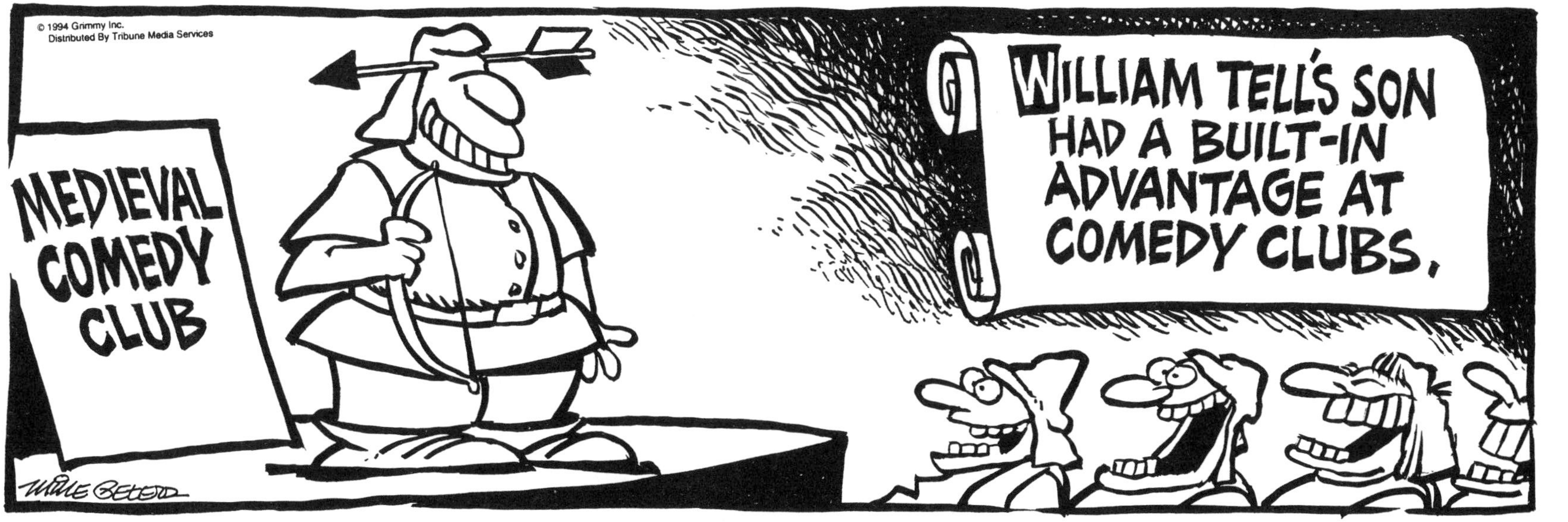
© 1994 Grimmy Inc.
Distributed By Tribune Media Services
WILLIAM TELL'S SON HAD A BUILT-IN ADVANTAGE AT COMEDY CLUBS.
MEDIEVAL COMEDY CLUB

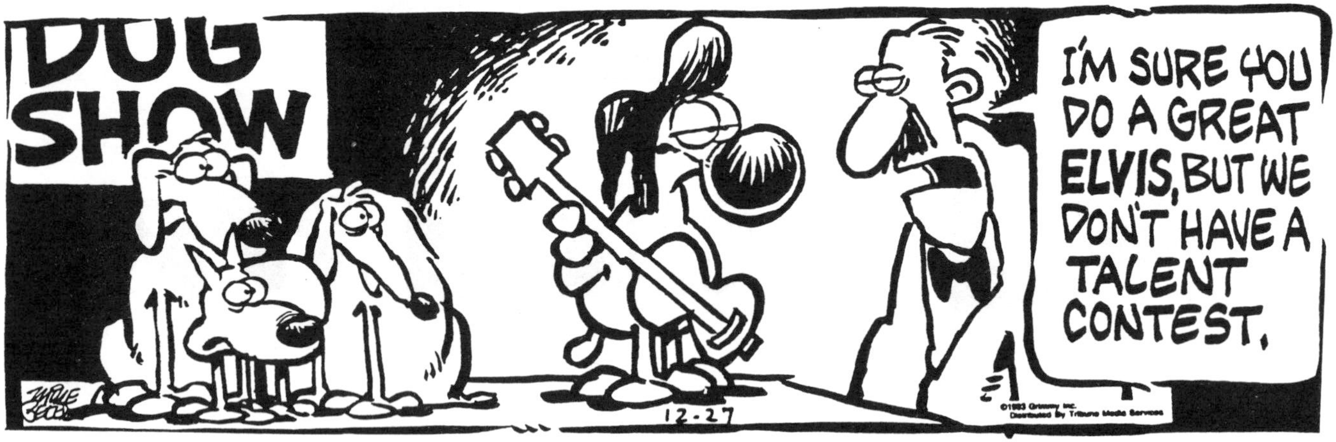
DOG SHOW
I'M SURE YOU DO A GREAT ELVIS, BUT WE DON'T HAVE A TALENT CONTEST.
12-27

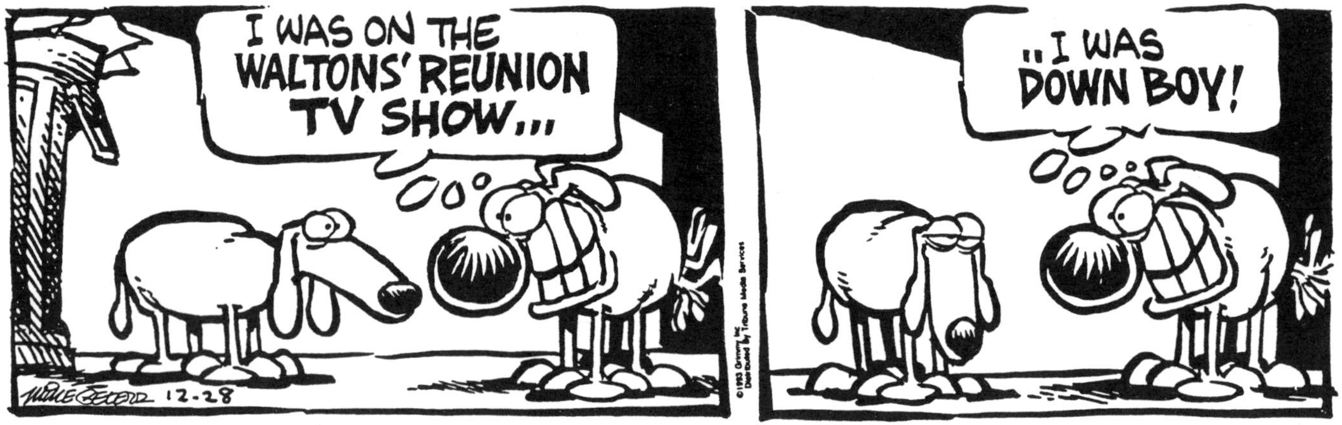
I WAS ON THE WALTONS' REUNION TV SHOW...
..I WAS DOWN BOY!
12-28

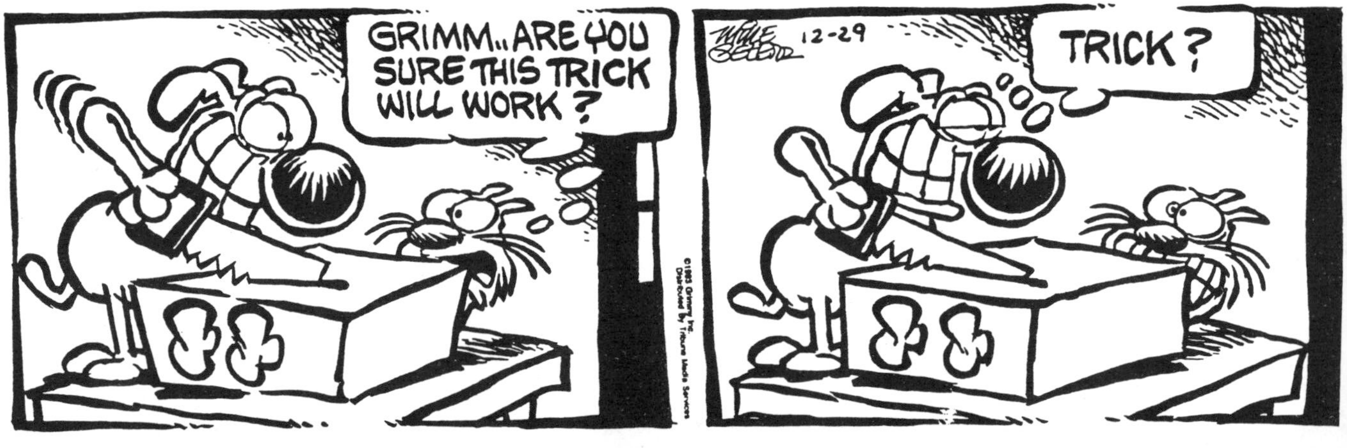
GRIMM.. ARE YOU SURE THIS TRICK WILL WORK?
12-29
TRICK?

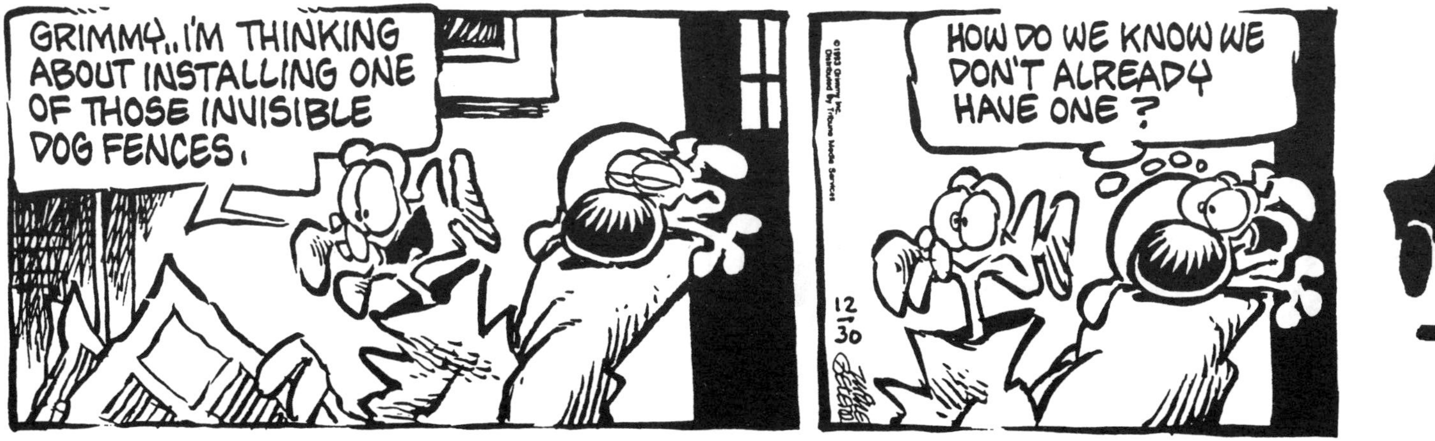
GRIMMY.. I'M THINKING ABOUT INSTALLING ONE OF THOSE INVISIBLE DOG FENCES.
© 1993 Grimmy Inc. Distributed by Tribune Media Services
HOW DO WE KNOW WE DON'T ALREADY HAVE ONE ?
12-30

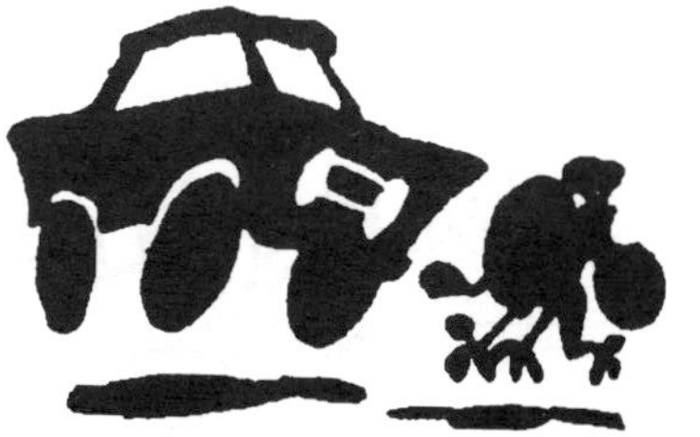

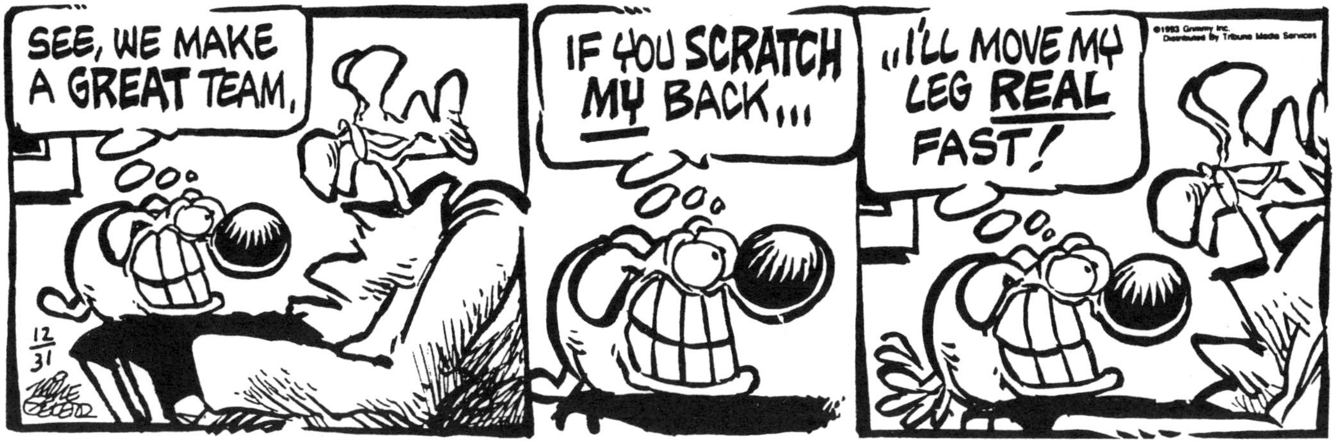
SEE, WE MAKE A GREAT TEAM.
12-31
IF YOU SCRATCH MY BACK...
..I'LL MOVE MY LEG REAL FAST!
© 1993 Grimmy Inc. Distributed By Tribune Media Services

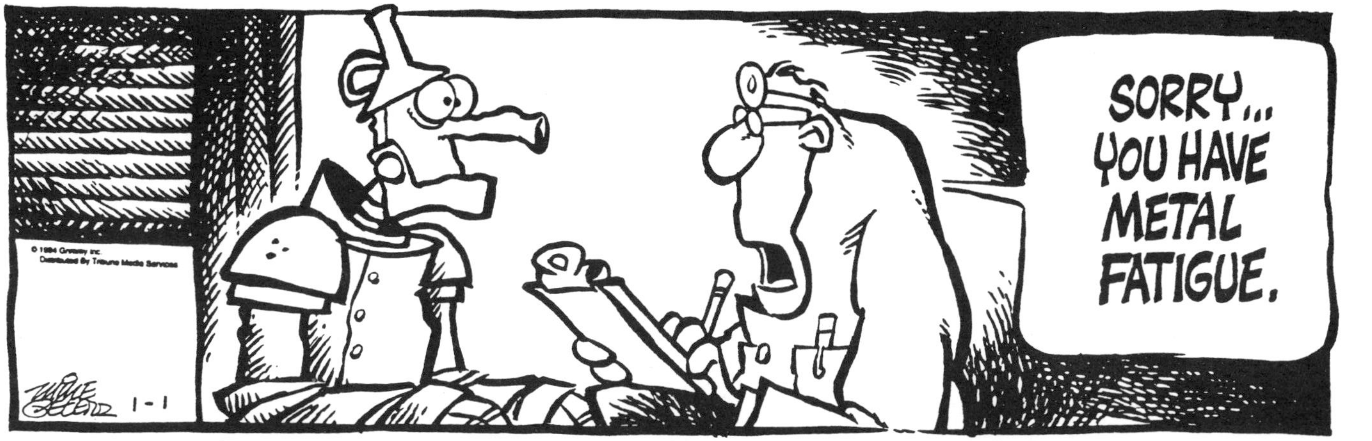
© 1994 Grimmy Inc. Distributed By Tribune Media Services
1-1
SORRY... YOU HAVE METAL FATIGUE.

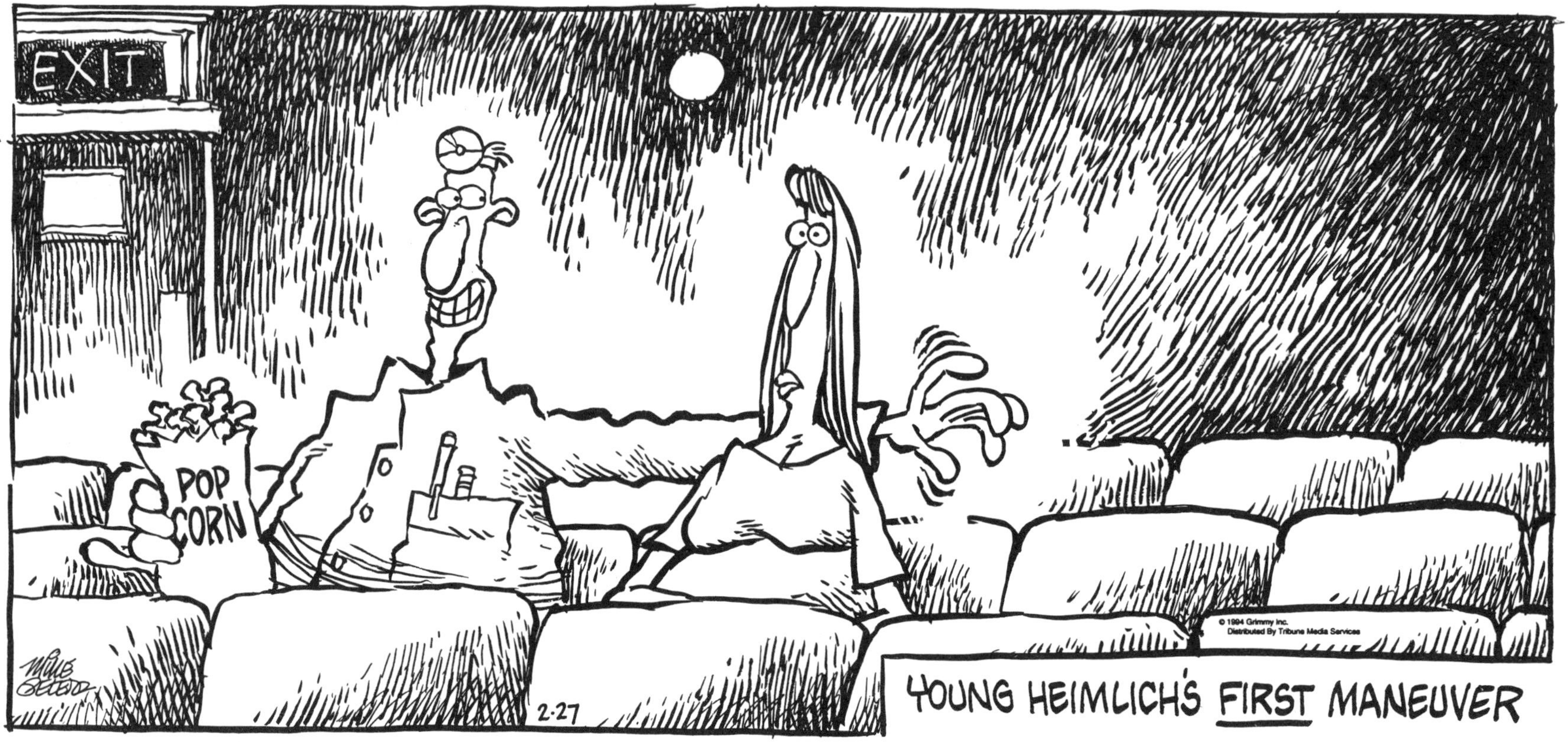
EXIT
POP CORN
2-27
© 1994 Grimmy Inc.
Distributed By Tribune Media Services

YOUNG HEIMLICH'S FIRST MANEUVER

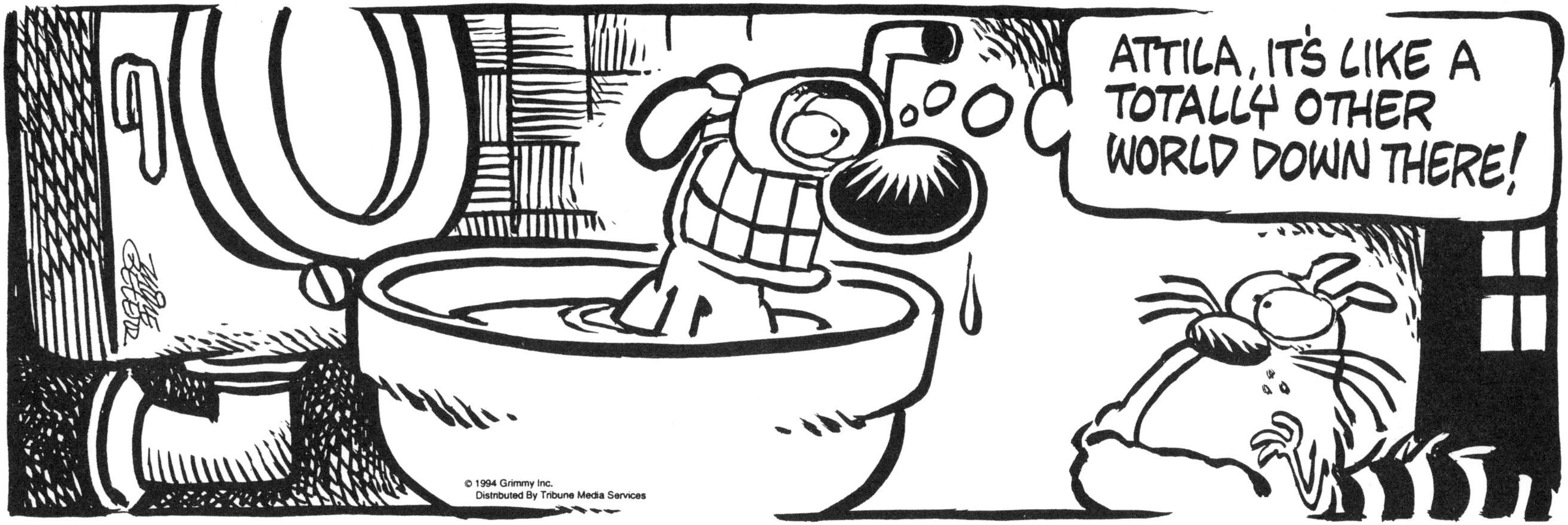
ATTILA, IT'S LIKE A TOTALLY OTHER WORLD DOWN THERE!
© 1994 Grimmy Inc.
Distributed By Tribune Media Services

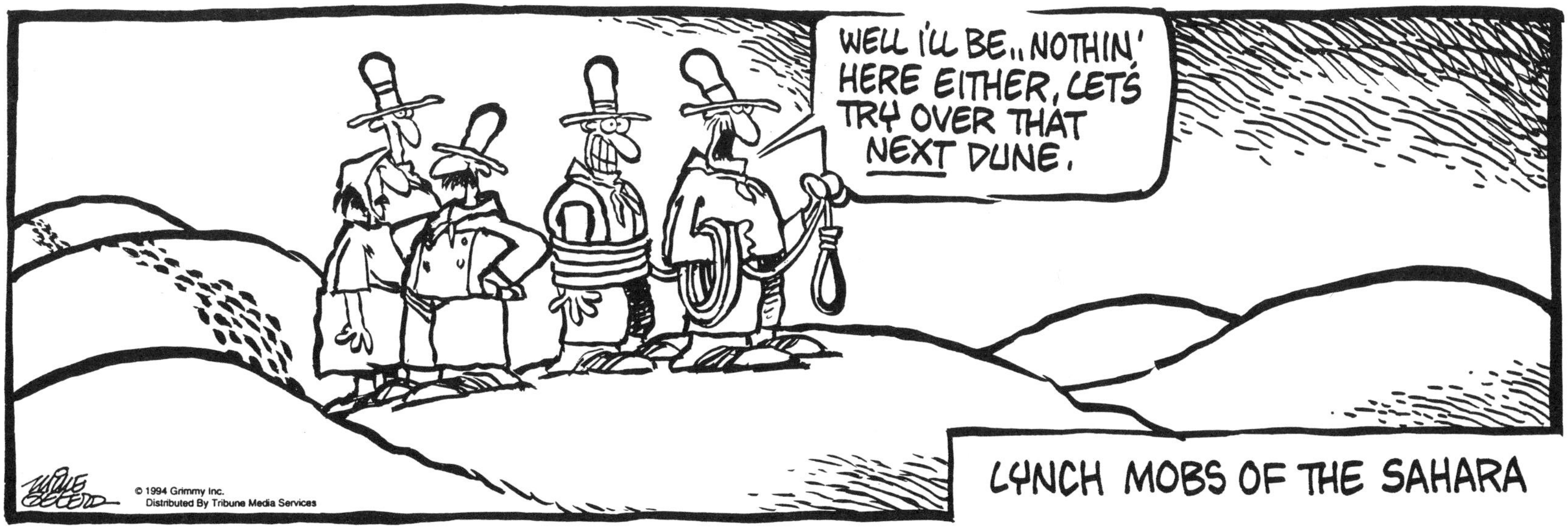
WELL I'LL BE.. NOTHIN' HERE EITHER, LET'S TRY OVER THAT NEXT DUNE.
LYNCH MOBS OF THE SAHARA
© 1994 Grimmy Inc.
Distributed By Tribune Media Services

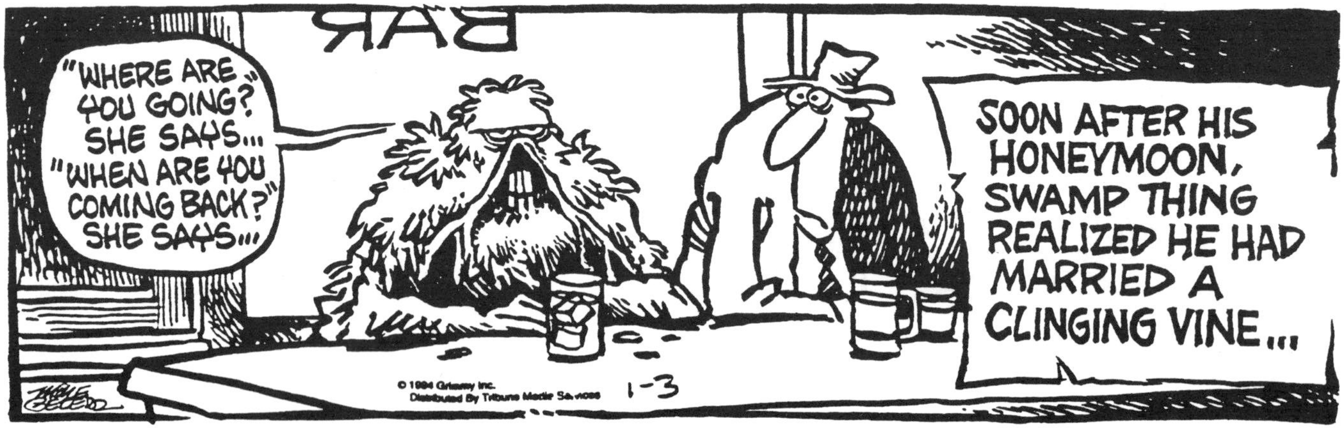
BAR
"WHERE ARE YOU GOING?" SHE SAYS... "WHEN ARE YOU COMING BACK?" SHE SAYS...
SOON AFTER HIS HONEYMOON, SWAMP THING REALIZED HE HAD MARRIED A CLINGING VINE...
© 1994 Grimmy Inc. Distributed By Tribune Media Services
1-3

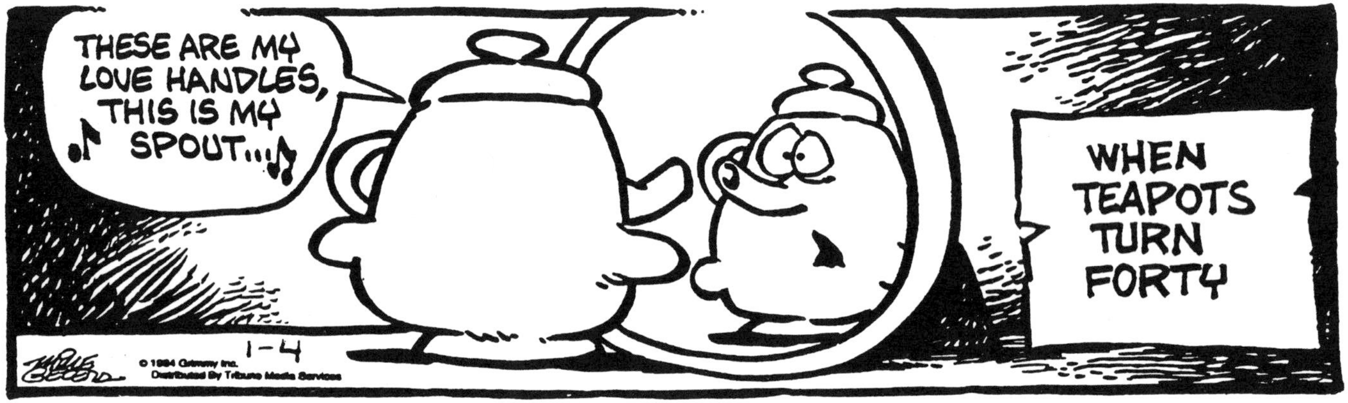
THESE ARE MY LOVE HANDLES, THIS IS MY SPOUT...
WHEN TEAPOTS TURN FORTY
© 1994 Grimmy Inc. Distributed By Tribune Media Services
1-4

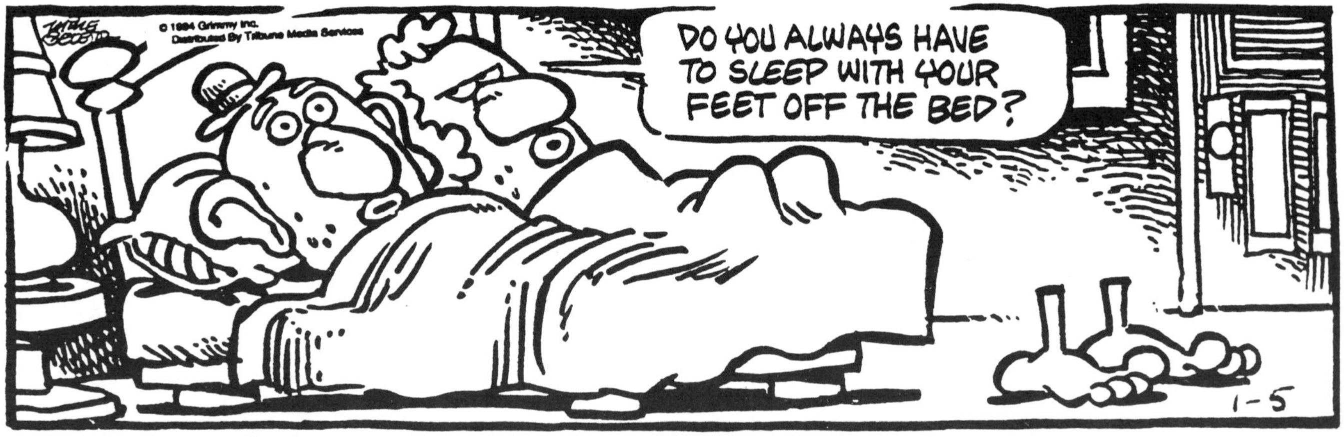
© 1994 Grimmy Inc. Distributed By Tribune Media Services
DO YOU ALWAYS HAVE TO SLEEP WITH YOUR FEET OFF THE BED?
1-5

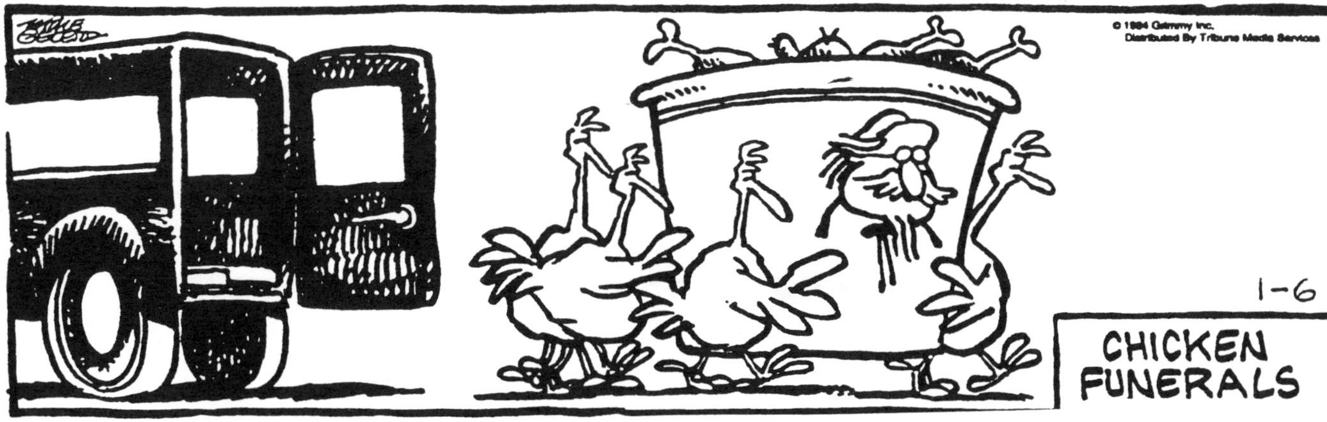
© 1994 Grimmy Inc.
Distributed By Tribune Media Services
1-6
CHICKEN FUNERALS

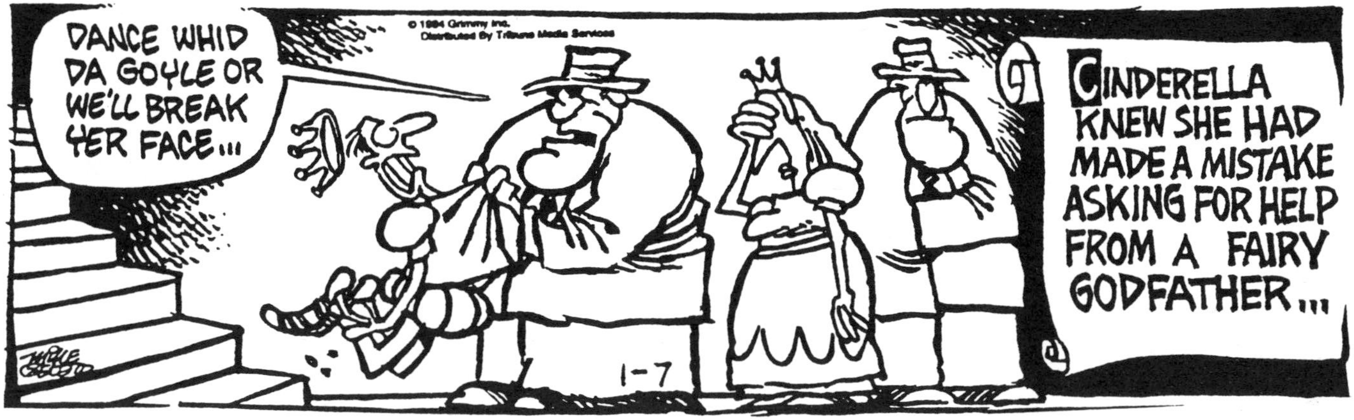
© 1994 Grimmy Inc.
Distributed By Tribune Media Services
DANCE WHID DA GOYLE OR WE'LL BREAK YER FACE...
CINDERELLA KNEW SHE HAD MADE A MISTAKE ASKING FOR HELP FROM A FAIRY GODFATHER...
1-7

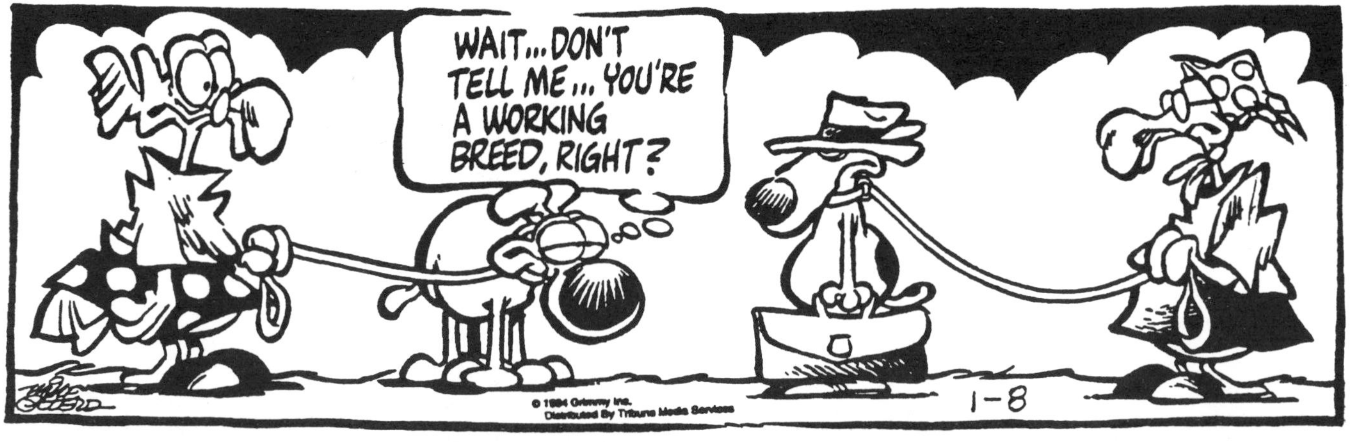
WAIT... DON'T TELL ME... YOU'RE A WORKING BREED, RIGHT?
© 1994 Grimmy Inc.
Distributed By Tribune Media Services
1-8

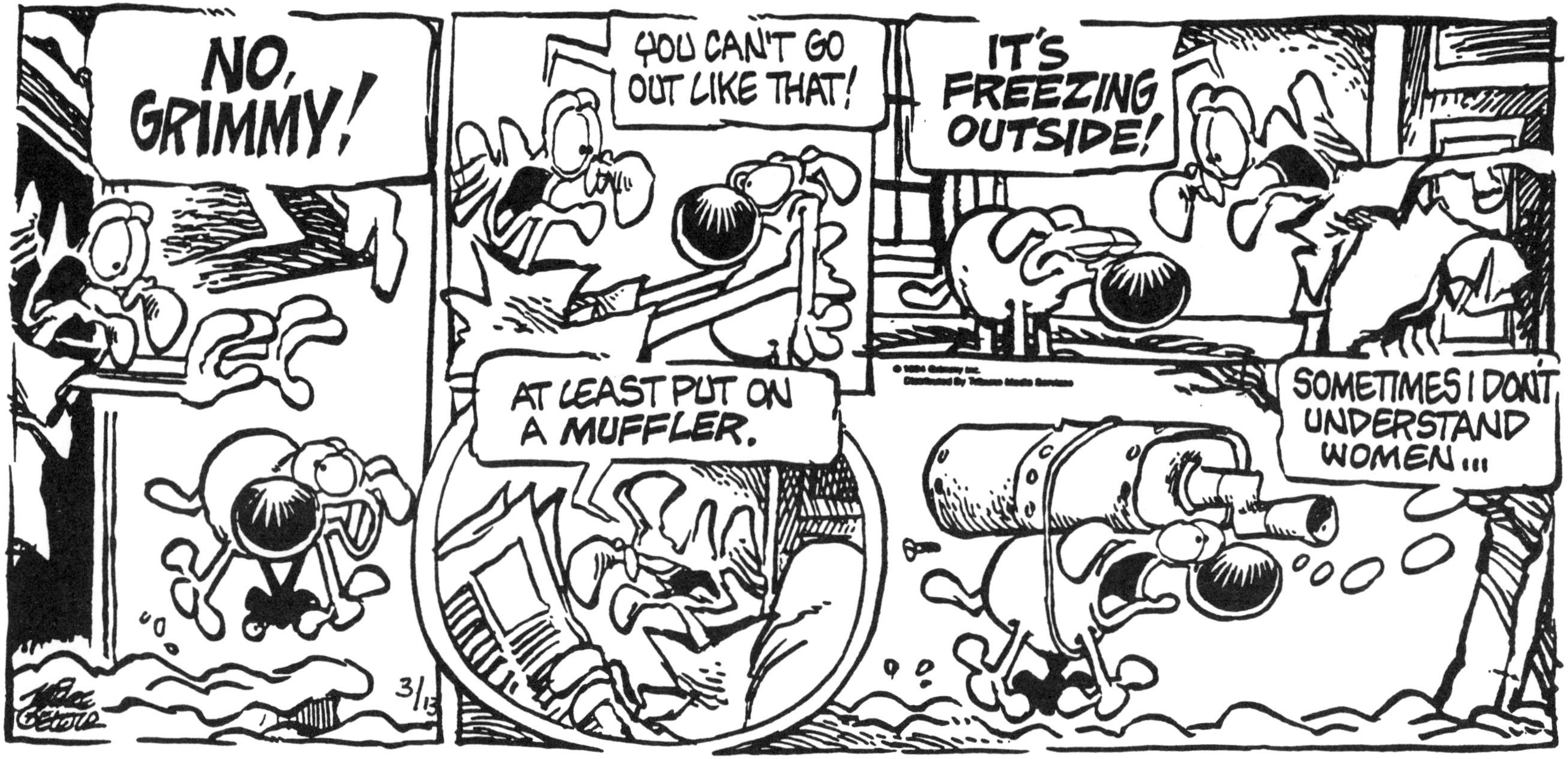
NO, GRIMMY!
YOU CAN'T GO OUT LIKE THAT!
IT'S FREEZING OUTSIDE!
AT LEAST PUT ON A MUFFLER.
SOMETIMES I DON'T UNDERSTAND WOMEN...
3/13

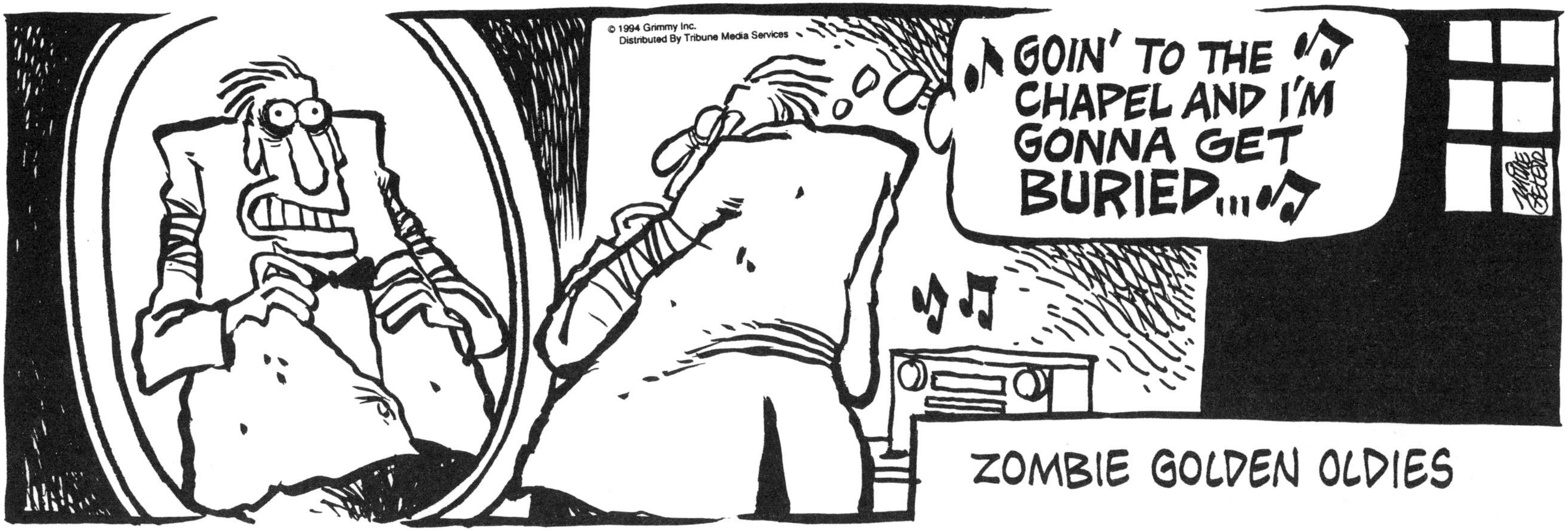
© 1994 Grimmy Inc.
Distributed By Tribune Media Services
GOIN' TO THE CHAPEL AND I'M GONNA GET BURIED...
ZOMBIE GOLDEN OLDIES

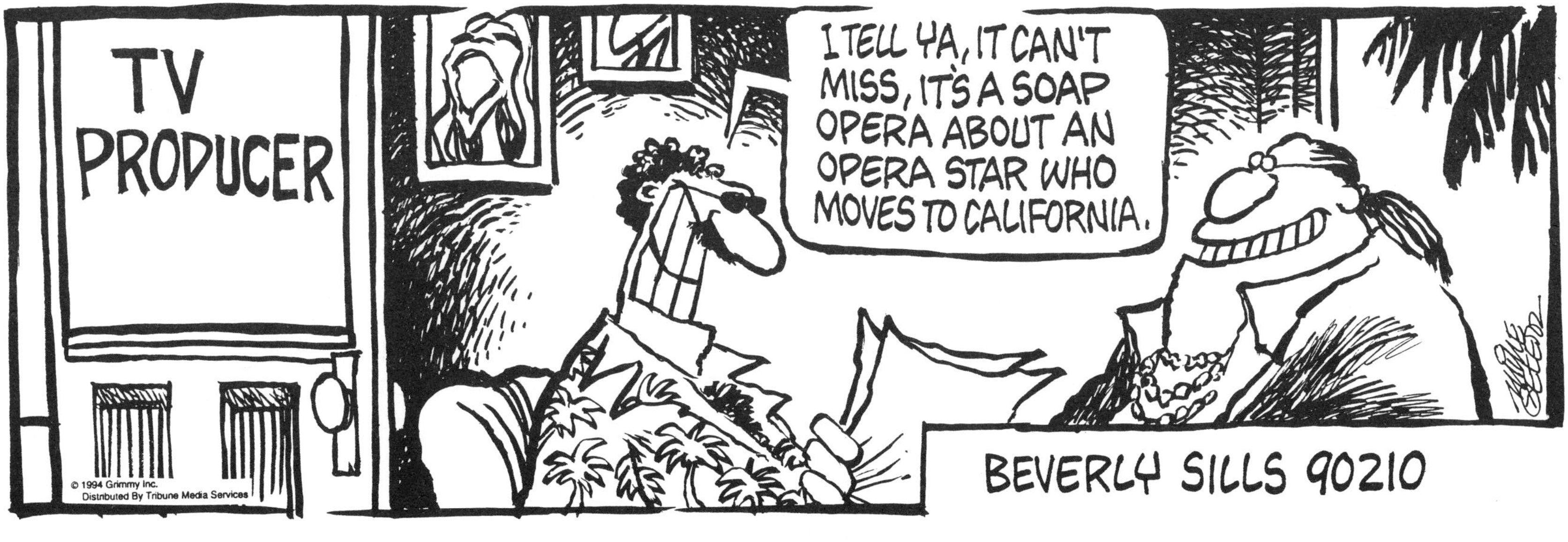
TV PRODUCER
I TELL YA, IT CAN'T MISS, IT'S A SOAP OPERA ABOUT AN OPERA STAR WHO MOVES TO CALIFORNIA.
© 1994 Grimmy Inc.
Distributed By Tribune Media Services
BEVERLY SILLS 90210

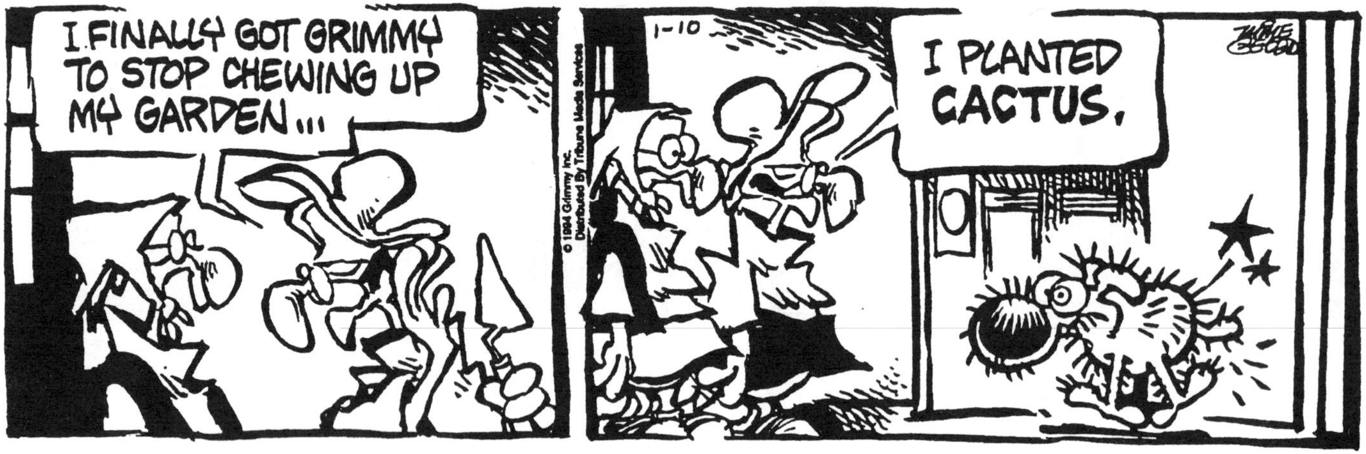
I FINALLY GOT GRIMMY TO STOP CHEWING UP MY GARDEN...
1-10
© 1994 Grimmy Inc.
Distributed By Tribune Media Services
I PLANTED CACTUS.

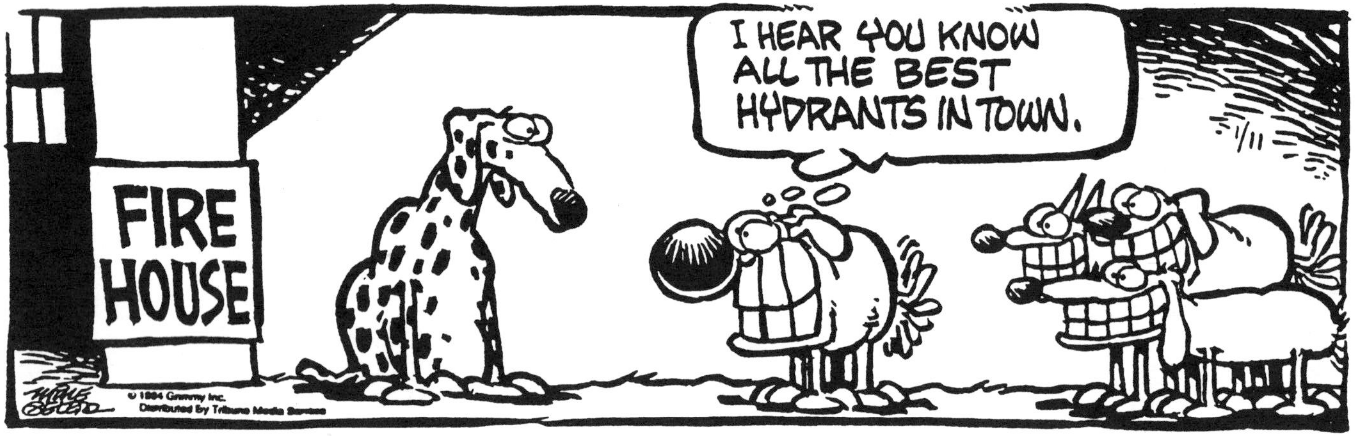
FIRE HOUSE
I HEAR YOU KNOW ALL THE BEST HYDRANTS IN TOWN.
1/11
© 1994 Grimmy Inc.
Distributed By Tribune Media Services

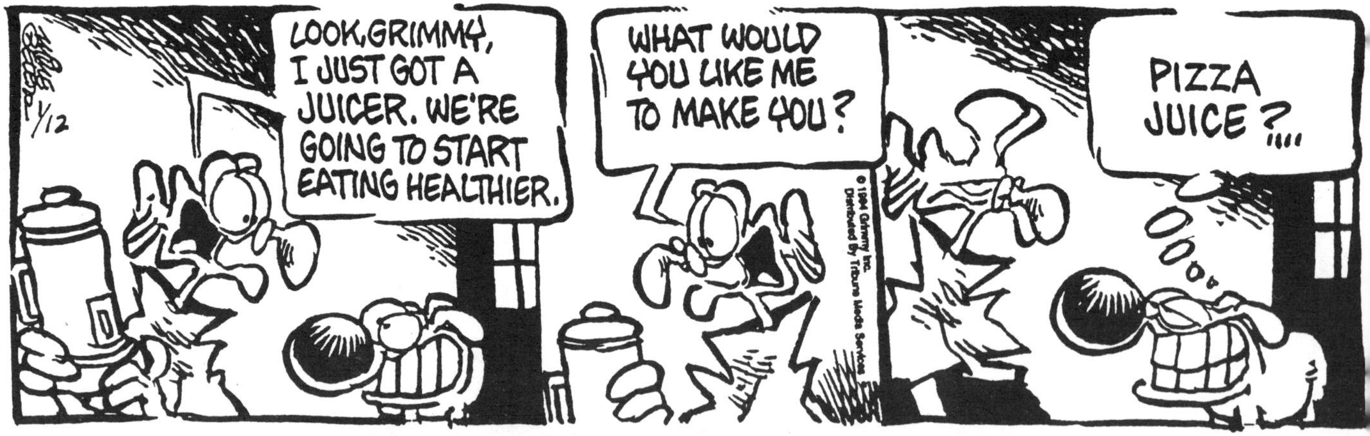
1/12
LOOK, GRIMMY, I JUST GOT A JUICER. WE'RE GOING TO START EATING HEALTHIER.
WHAT WOULD YOU LIKE ME TO MAKE YOU?
© 1994 Grimmy Inc.
Distributed By Tribune Media Services
PIZZA JUICE?....

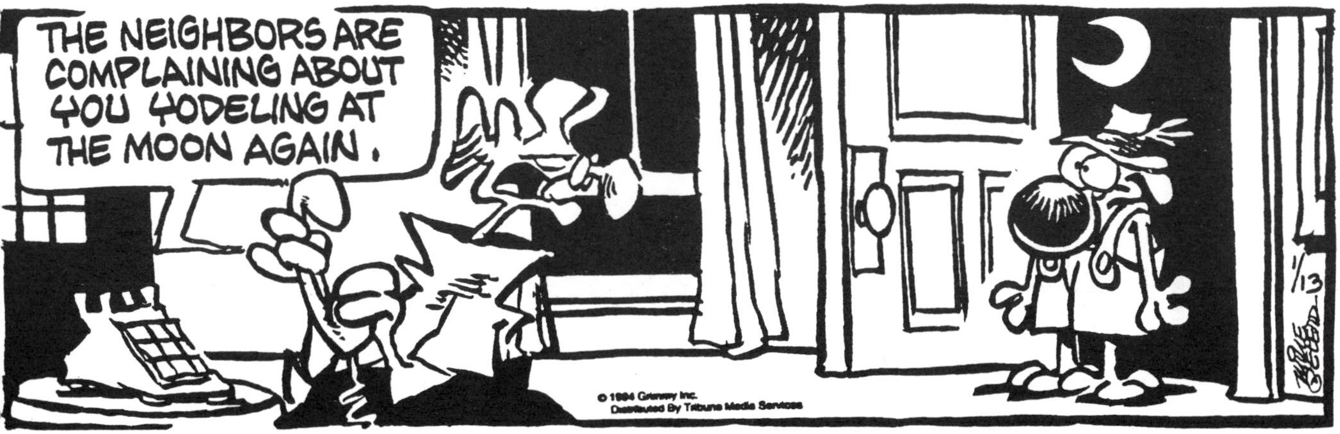
THE NEIGHBORS ARE COMPLAINING ABOUT YOU YODELING AT THE MOON AGAIN.
© 1994 Grimmy Inc.
Distributed By Tribune Media Services
1/13

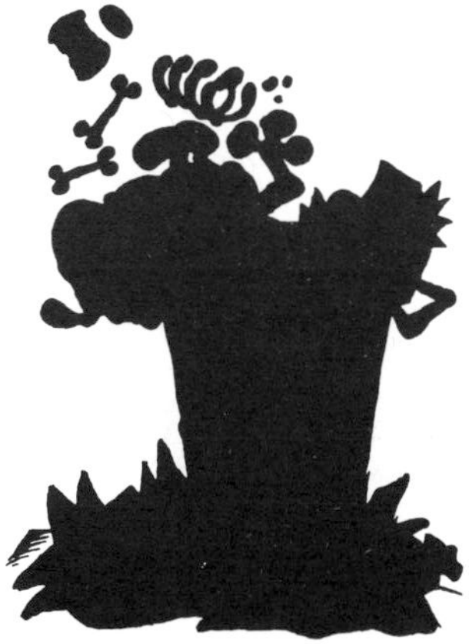

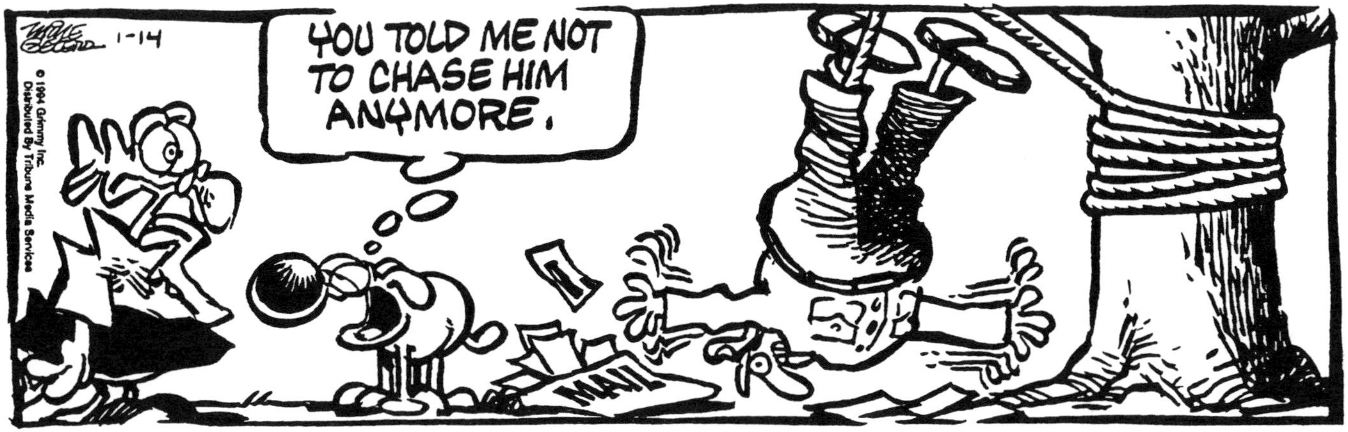
1-14
© 1994 Grimmy Inc.
Distributed By Tribune Media Services
YOU TOLD ME NOT TO CHASE HIM ANYMORE.
MAIL

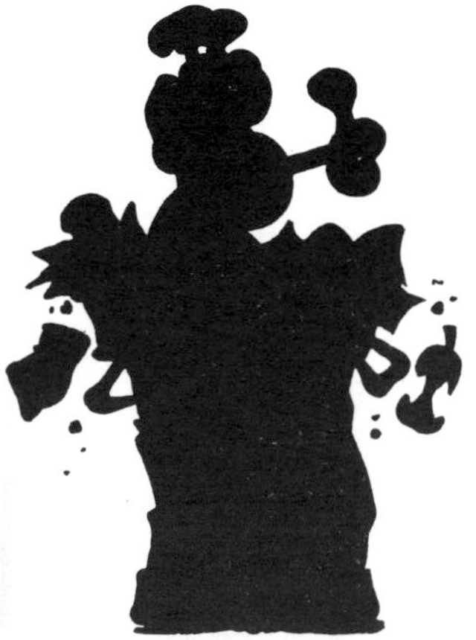

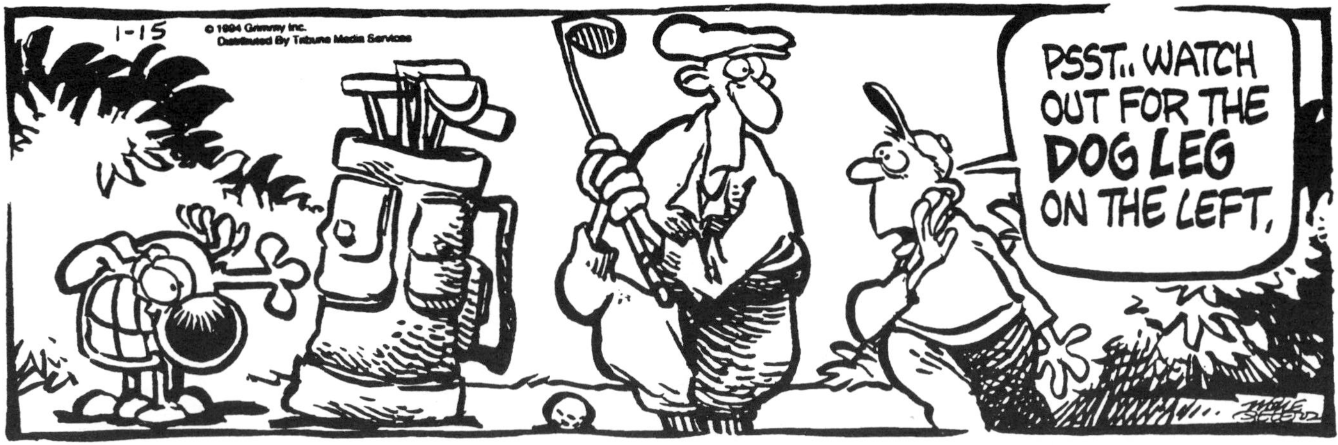
1-15
© 1994 Grimmy Inc.
Distributed By Tribune Media Services
PSST.. WATCH OUT FOR THE **DOG LEG** ON THE LEFT.

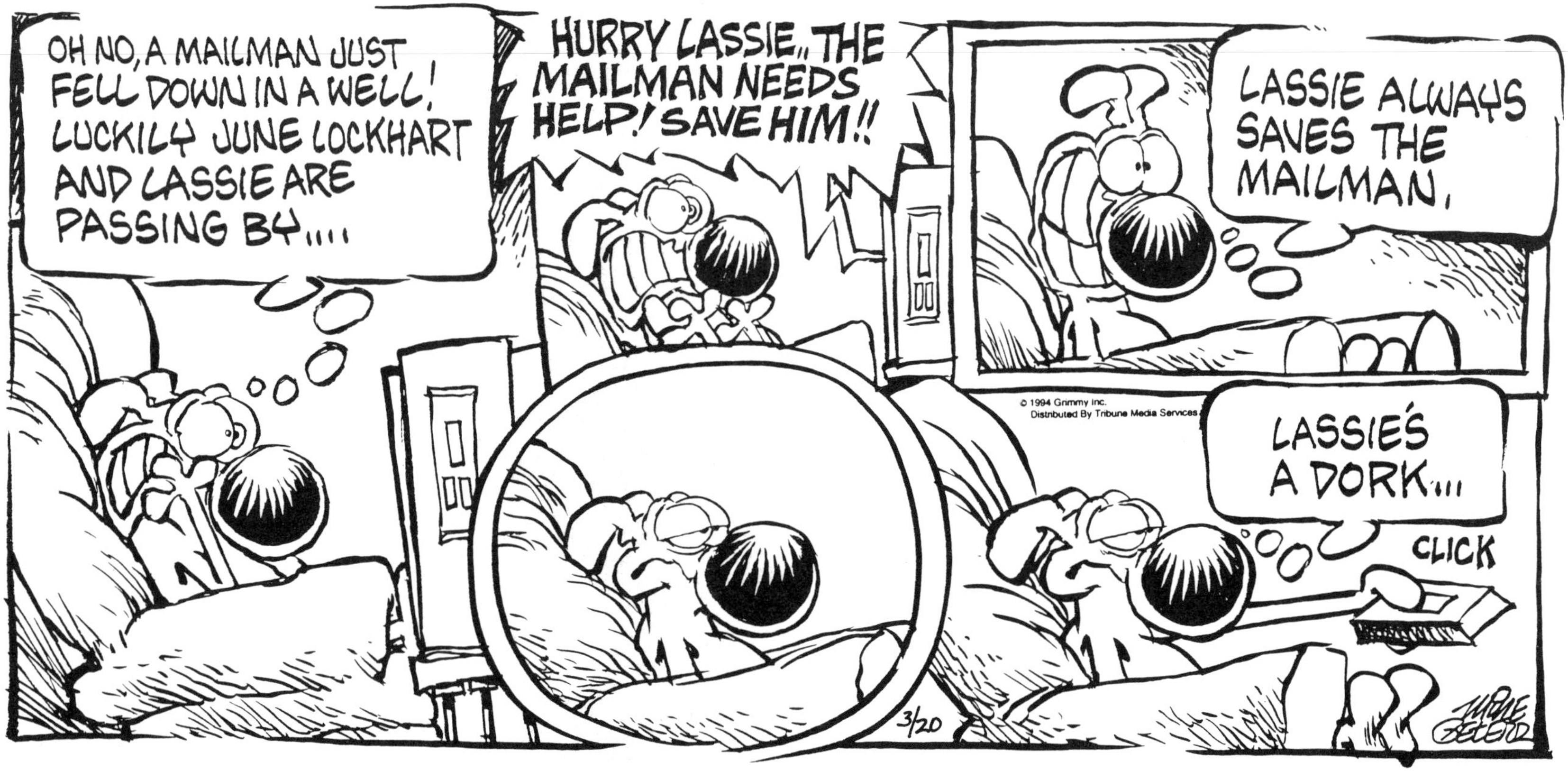
OH NO, A MAILMAN JUST FELL DOWN IN A WELL! LUCKILY JUNE LOCKHART AND LASSIE ARE PASSING BY....
HURRY LASSIE.. THE MAILMAN NEEDS HELP! SAVE HIM!!
LASSIE ALWAYS SAVES THE MAILMAN.
© 1994 Grimmy Inc.
Distributed By Tribune Media Services
LASSIE'S A DORK...
CLICK
3/20

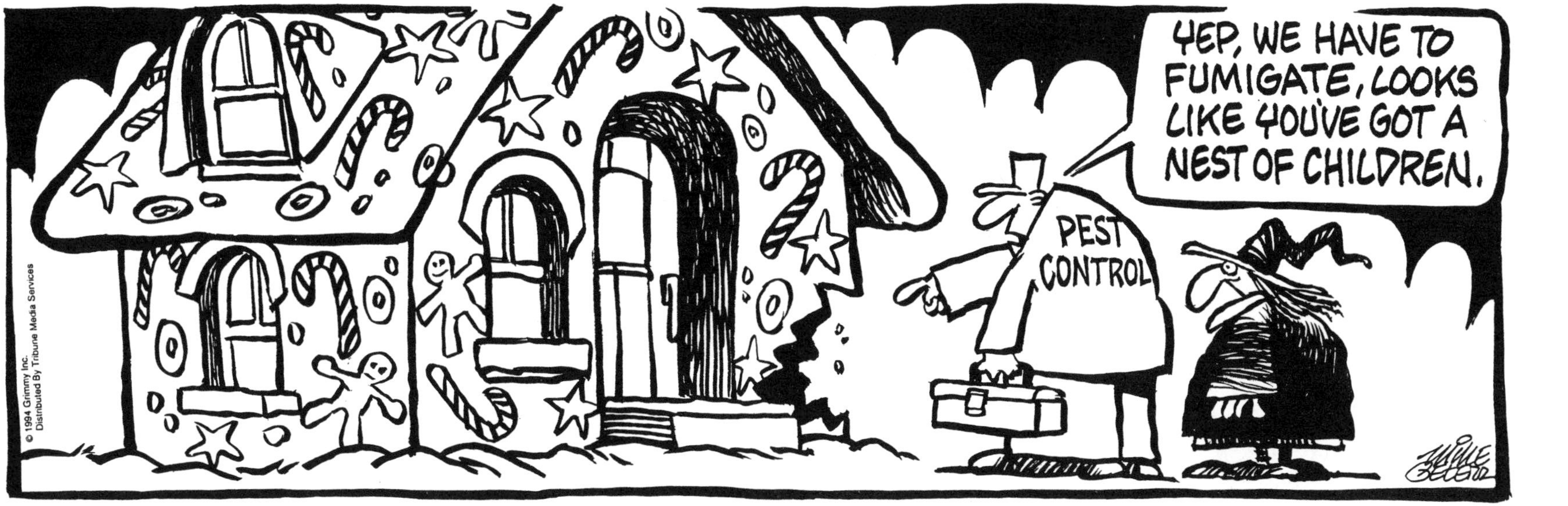
© 1994 Grimmy Inc.
Distributed By Tribune Media Services
YEP, WE HAVE TO FUMIGATE, LOOKS LIKE YOU'VE GOT A NEST OF CHILDREN.
PEST CONTROL

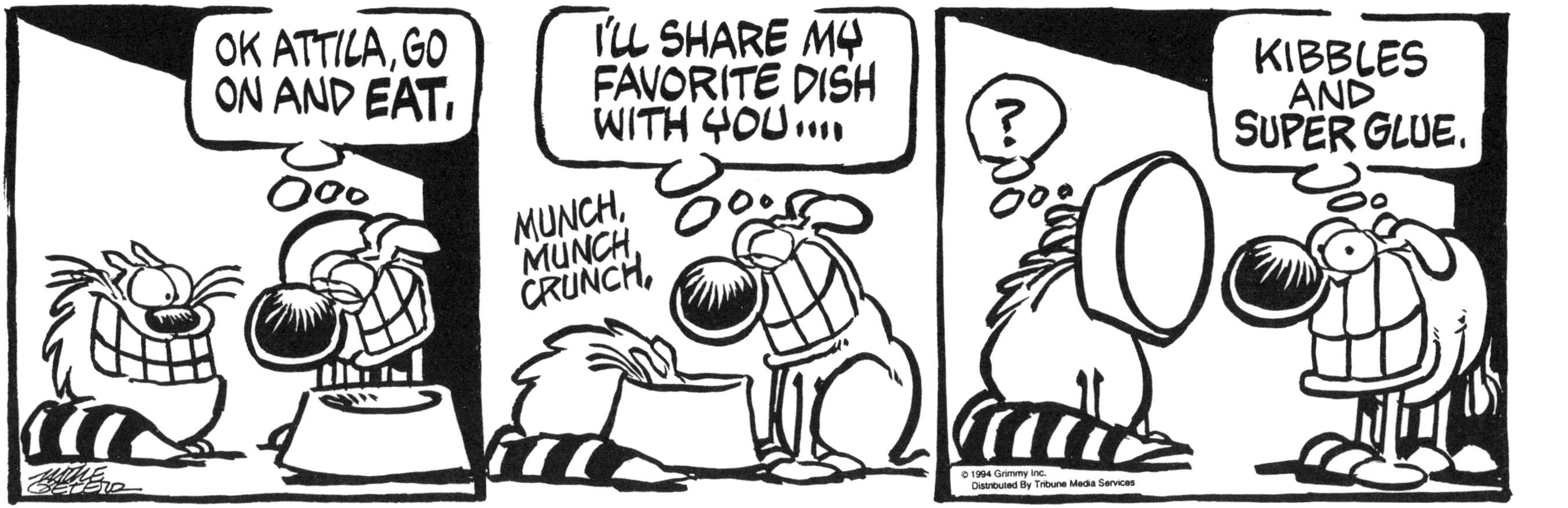
OK ATTILA, GO ON AND EAT.
I'LL SHARE MY FAVORITE DISH WITH YOU....
MUNCH, MUNCH CRUNCH.
?
KIBBLES AND SUPER GLUE.
© 1994 Grimmy Inc.
Distributed By Tribune Media Services

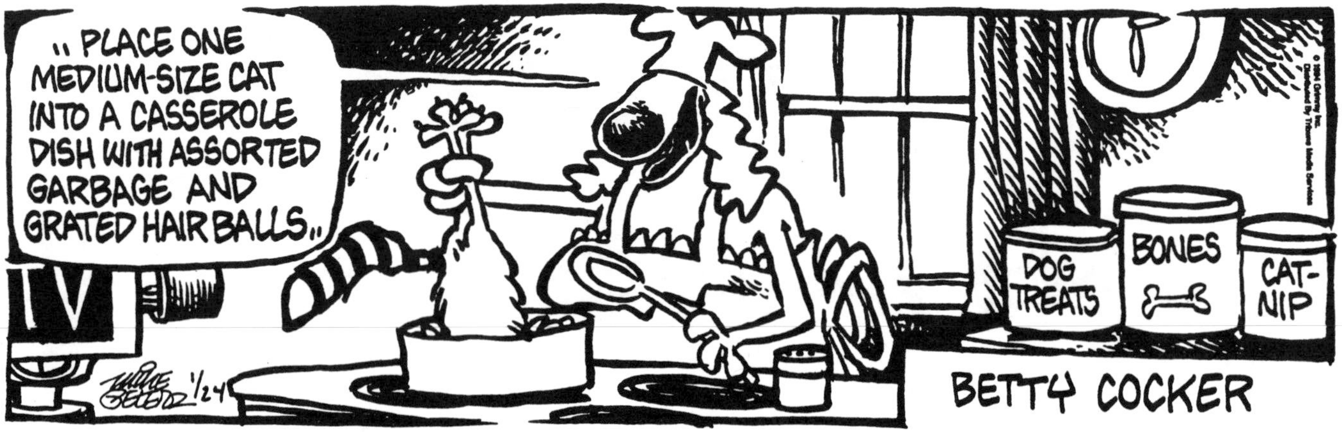
.. PLACE ONE MEDIUM-SIZE CAT INTO A CASSEROLE DISH WITH ASSORTED GARBAGE AND GRATED HAIR BALLS..
DOG TREATS
BONES
CAT-NIP
© 1984 Grimmy Inc. Distributed By Tribune Media Services

BETTY COCKER

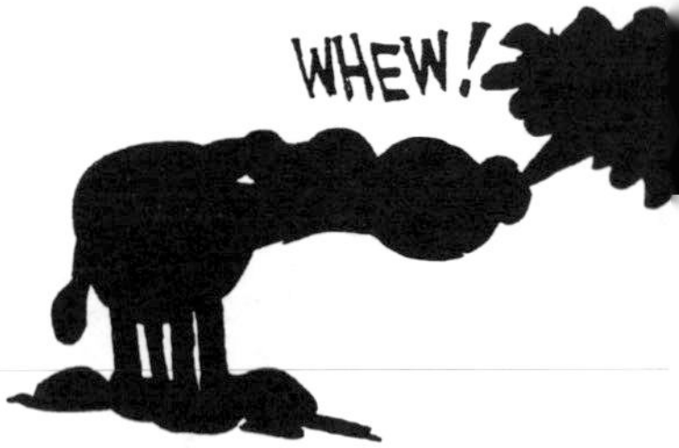
WHEW!

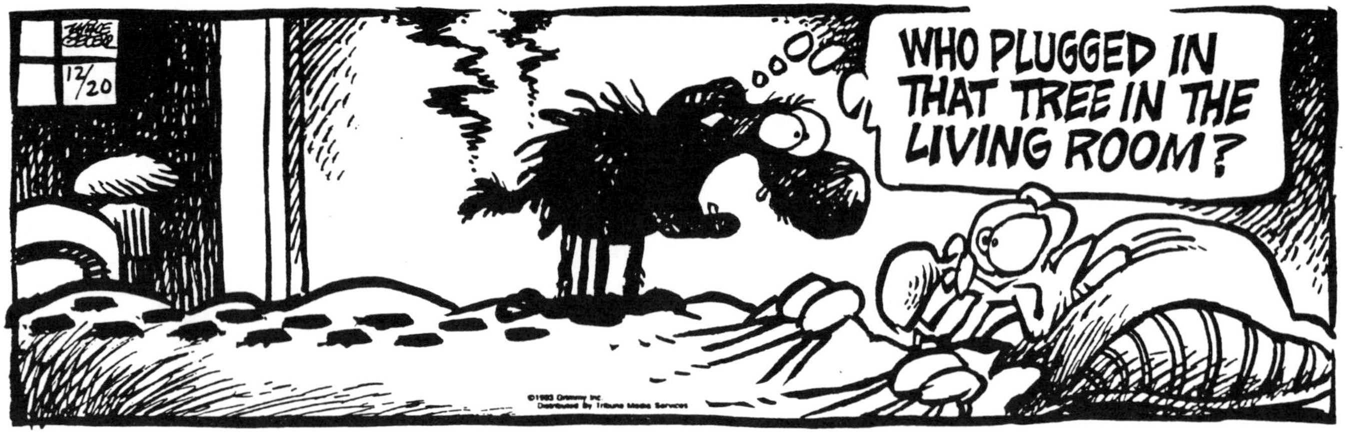
WHO PLUGGED IN THAT TREE IN THE LIVING ROOM?
©1983 Grimmy Inc. Distributed By Tribune Media Services

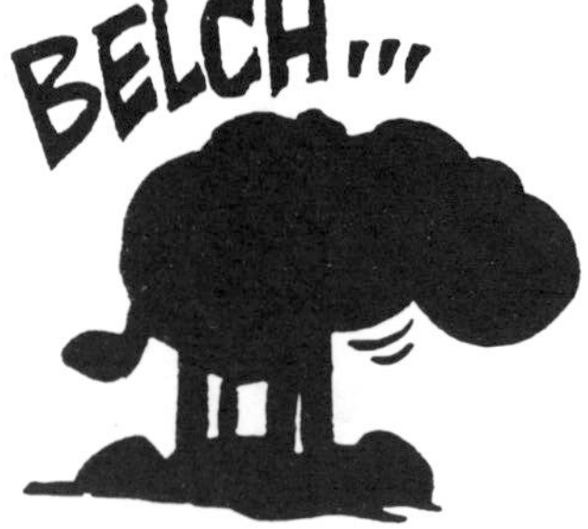
BELCH...

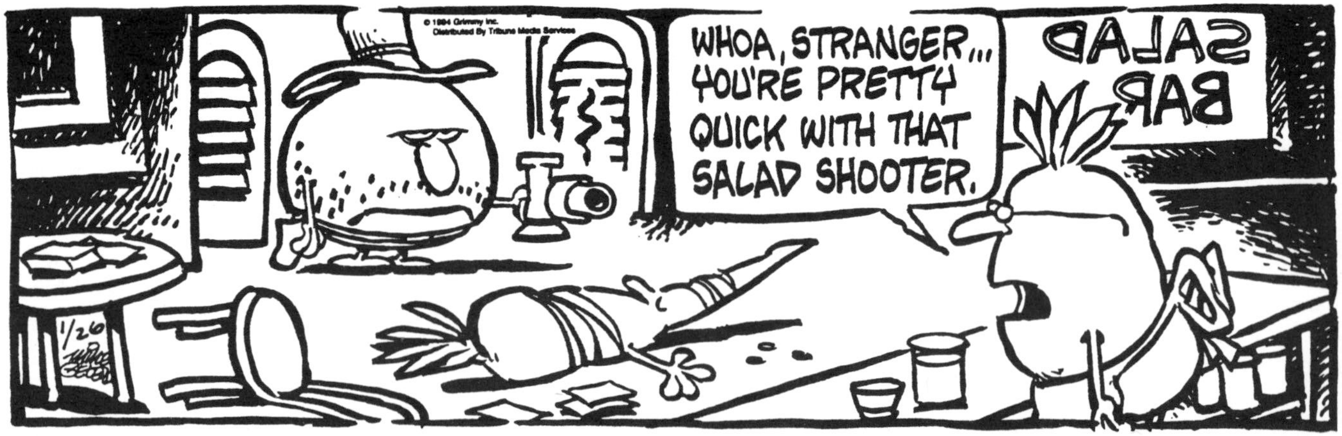
© 1984 Grimmy Inc. Distributed By Tribune Media Services
WHOA, STRANGER... YOU'RE PRETTY QUICK WITH THAT SALAD SHOOTER.
SALAD BAR

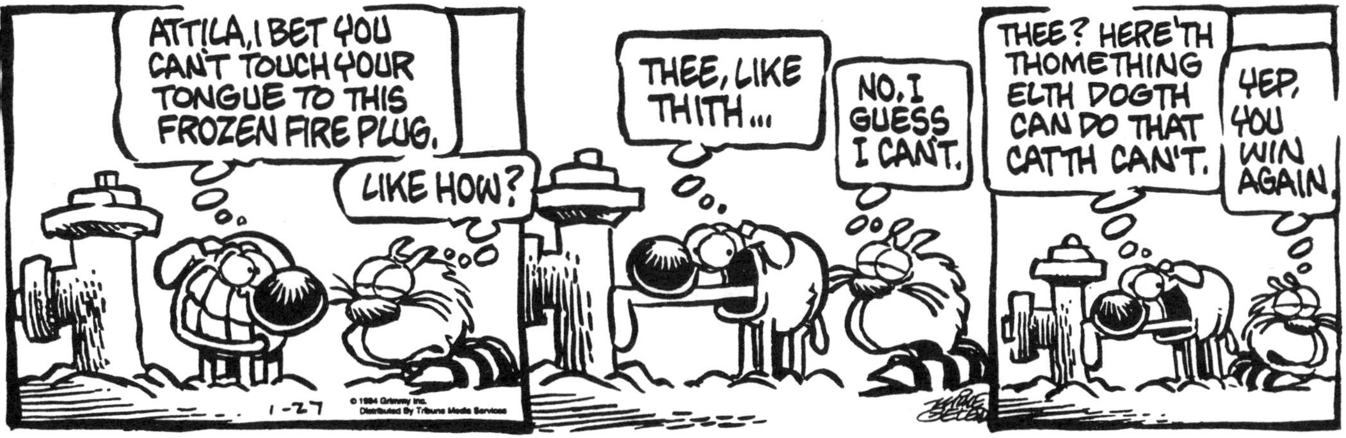
ATTILA, I BET YOU CAN'T TOUCH YOUR TONGUE TO THIS FROZEN FIRE PLUG.
LIKE HOW?
THEE, LIKE THITH...
NO, I GUESS I CAN'T.
THEE? HERE'TH THOMETHING ELTH DOGTH CAN DO THAT CATTH CAN'T.
YEP, YOU WIN AGAIN.
1-27
© 1984 Grimmy Inc. Distributed By Tribune Media Services

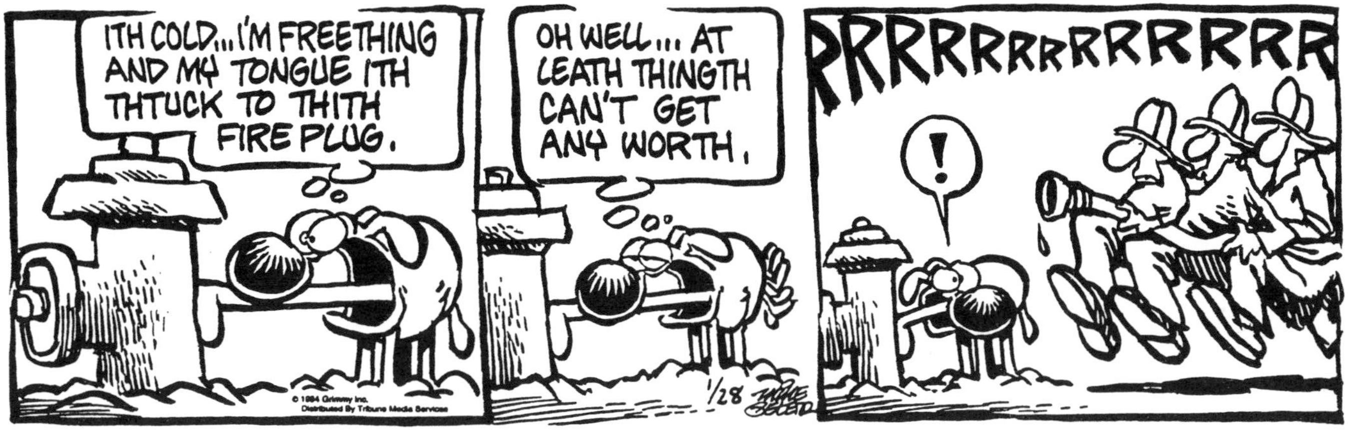
ITH COLD... I'M FREETHING AND MY TONGUE ITH THTUCK TO THITH FIRE PLUG.
© 1984 Grimmy Inc. Distributed By Tribune Media Services
OH WELL... AT LEATH THINGTH CAN'T GET ANY WORTH.
1/28
RRRRRRRRRRRRR
!

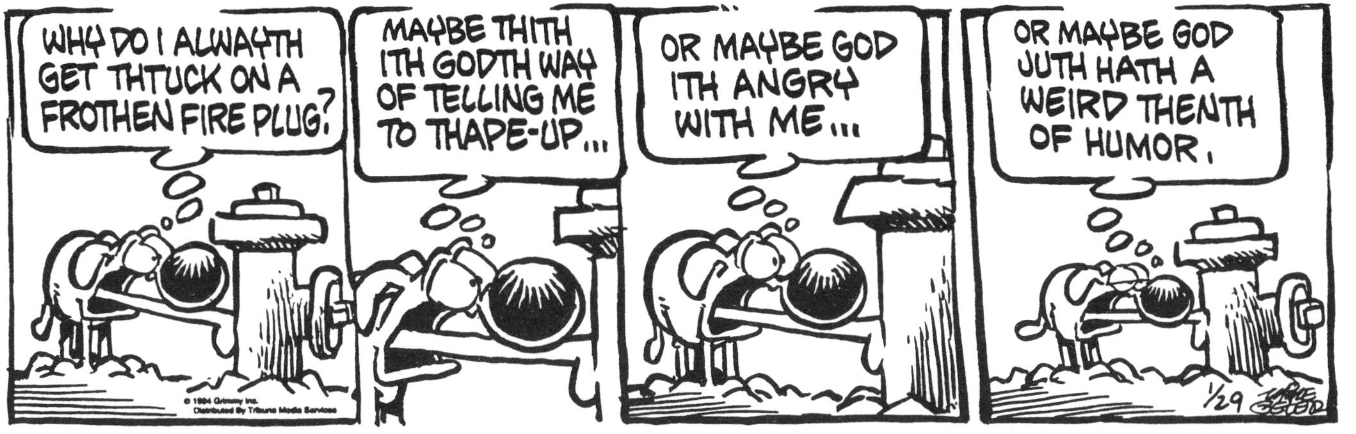
WHY DO I ALWAYTH GET THTUCK ON A FROTHEN FIRE PLUG?
© 1984 Grimmy Inc. Distributed By Tribune Media Services
MAYBE THITH ITH GODTH WAY OF TELLING ME TO THAPE-UP...
OR MAYBE GOD ITH ANGRY WITH ME...
OR MAYBE GOD JUTH HATH A WEIRD THENTH OF HUMOR.
1/29

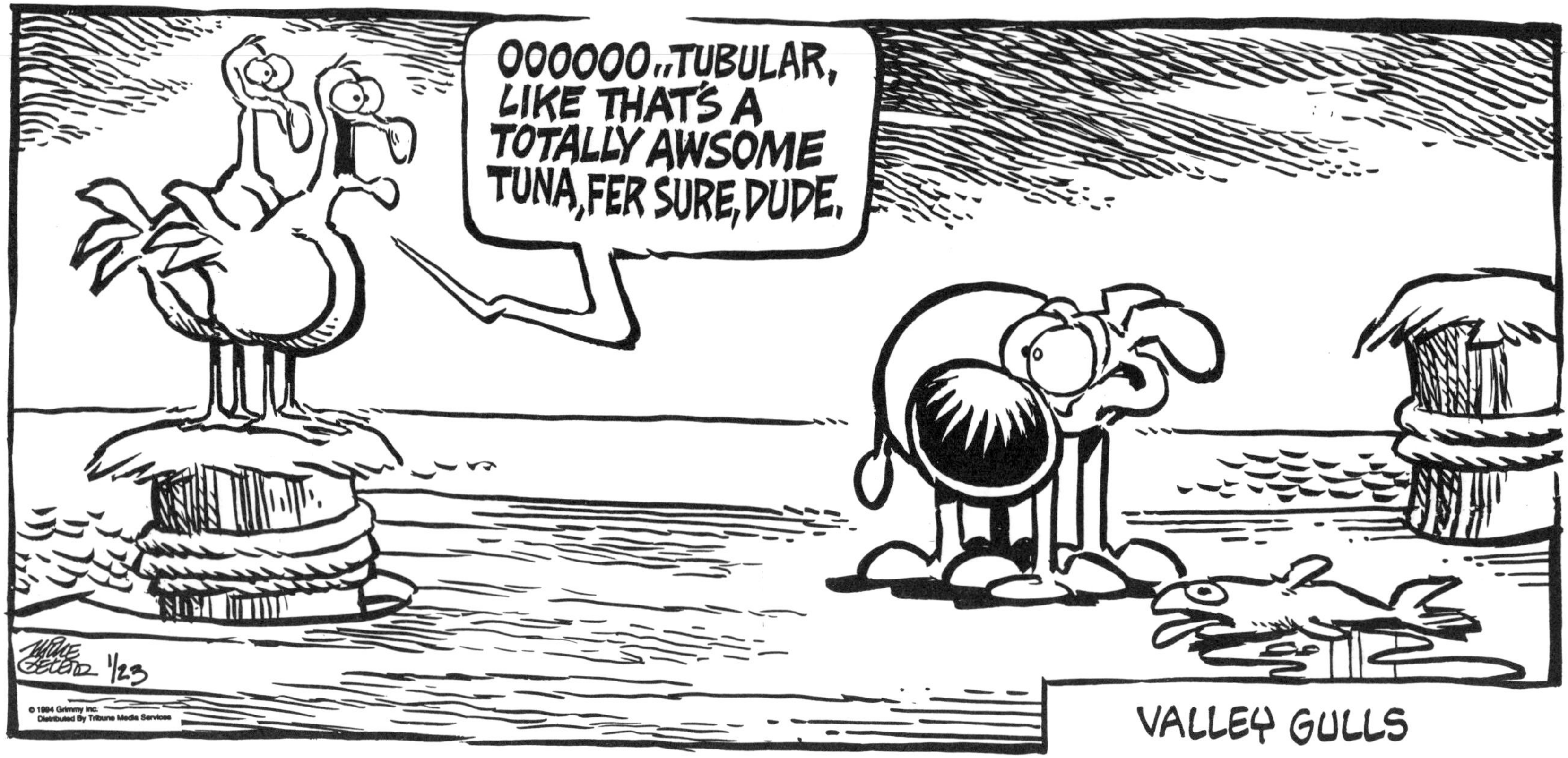
OOOOOO.,TUBULAR, LIKE THAT'S A TOTALLY AWSOME TUNA, FER SURE, DUDE.
1/23
© 1994 Grimmy Inc.
Distributed By Tribune Media Services
VALLEY GULLS

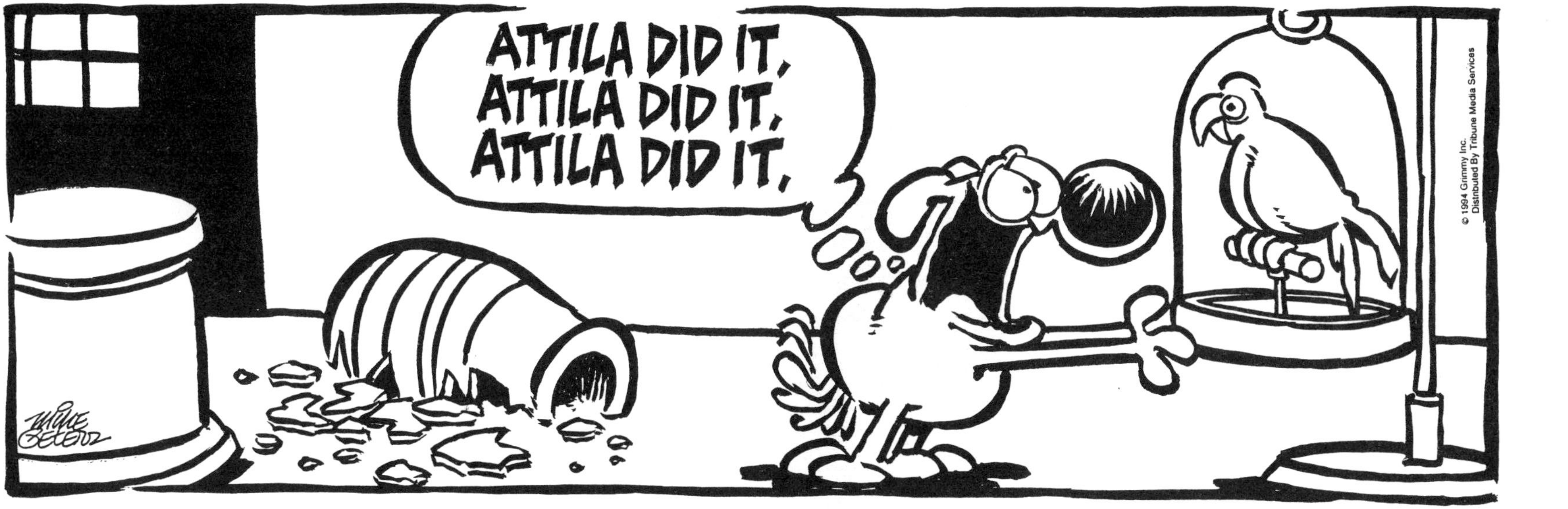
ATTILA DID IT, ATTILA DID IT, ATTILA DID IT.
© 1994 Grimmy Inc. Distributed By Tribune Media Services

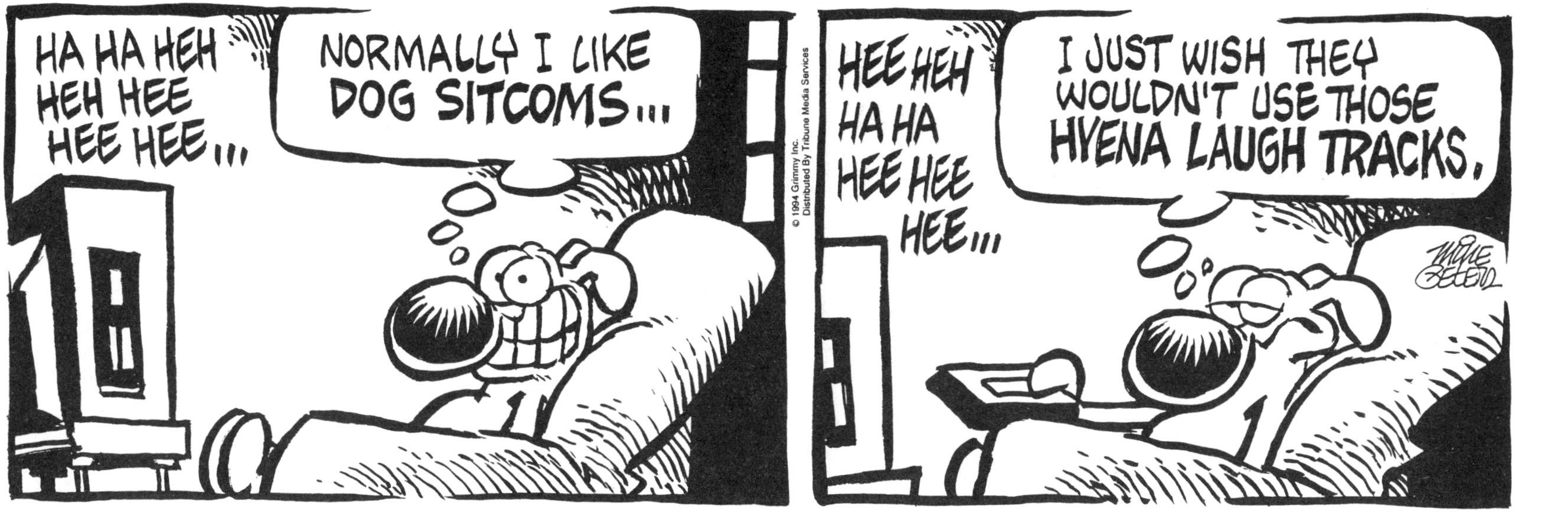
HA HA HEH HEH HEE HEE HEE...
NORMALLY I LIKE DOG SITCOMS...
© 1994 Grimmy Inc. Distributed By Tribune Media Services
HEE HEH HA HA HEE HEE HEE...
I JUST WISH THEY WOULDN'T USE THOSE HYENA LAUGH TRACKS.

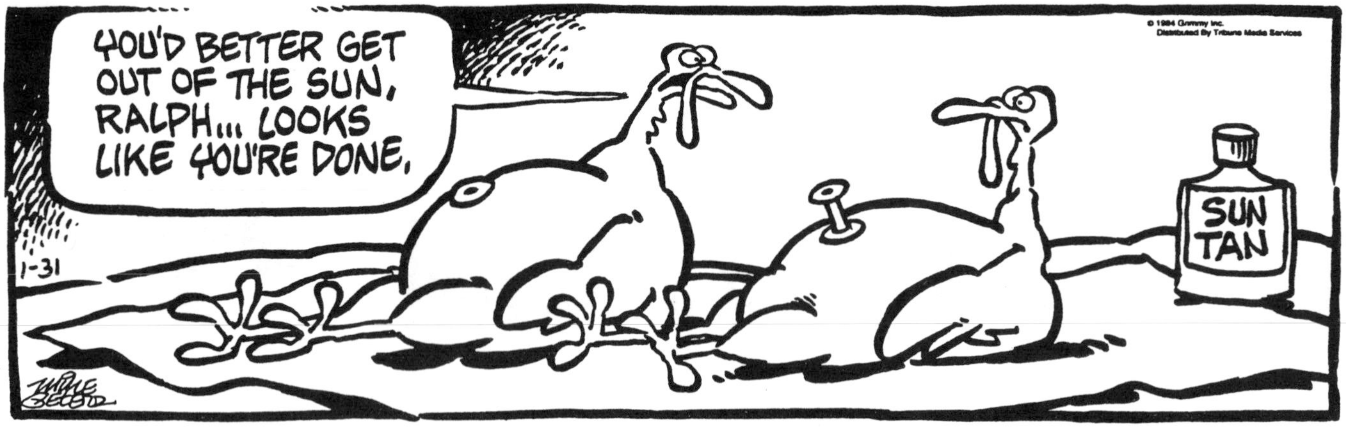
YOU'D BETTER GET OUT OF THE SUN, RALPH... LOOKS LIKE YOU'RE DONE.
SUN TAN
1-31

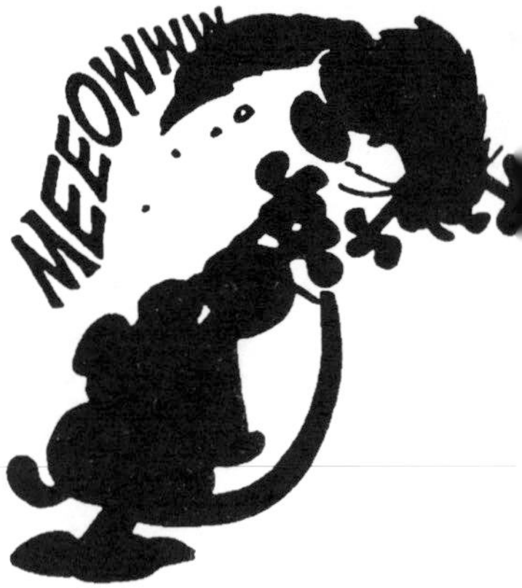
MEEOWWW

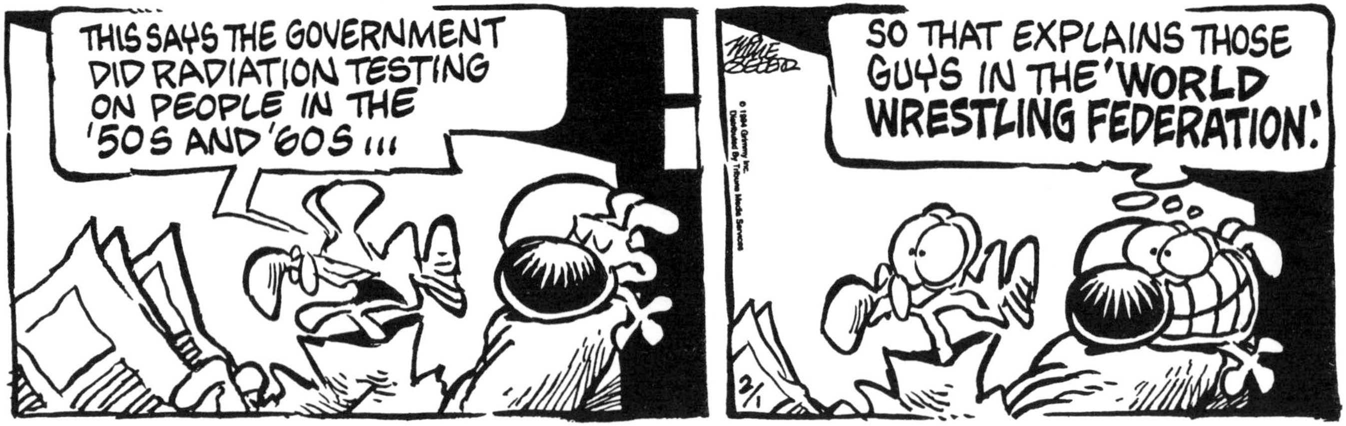
THIS SAYS THE GOVERNMENT DID RADIATION TESTING ON PEOPLE IN THE '50S AND '60S...
SO THAT EXPLAINS THOSE GUYS IN THE 'WORLD WRESTLING FEDERATION.'
2/1

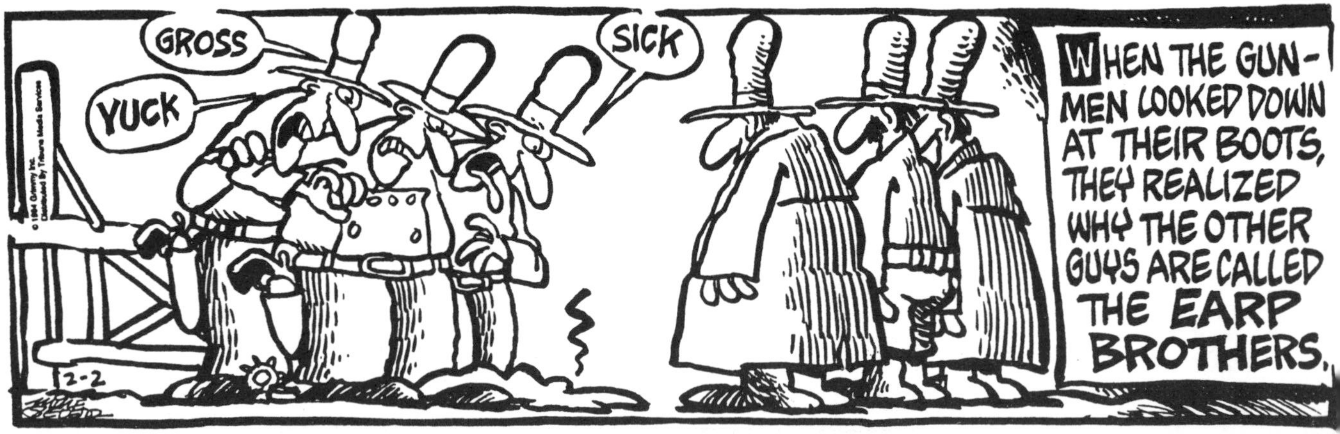
GROSS
YUCK
SICK
WHEN THE GUNMEN LOOKED DOWN AT THEIR BOOTS, THEY REALIZED WHY THE OTHER GUYS ARE CALLED THE EARP BROTHERS.
2-2

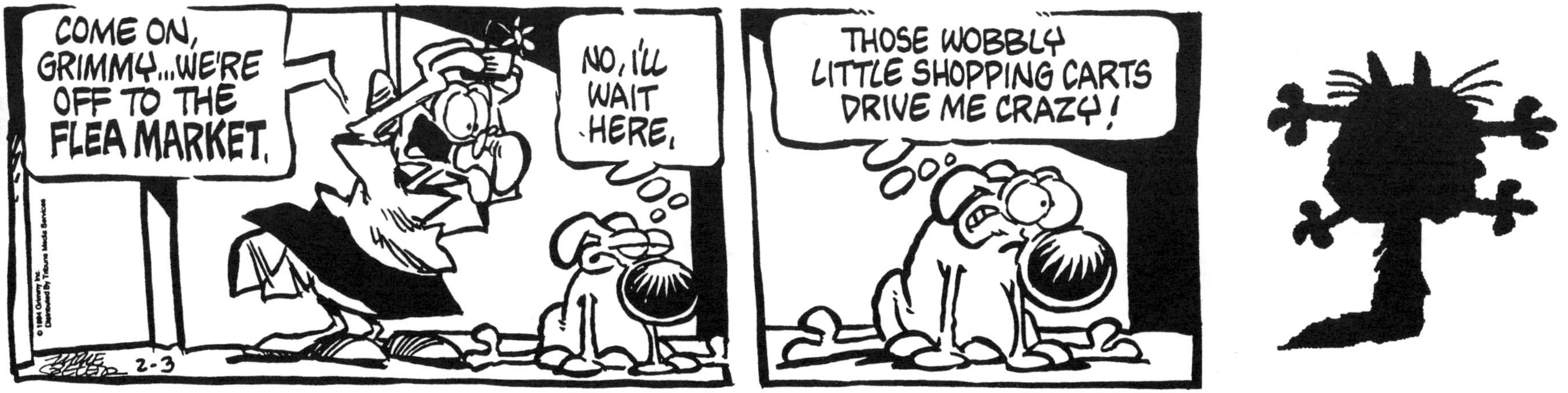
COME ON, GRIMMY...WE'RE OFF TO THE FLEA MARKET.
NO, I'LL WAIT HERE.
THOSE WOBBLY LITTLE SHOPPING CARTS DRIVE ME CRAZY!
© 1994 Grimmy Inc. Distributed By Tribune Media Services
2-3

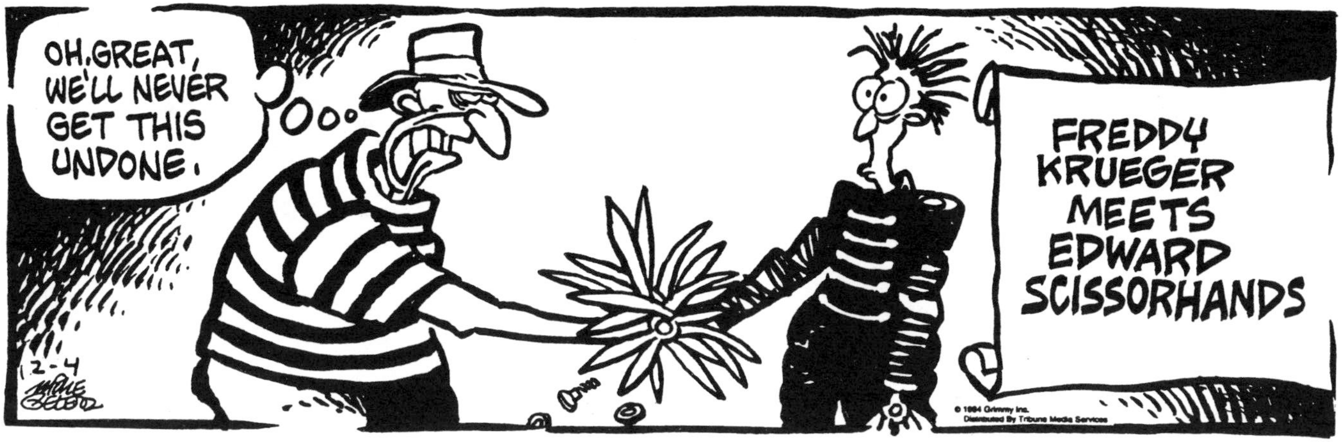
OH, GREAT, WE'LL NEVER GET THIS UNDONE.
FREDDY KRUEGER MEETS EDWARD SCISSORHANDS
© 1994 Grimmy Inc. Distributed By Tribune Media Services
2-4

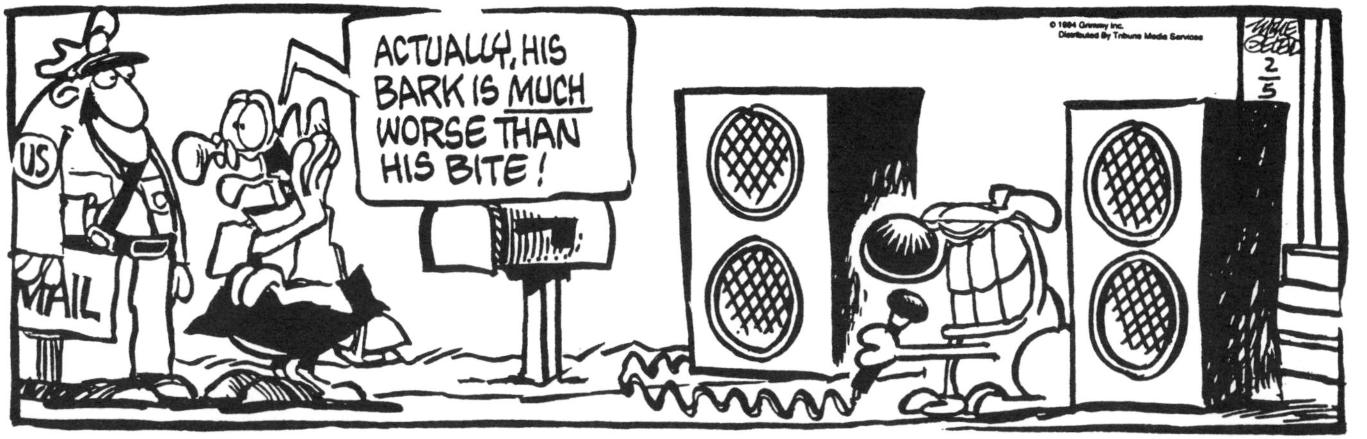
US
MAIL
ACTUALLY, HIS BARK IS MUCH WORSE THAN HIS BITE!
© 1994 Grimmy Inc. Distributed By Tribune Media Services
2/5

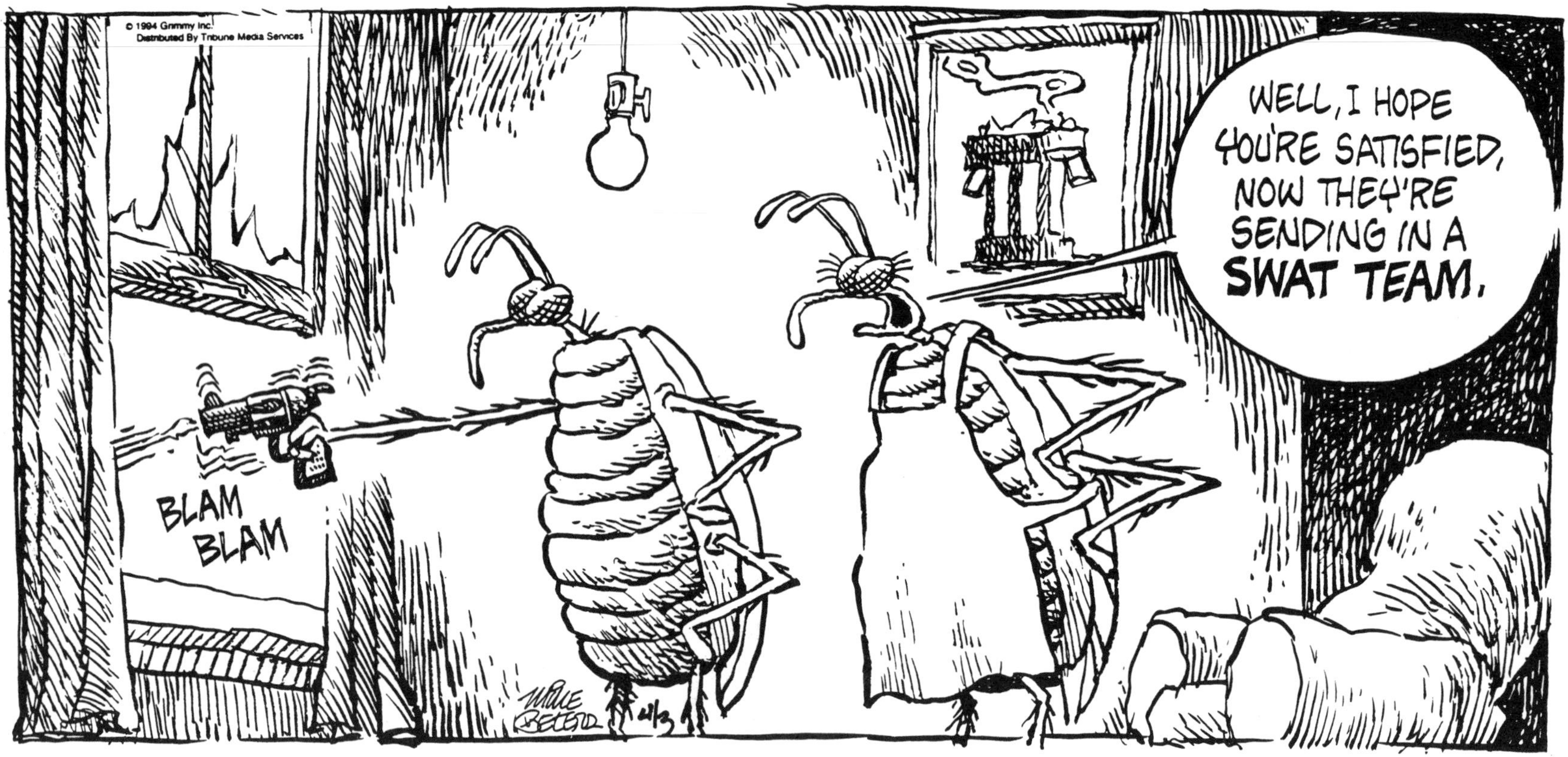
© 1994 Grimmy Inc.
Distributed By Tribune Media Services
BLAM
BLAM
WELL, I HOPE YOU'RE SATISFIED, NOW THEY'RE SENDING IN A SWAT TEAM.
MIKE PETERS

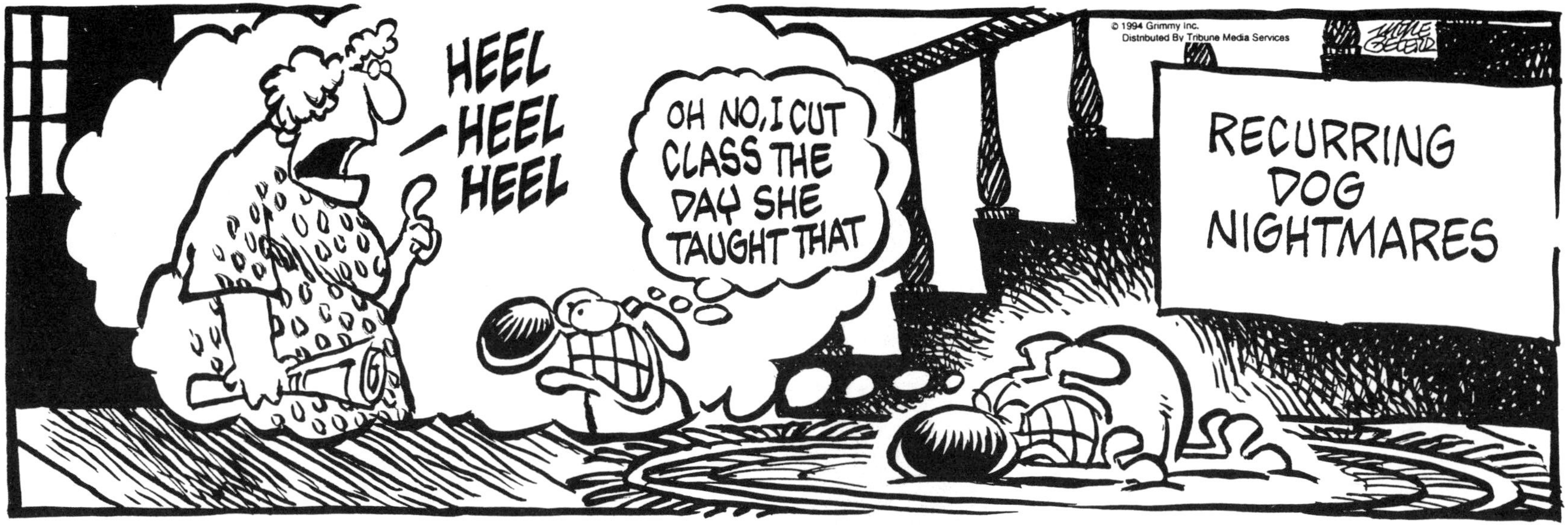
© 1994 Grimmy Inc.
Distributed By Tribune Media Services
HEEL HEEL HEEL
OH NO, I CUT CLASS THE DAY SHE TAUGHT THAT
RECURRING DOG NIGHTMARES

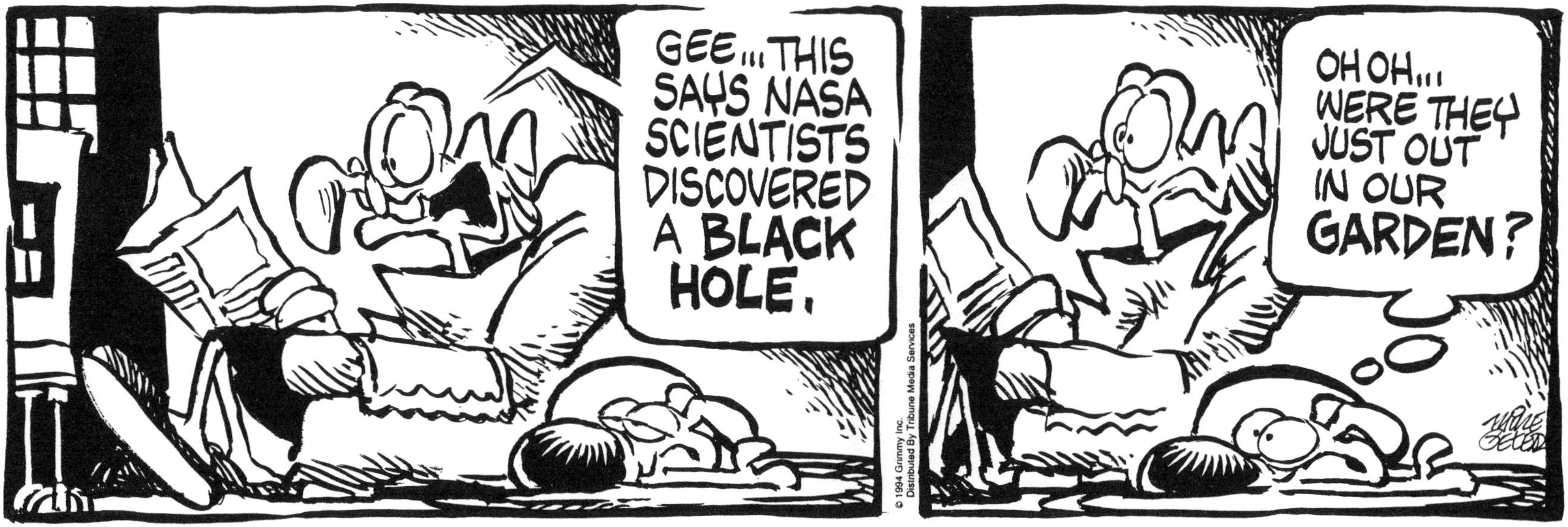
GEE... THIS SAYS NASA SCIENTISTS DISCOVERED A BLACK HOLE.
© 1994 Grimmy Inc.
Distributed By Tribune Media Services
OH OH... WERE THEY JUST OUT IN OUR GARDEN?

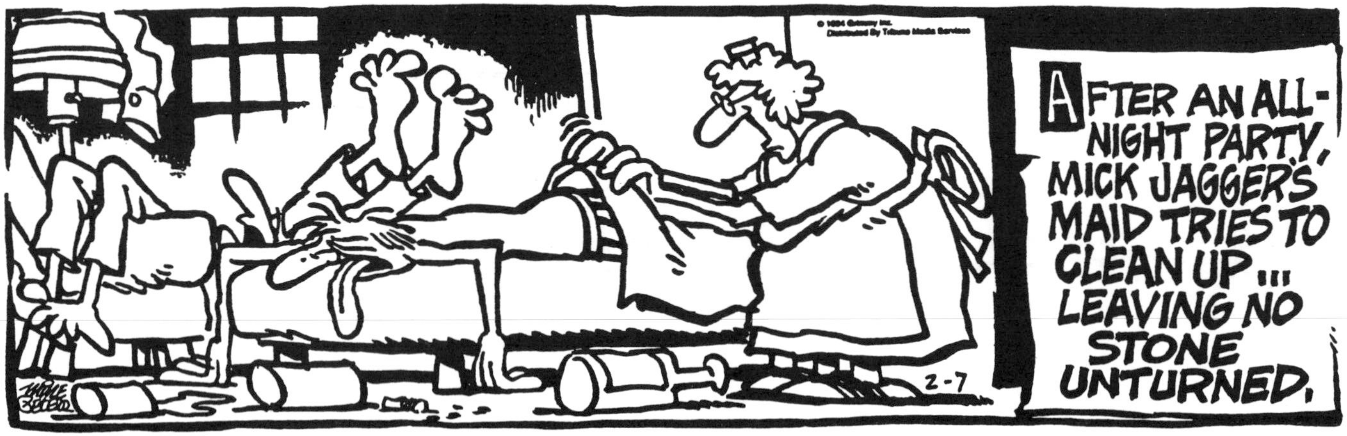
2-7
AFTER AN ALL-NIGHT PARTY, MICK JAGGER'S MAID TRIES TO CLEAN UP... LEAVING NO STONE UNTURNED.

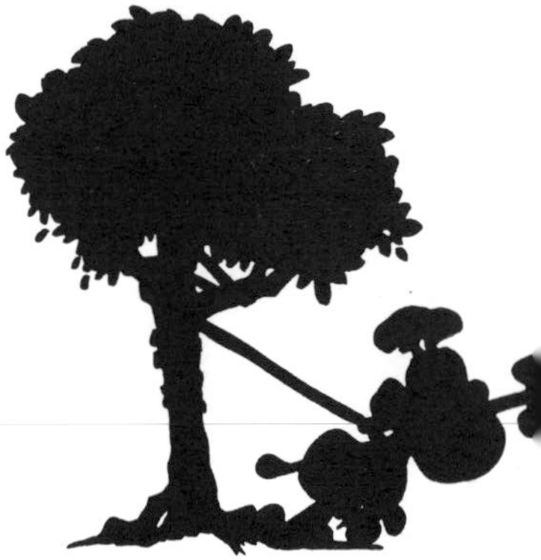

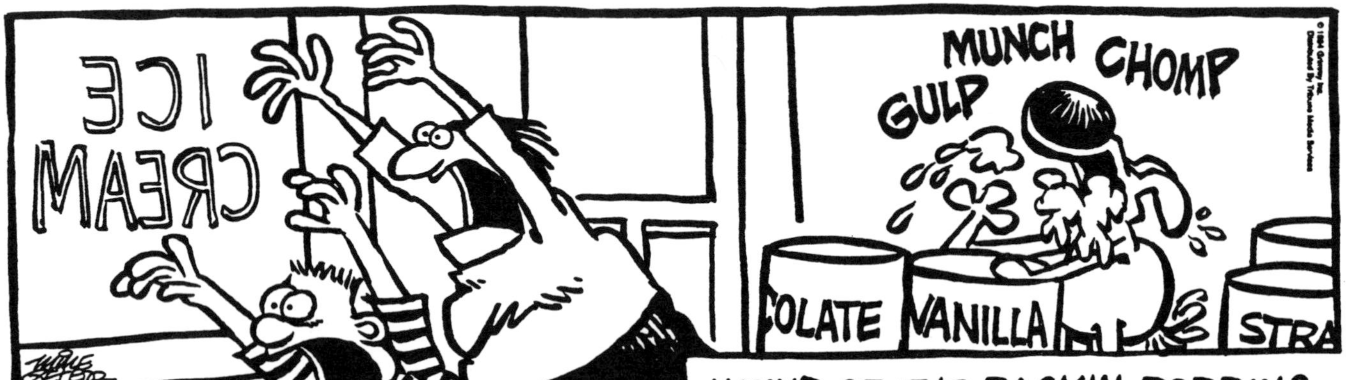
ICE CREAM
2-8
MUNCH
CHOMP
GULP
COLATE
VANILLA
STRA

HOUND OF THE BASKIN-ROBBINS

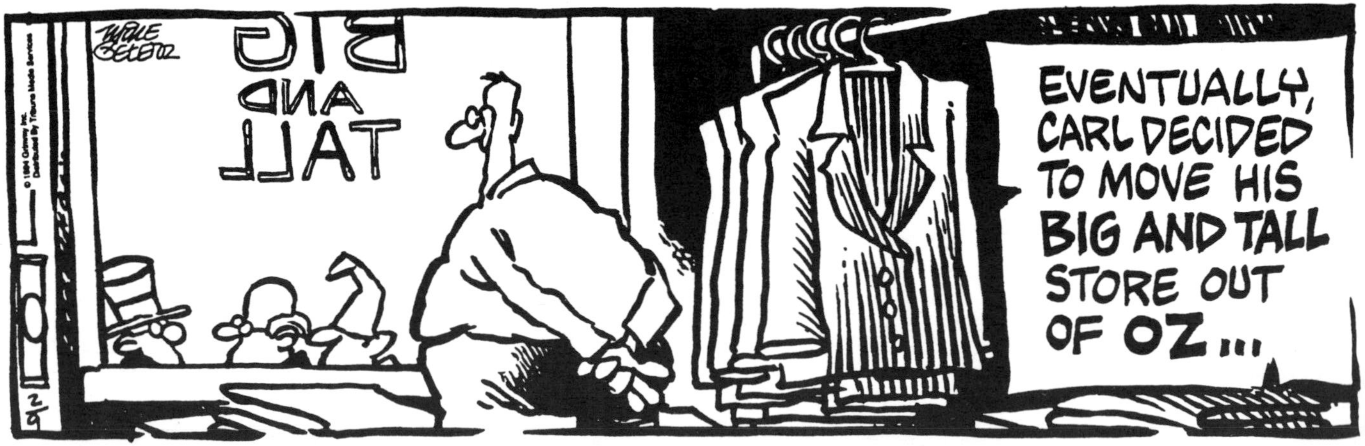
BIG AND TALL
2/9
EVENTUALLY, CARL DECIDED TO MOVE HIS BIG AND TALL STORE OUT OF OZ...

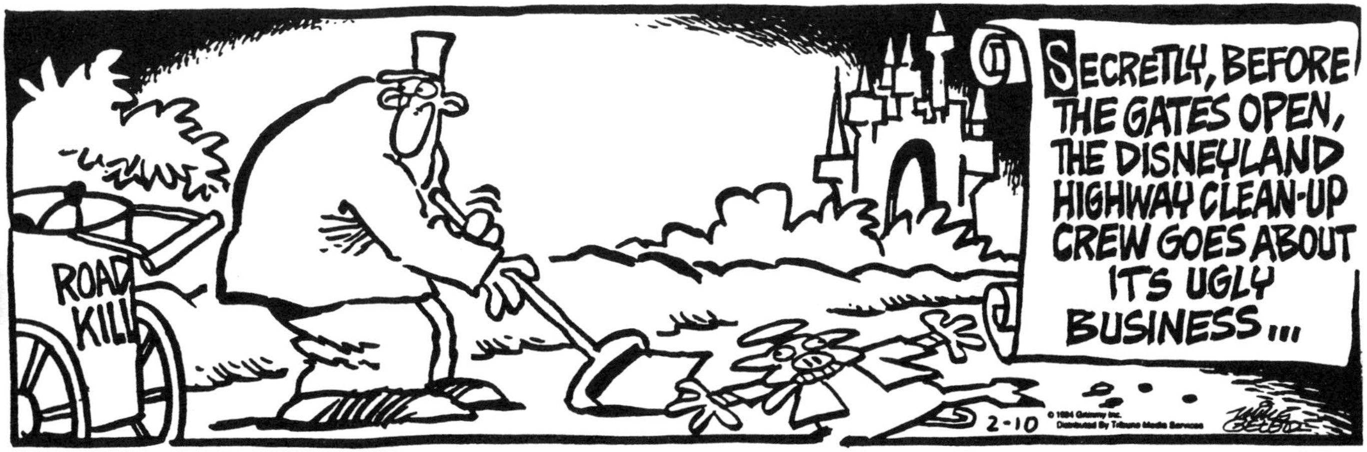
SECRETLY, BEFORE THE GATES OPEN, THE DISNEYLAND HIGHWAY CLEAN-UP CREW GOES ABOUT ITS UGLY BUSINESS...
ROAD KILL
2-10
© 1994 Grimmy Inc.
Distributed By Tribune Media Services

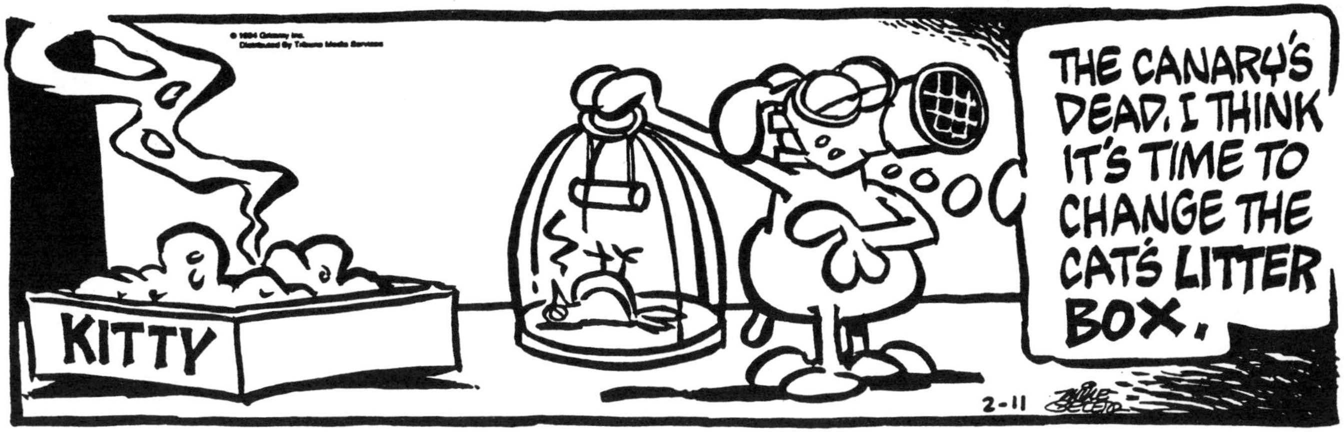
THE CANARY'S DEAD. I THINK IT'S TIME TO CHANGE THE CAT'S LITTER BOX.
KITTY
2-11
© 1994 Grimmy Inc.
Distributed By Tribune Media Services

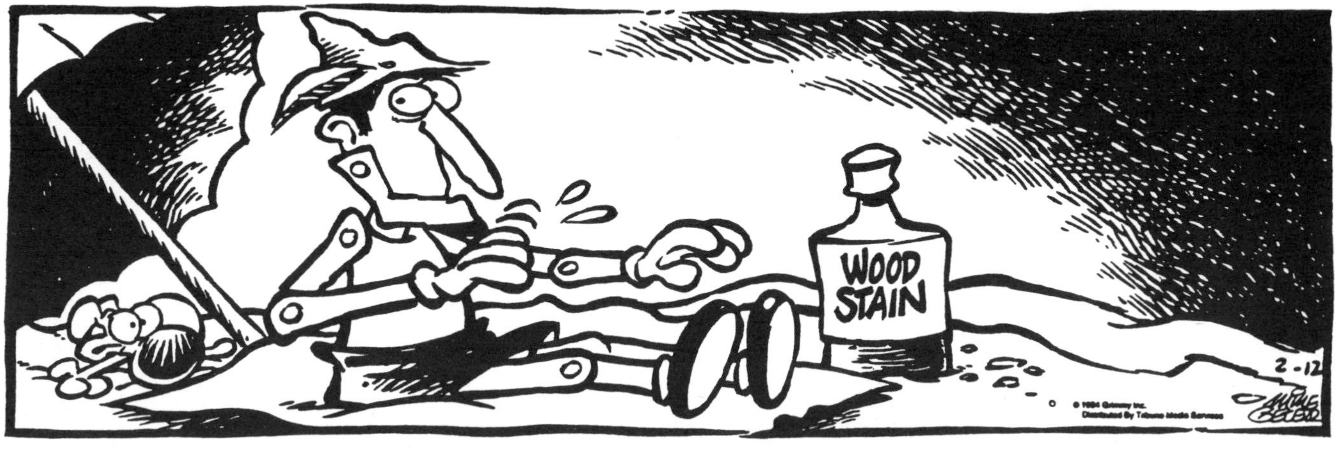
WOOD STAIN
2-12
© 1994 Grimmy Inc.
Distributed By Tribune Media Services

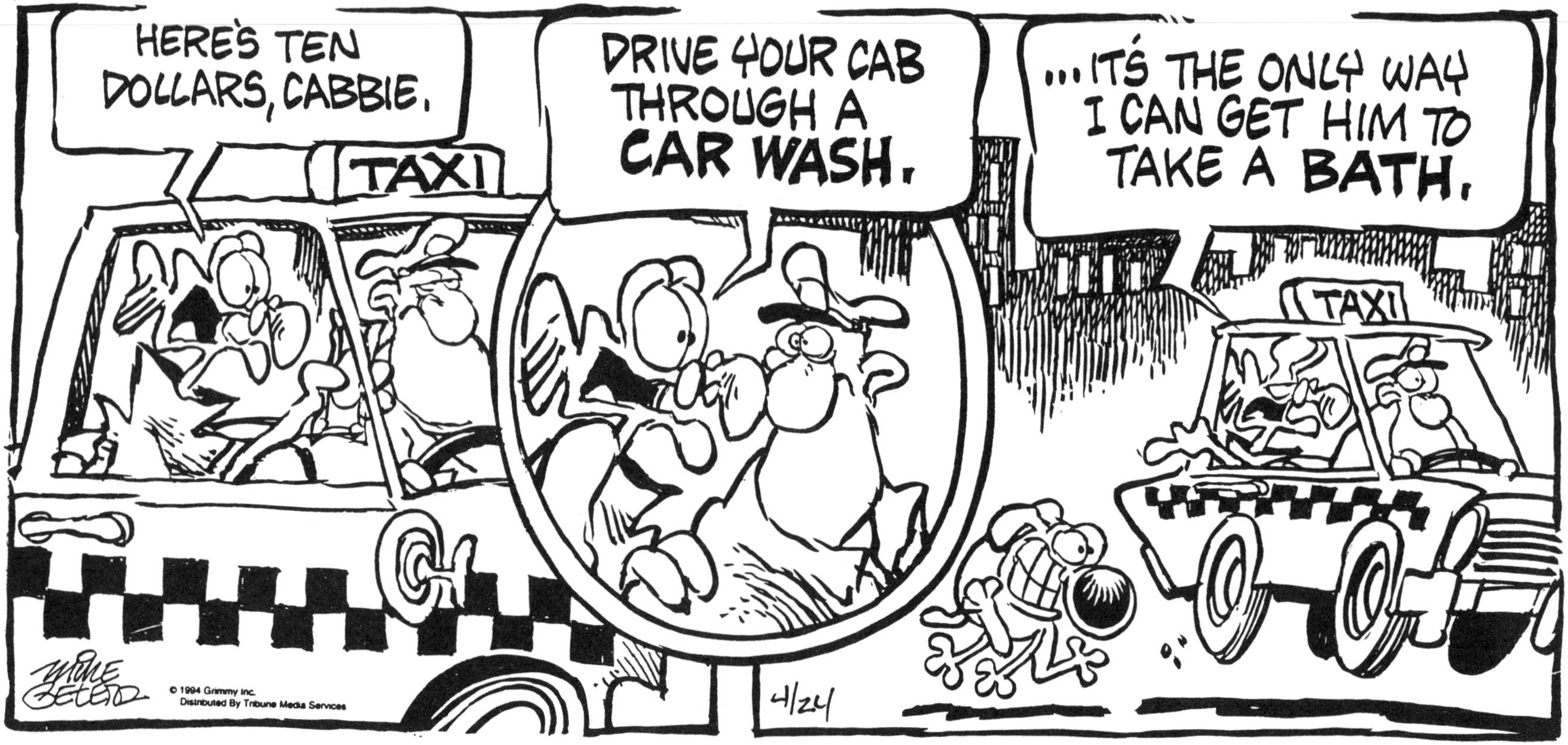
HERE'S TEN DOLLARS, CABBIE.
TAXI
DRIVE YOUR CAB THROUGH A CAR WASH.
...IT'S THE ONLY WAY I CAN GET HIM TO TAKE A BATH.
TAXI
MIKE PETERS
© 1994 Grimmy Inc.
Distributed By Tribune Media Services
4/24

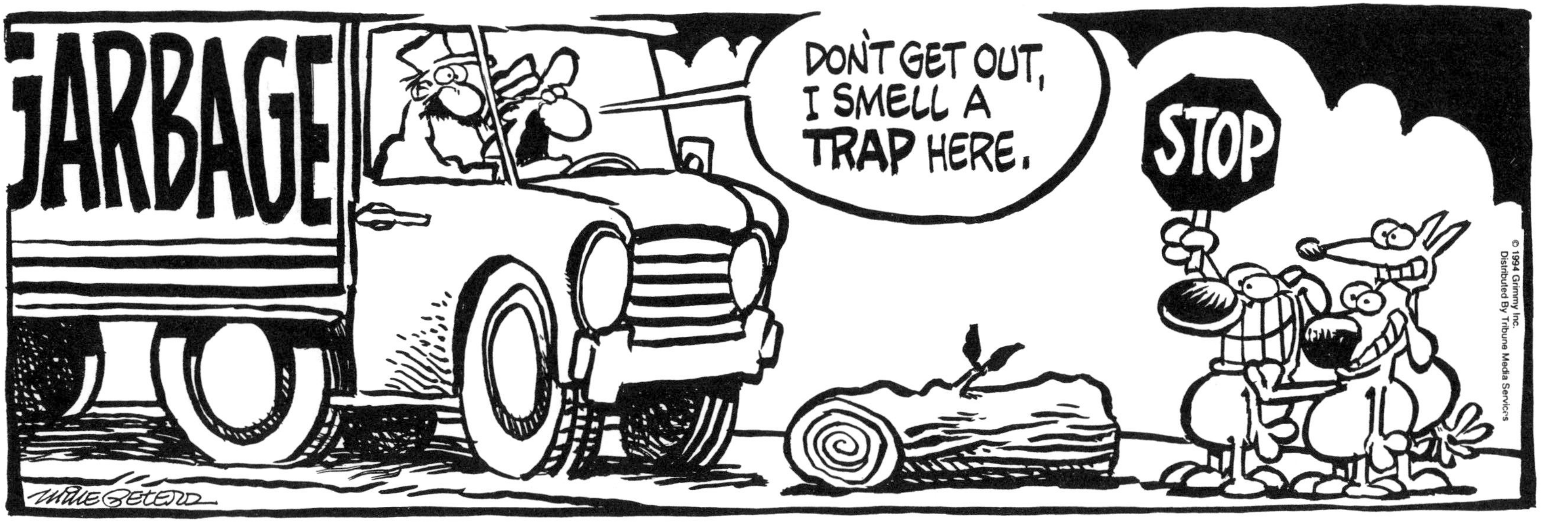
GARBAGE
DON'T GET OUT, I SMELL A TRAP HERE.
STOP
© 1994 Grimmy Inc. Distributed By Tribune Media Services

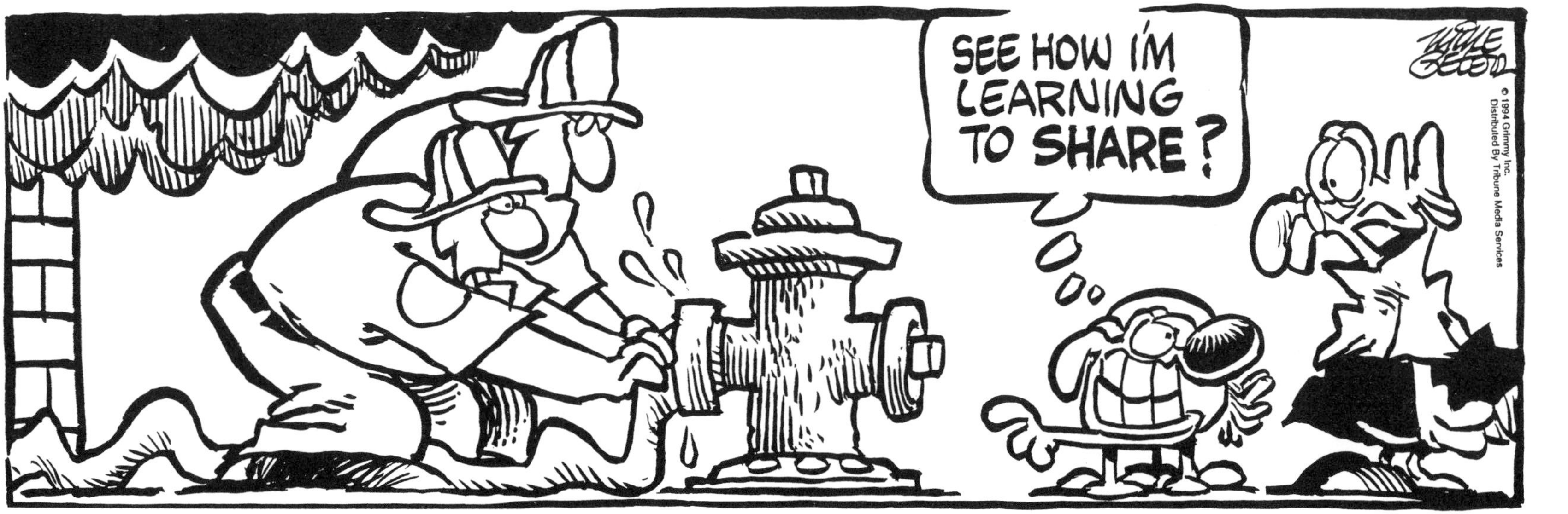
SEE HOW I'M LEARNING TO SHARE?
© 1994 Grimmy Inc. Distributed By Tribune Media Services

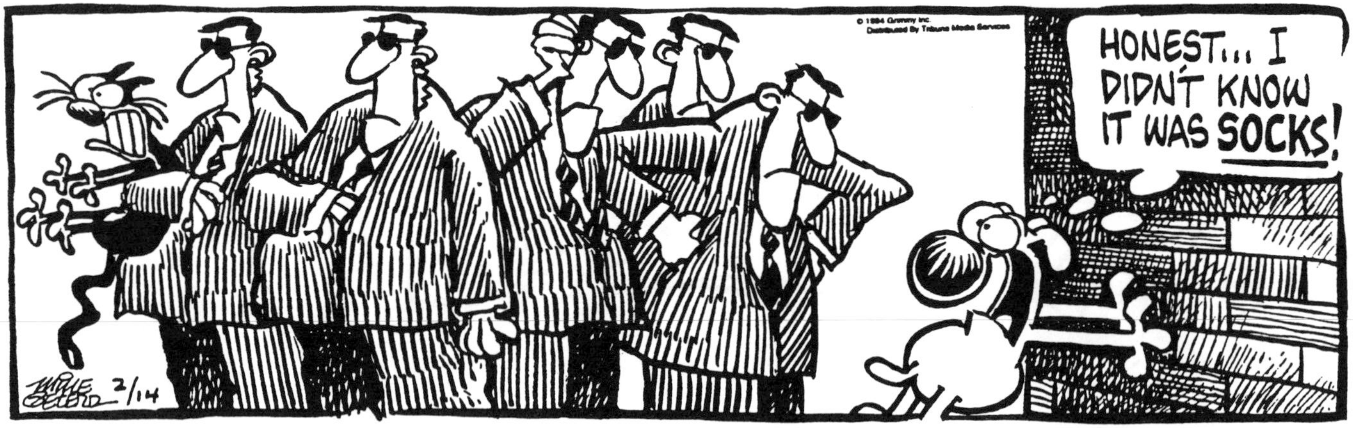
© 1994 Grimmy Inc.
Distributed By Tribune Media Services
2/14
HONEST... I DIDN'T KNOW IT WAS SOCKS!

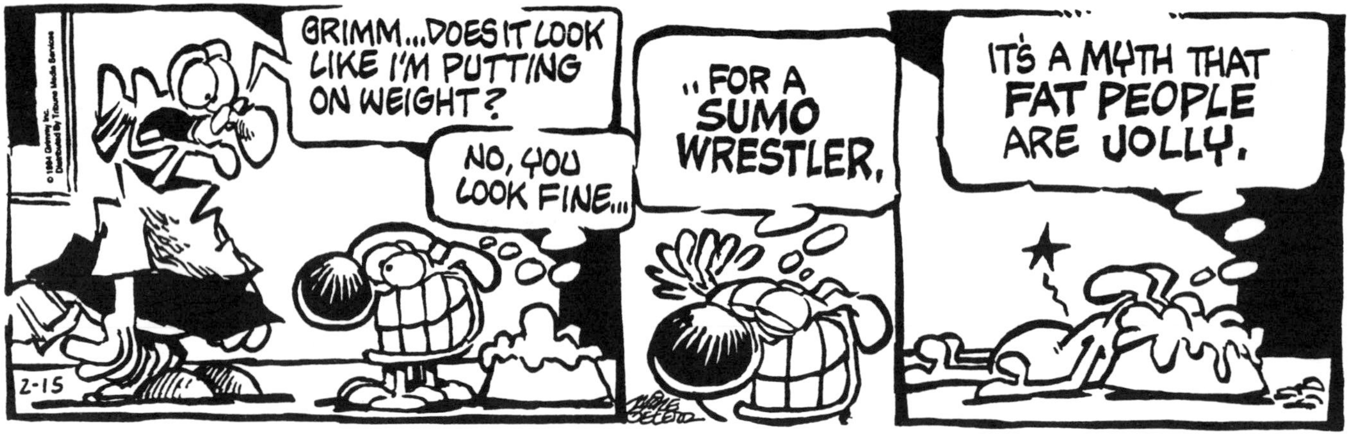
© 1994 Grimmy Inc.
Distributed By Tribune Media Services
2-15
GRIMM...DOES IT LOOK LIKE I'M PUTTING ON WEIGHT?
NO, YOU LOOK FINE...
..FOR A SUMO WRESTLER.
IT'S A MYTH THAT FAT PEOPLE ARE JOLLY.

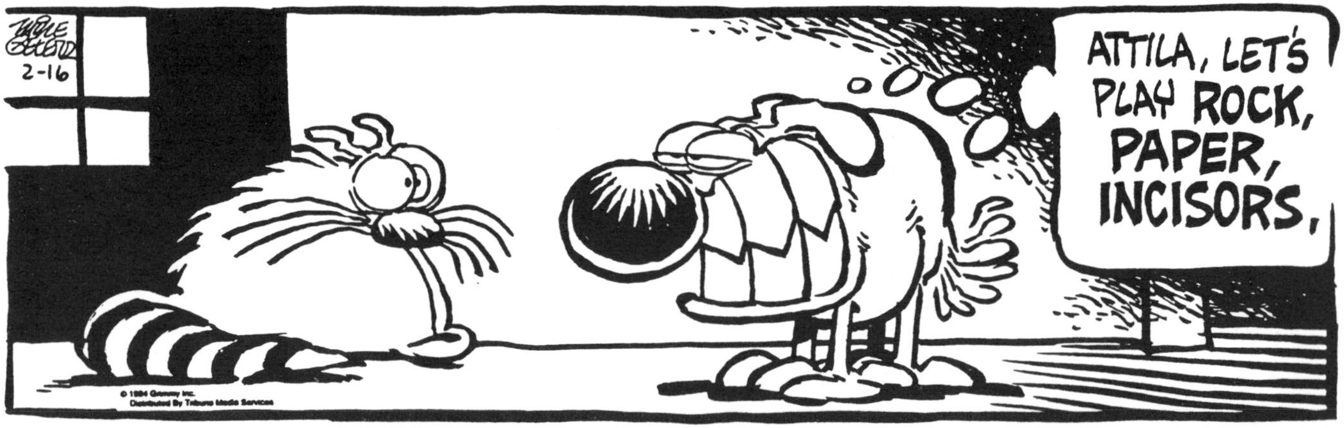
2-16
ATTILA, LET'S PLAY ROCK, PAPER, INCISORS.
© 1994 Grimmy Inc.
Distributed By Tribune Media Services

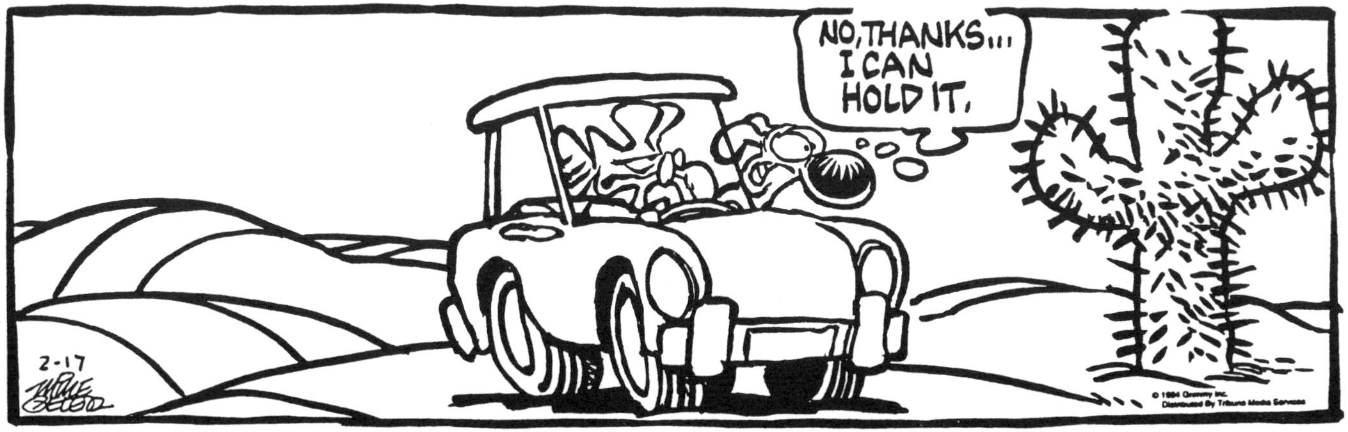
NO, THANKS... I CAN HOLD IT.
2-17

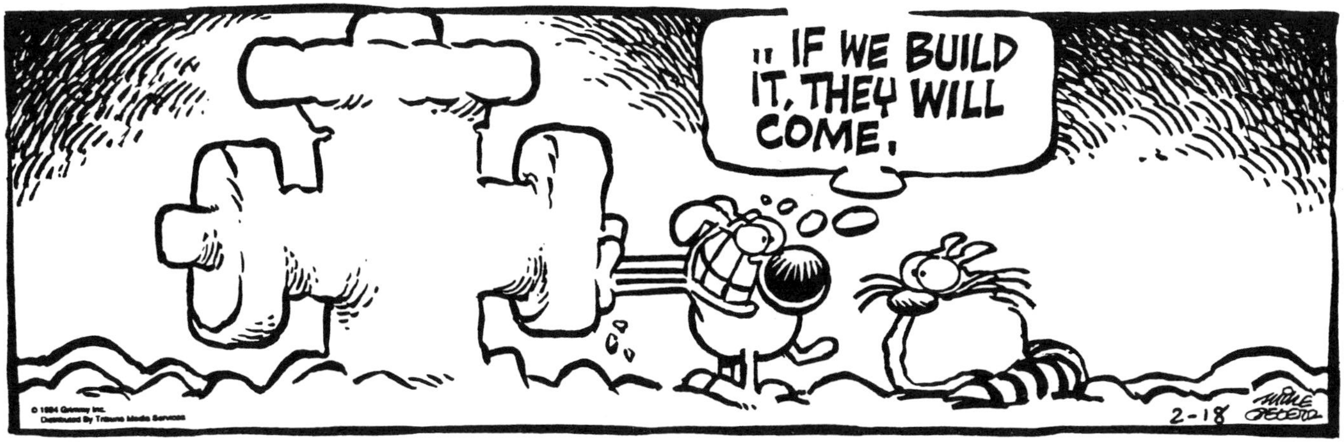
.. IF WE BUILD IT, THEY WILL COME.
2-18

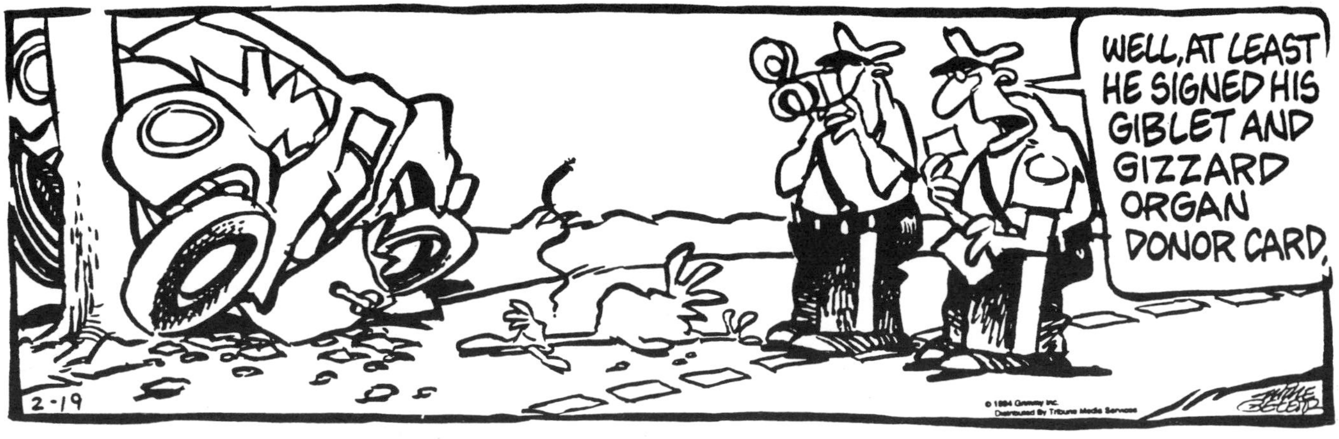
WELL, AT LEAST HE SIGNED HIS GIBLET AND GIZZARD ORGAN DONOR CARD.
2-19

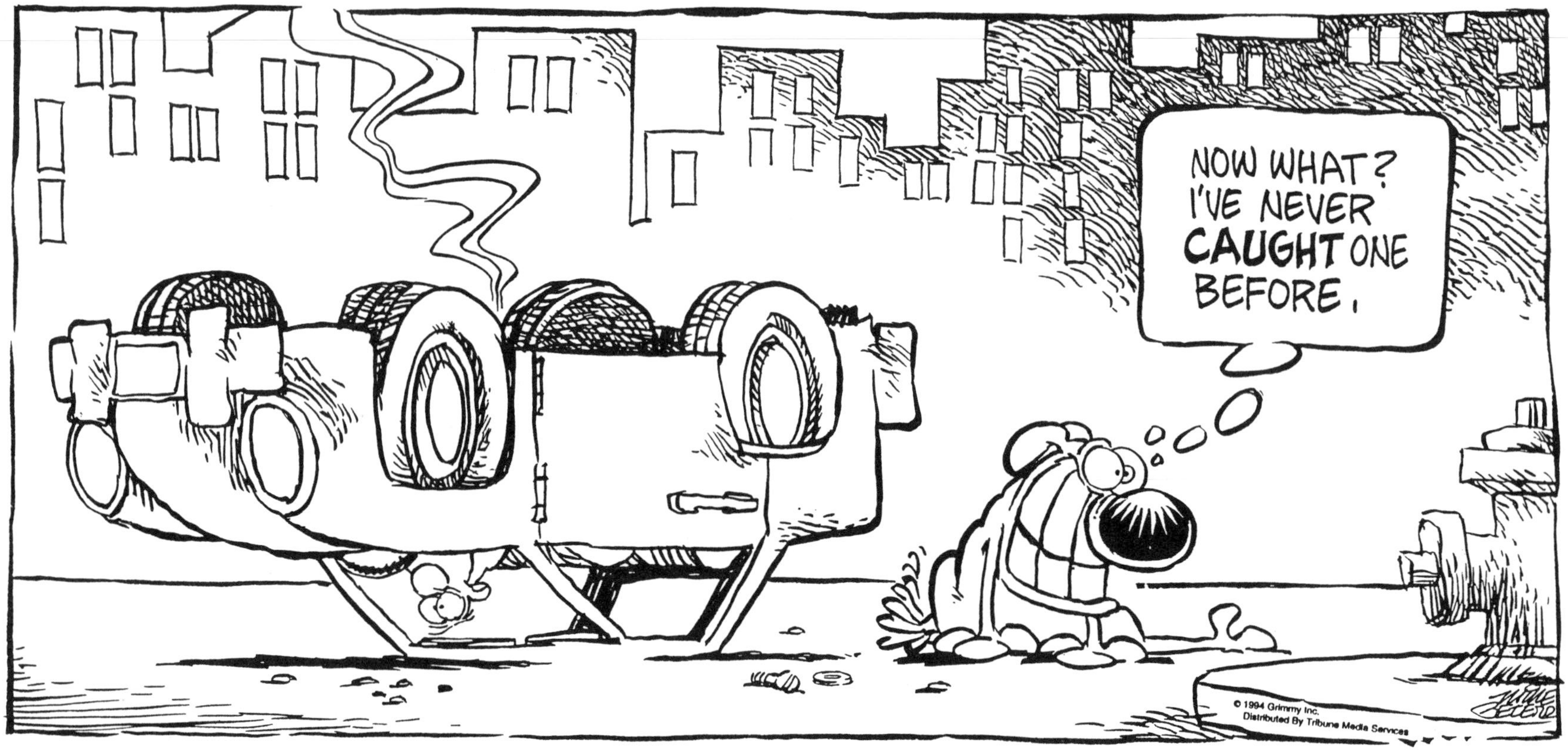
NOW WHAT? I'VE NEVER **CAUGHT** ONE BEFORE.
© 1994 Grimmy Inc.
Distributed By Tribune Media Services

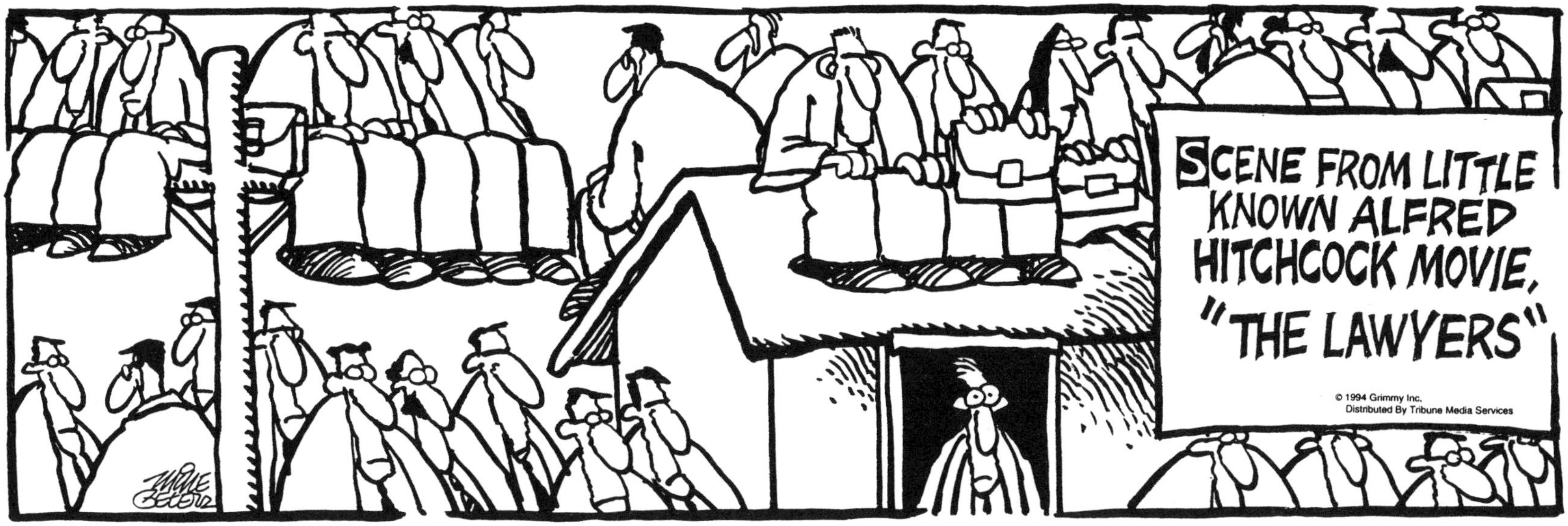
SCENE FROM LITTLE KNOWN ALFRED HITCHCOCK MOVIE, "THE LAWYERS"
© 1994 Grimmy Inc.
Distributed By Tribune Media Services

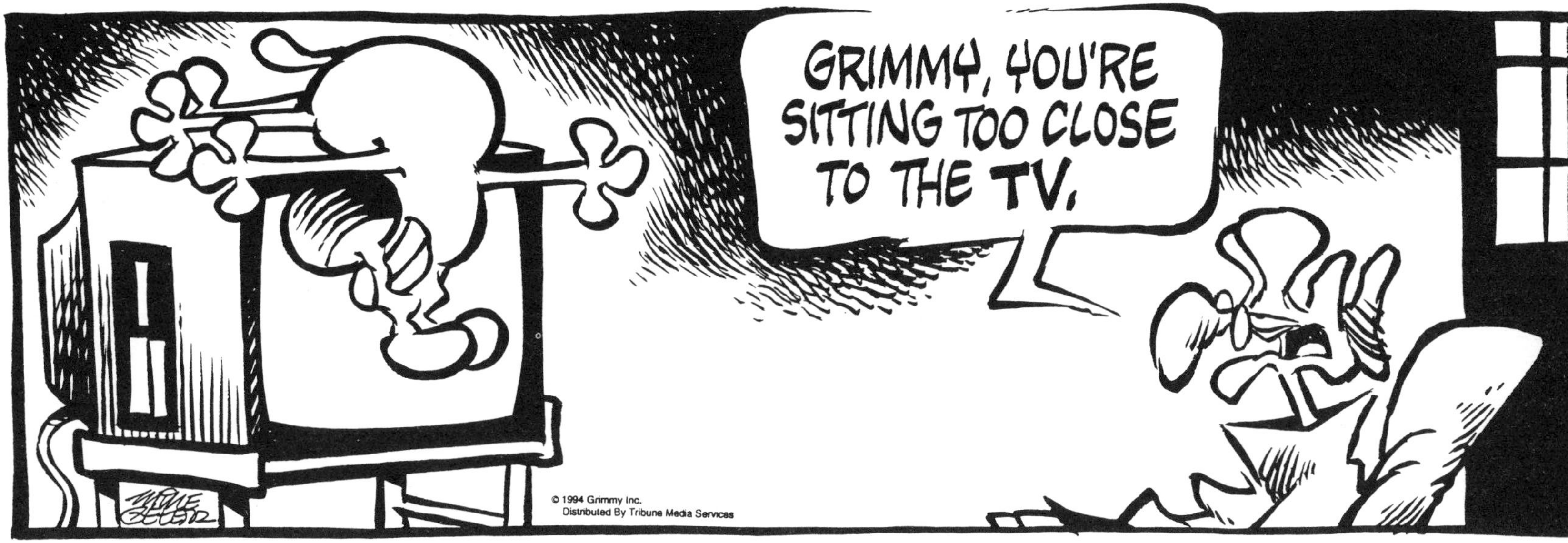
GRIMMY, YOU'RE SITTING TOO CLOSE TO THE TV.
© 1994 Grimmy Inc.
Distributed By Tribune Media Services

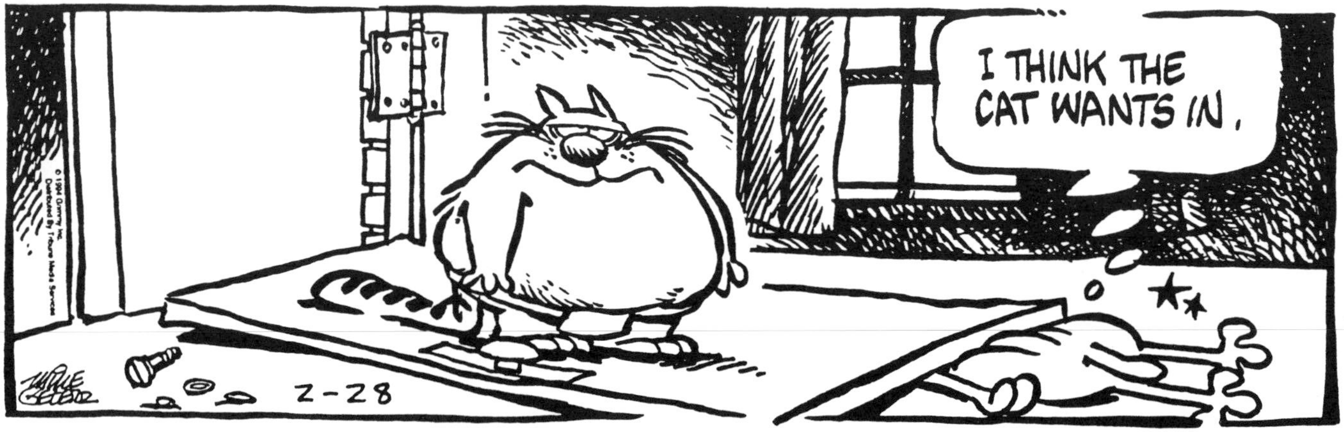
I THINK THE CAT WANTS IN.
2-28

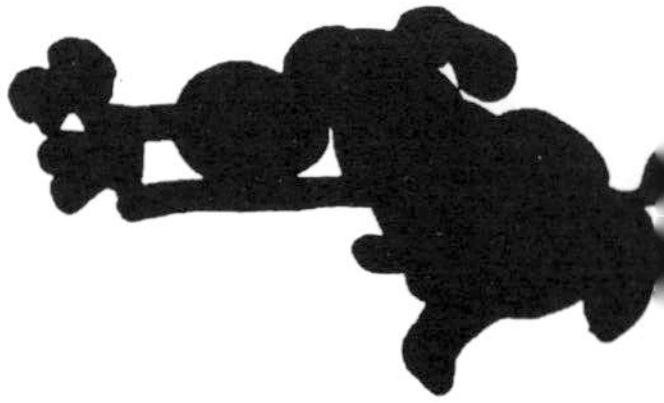

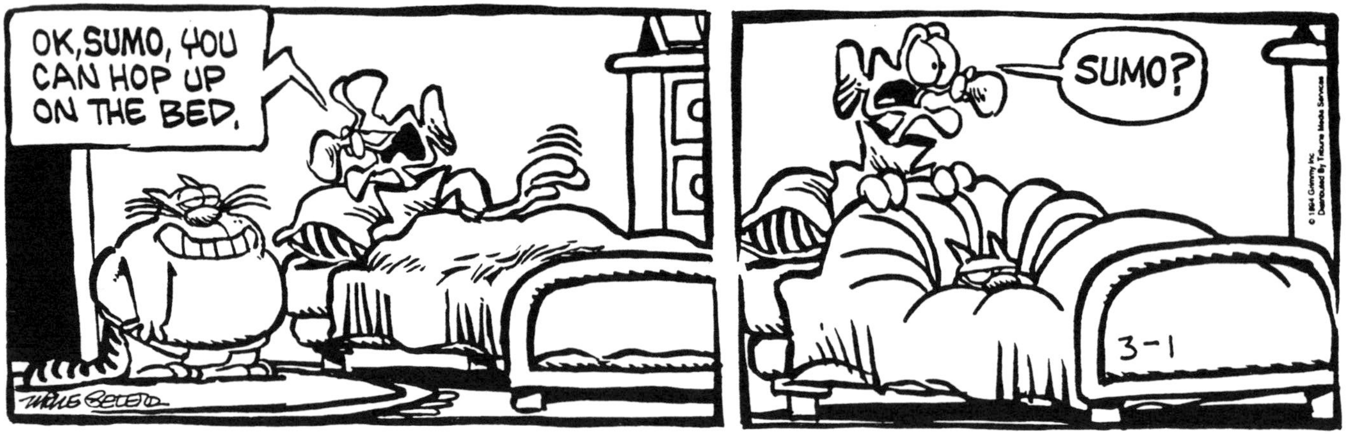
OK, SUMO, YOU CAN HOP UP ON THE BED.
SUMO?
3-1

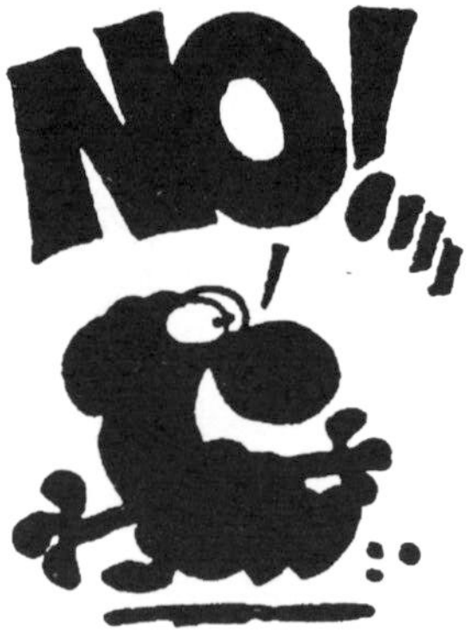
NO!

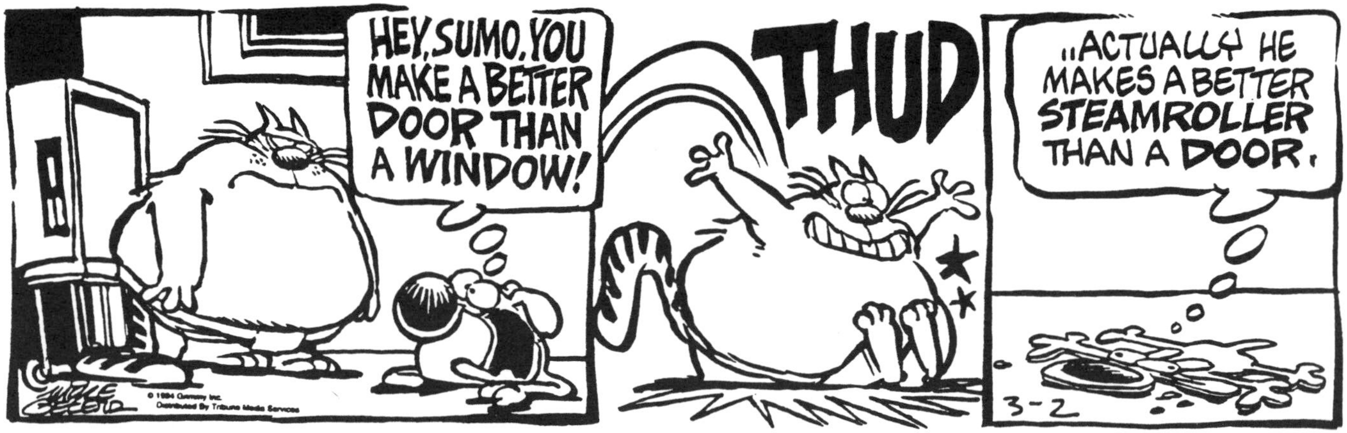
HEY, SUMO, YOU MAKE A BETTER DOOR THAN A WINDOW!
THUD
..ACTUALLY HE MAKES A BETTER STEAMROLLER THAN A DOOR.
3-2

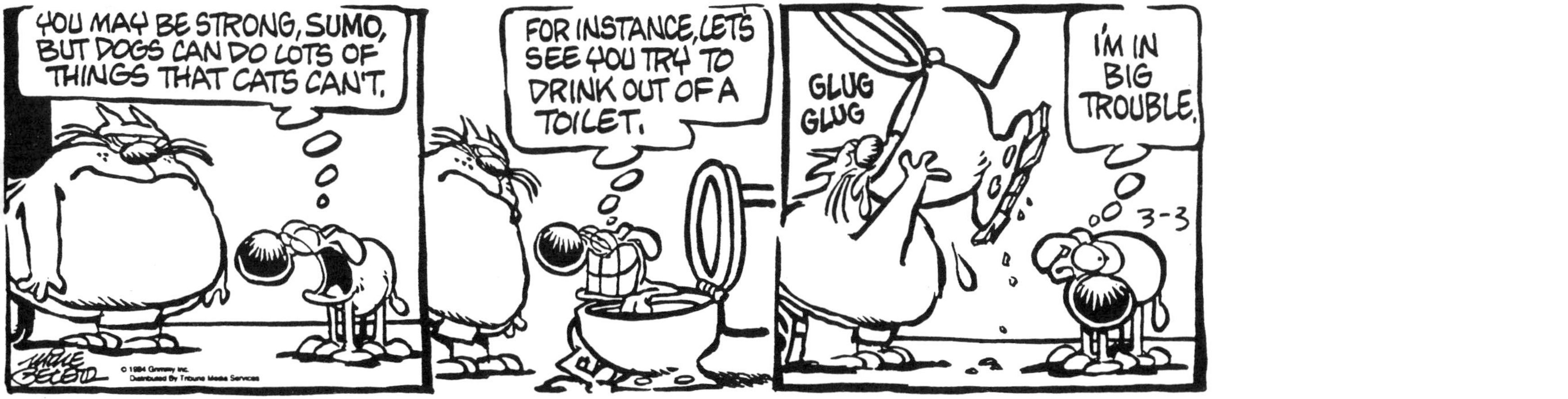
YOU MAY BE STRONG, SUMO, BUT DOGS CAN DO LOTS OF THINGS THAT CATS CAN'T.
FOR INSTANCE, LET'S SEE YOU TRY TO DRINK OUT OF A TOILET.
GLUG GLUG
I'M IN BIG TROUBLE.
3-3

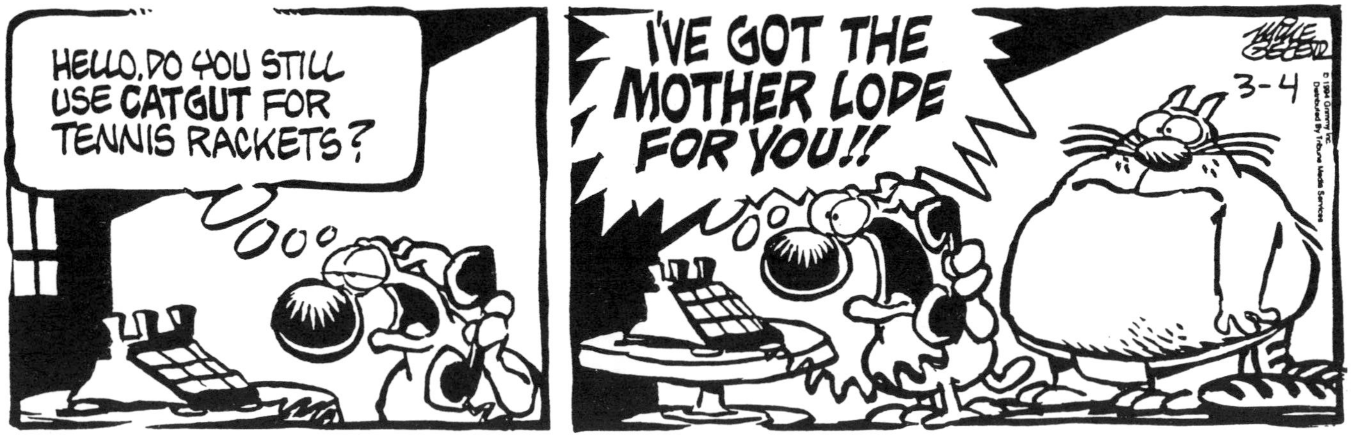
HELLO, DO YOU STILL USE CATGUT FOR TENNIS RACKETS?
I'VE GOT THE MOTHER LODE FOR YOU!!
3-4

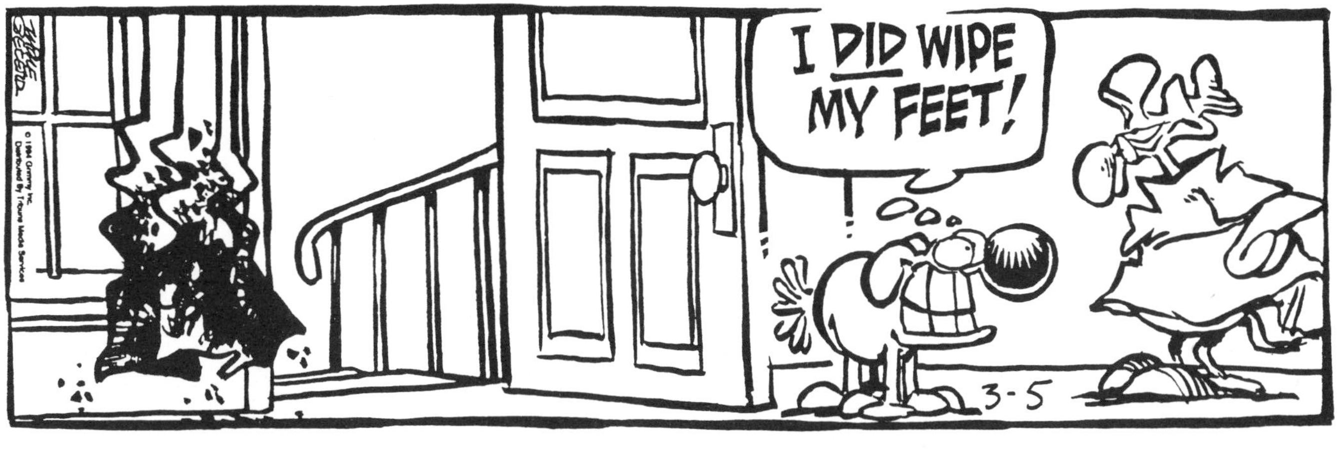
I DID WIPE MY FEET!
3-5

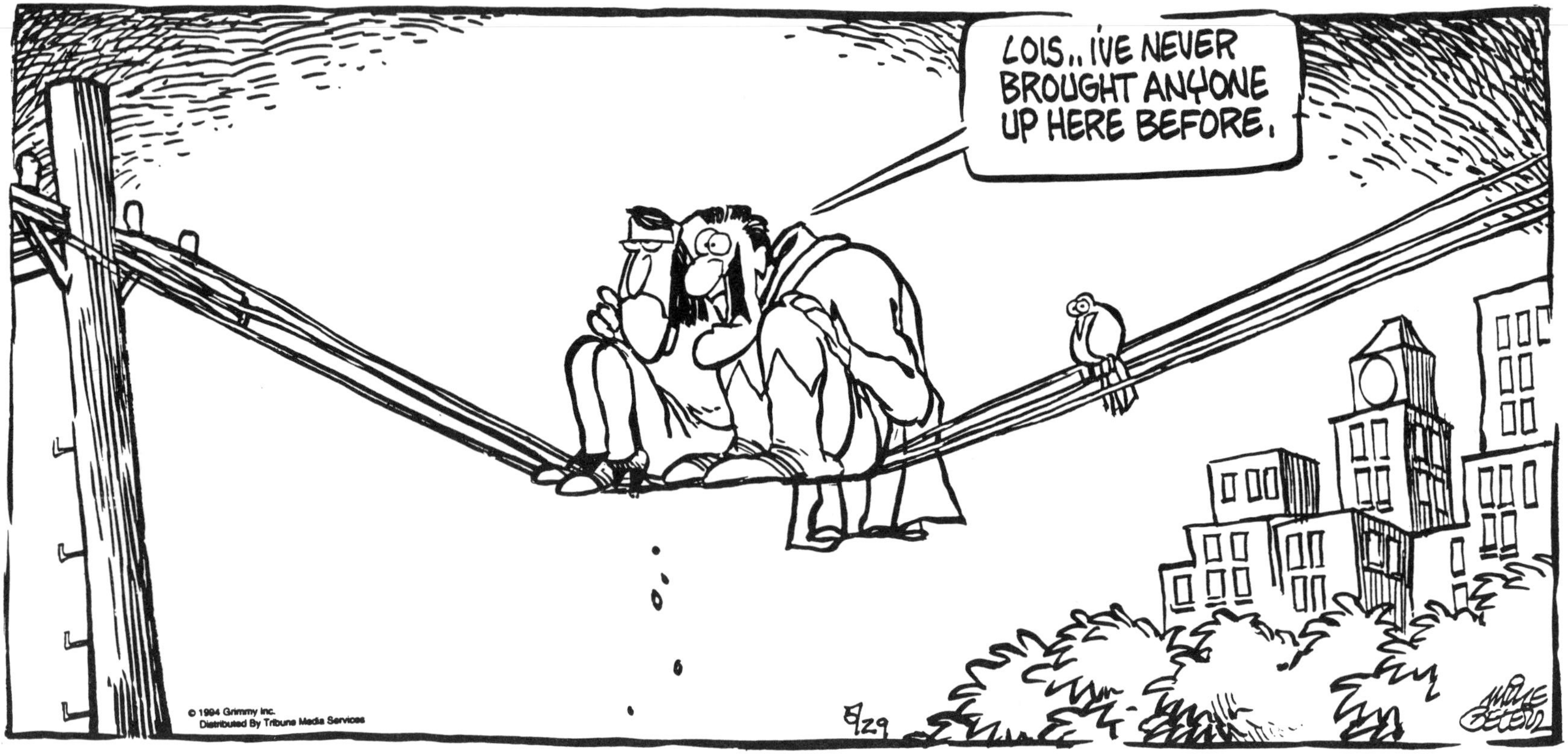
LOIS.. I'VE NEVER BROUGHT ANYONE UP HERE BEFORE.
© 1994 Grimmy Inc.
Distributed By Tribune Media Services
9/29

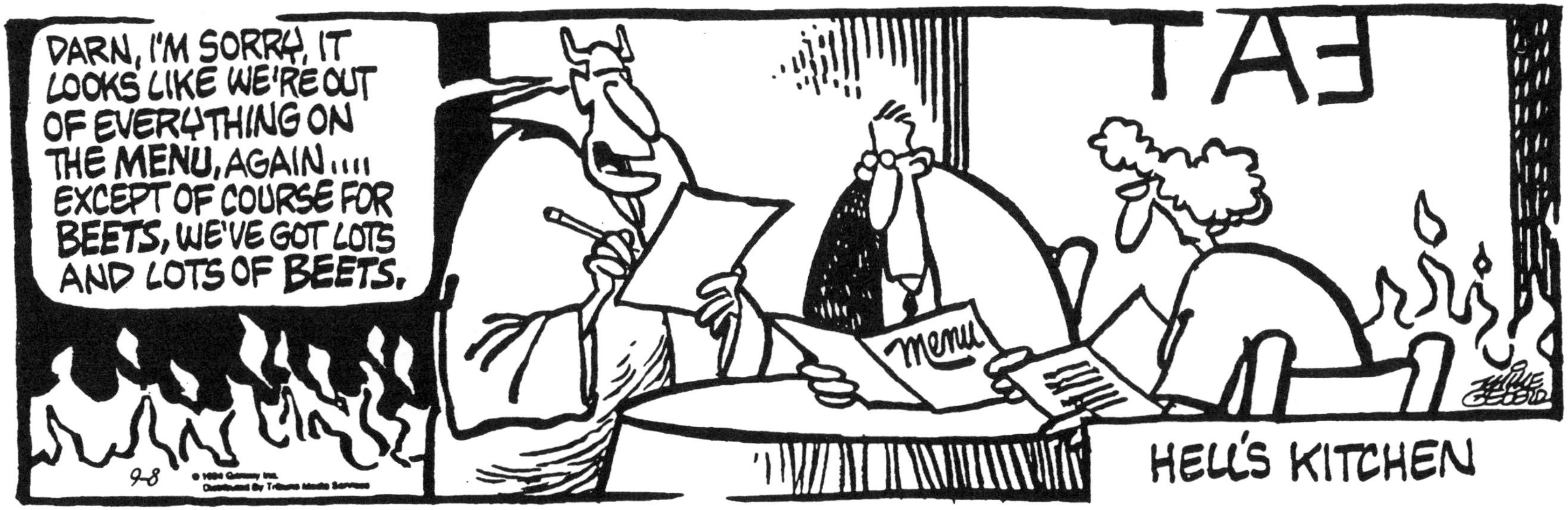
DARN, I'M SORRY, IT LOOKS LIKE WE'RE OUT OF EVERYTHING ON THE MENU, AGAIN.... EXCEPT OF COURSE FOR BEETS, WE'VE GOT LOTS AND LOTS OF BEETS.
EAT
menu
9-8

HELL'S KITCHEN

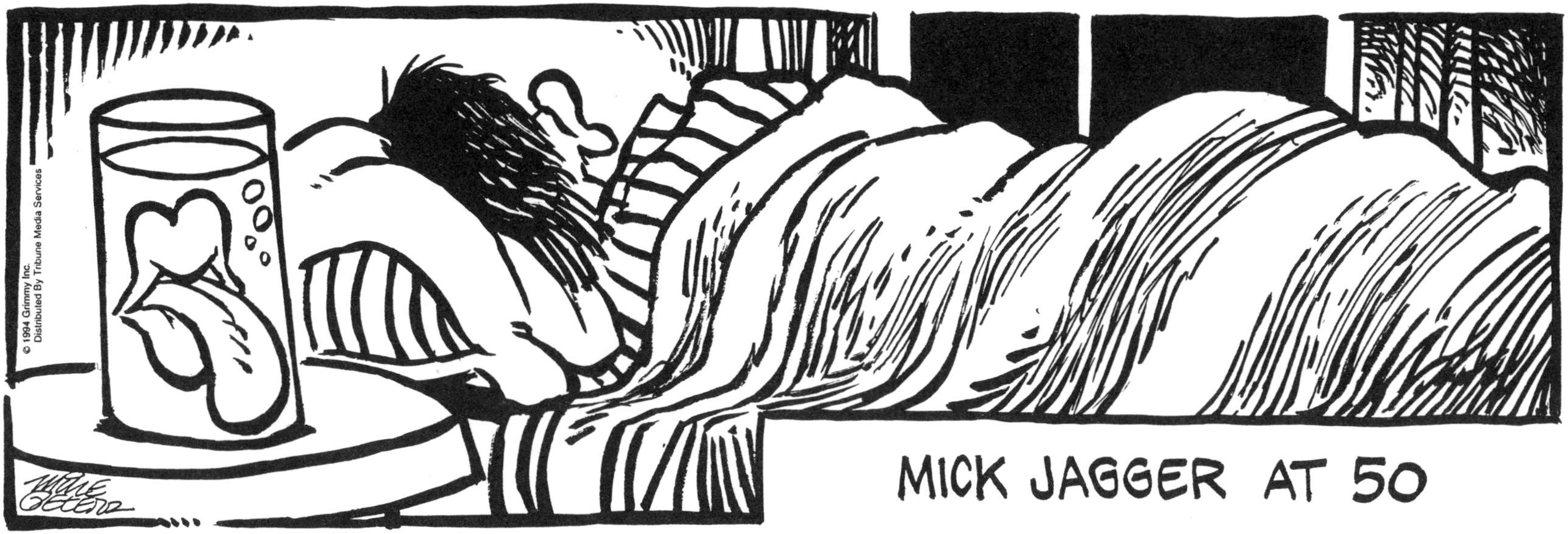

MICK JAGGER AT 50

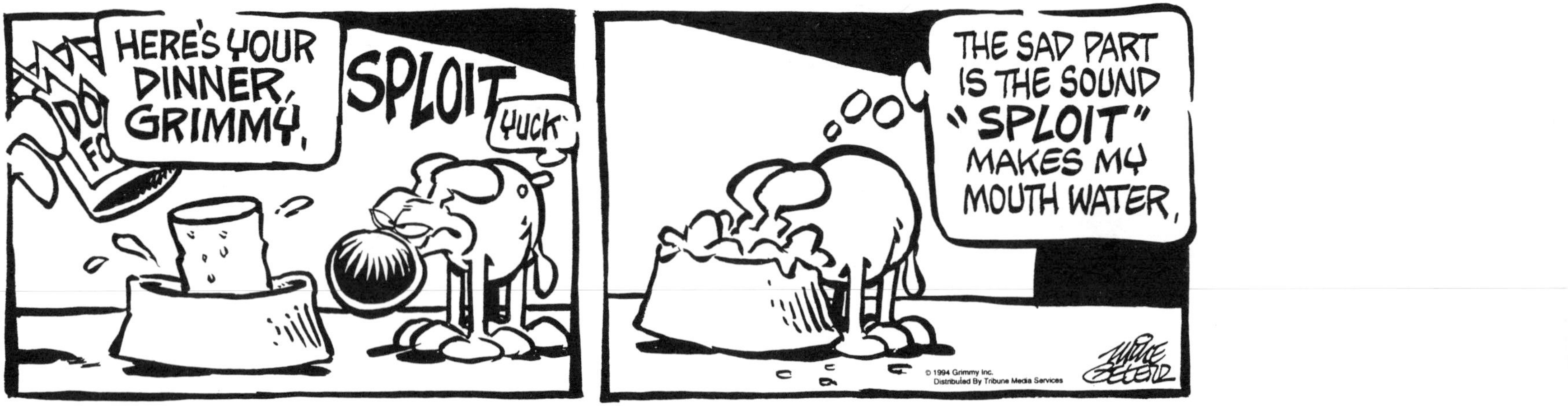
HERE'S YOUR DINNER, GRIMMY.
SPLOIT
YUCK
THE SAD PART IS THE SOUND "SPLOIT" MAKES MY MOUTH WATER.
© 1994 Grimmy Inc.
Distributed By Tribune Media Services

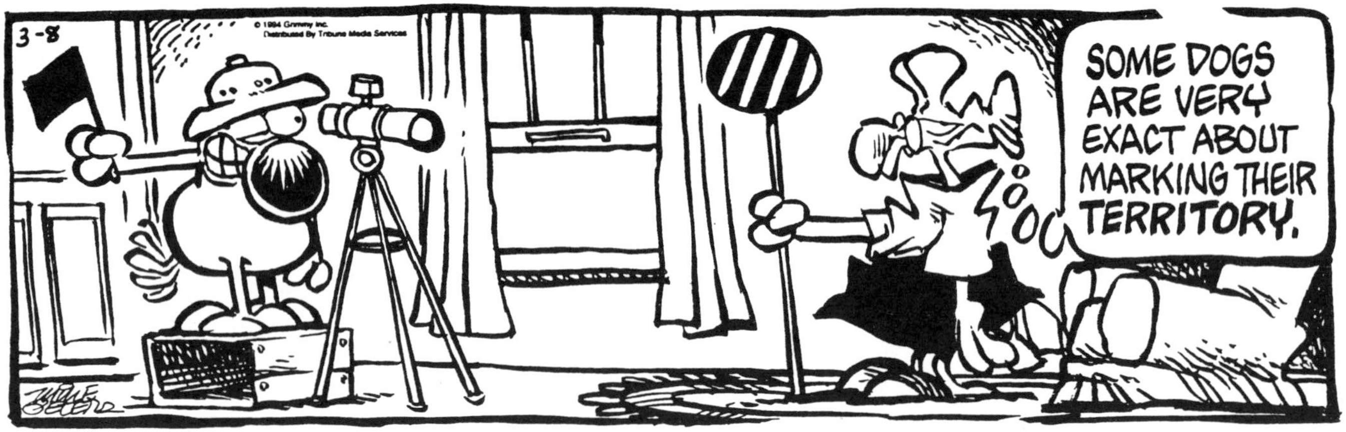
3-8
© 1994 Grimmy Inc.
Distributed By Tribune Media Services
SOME DOGS ARE VERY EXACT ABOUT MARKING THEIR TERRITORY.

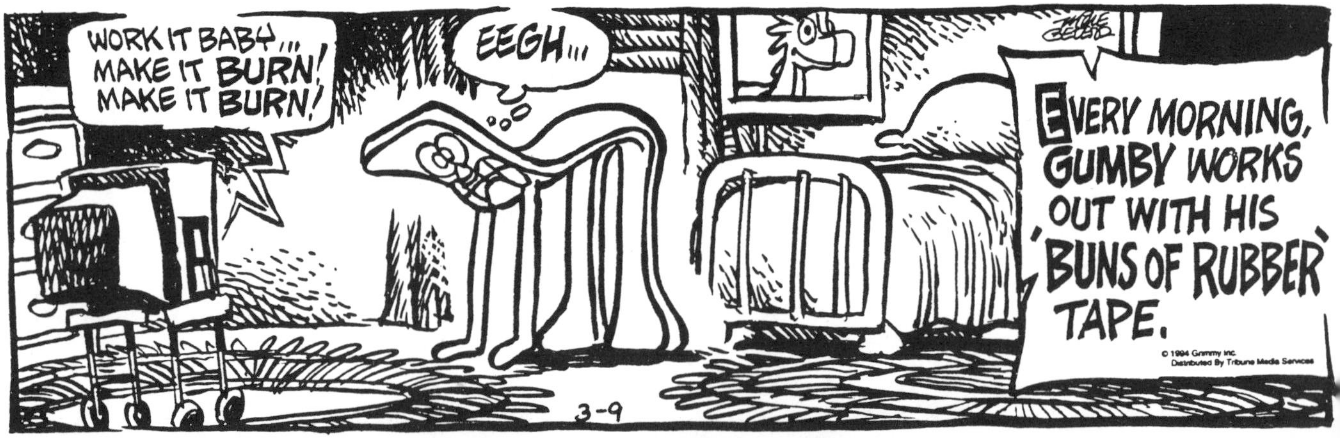
WORK IT BABY... MAKE IT BURN! MAKE IT BURN!
EEGH...
EVERY MORNING, GUMBY WORKS OUT WITH HIS 'BUNS OF RUBBER' TAPE.
© 1994 Grimmy Inc.
Distributed By Tribune Media Services
3-9

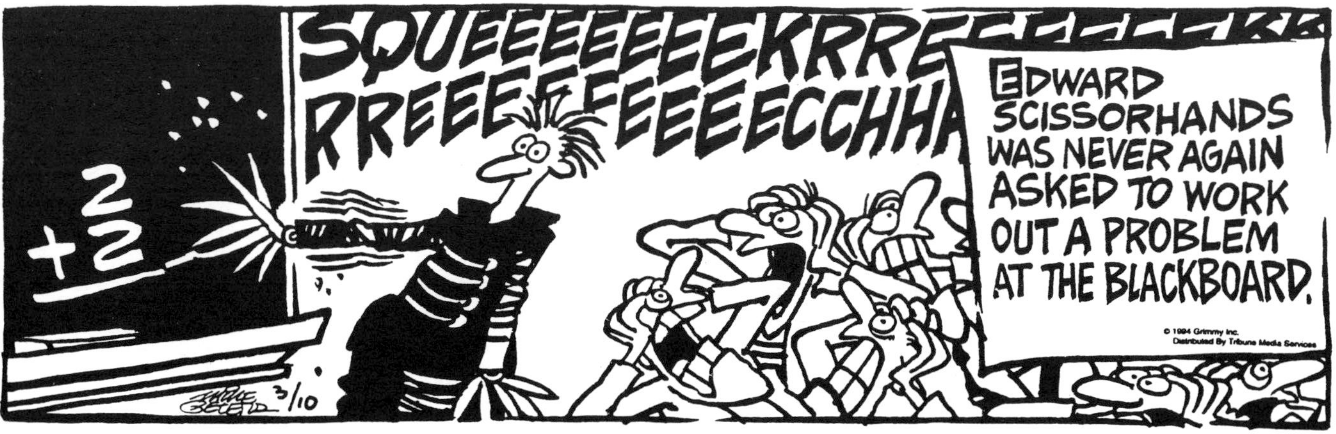
SQUEEEEEEEEKRRE
RREEEFFEEEEECCHHA
EDWARD SCISSORHANDS WAS NEVER AGAIN ASKED TO WORK OUT A PROBLEM AT THE BLACKBOARD.
© 1994 Grimmy Inc.
Distributed By Tribune Media Services
3/10

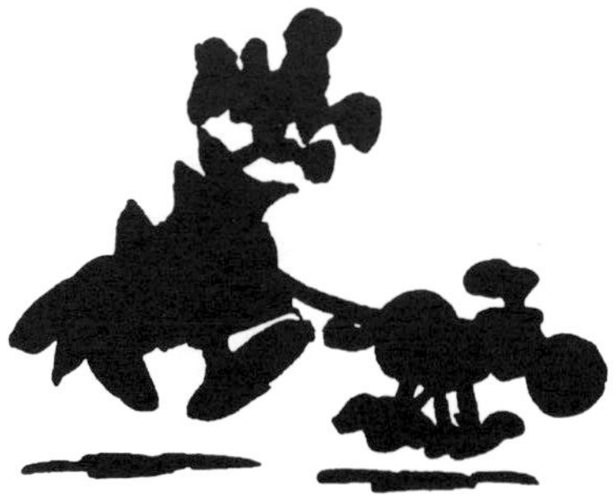

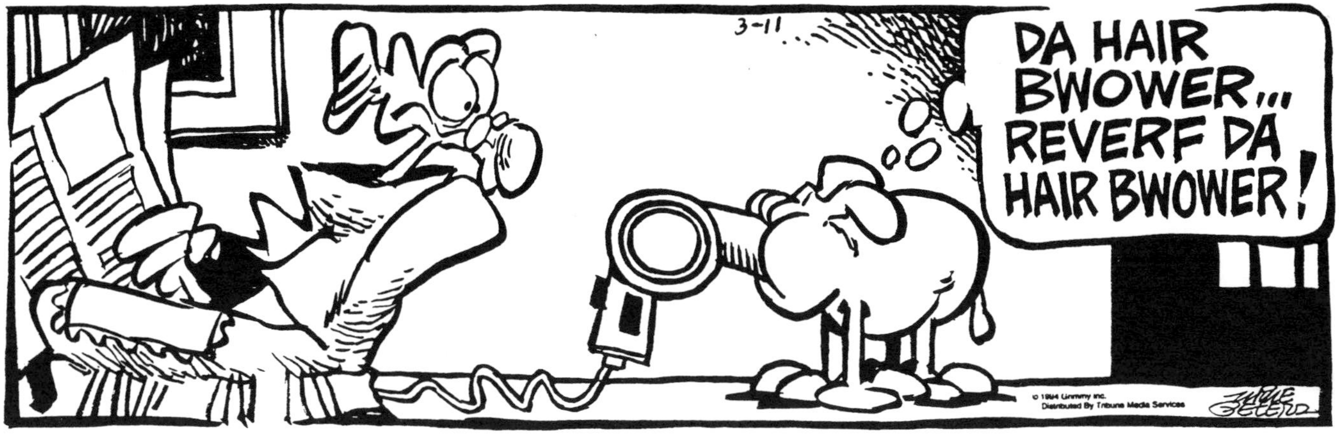
3-11
DA HAIR BWOWER... REVERF DA HAIR BWOWER!
© 1994 Grimmy Inc.
Distributed By Tribune Media Services

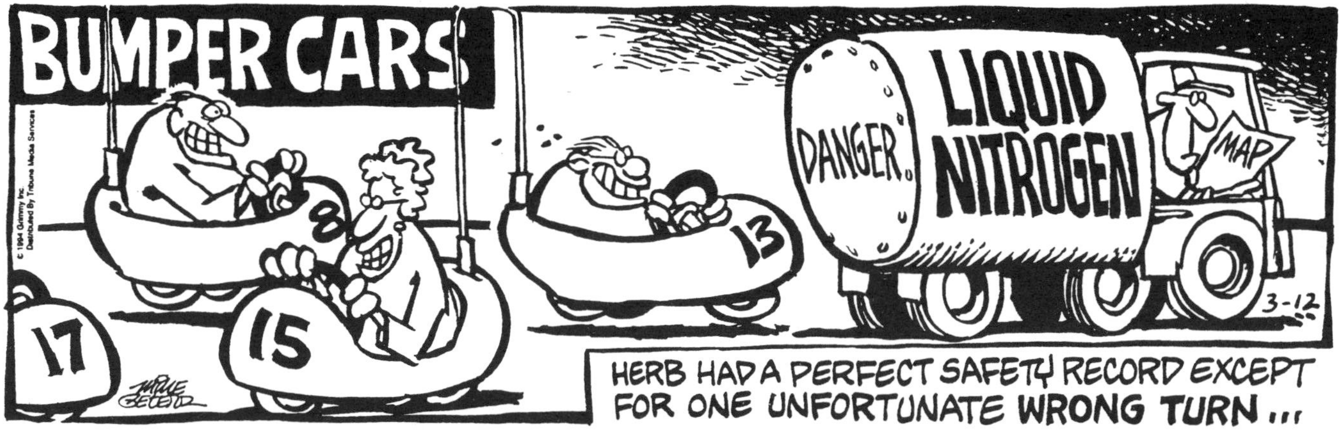
BUMPER CARS
DANGER
LIQUID NITROGEN
MAP
8
13
15
17
3-12
© 1994 Grimmy Inc.
Distributed By Tribune Media Services
HERB HAD A PERFECT SAFETY RECORD EXCEPT FOR ONE UNFORTUNATE WRONG TURN...

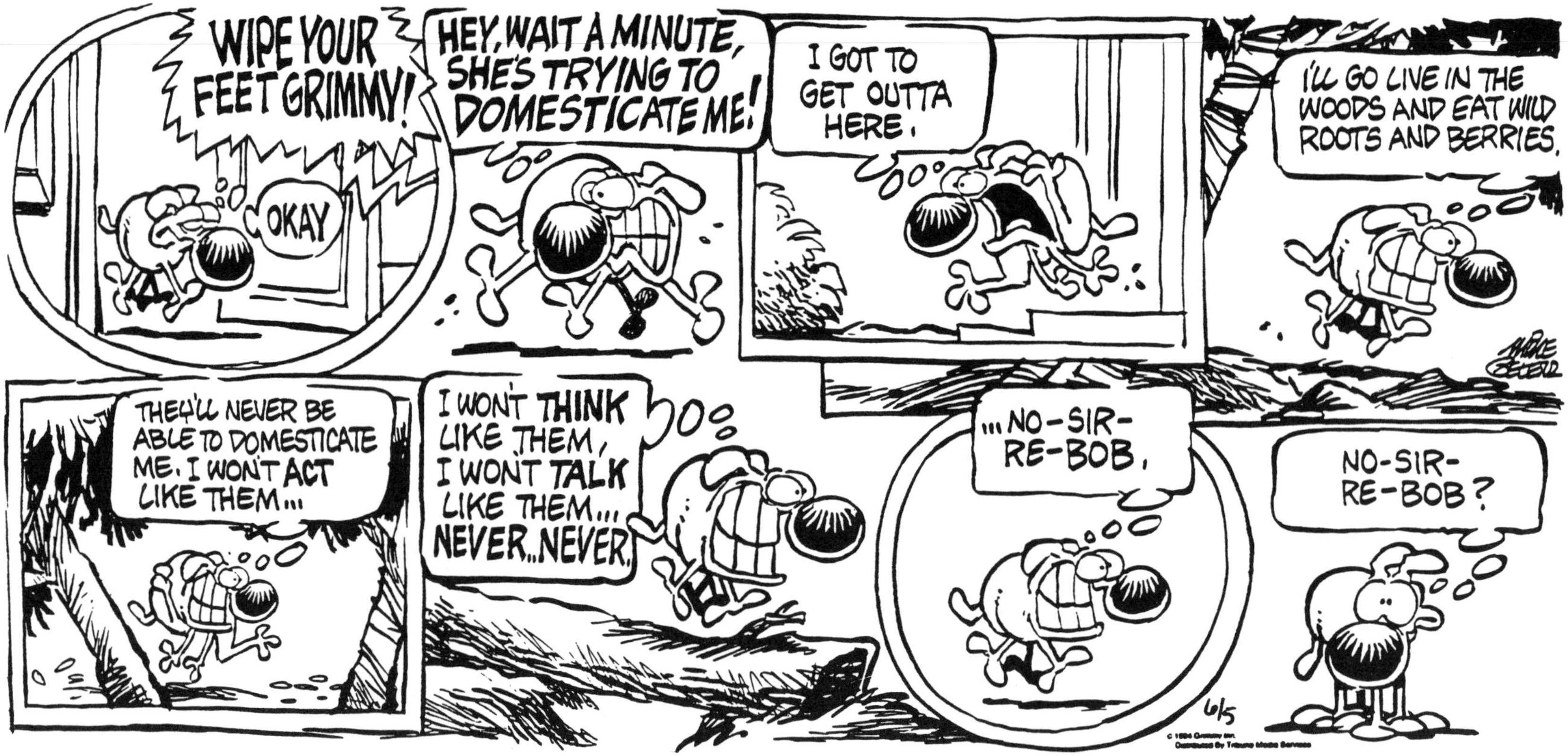
WIPE YOUR FEET GRIMMY!
OKAY
HEY, WAIT A MINUTE, SHE'S TRYING TO DOMESTICATE ME!
I GOT TO GET OUTTA HERE.
I'LL GO LIVE IN THE WOODS AND EAT WILD ROOTS AND BERRIES.
THEY'LL NEVER BE ABLE TO DOMESTICATE ME. I WON'T ACT LIKE THEM...
I WON'T THINK LIKE THEM, I WON'T TALK LIKE THEM... NEVER...NEVER.
...NO-SIR-RE-BOB.
NO-SIR-RE-BOB?
6/5

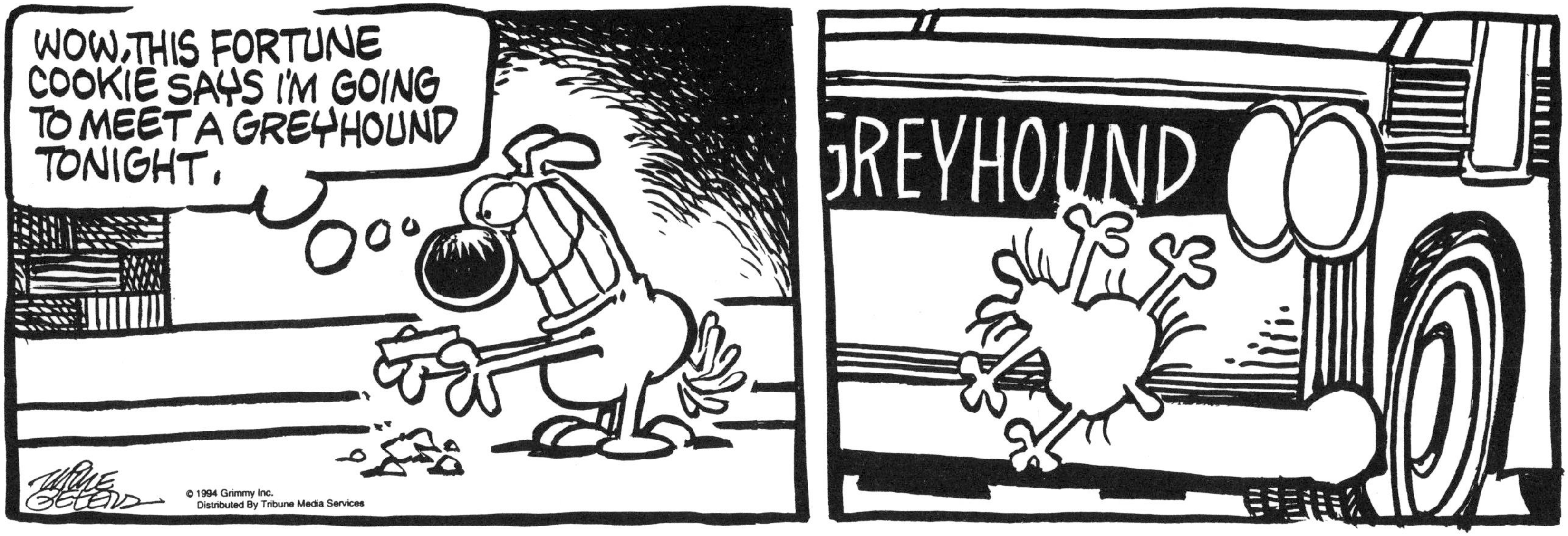
WOW, THIS FORTUNE COOKIE SAYS I'M GOING TO MEET A GREYHOUND TONIGHT.
© 1994 Grimmy Inc.
Distributed By Tribune Media Services
GREYHOUND

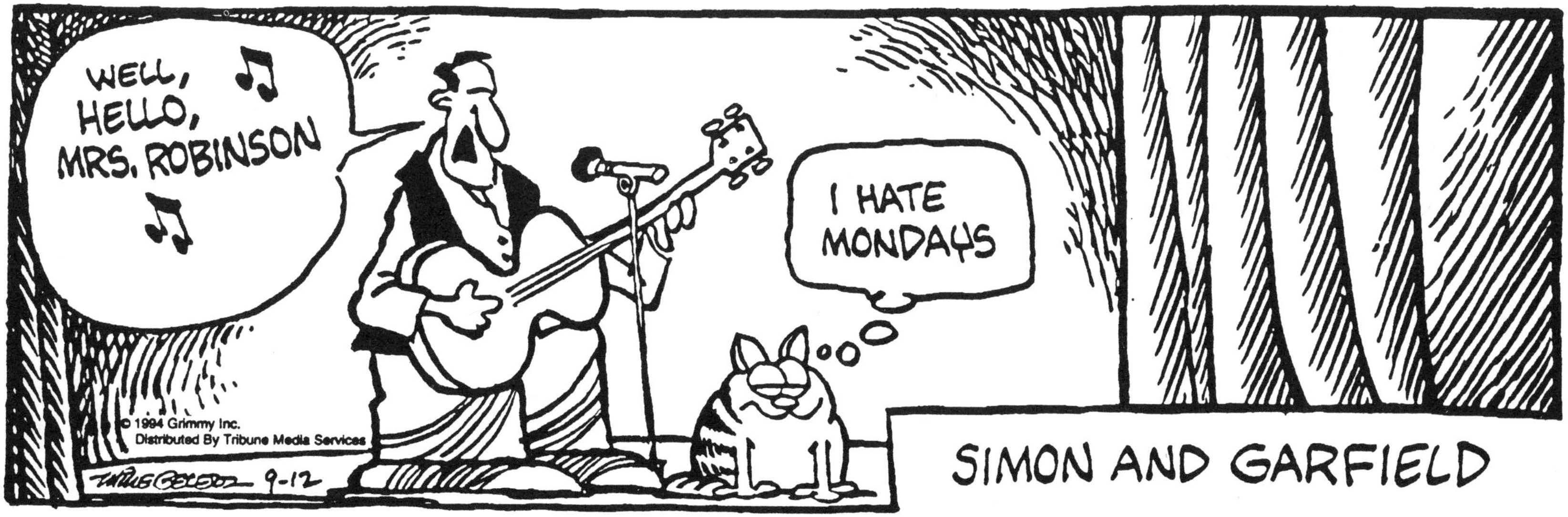
WELL, HELLO, MRS. ROBINSON
I HATE MONDAYS
© 1994 Grimmy Inc.
Distributed By Tribune Media Services
9-12
SIMON AND GARFIELD

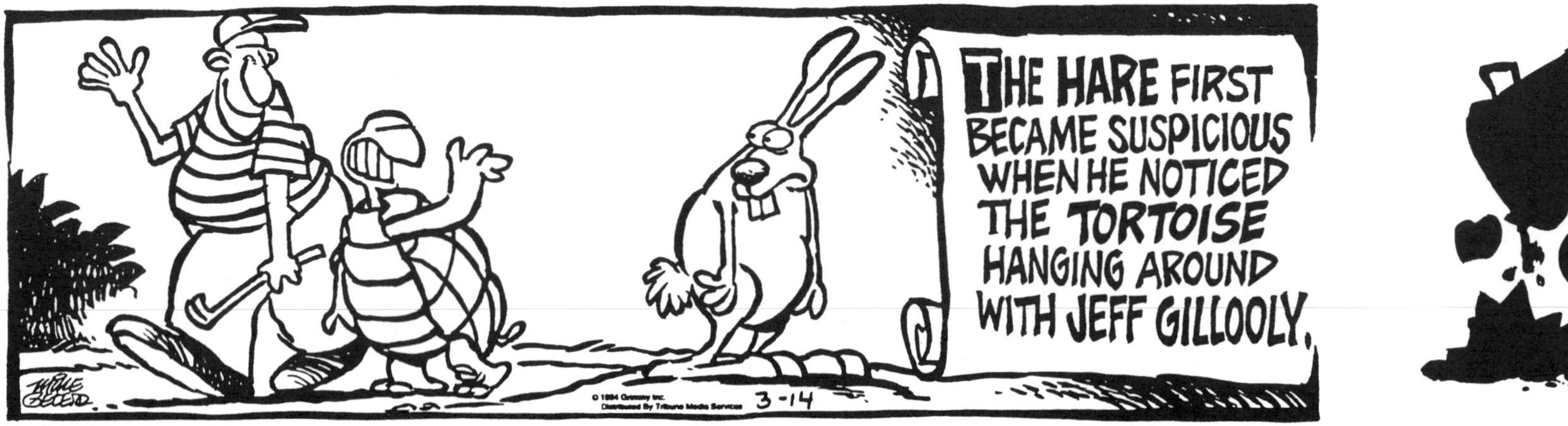
THE HARE FIRST BECAME SUSPICIOUS WHEN HE NOTICED THE TORTOISE HANGING AROUND WITH JEFF GILLOOLY.
© 1994 Grimmy Inc. Distributed By Tribune Media Services
3-14

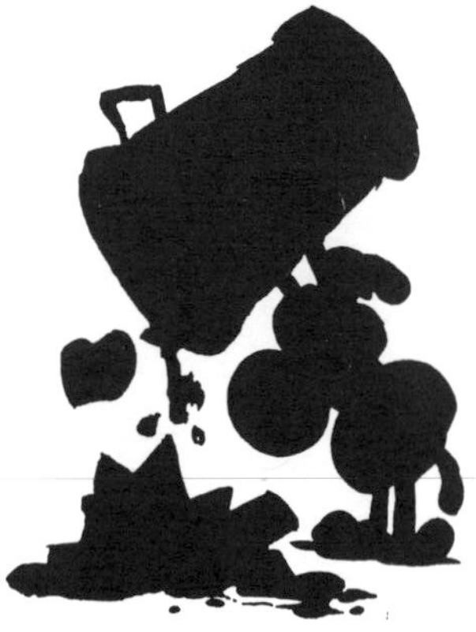

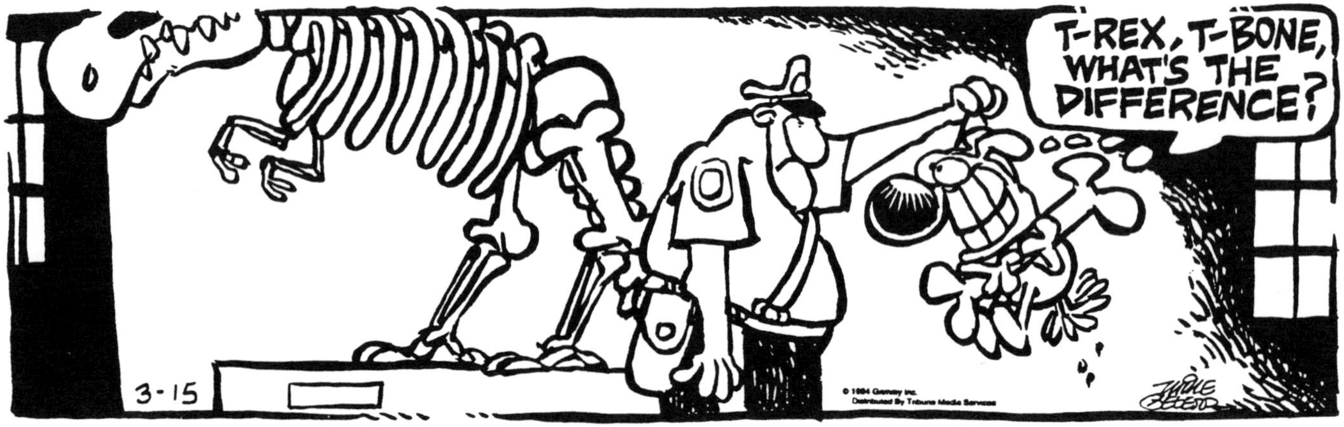
T-REX, T-BONE, WHAT'S THE DIFFERENCE?
3-15
© 1994 Grimmy Inc. Distributed By Tribune Media Services

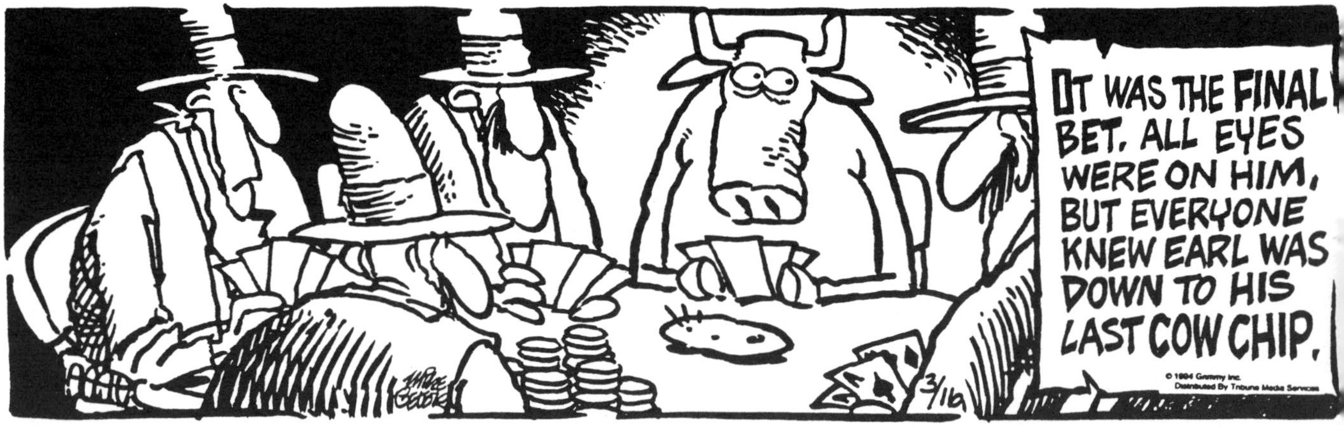
IT WAS THE FINAL BET. ALL EYES WERE ON HIM, BUT EVERYONE KNEW EARL WAS DOWN TO HIS LAST COW CHIP.
3/16
© 1994 Grimmy Inc. Distributed By Tribune Media Services

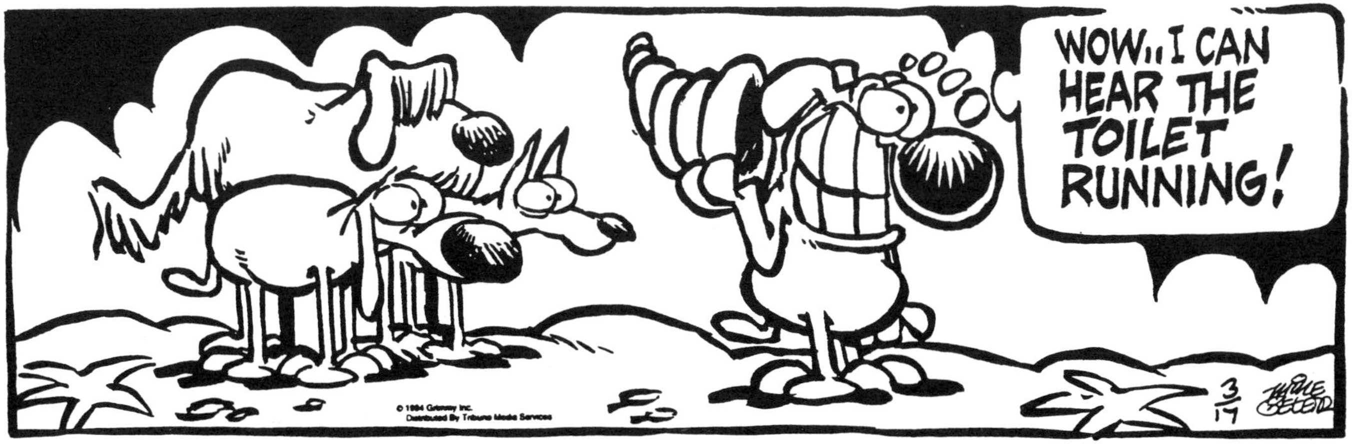
WOW.. I CAN HEAR THE TOILET RUNNING!
© 1984 Grimmy Inc. Distributed By Tribune Media Services
3/17

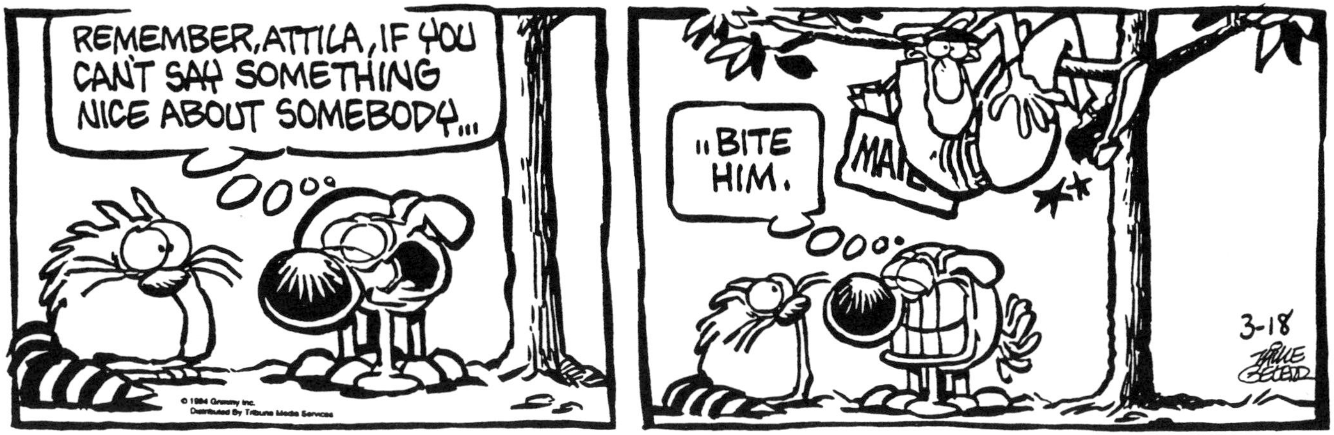
REMEMBER, ATTILA, IF YOU CAN'T SAY SOMETHING NICE ABOUT SOMEBODY...
© 1984 Grimmy Inc. Distributed By Tribune Media Services
..BITE HIM.
MAIL
3-18

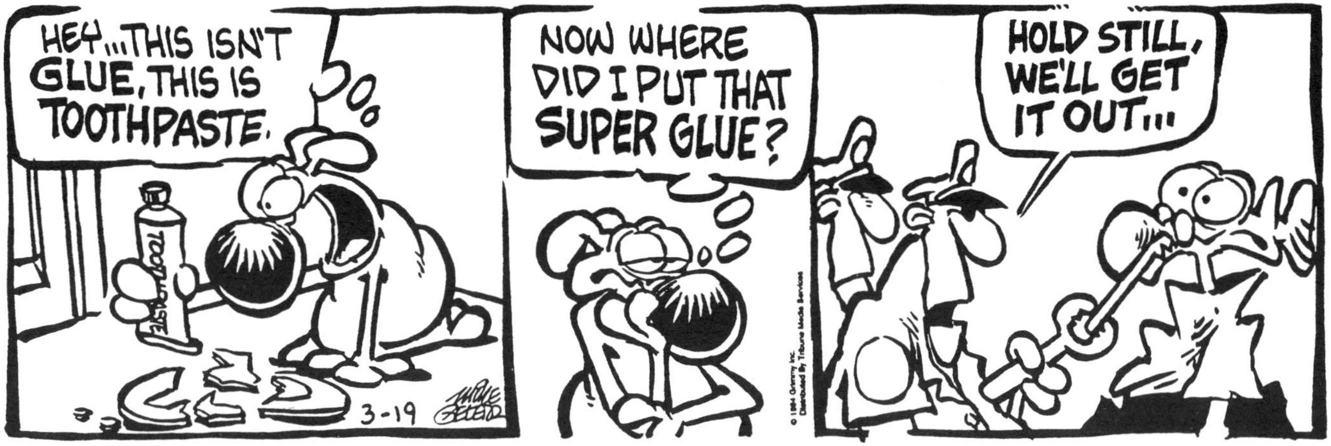
HEY...THIS ISN'T GLUE, THIS IS TOOTHPASTE.
3-19
NOW WHERE DID I PUT THAT SUPER GLUE?
© 1984 Grimmy Inc. Distributed By Tribune Media Services
HOLD STILL, WE'LL GET IT OUT...

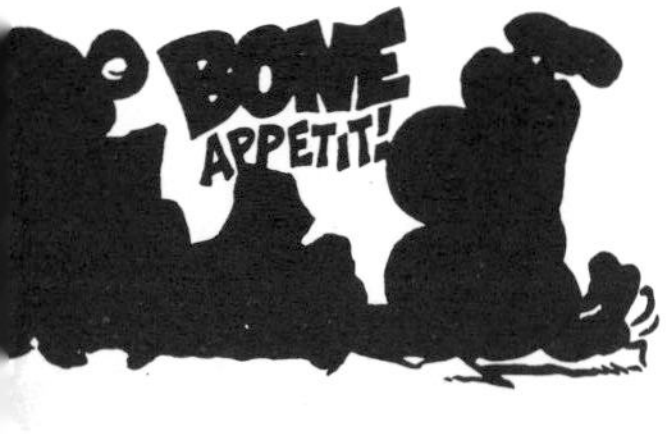
BONE APPETIT!

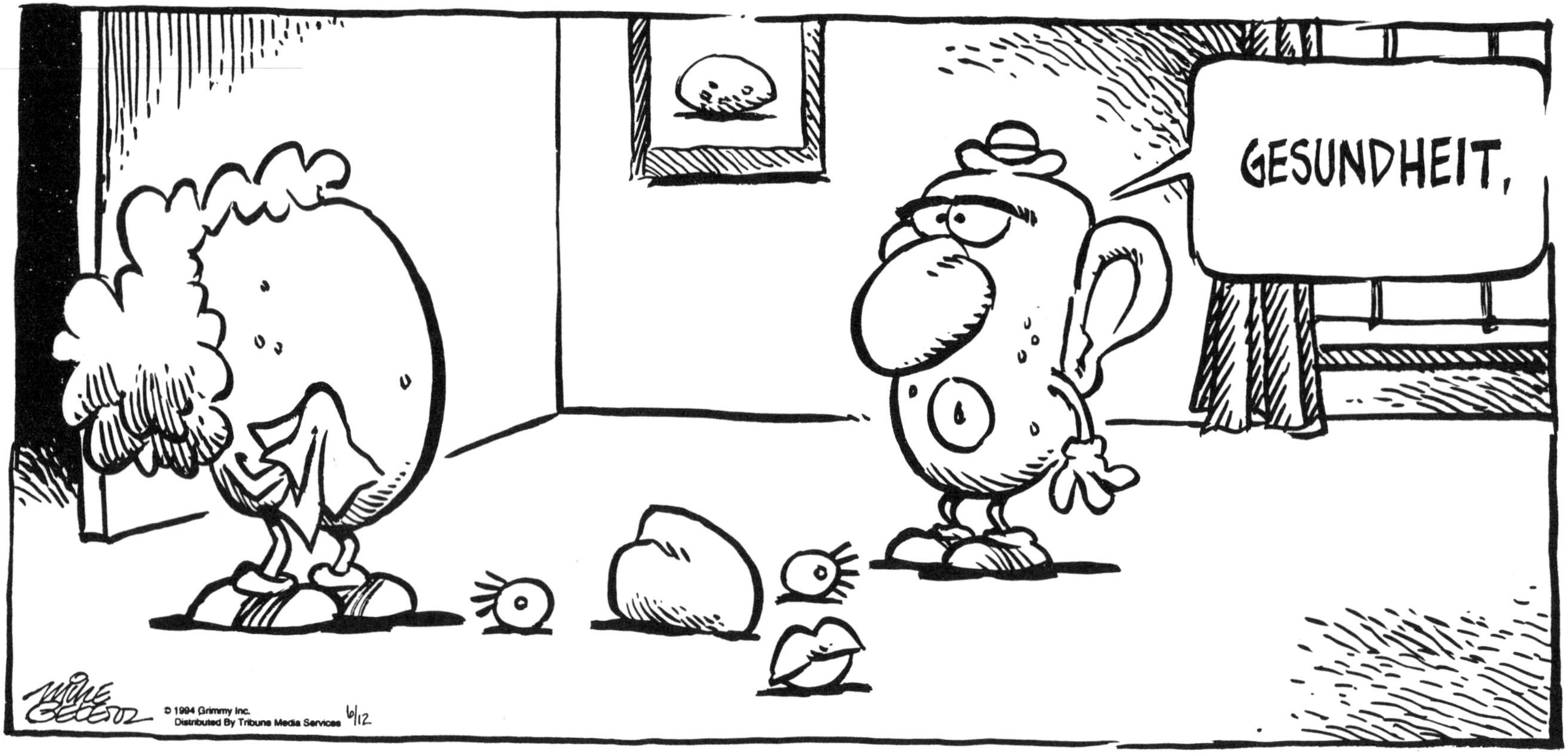
GESUNDHEIT,
© 1994 Grimmy Inc.
Distributed By Tribune Media Services
6/12

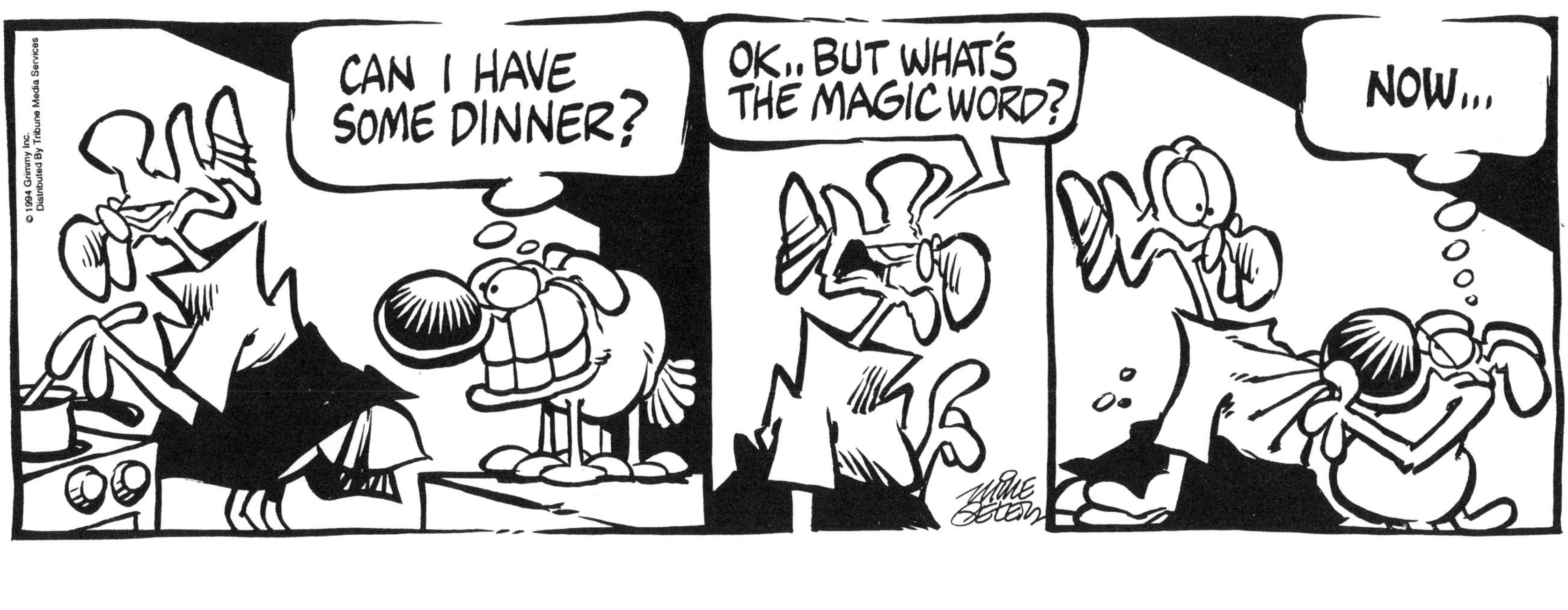
© 1994 Grimmy Inc.
Distributed By Tribune Media Services
CAN I HAVE SOME DINNER?
OK.. BUT WHAT'S THE MAGIC WORD?
NOW...

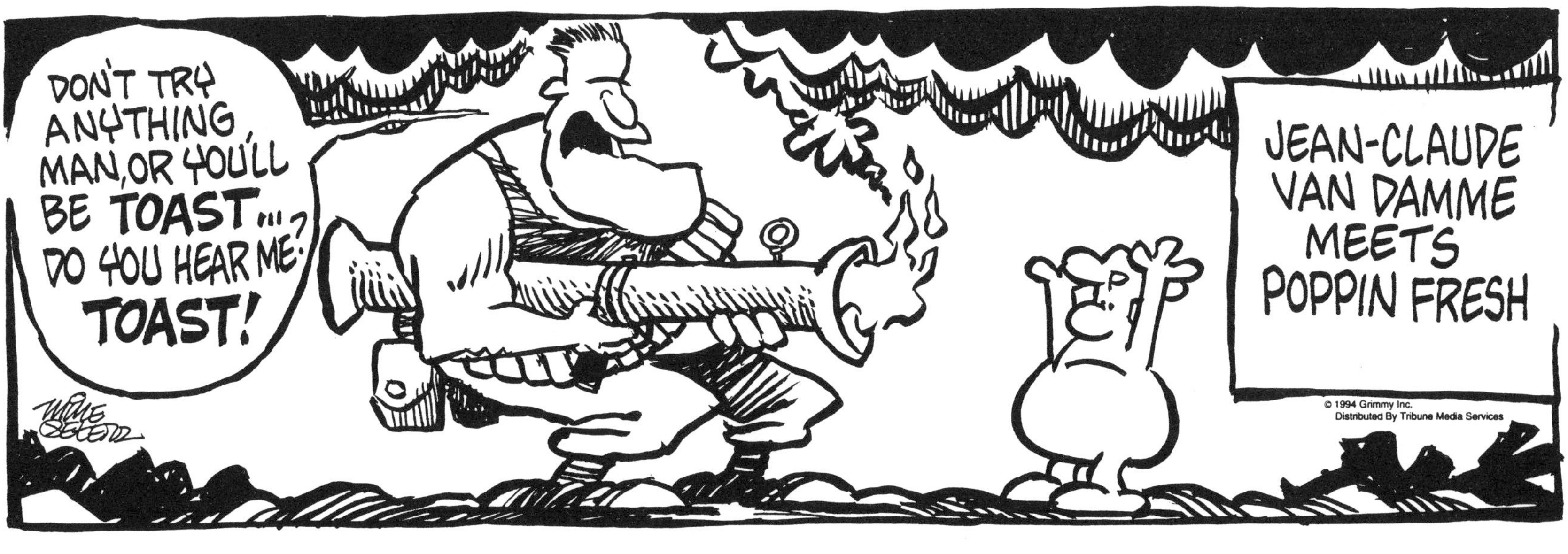
DON'T TRY ANYTHING MAN, OR YOU'LL BE **TOAST**...? DO YOU HEAR ME? **TOAST!**
JEAN-CLAUDE VAN DAMME MEETS POPPIN FRESH
© 1994 Grimmy Inc.
Distributed By Tribune Media Services

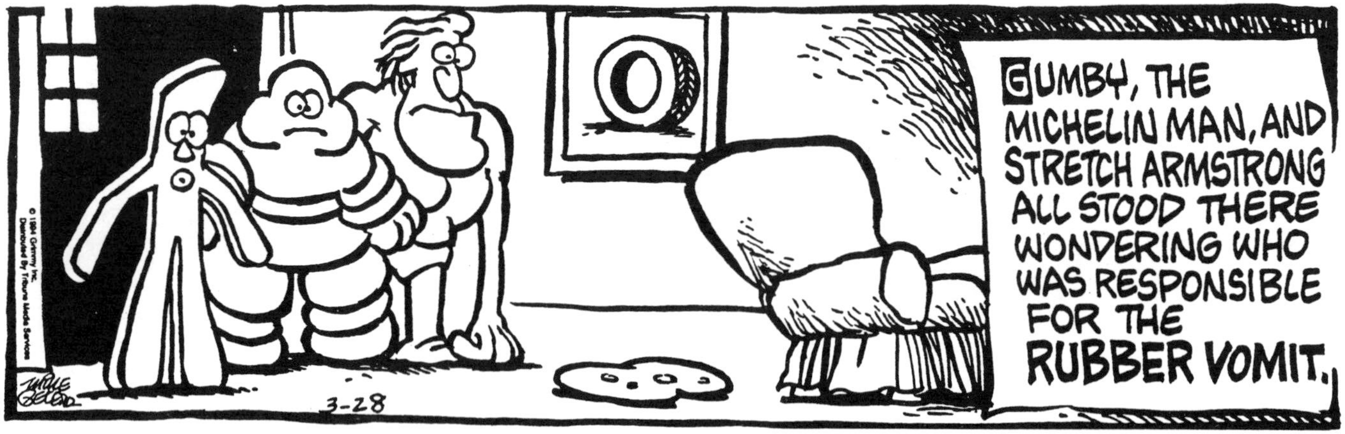
GUMBY, THE MICHELIN MAN, AND STRETCH ARMSTRONG ALL STOOD THERE WONDERING WHO WAS RESPONSIBLE FOR THE RUBBER VOMIT.
3-28

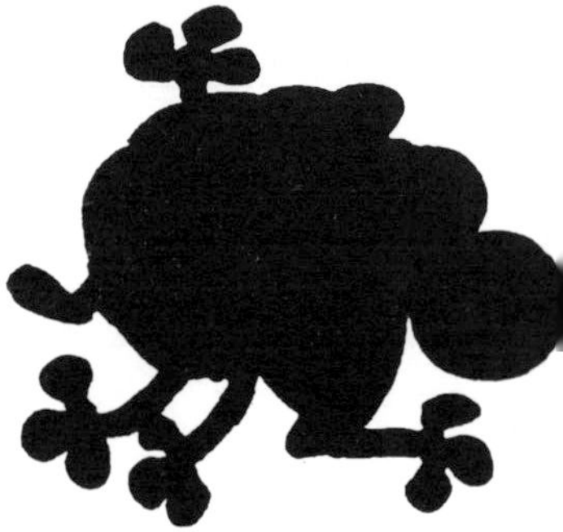

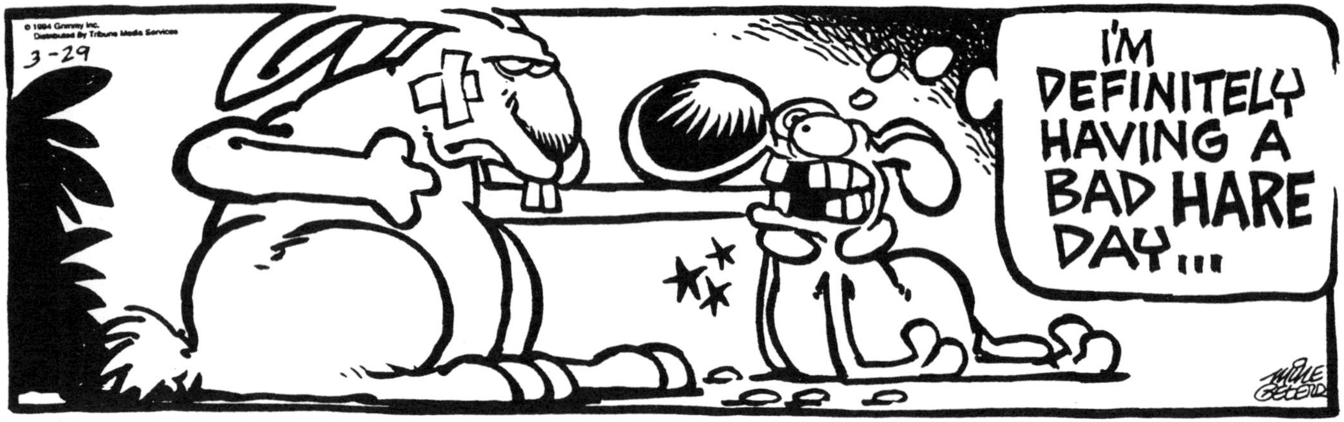
© 1994 Grimmy Inc.
Distributed By Tribune Media Services
3-29
I'M DEFINITELY HAVING A BAD HARE DAY...

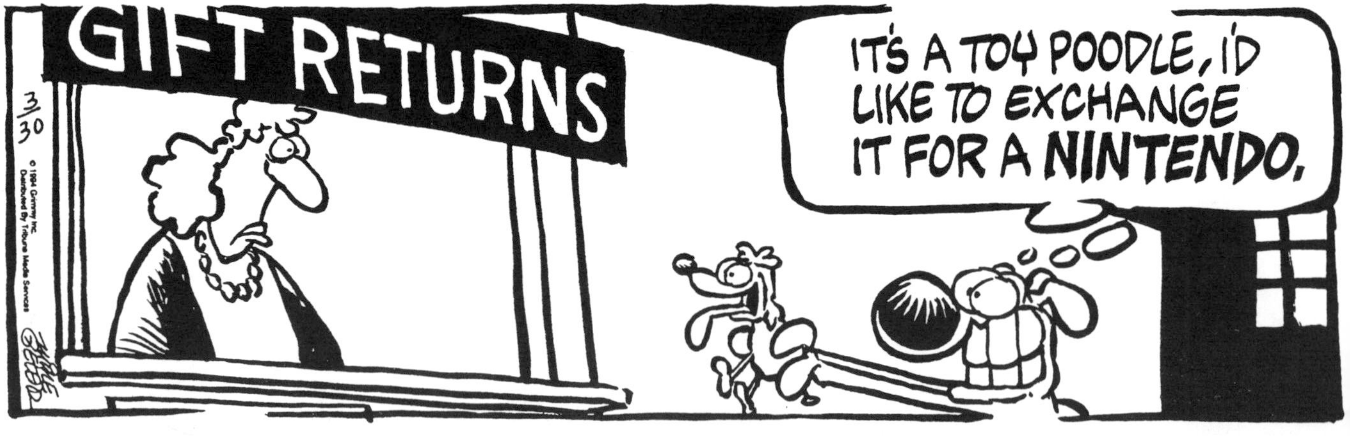
GIFT RETURNS
3/30
IT'S A TOY POODLE, I'D LIKE TO EXCHANGE IT FOR A NINTENDO.

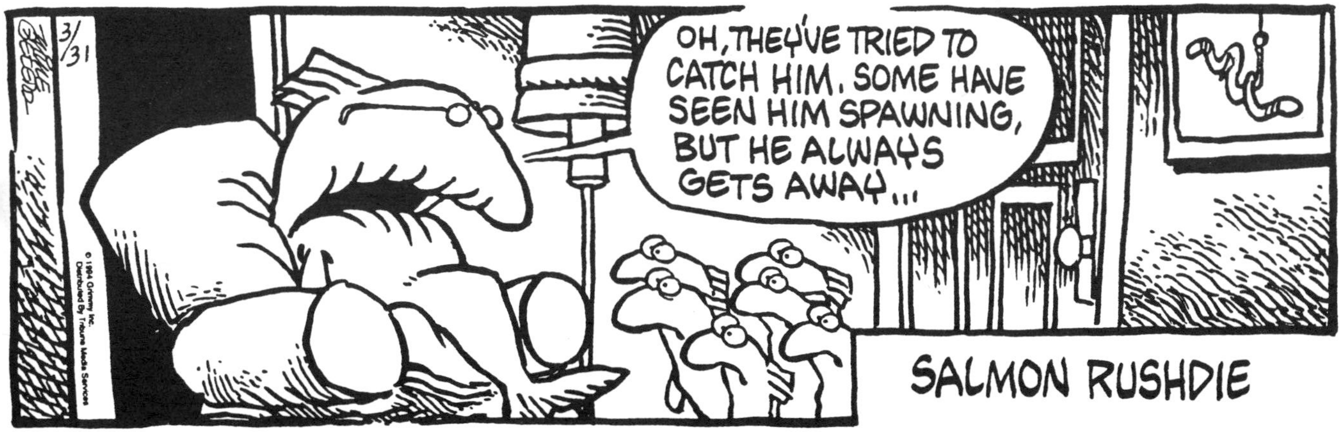
3/31
© 1994 Grimmy Inc.
Distributed By Tribune Media Services
OH, THEY'VE TRIED TO CATCH HIM. SOME HAVE SEEN HIM SPAWNING, BUT HE ALWAYS GETS AWAY...
SALMON RUSHDIE

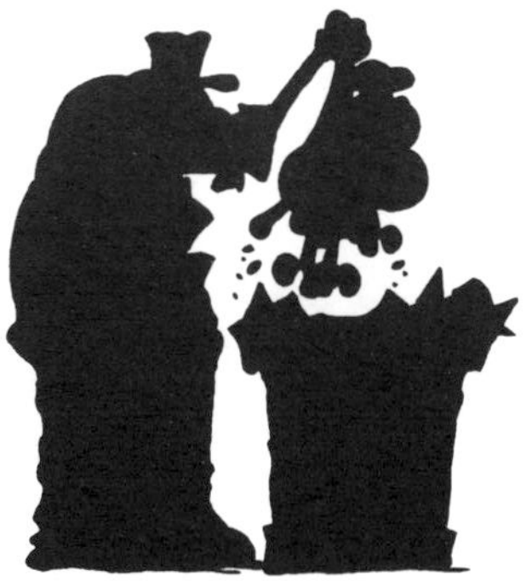

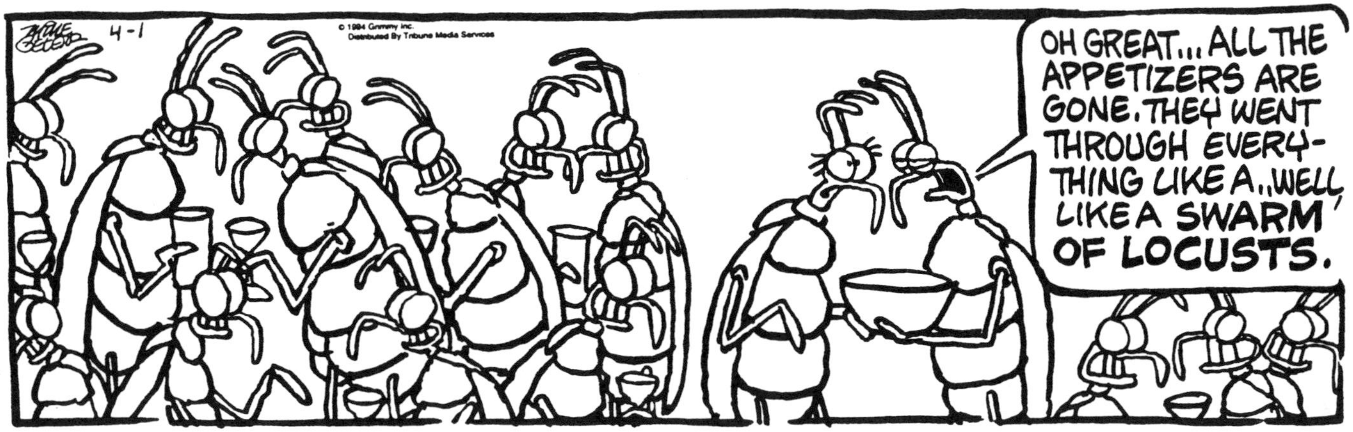
4-1
© 1994 Grimmy Inc.
Distributed By Tribune Media Services
OH GREAT... ALL THE APPETIZERS ARE GONE. THEY WENT THROUGH EVERYTHING LIKE A.. WELL, LIKE A SWARM OF LOCUSTS.

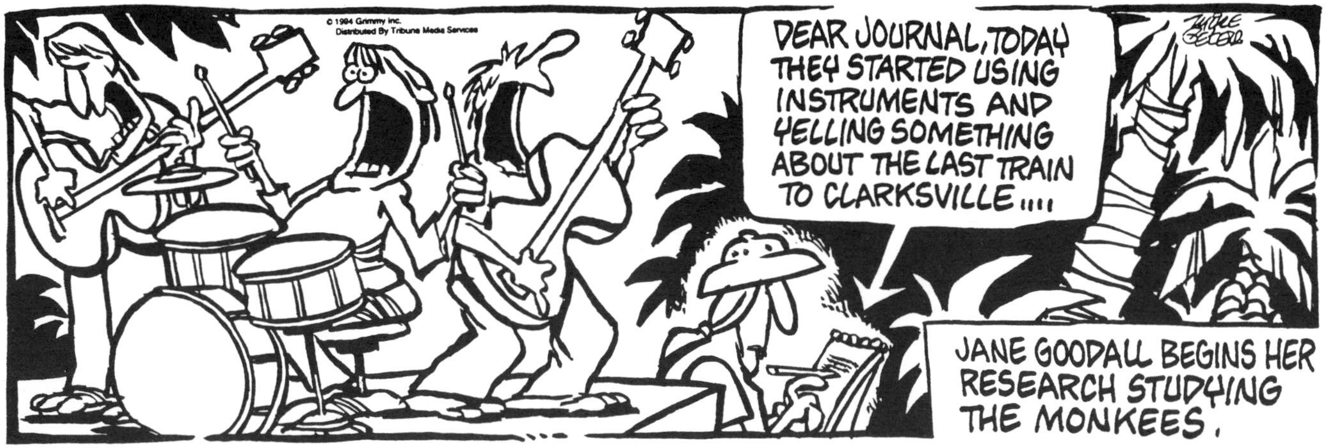
© 1994 Grimmy Inc.
Distributed By Tribune Media Services
DEAR JOURNAL, TODAY THEY STARTED USING INSTRUMENTS AND YELLING SOMETHING ABOUT THE LAST TRAIN TO CLARKSVILLE....
JANE GOODALL BEGINS HER RESEARCH STUDYING THE MONKEES.

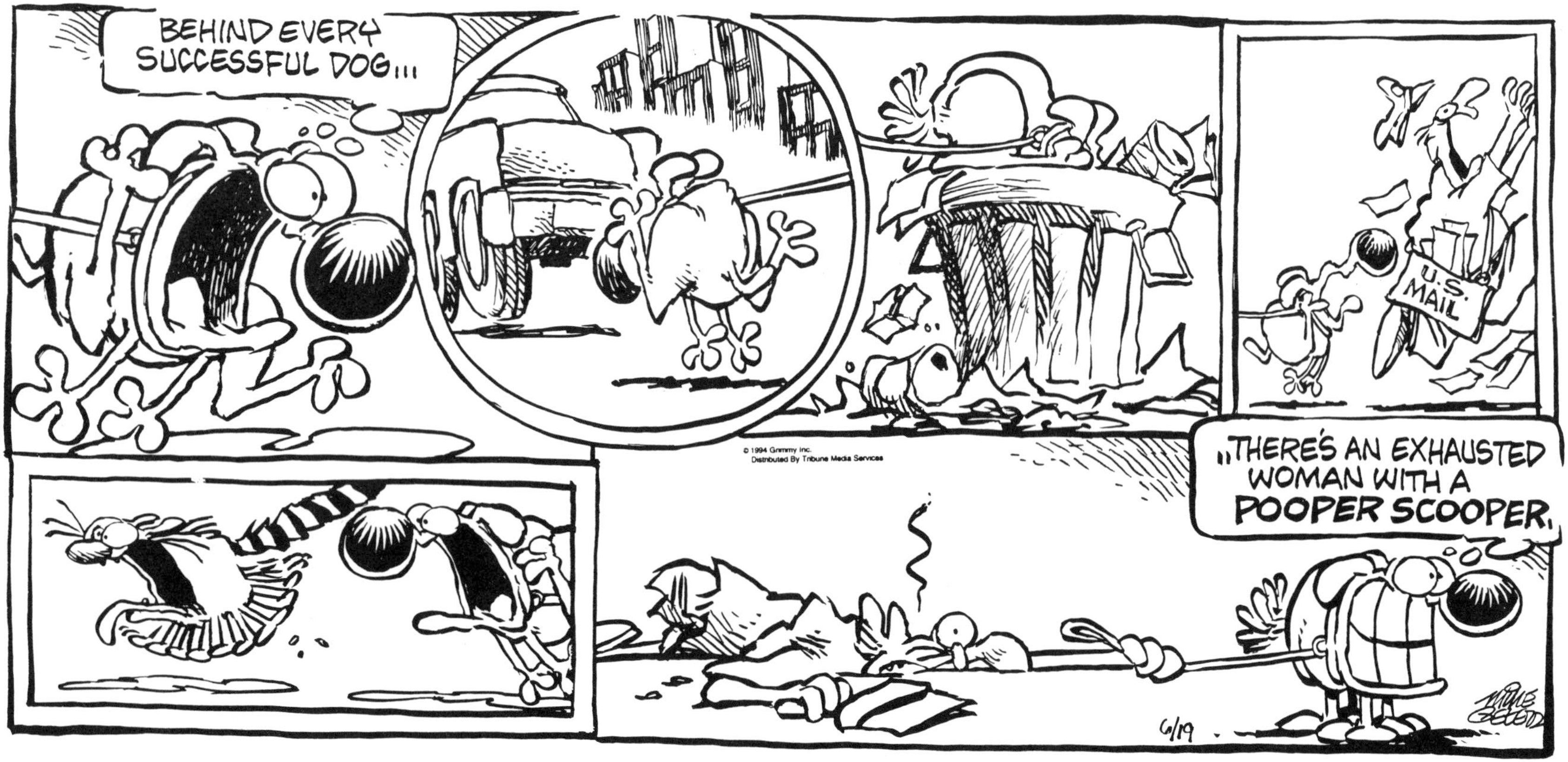
BEHIND EVERY SUCCESSFUL DOG...
U.S. MAIL
© 1994 Grimmy Inc.
Distributed By Tribune Media Services
...THERE'S AN EXHAUSTED WOMAN WITH A POOPER SCOOPER.
6/19

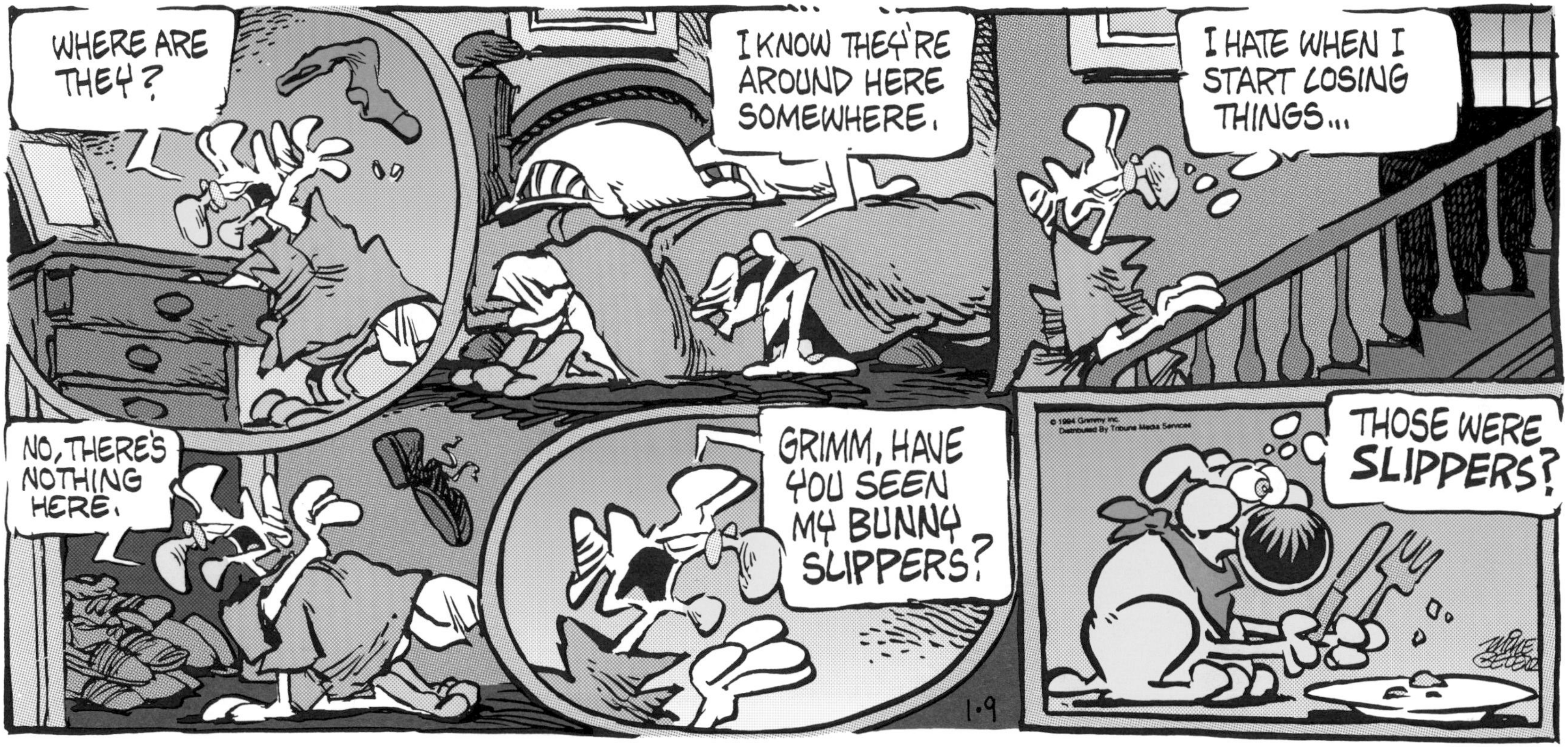
WHERE ARE THEY?
I KNOW THEY'RE AROUND HERE SOMEWHERE.
I HATE WHEN I START LOSING THINGS...
NO, THERE'S NOTHING HERE.
GRIMM, HAVE YOU SEEN MY **BUNNY** SLIPPERS?
© 1994 Grimmy Inc.
Distributed By Tribune Media Services
THOSE WERE **SLIPPERS**?
1·9

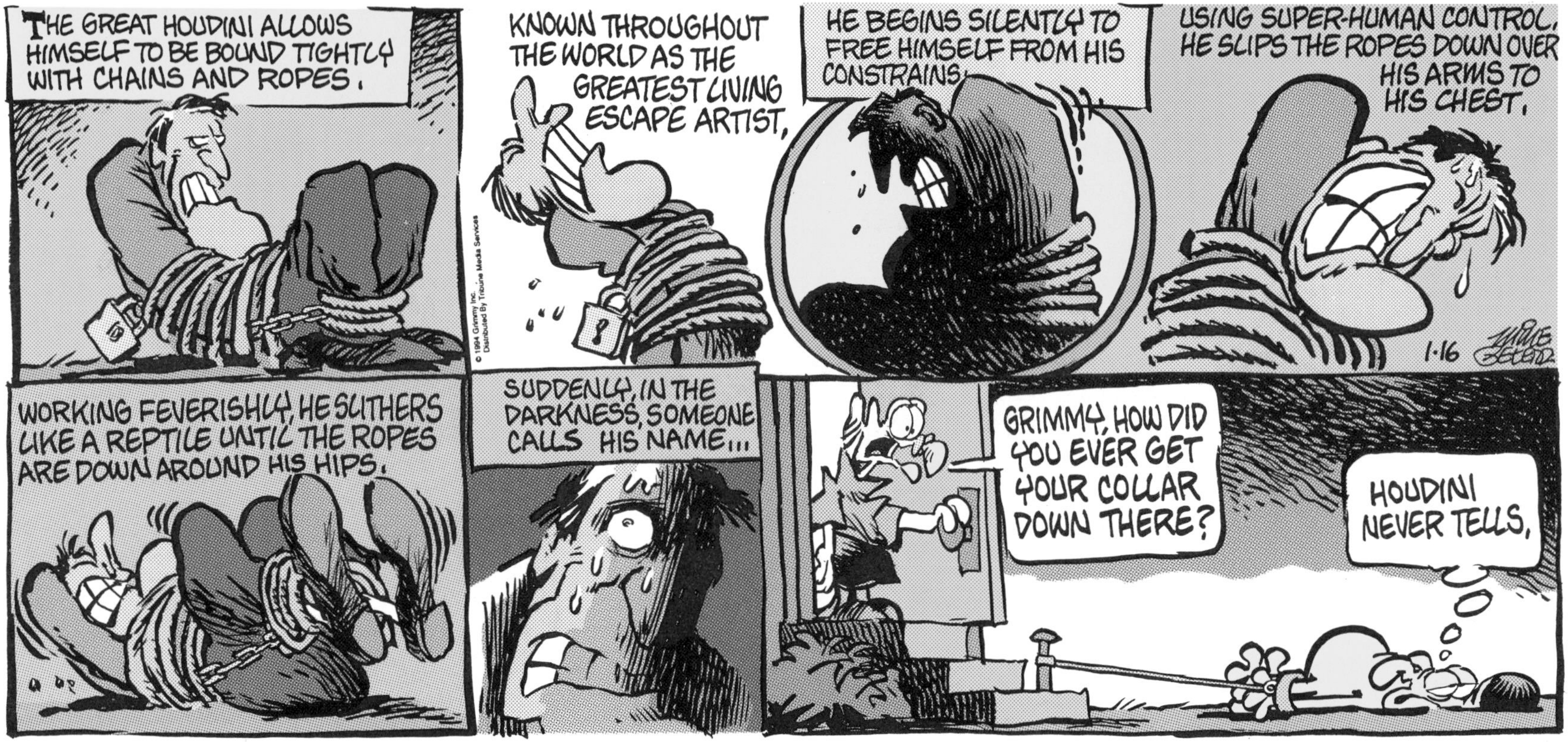
THE GREAT HOUDINI ALLOWS HIMSELF TO BE BOUND TIGHTLY WITH CHAINS AND ROPES.
KNOWN THROUGHOUT THE WORLD AS THE GREATEST LIVING ESCAPE ARTIST,
© 1994 Grimmy Inc. Distributed By Tribune Media Services
HE BEGINS SILENTLY TO FREE HIMSELF FROM HIS CONSTRAINS.
USING SUPER-HUMAN CONTROL, HE SLIPS THE ROPES DOWN OVER HIS ARMS TO HIS CHEST.
1·16
WORKING FEVERISHLY, HE SLITHERS LIKE A REPTILE UNTIL THE ROPES ARE DOWN AROUND HIS HIPS.
SUDDENLY, IN THE DARKNESS, SOMEONE CALLS HIS NAME...
GRIMMY, HOW DID YOU EVER GET YOUR COLLAR DOWN THERE?
HOUDINI NEVER TELLS.

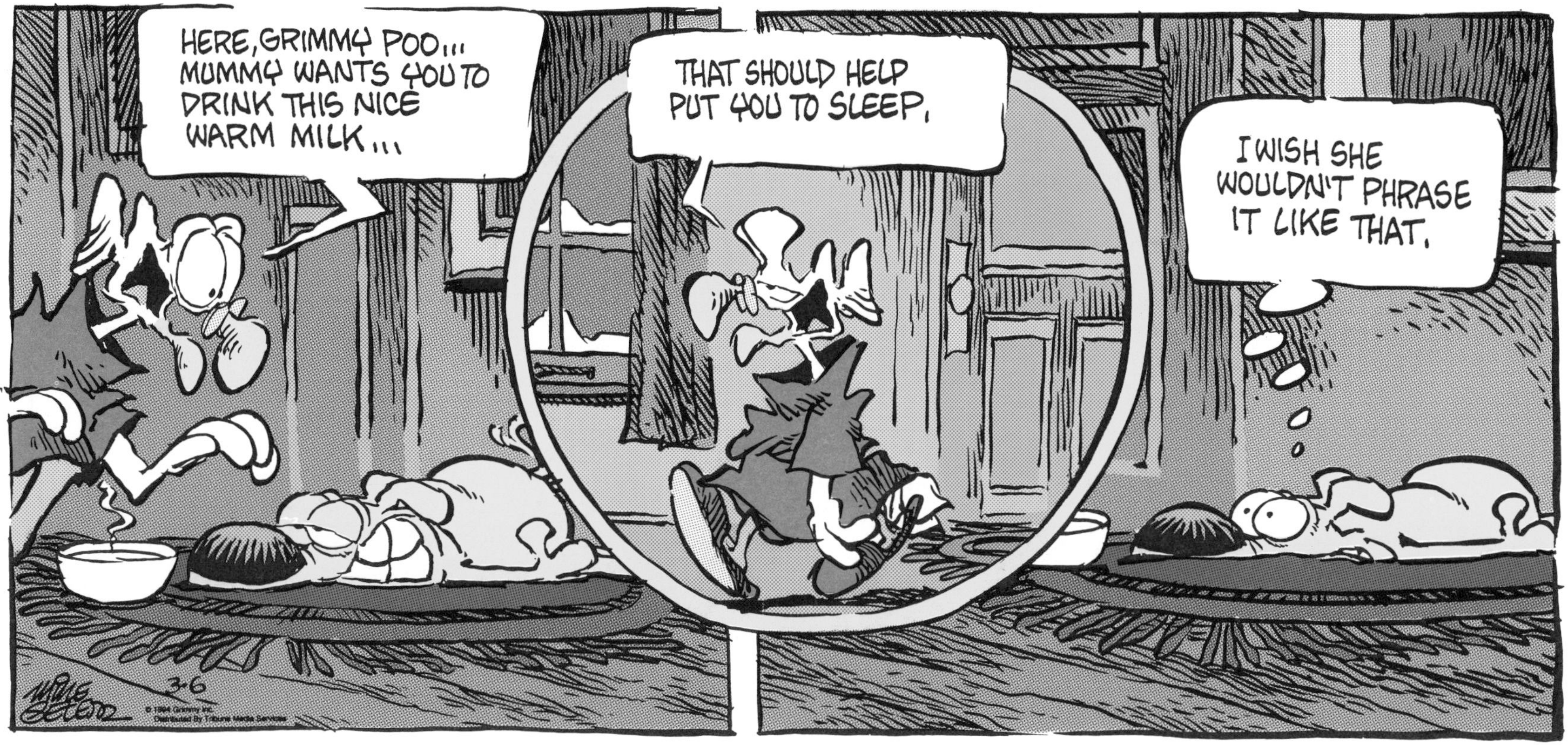
HERE, GRIMMY POO... MUMMY WANTS YOU TO DRINK THIS NICE WARM MILK...
THAT SHOULD HELP PUT YOU TO SLEEP.
I WISH SHE WOULDN'T PHRASE IT LIKE THAT.

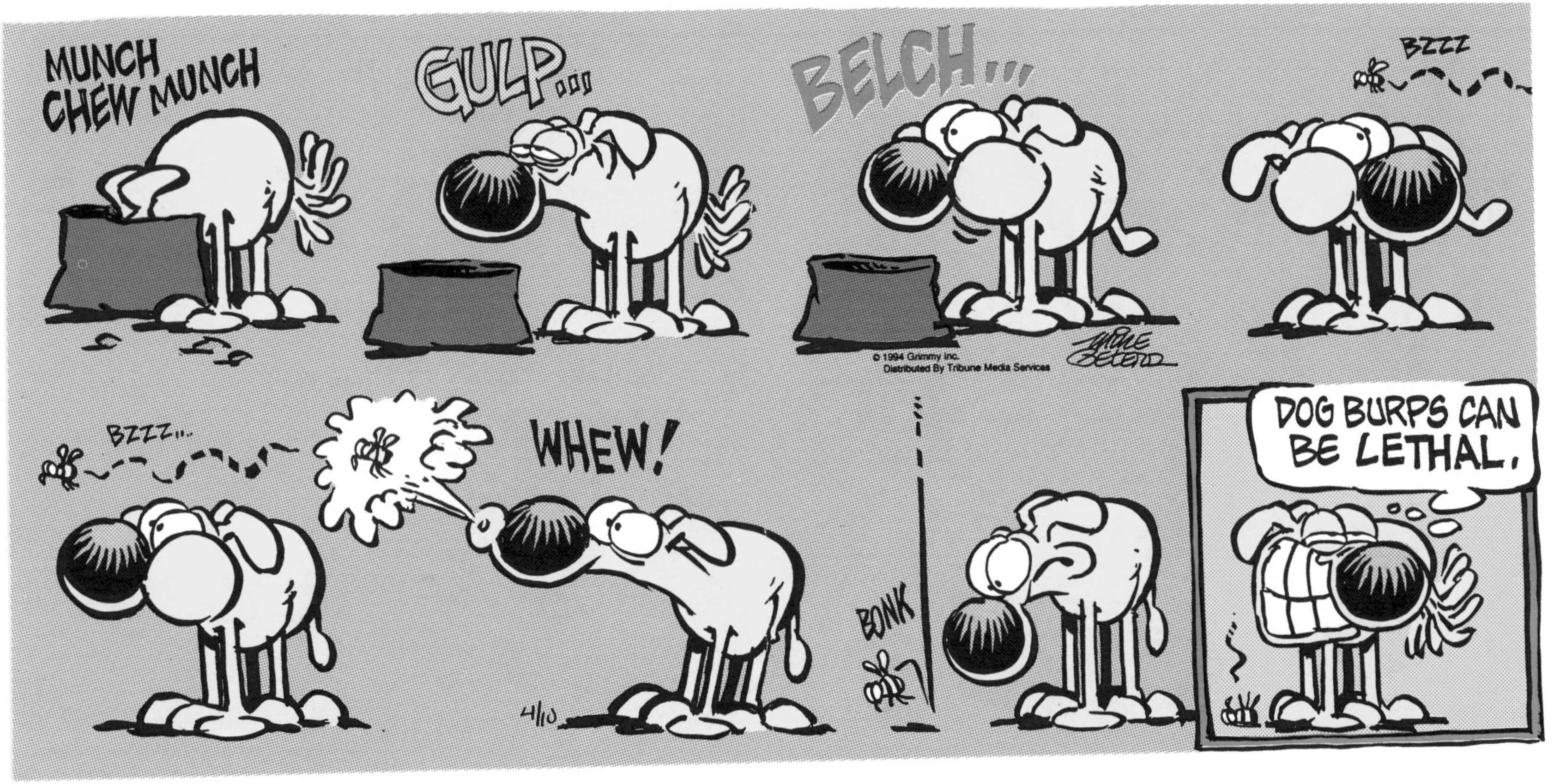
MUNCH
CHEW MUNCH
GULP...
BELCH...
BZZZ
© 1994 Grimmy Inc.
Distributed By Tribune Media Services
BZZZ...
WHEW!
4/10
BONK
DOG BURPS CAN BE LETHAL.

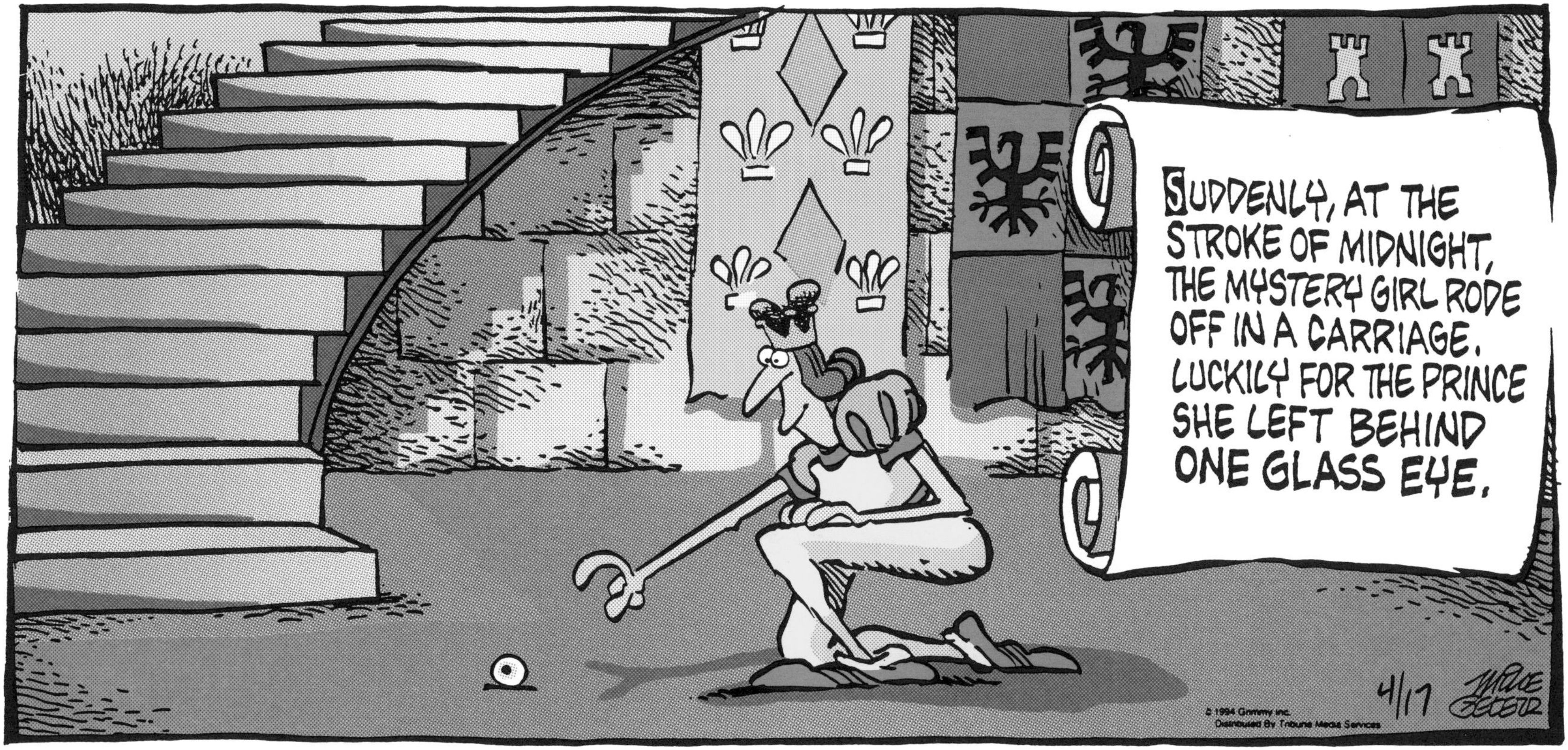
SUDDENLY, AT THE STROKE OF MIDNIGHT, THE MYSTERY GIRL RODE OFF IN A CARRIAGE. LUCKILY FOR THE PRINCE SHE LEFT BEHIND ONE GLASS EYE.
4/17
© 1994 Grimmy Inc.
Distributed By Tribune Media Services

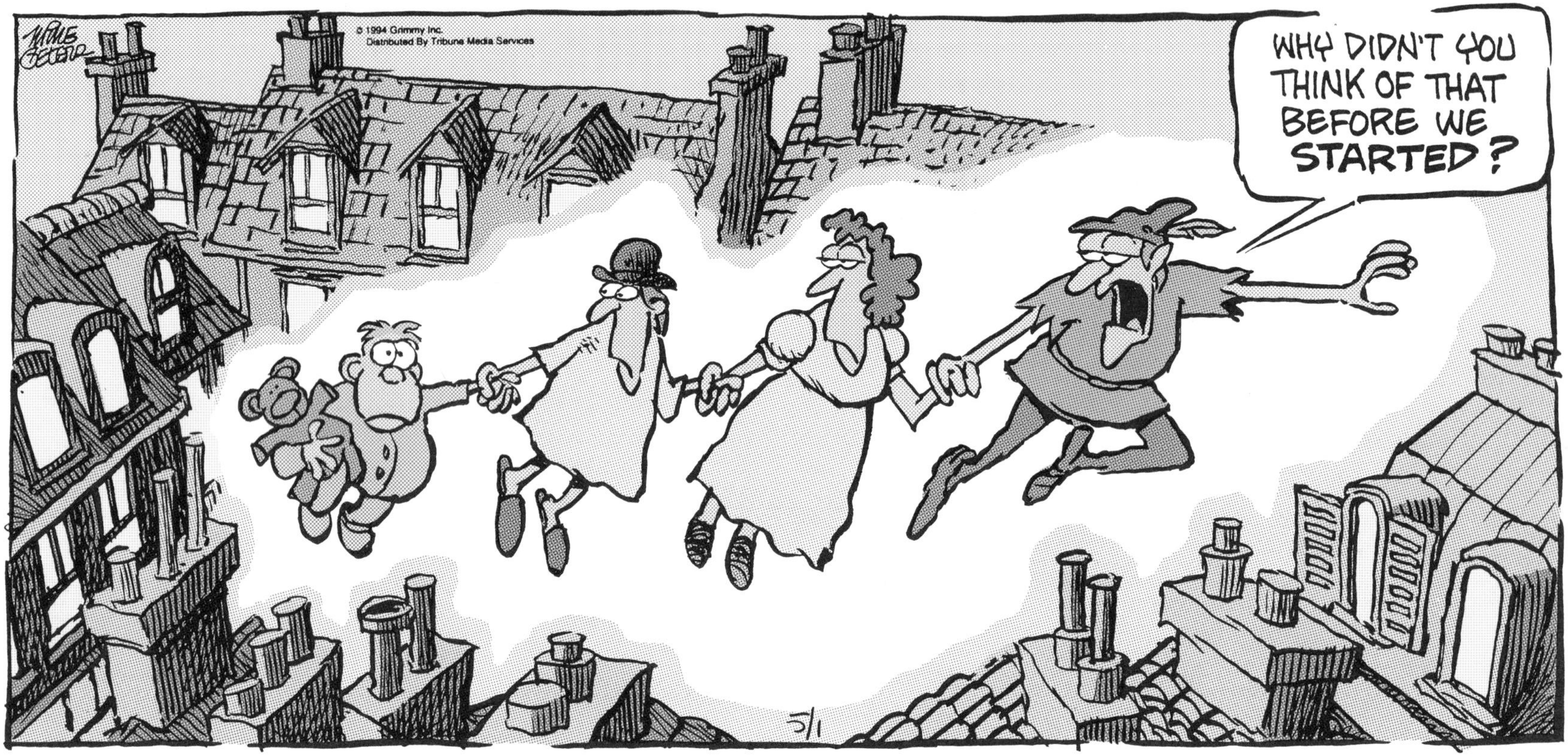
© 1994 Grimmy Inc.
Distributed By Tribune Media Services
WHY DIDN'T YOU THINK OF THAT BEFORE WE STARTED?
5/1

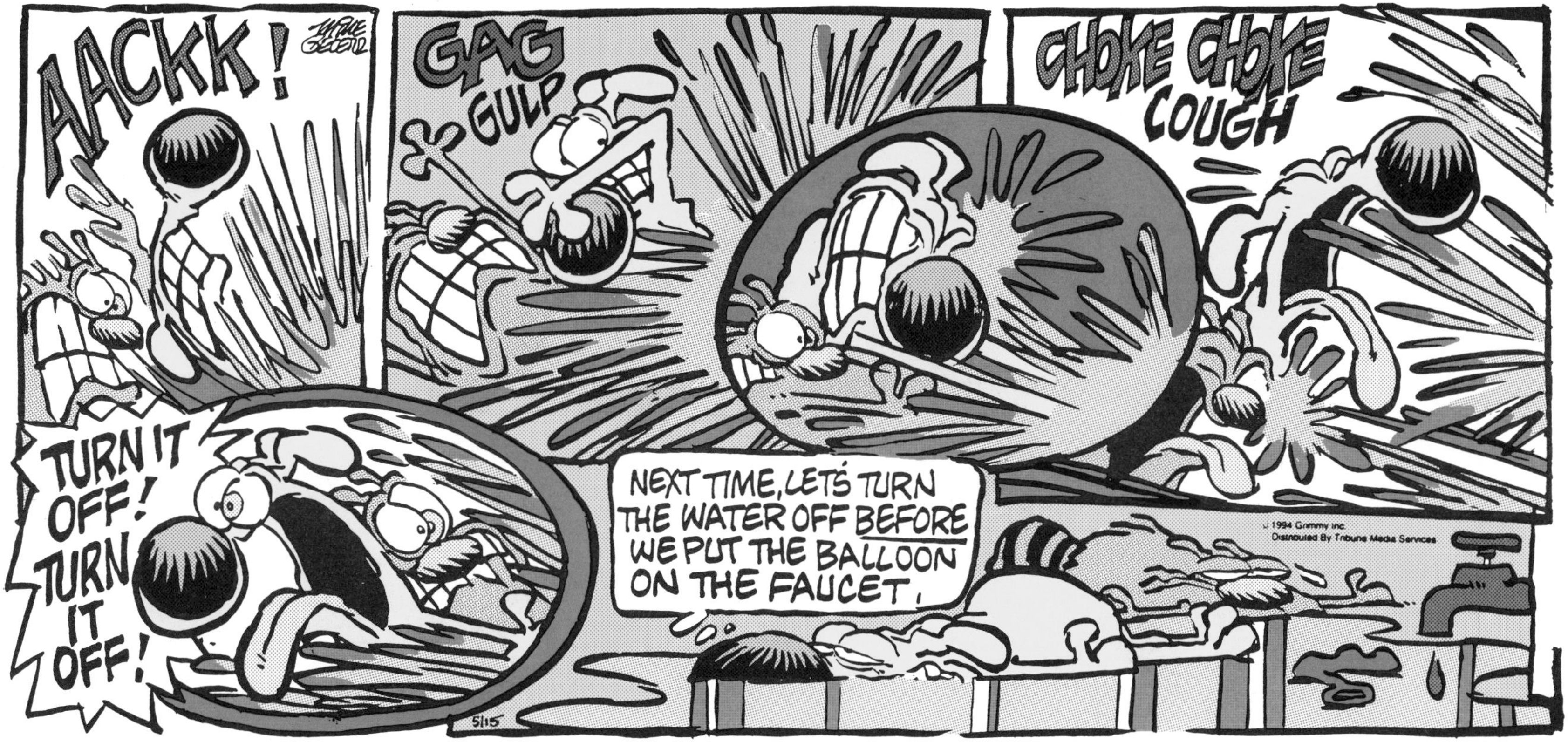
AACKK!
GAG
GULP
CHOKE CHOKE
COUGH
TURN IT OFF! TURN IT OFF!
NEXT TIME, LET'S TURN THE WATER OFF BEFORE WE PUT THE BALLOON ON THE FAUCET.
© 1994 Grimmy Inc.
Distributed By Tribune Media Services
5/15

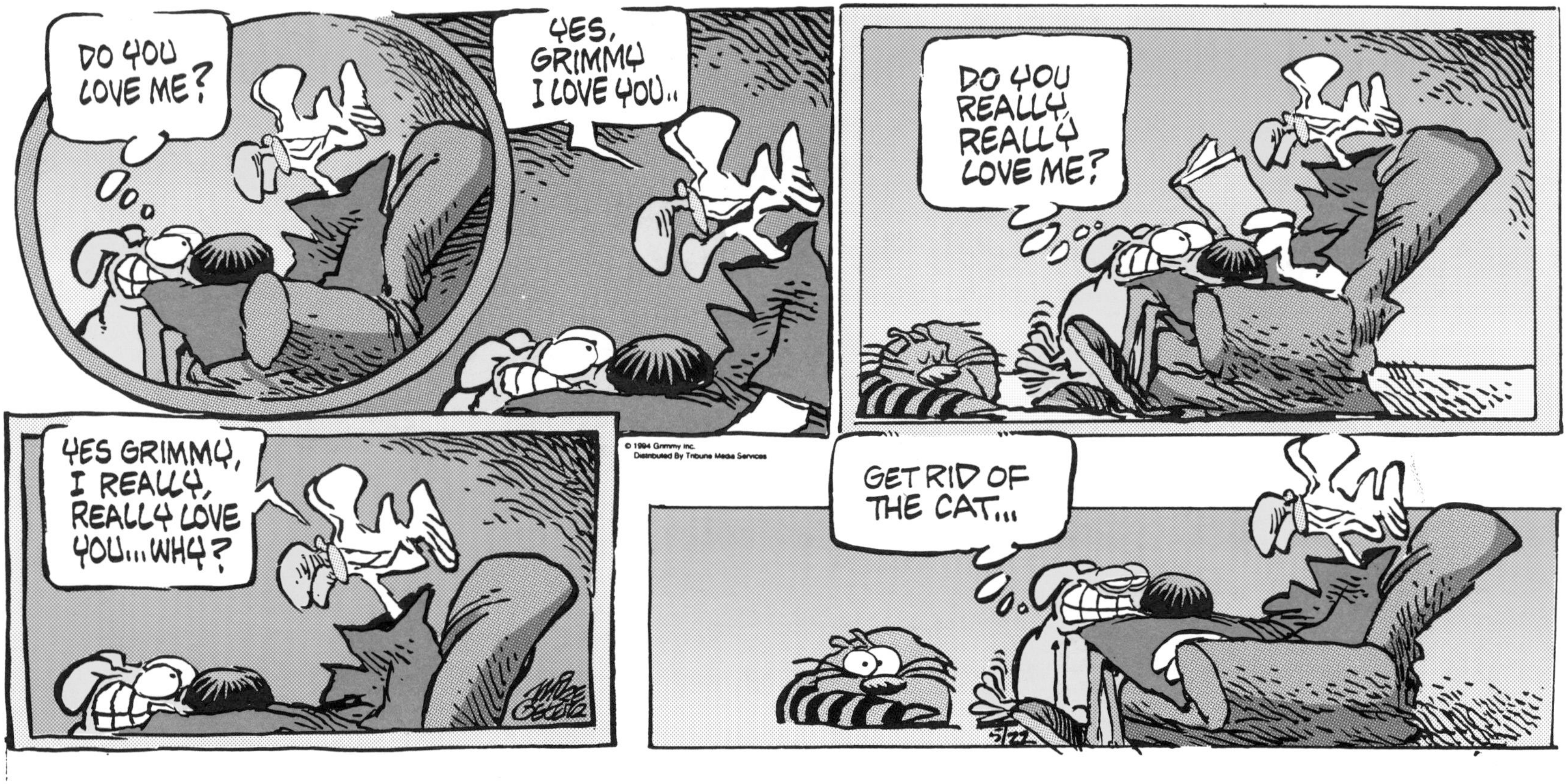
DO YOU LOVE ME?
YES, GRIMMY I LOVE YOU..
DO YOU REALLY, REALLY LOVE ME?
YES GRIMMY, I REALLY, REALLY LOVE YOU...WHY?
GET RID OF THE CAT...
5/22

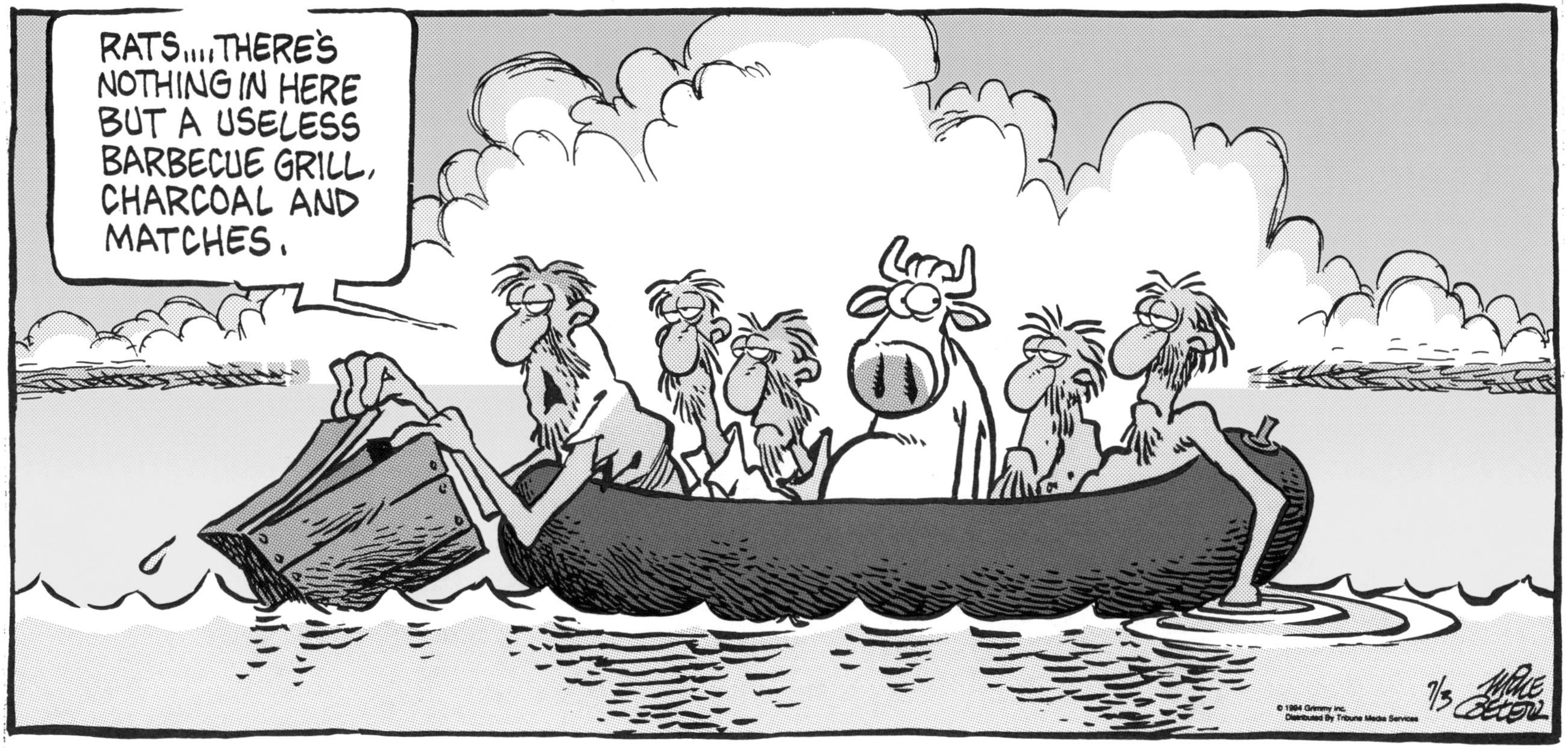
RATS....THERE'S NOTHING IN HERE BUT A USELESS BARBECUE GRILL, CHARCOAL AND MATCHES.
© 1994 Grimmy Inc.
Distributed By Tribune Media Services
7/3
MIKE PETERS

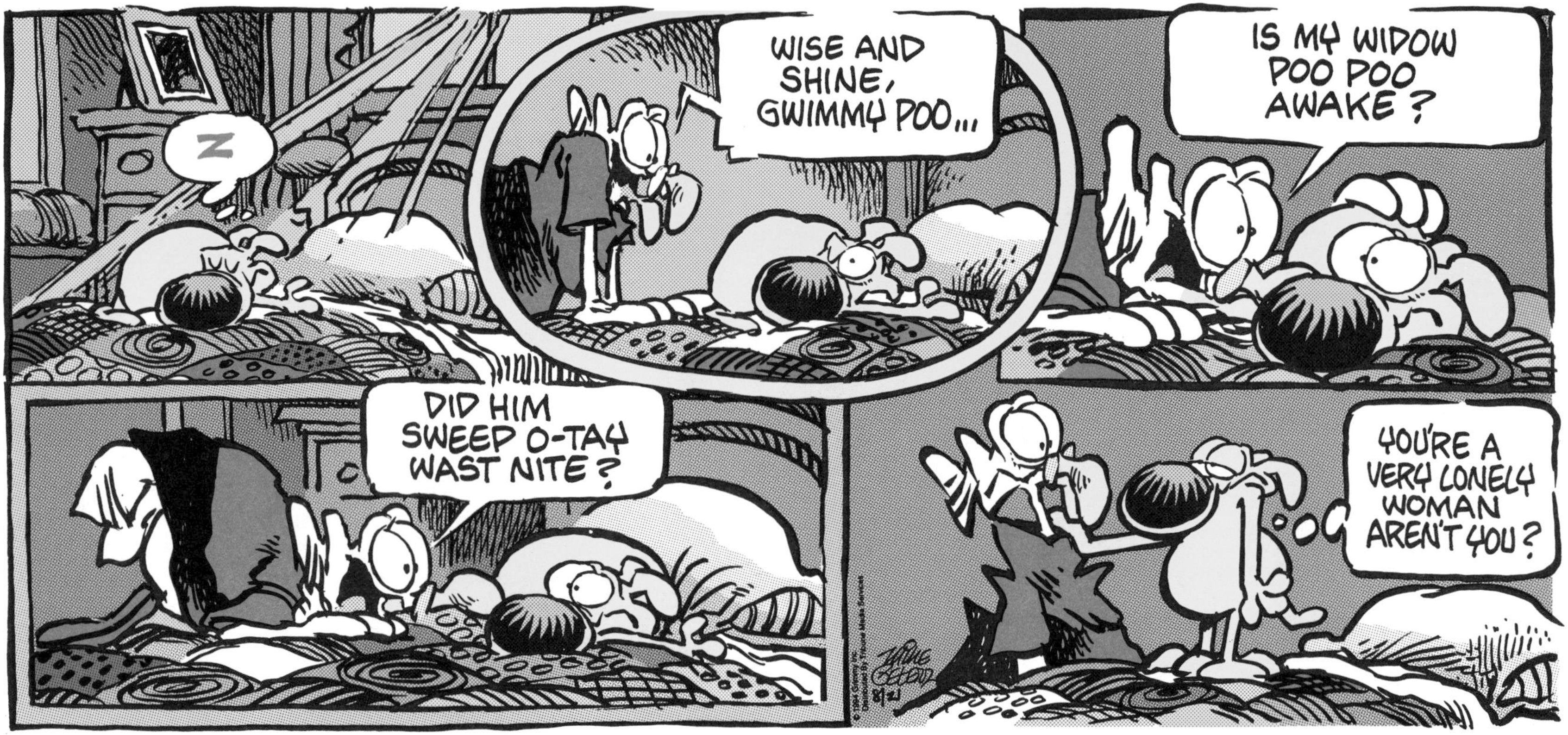
Z
WISE AND SHINE, GWIMMY POO...
IS MY WIDOW POO POO AWAKE?
DID HIM SWEEP O-TAY WAST NITE?
YOU'RE A VERY LONELY WOMAN AREN'T YOU?

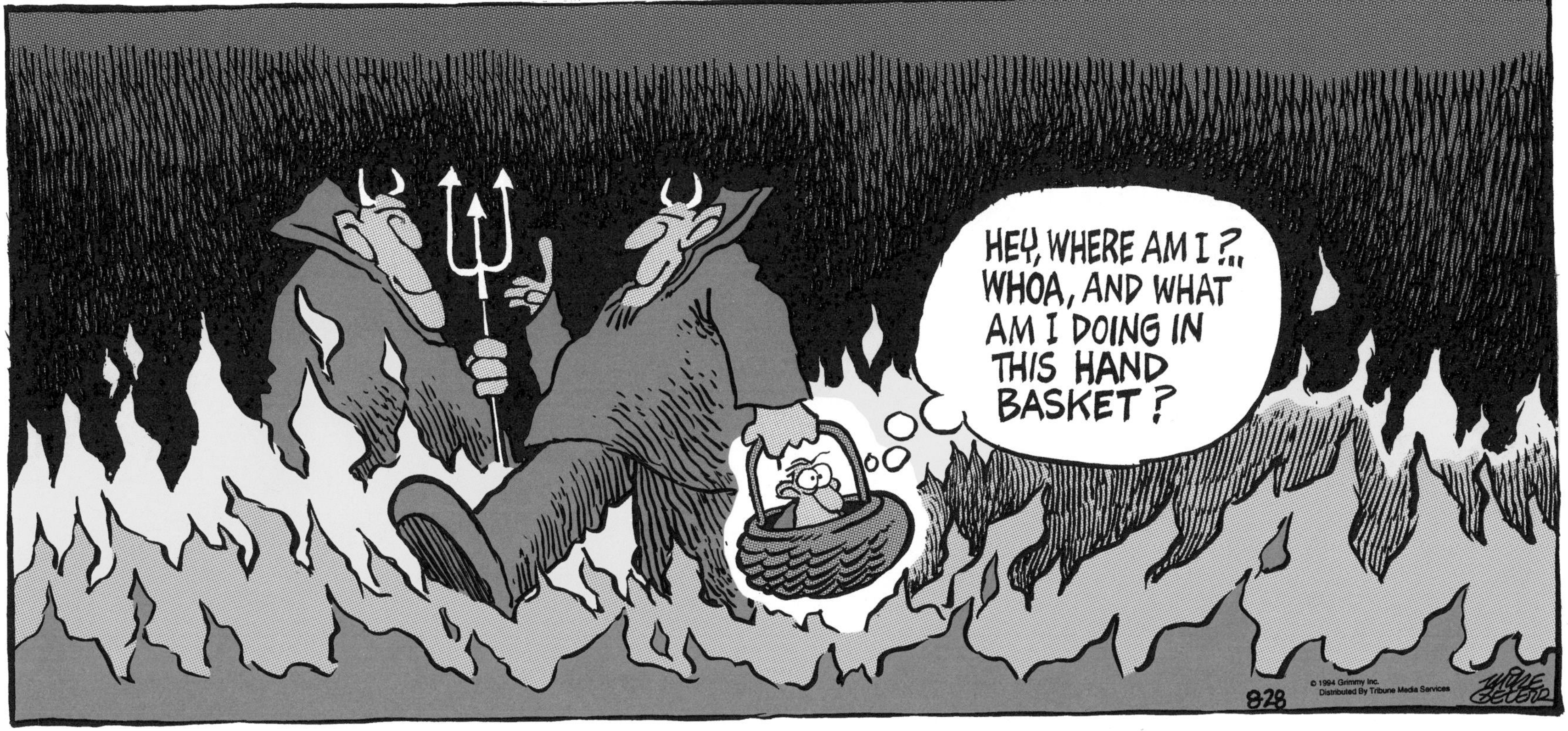
HEY, WHERE AM I?... WHOA, AND WHAT AM I DOING IN THIS HAND BASKET?
8-28
© 1994 Grimmy Inc.
Distributed By Tribune Media Services

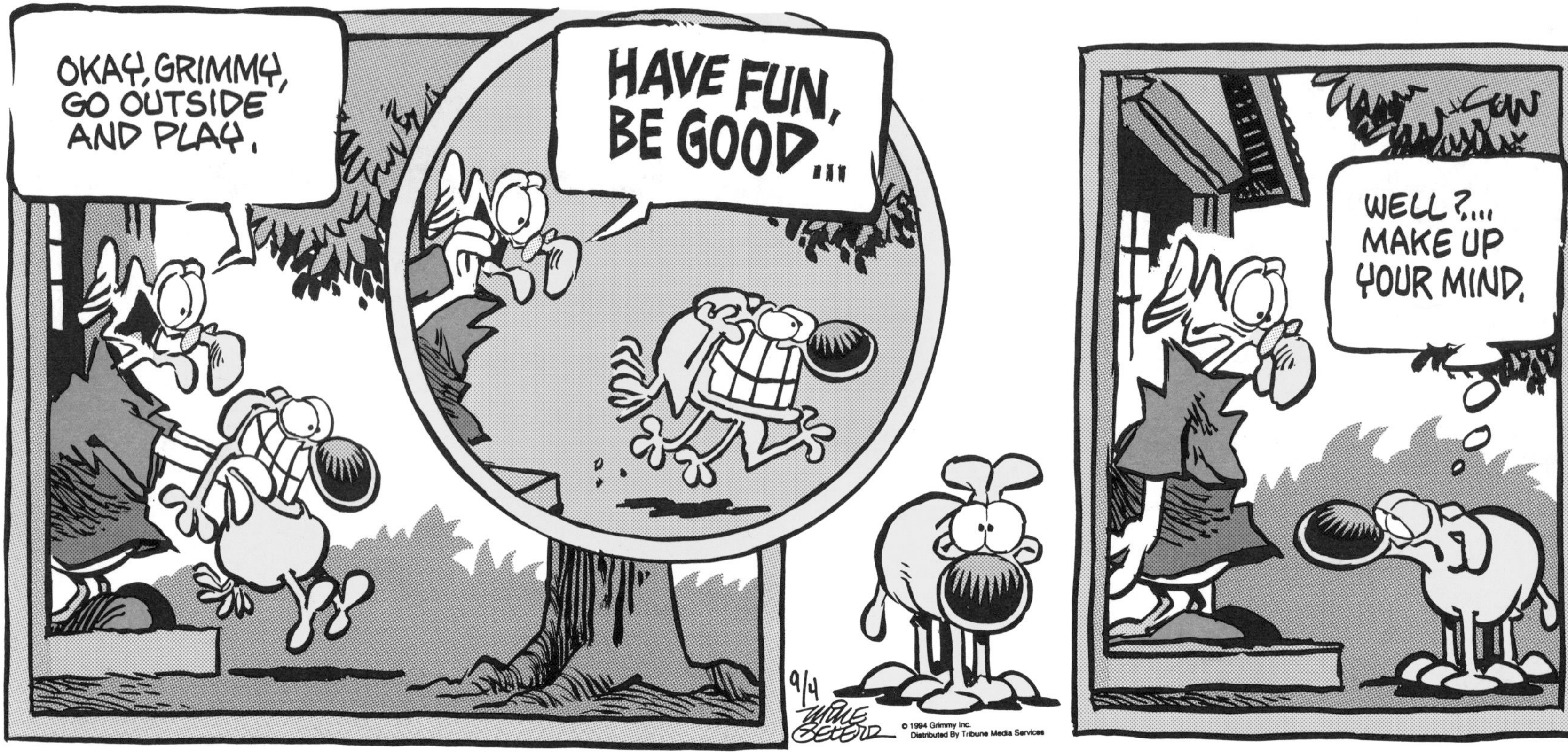
OKAY, GRIMMY, GO OUTSIDE AND PLAY.
HAVE FUN, BE GOOD...
WELL?... MAKE UP YOUR MIND.
9/4
© 1994 Grimmy Inc.
Distributed By Tribune Media Services

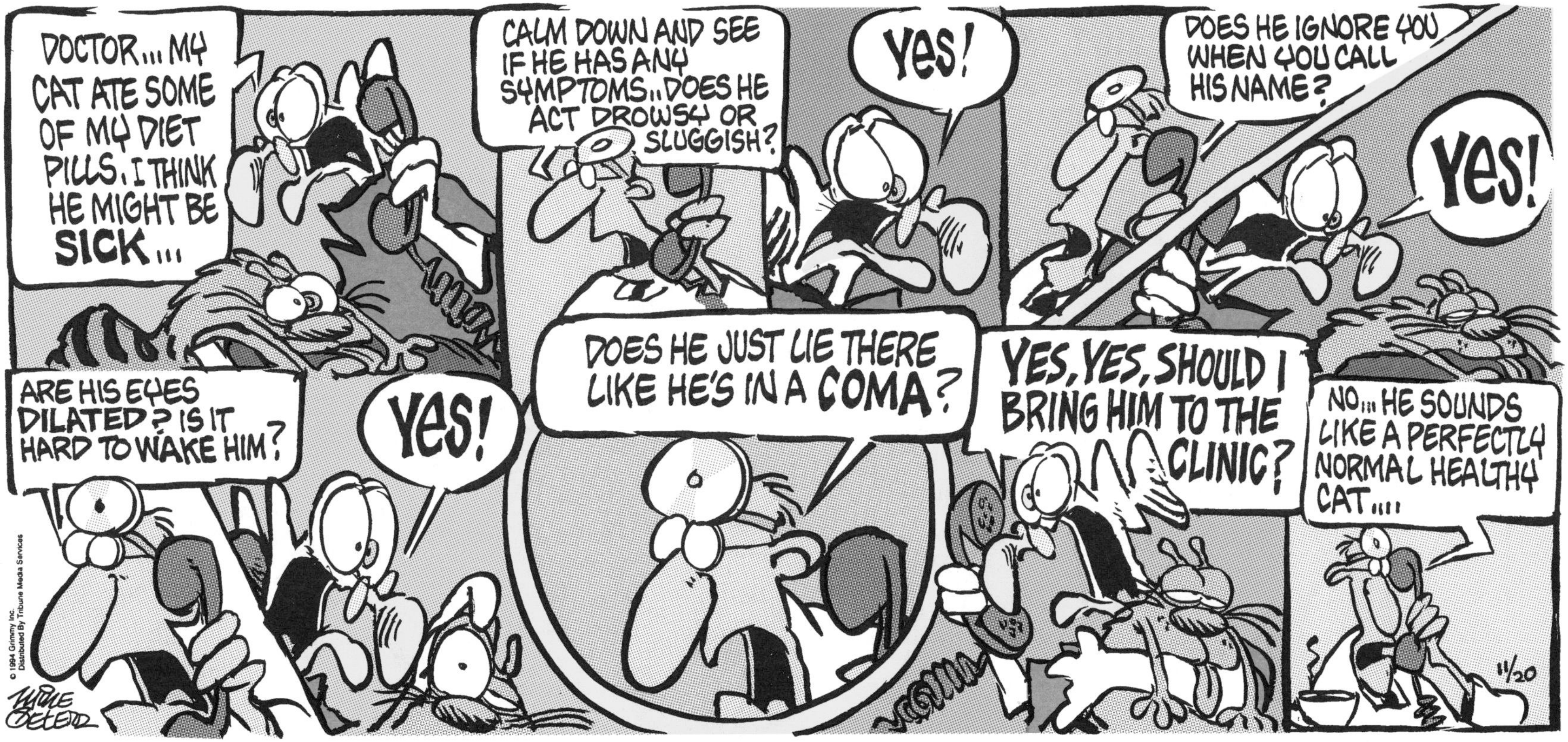
DOCTOR... MY CAT ATE SOME OF MY DIET PILLS. I THINK HE MIGHT BE **SICK**...
CALM DOWN AND SEE IF HE HAS ANY SYMPTOMS.. DOES HE ACT DROWSY OR SLUGGISH?
YES!
DOES HE IGNORE YOU WHEN YOU CALL HIS NAME?
YES!
ARE HIS EYES **DILATED**? IS IT HARD TO **WAKE** HIM?
YES!
DOES HE JUST LIE THERE LIKE HE'S IN A **COMA**?
YES, YES, SHOULD I BRING HIM TO THE CLINIC?
NO... HE SOUNDS LIKE A PERFECTLY NORMAL HEALTHY CAT....
© 1994 Grimmy Inc.
Distributed By Tribune Media Services
11/20

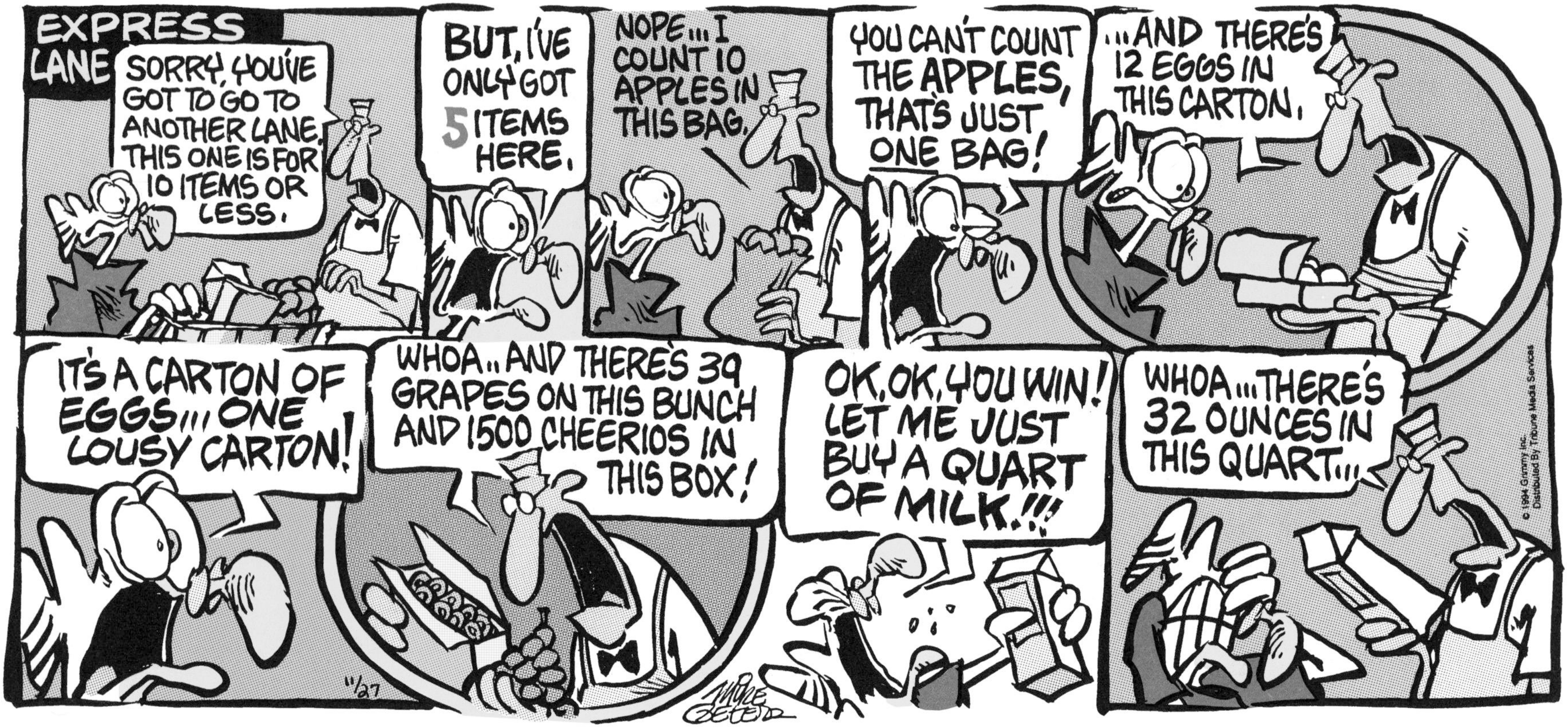
EXPRESS LANE
SORRY, YOU'VE GOT TO GO TO ANOTHER LANE, THIS ONE IS FOR 10 ITEMS OR LESS.
BUT, I'VE ONLY GOT 5 ITEMS HERE.
NOPE... I COUNT 10 APPLES IN THIS BAG.
YOU CAN'T COUNT THE APPLES, THAT'S JUST ONE BAG!
...AND THERE'S 12 EGGS IN THIS CARTON.
IT'S A CARTON OF EGGS... ONE LOUSY CARTON!
WHOA.. AND THERE'S 39 GRAPES ON THIS BUNCH AND 1500 CHEERIOS IN THIS BOX!
OK, OK, YOU WIN! LET ME JUST BUY A QUART OF MILK!!!
WHOA... THERE'S 32 OUNCES IN THIS QUART...
11/27
© 1994 Grimmy Inc. Distributed By Tribune Media Services

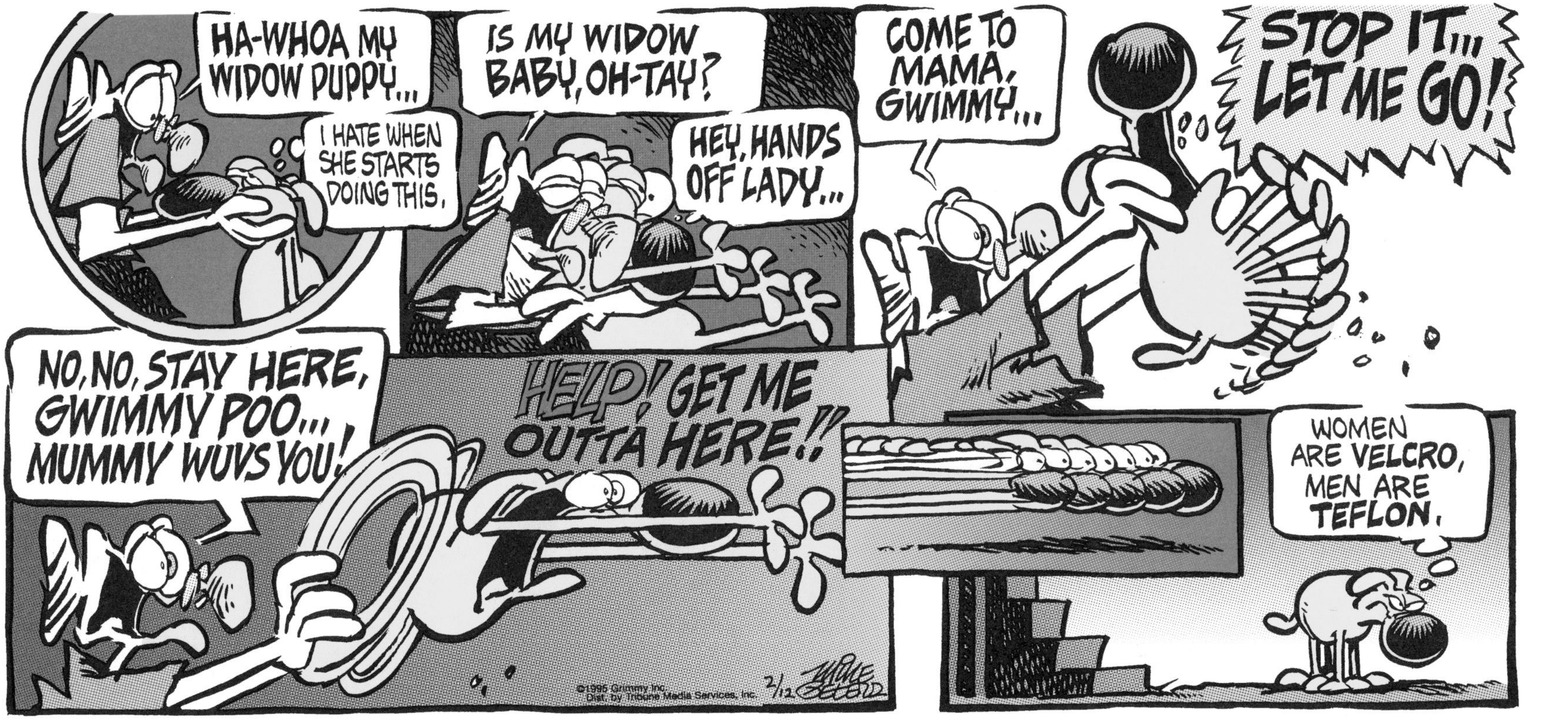
HA-WHOA MY WIDOW PUPPY...
I HATE WHEN SHE STARTS DOING THIS.
IS MY WIDOW BABY, OH-TAY?
HEY, HANDS OFF LADY...
COME TO MAMA, GWIMMY...
STOP IT... LET ME GO!
NO, NO, STAY HERE, GWIMMY POO... MUMMY WUVS YOU!
HELP! GET ME OUTTA HERE!!
WOMEN ARE VELCRO, MEN ARE TEFLON.
©1995 Grimmy Inc.
Dist. by Tribune Media Services, Inc.
2/12

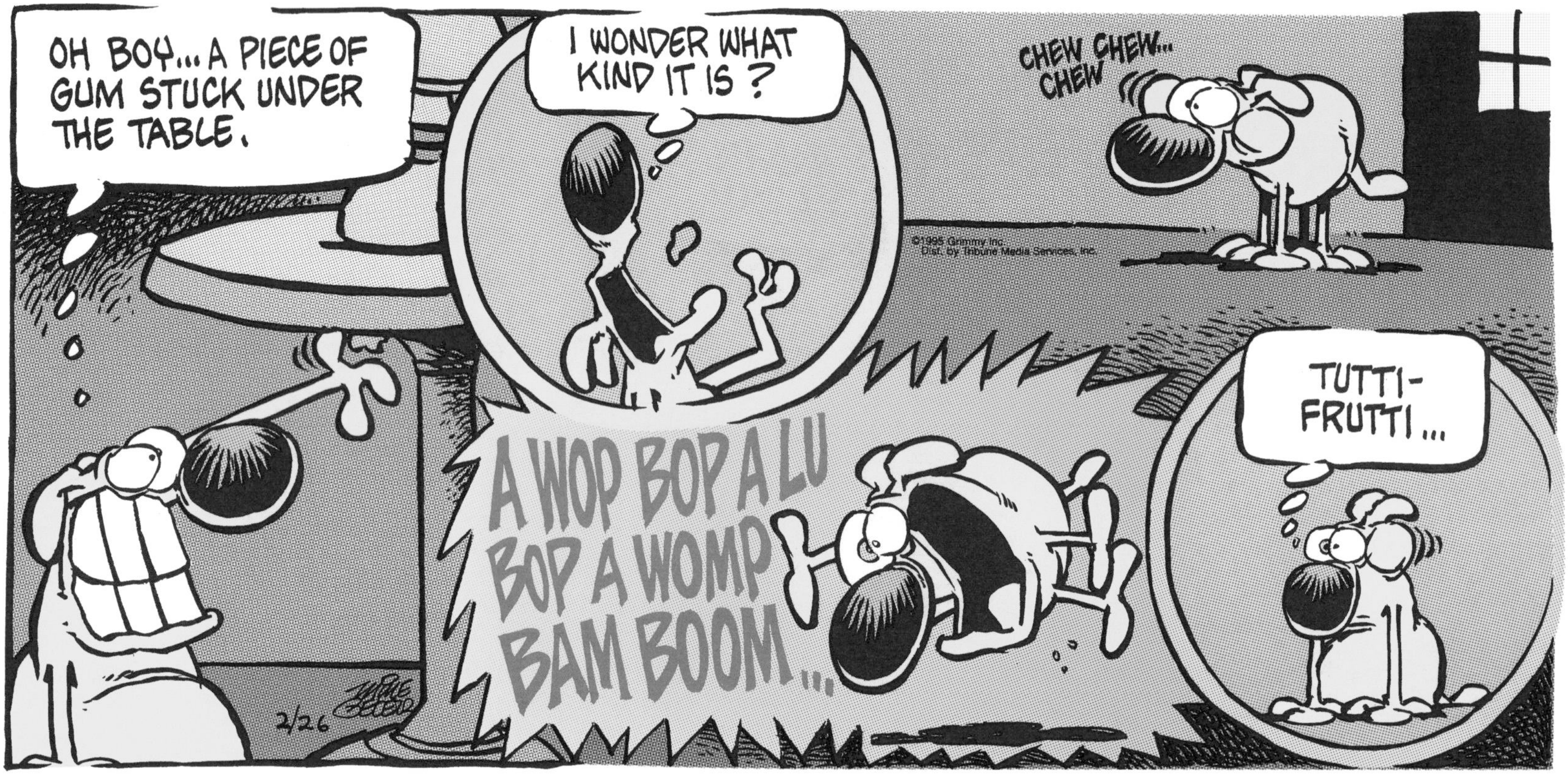
OH BOY... A PIECE OF GUM STUCK UNDER THE TABLE.
I WONDER WHAT KIND IT IS ?
CHEW CHEW... CHEW
©1995 Grimmy Inc. Dist. by Tribune Media Services, Inc.
A WOP BOP A LU BOP A WOMP BAM BOOM...
TUTTI-FRUTTI...
2/26

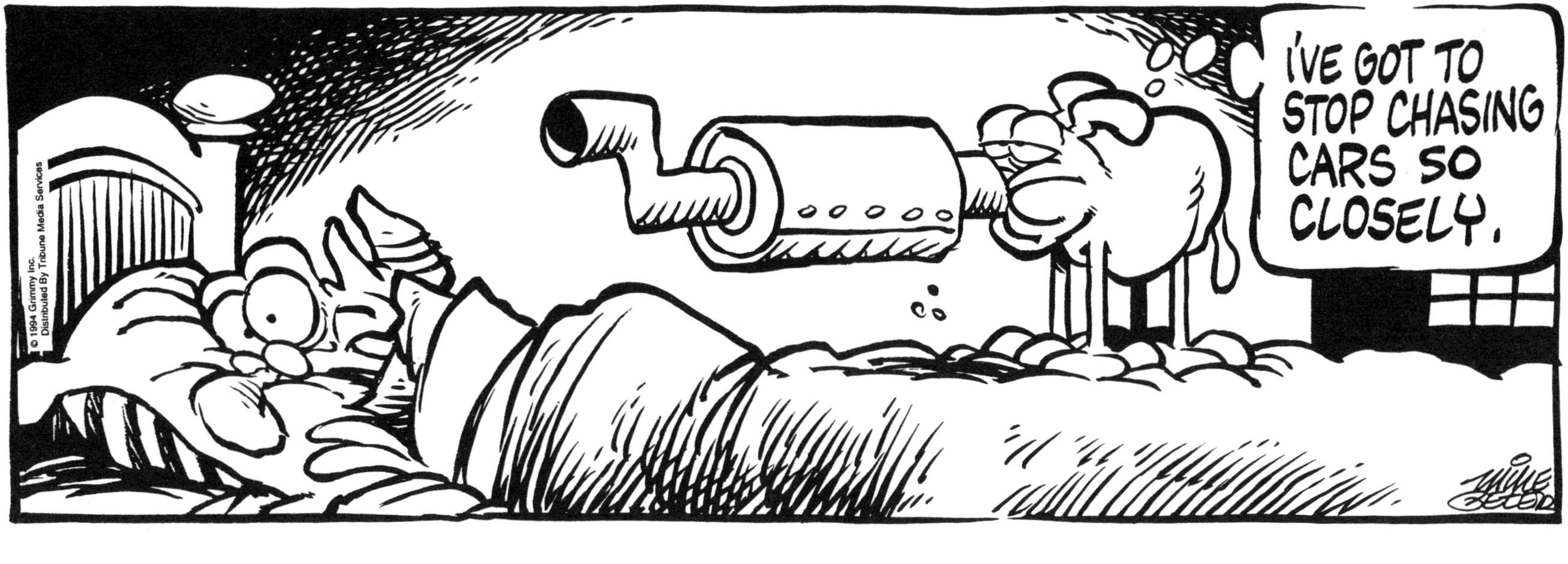
© 1994 Grimmy Inc.
Distributed By Tribune Media Services
I'VE GOT TO STOP CHASING CARS SO CLOSELY.

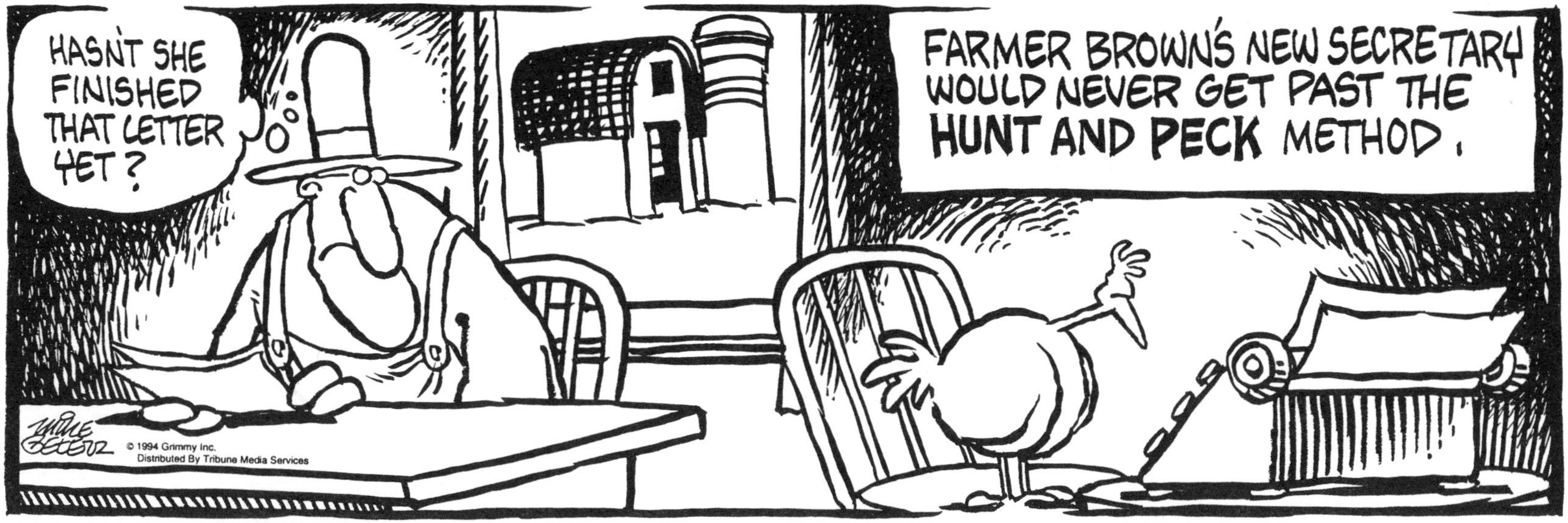
HASN'T SHE FINISHED THAT LETTER YET?
FARMER BROWN'S NEW SECRETARY WOULD NEVER GET PAST THE HUNT AND PECK METHOD.
© 1994 Grimmy Inc.
Distributed By Tribune Media Services

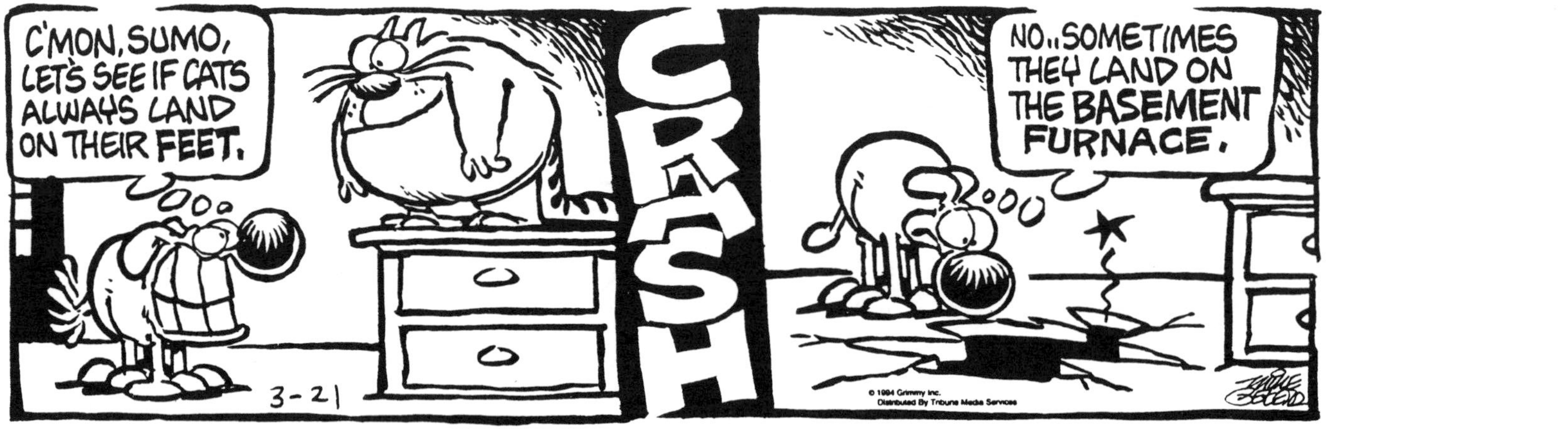
C'MON, SUMO, LET'S SEE IF CATS ALWAYS LAND ON THEIR FEET.
3-21
CRASH
NO.. SOMETIMES THEY LAND ON THE BASEMENT FURNACE.
© 1994 Grimmy Inc. Distributed By Tribune Media Services

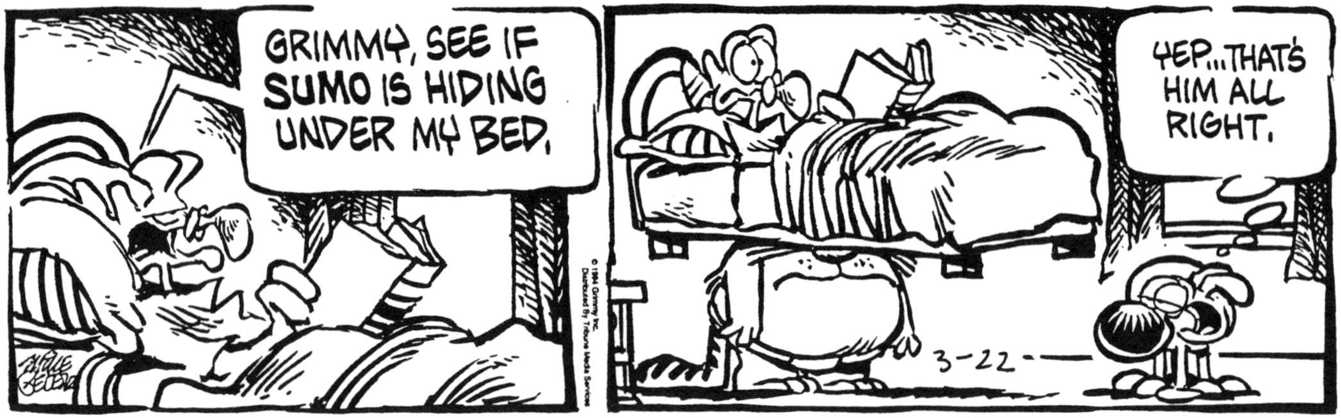
GRIMMY, SEE IF SUMO IS HIDING UNDER MY BED.
© 1994 Grimmy Inc. Distributed By Tribune Media Services
YEP... THAT'S HIM ALL RIGHT.
3-22

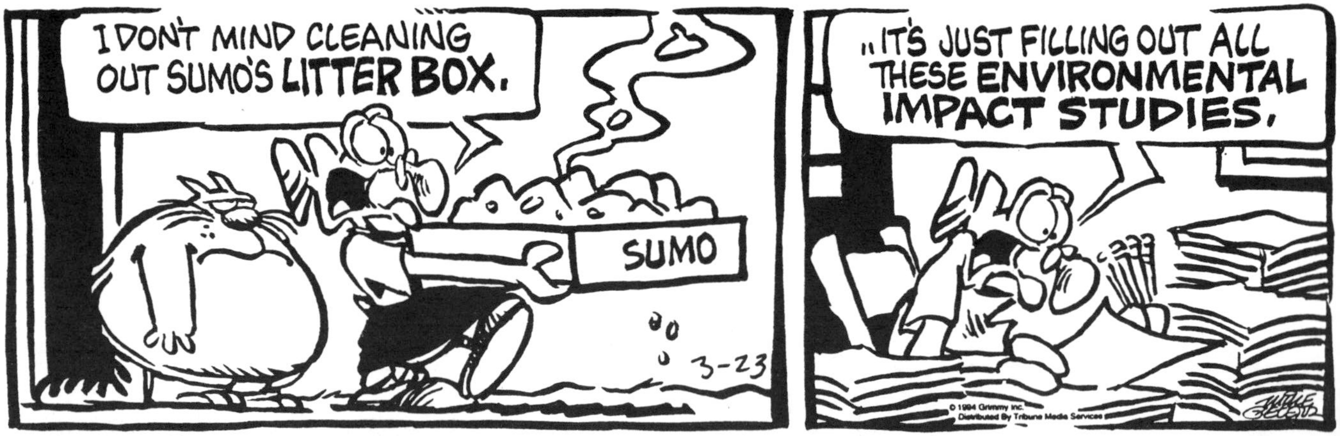
I DON'T MIND CLEANING OUT SUMO'S LITTER BOX.
SUMO
3-23
..IT'S JUST FILLING OUT ALL THESE ENVIRONMENTAL IMPACT STUDIES.
© 1994 Grimmy Inc. Distributed By Tribune Media Services

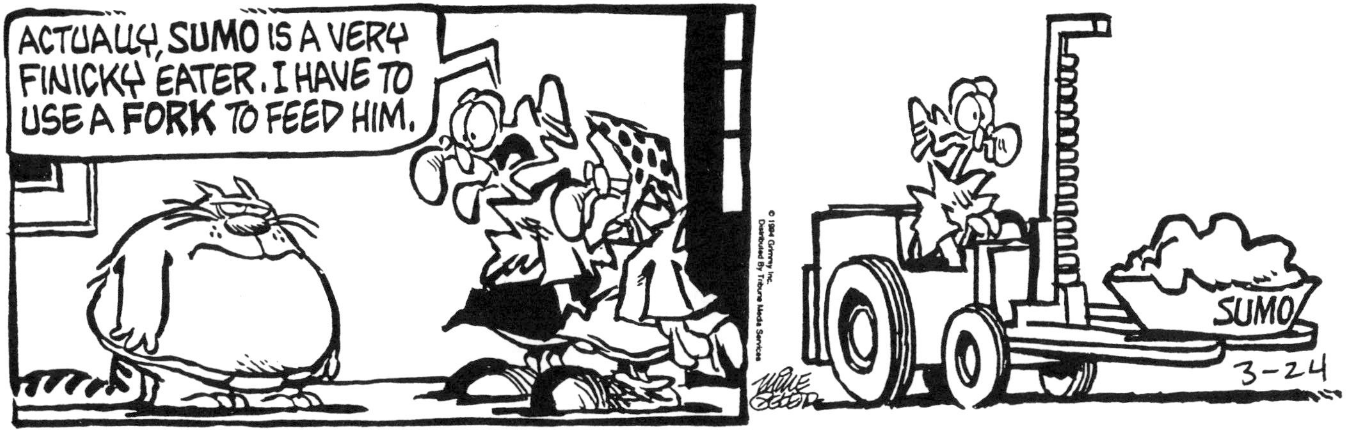
ACTUALLY, SUMO IS A VERY FINICKY EATER. I HAVE TO USE A FORK TO FEED HIM.
SUMO
3-24

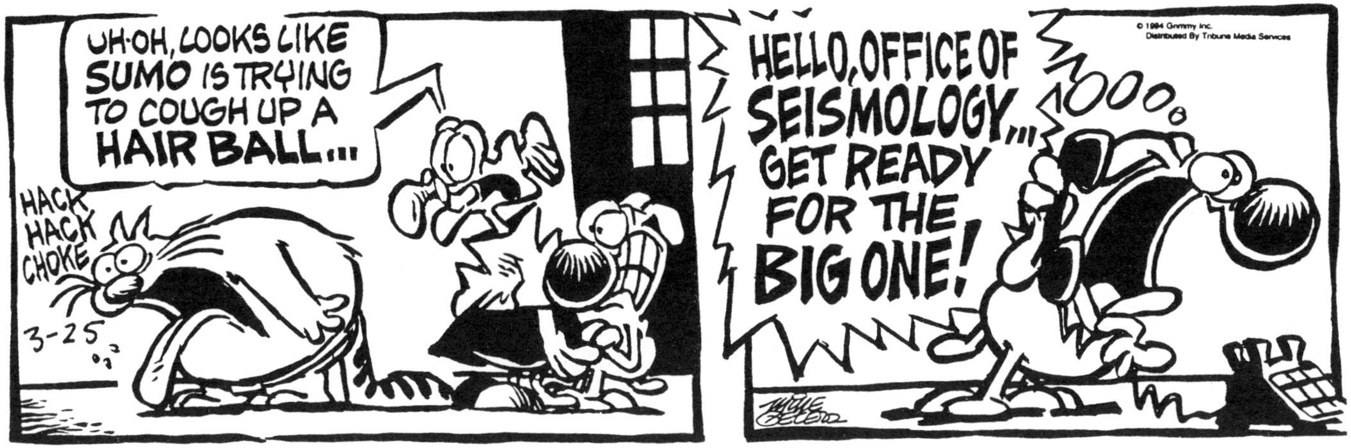
UH-OH, LOOKS LIKE SUMO IS TRYING TO COUGH UP A HAIR BALL...
HACK HACK CHOKE
3-25
© 1994 Grimmy Inc. Distributed By Tribune Media Services
HELLO, OFFICE OF SEISMOLOGY... GET READY FOR THE BIG ONE!

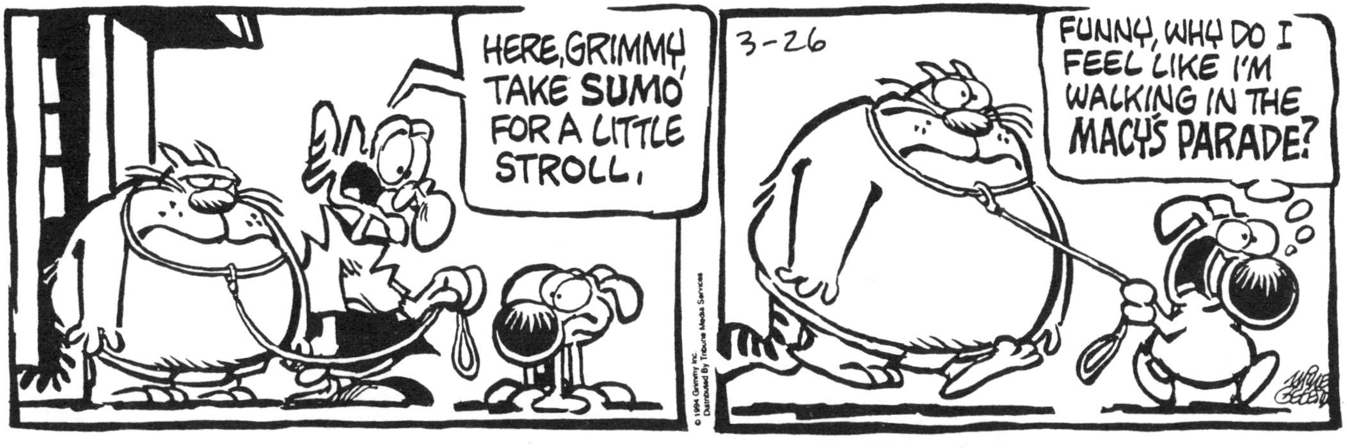
HERE, GRIMMY, TAKE SUMO FOR A LITTLE STROLL.
3-26
FUNNY, WHY DO I FEEL LIKE I'M WALKING IN THE MACY'S PARADE?

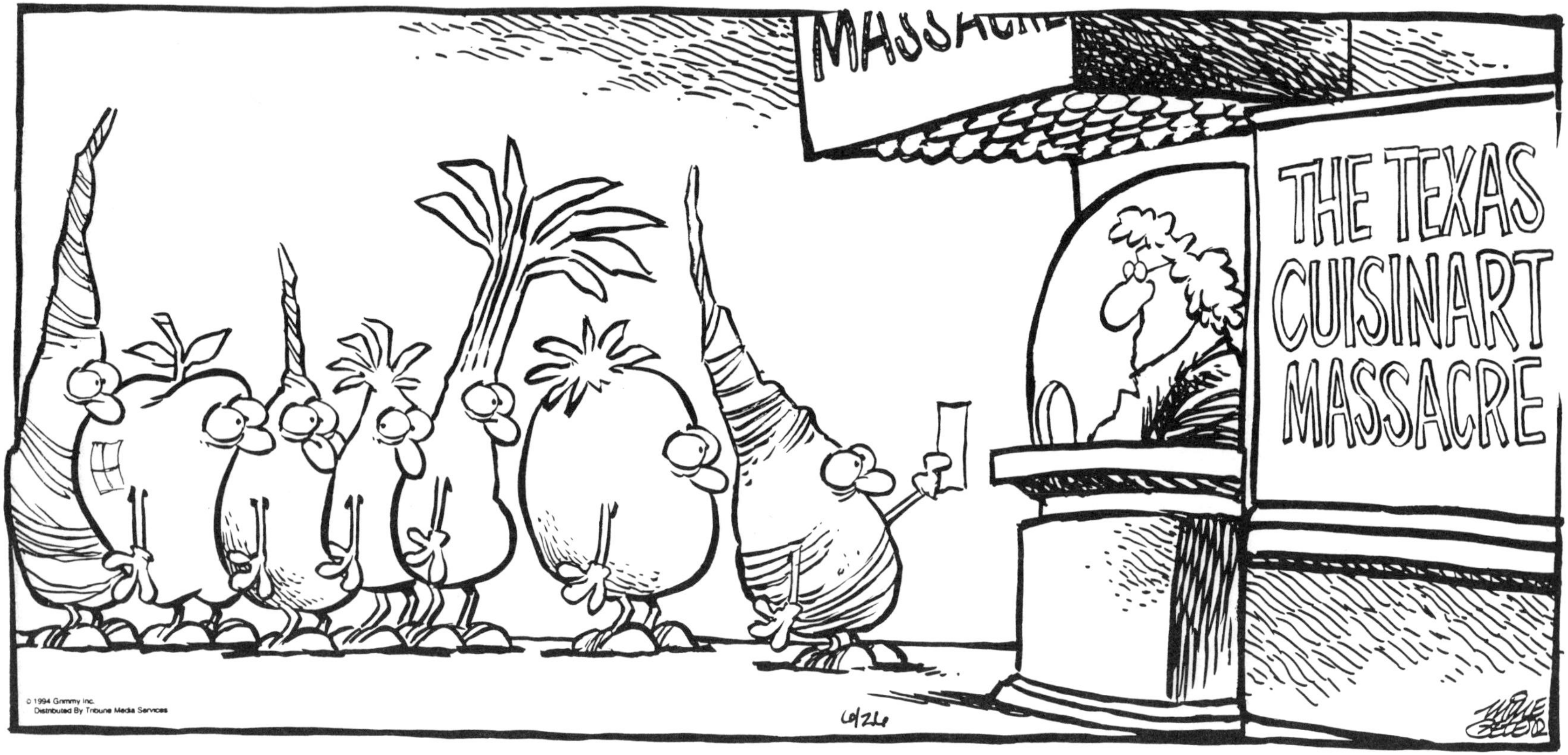
THE TEXAS
CUISINART
MASSACRE
6/26

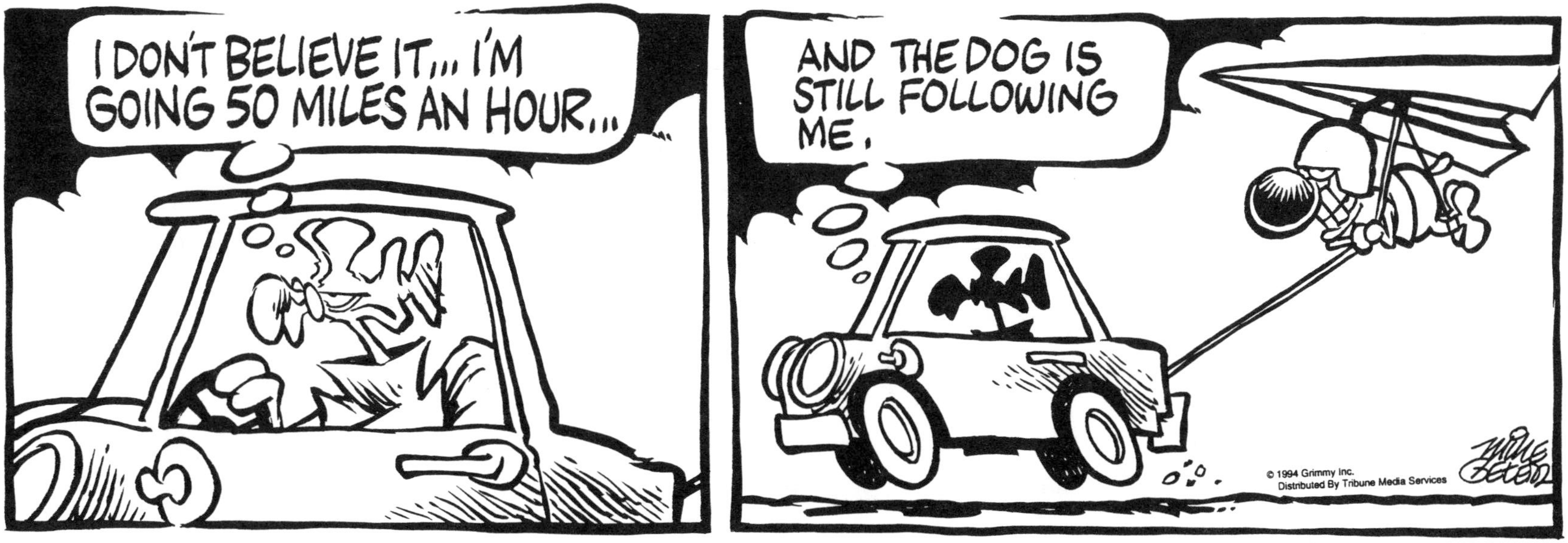
I DON'T BELIEVE IT... I'M GOING 50 MILES AN HOUR...
AND THE DOG IS STILL FOLLOWING ME.
© 1994 Grimmy Inc. Distributed By Tribune Media Services

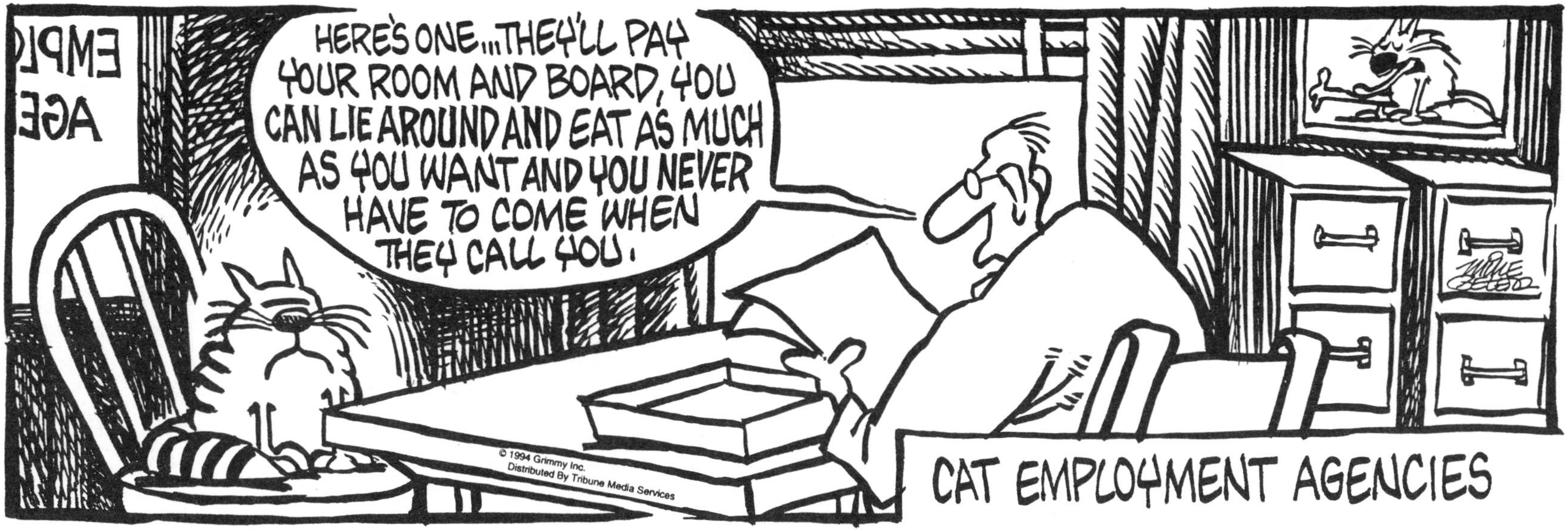
HERE'S ONE...THEY'LL PAY YOUR ROOM AND BOARD, YOU CAN LIE AROUND AND EAT AS MUCH AS YOU WANT AND YOU NEVER HAVE TO COME WHEN THEY CALL YOU.
© 1994 Grimmy Inc. Distributed By Tribune Media Services
CAT EMPLOYMENT AGENCIES

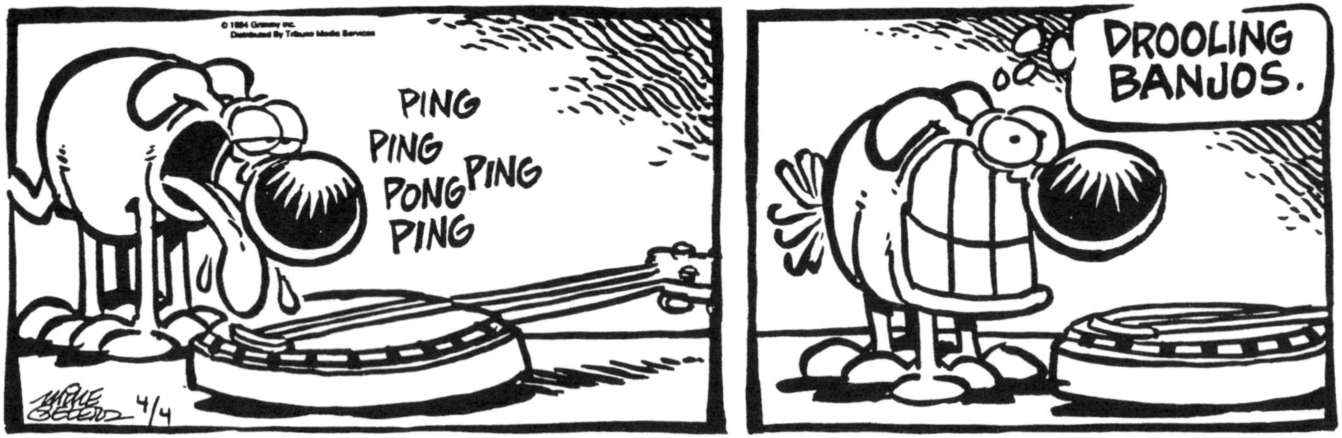
PING
PING
PONG PING
PING
4/4
DROOLING BANJOS.

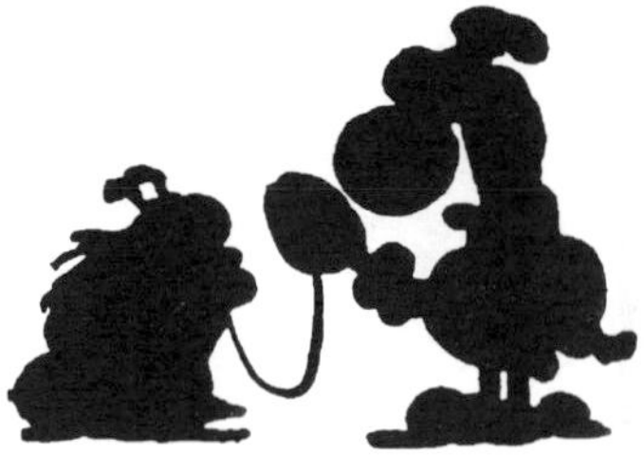

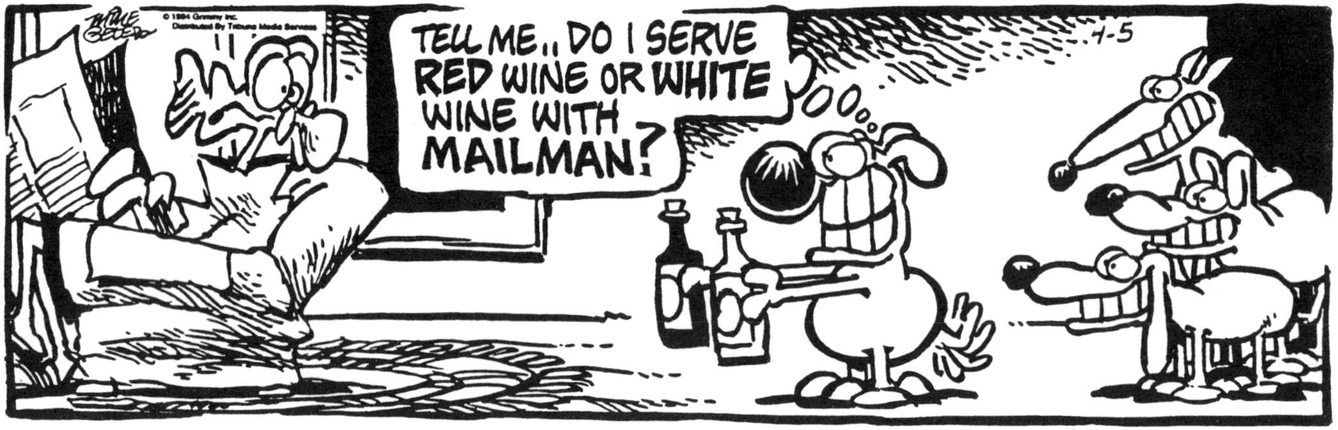
TELL ME.. DO I SERVE RED WINE OR WHITE WINE WITH MAILMAN?
4-5

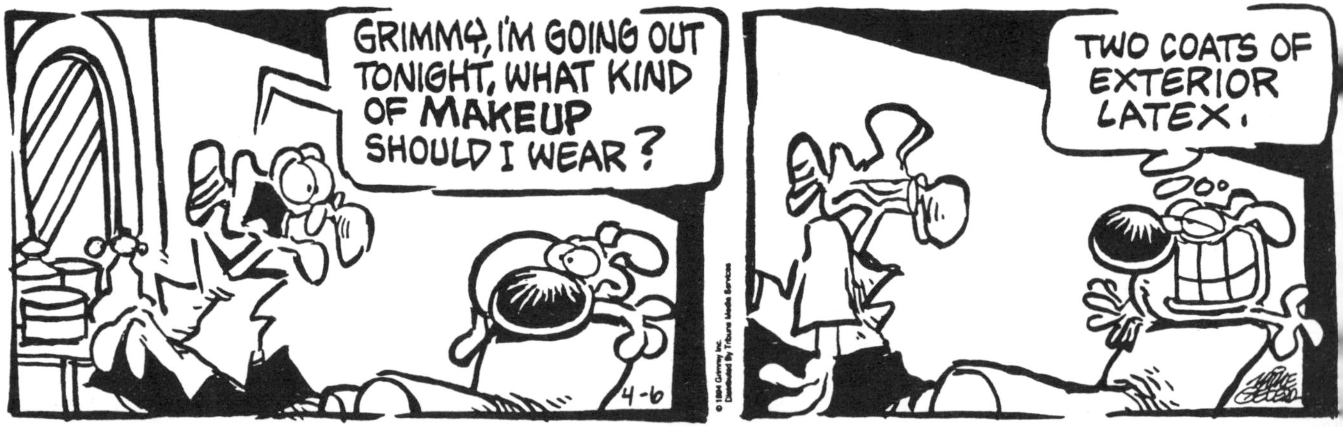
GRIMMY, I'M GOING OUT TONIGHT, WHAT KIND OF MAKEUP SHOULD I WEAR?
4-6
TWO COATS OF EXTERIOR LATEX.

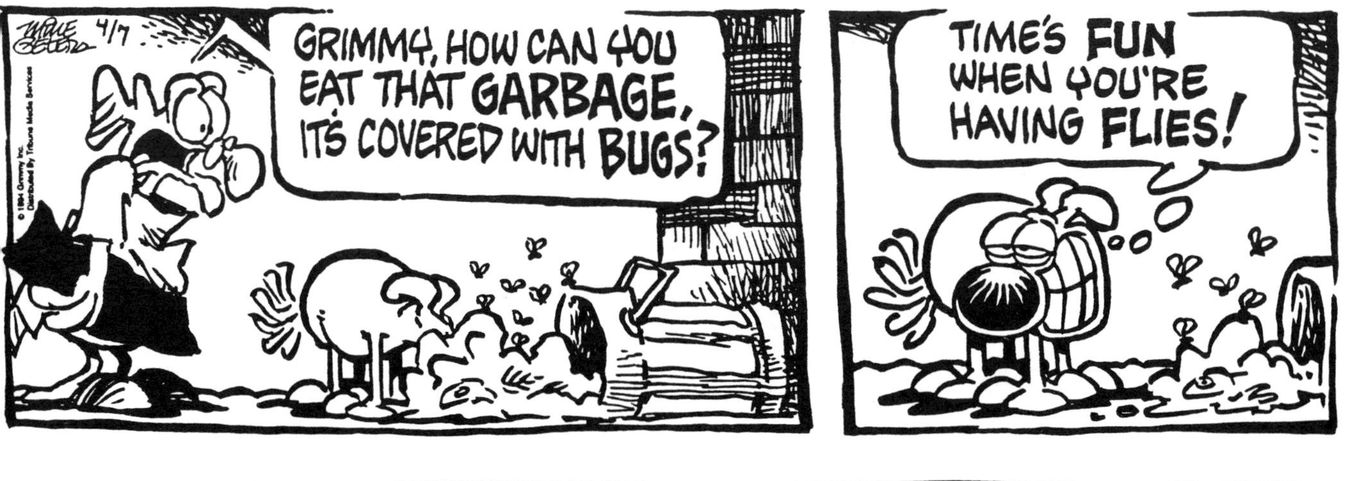
4/7
GRIMMY, HOW CAN YOU EAT THAT GARBAGE, IT'S COVERED WITH BUGS?
TIME'S FUN WHEN YOU'RE HAVING FLIES!

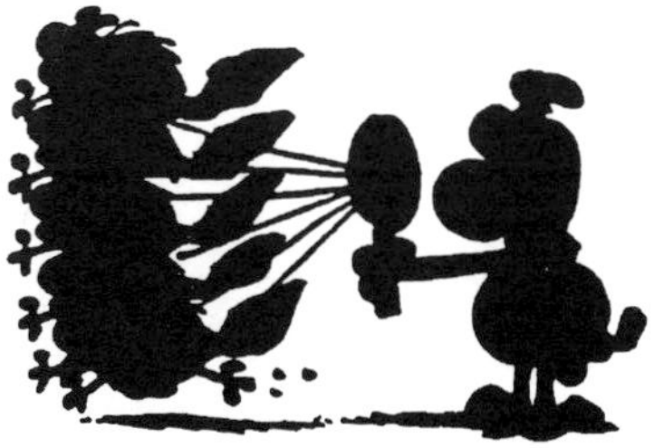

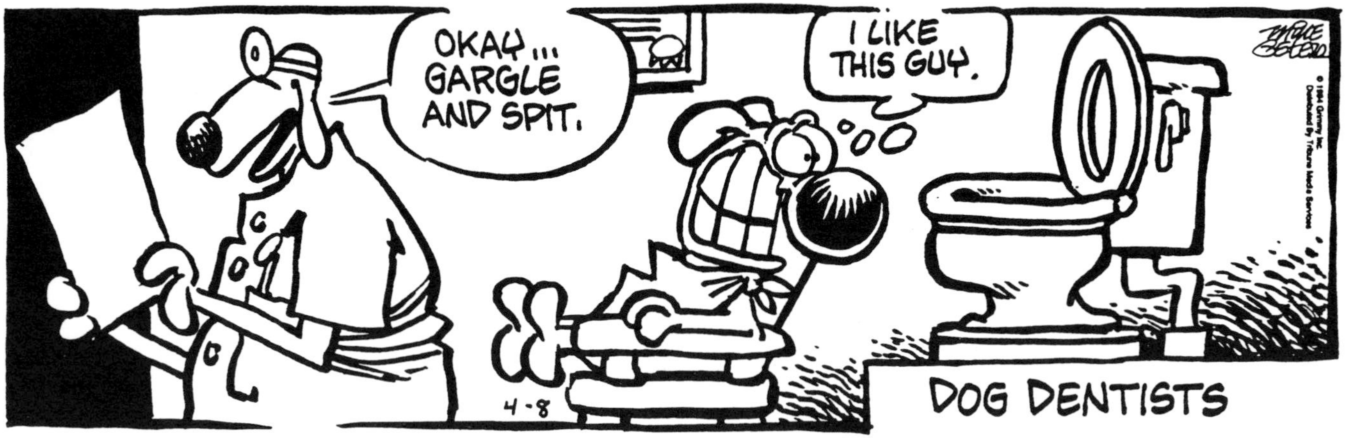
OKAY... GARGLE AND SPIT.
I LIKE THIS GUY.
4-8
DOG DENTISTS

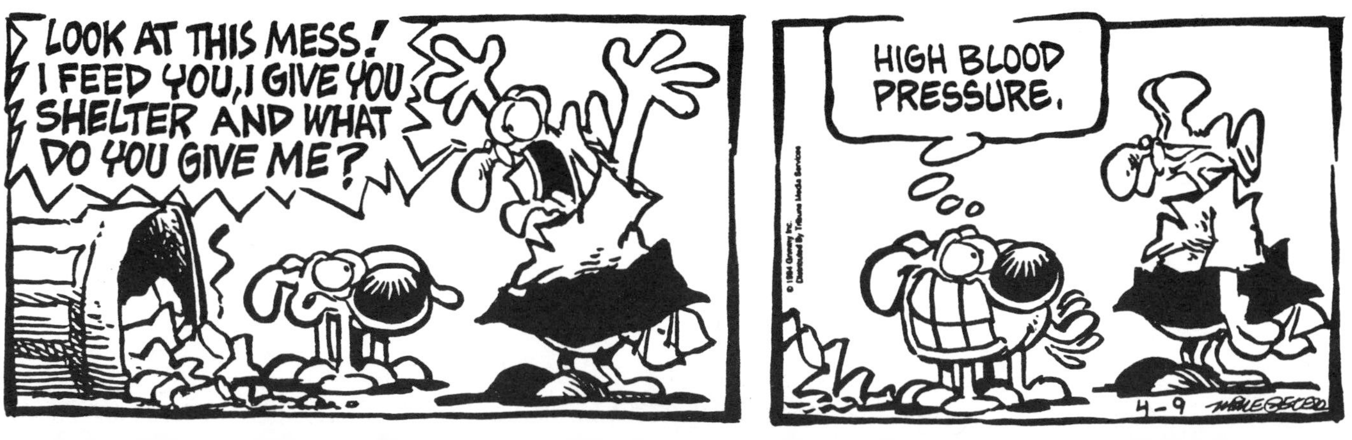
LOOK AT THIS MESS! I FEED YOU, I GIVE YOU SHELTER AND WHAT DO YOU GIVE ME?
HIGH BLOOD PRESSURE.
4-9

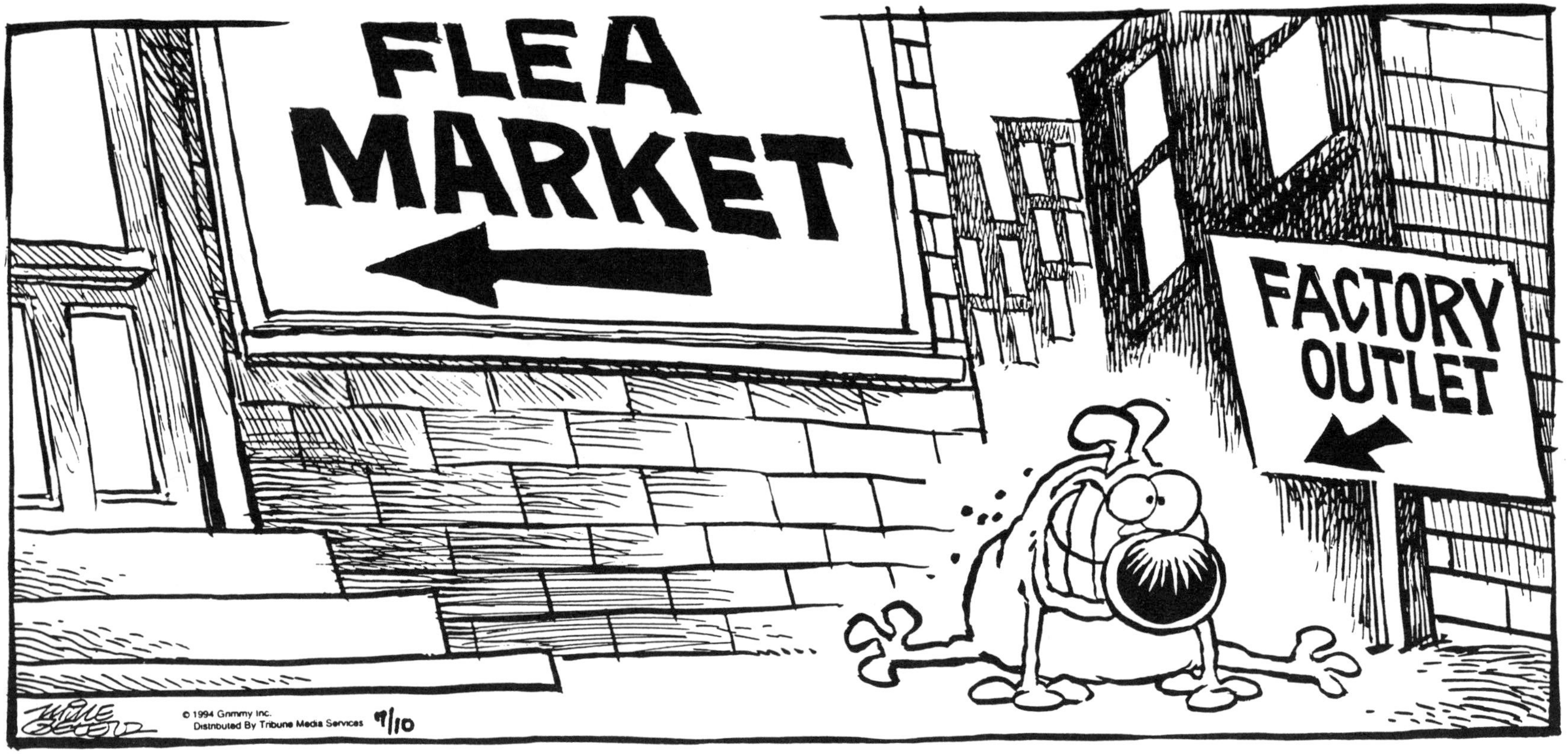
FLEA MARKET
FACTORY OUTLET
© 1994 Grimmy Inc.
Distributed By Tribune Media Services
9/10

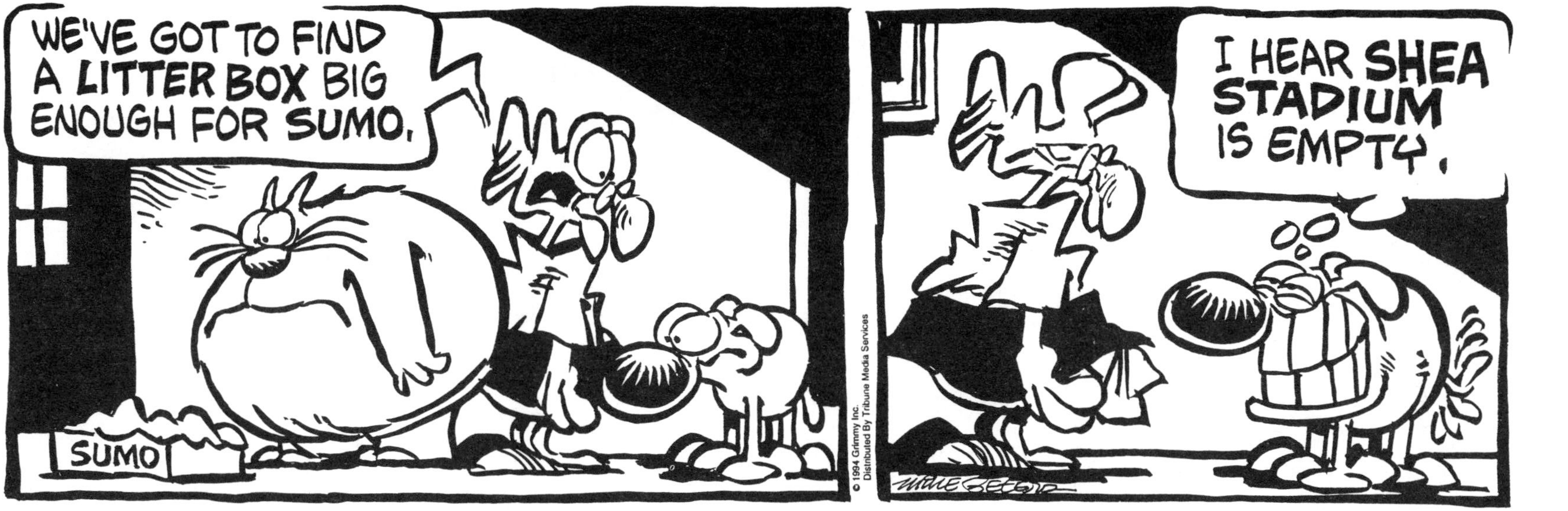
WE'VE GOT TO FIND A LITTER BOX BIG ENOUGH FOR SUMO.
SUMO
© 1994 Grimmy Inc. Distributed By Tribune Media Services
I HEAR SHEA STADIUM IS EMPTY.

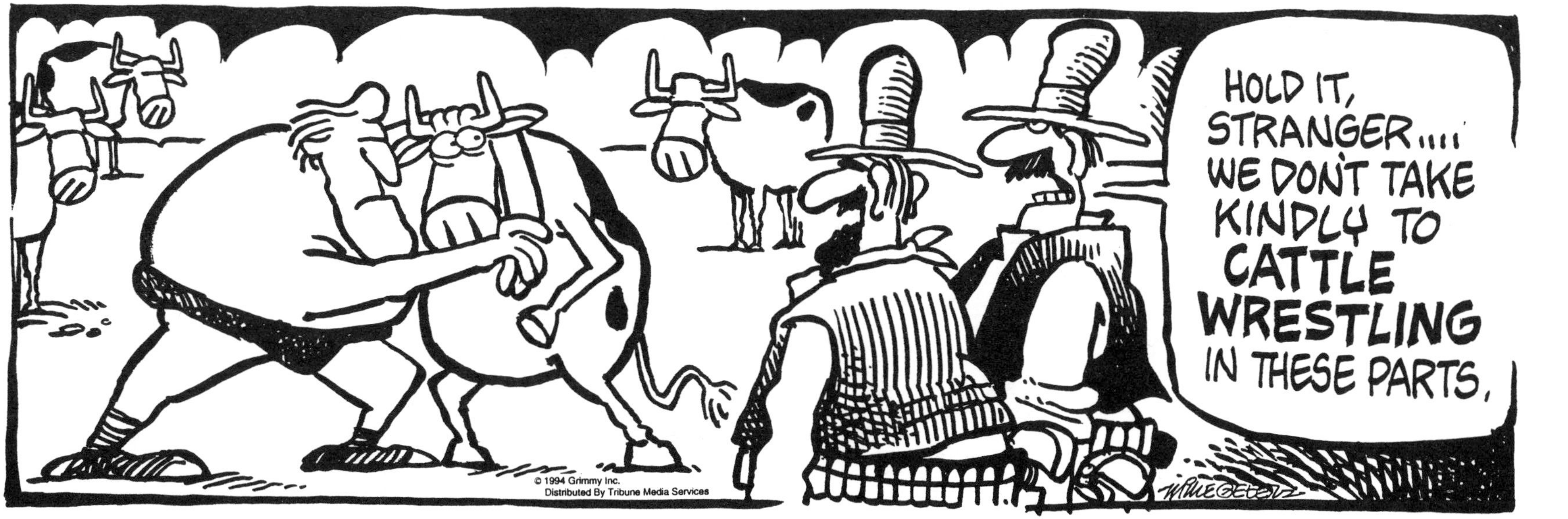
HOLD IT, STRANGER.... WE DON'T TAKE KINDLY TO CATTLE WRESTLING IN THESE PARTS.
© 1994 Grimmy Inc. Distributed By Tribune Media Services

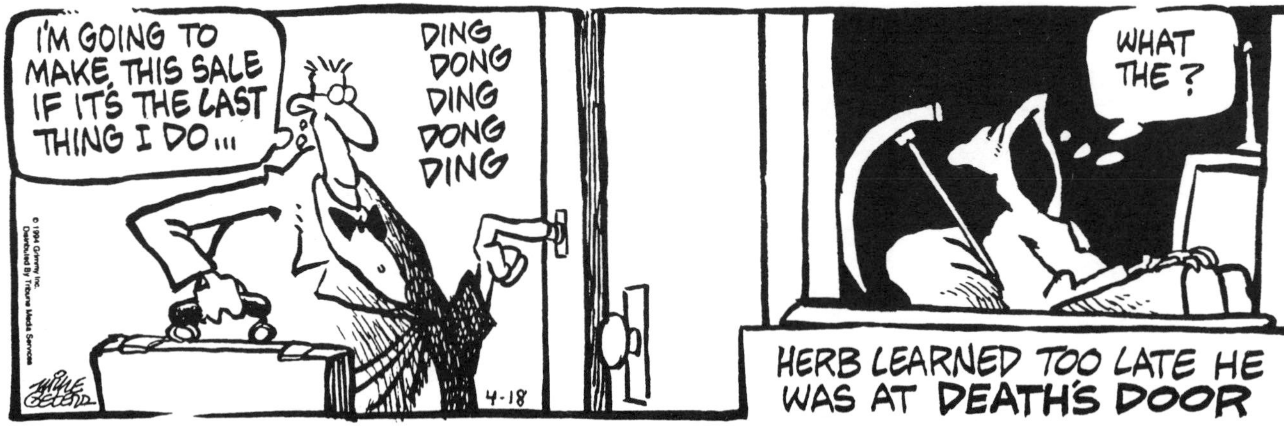
I'M GOING TO MAKE THIS SALE IF IT'S THE LAST THING I DO...
DING DONG DING DONG DING
© 1984 Grimmy Inc. Distributed By Tribune Media Services
4-18
WHAT THE ?
HERB LEARNED TOO LATE HE WAS AT DEATH'S DOOR

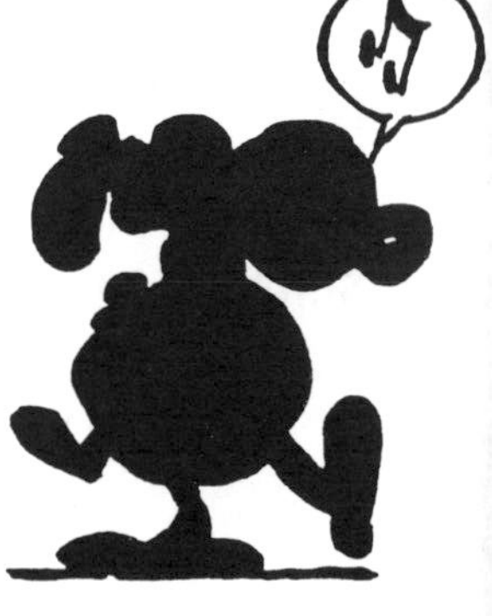

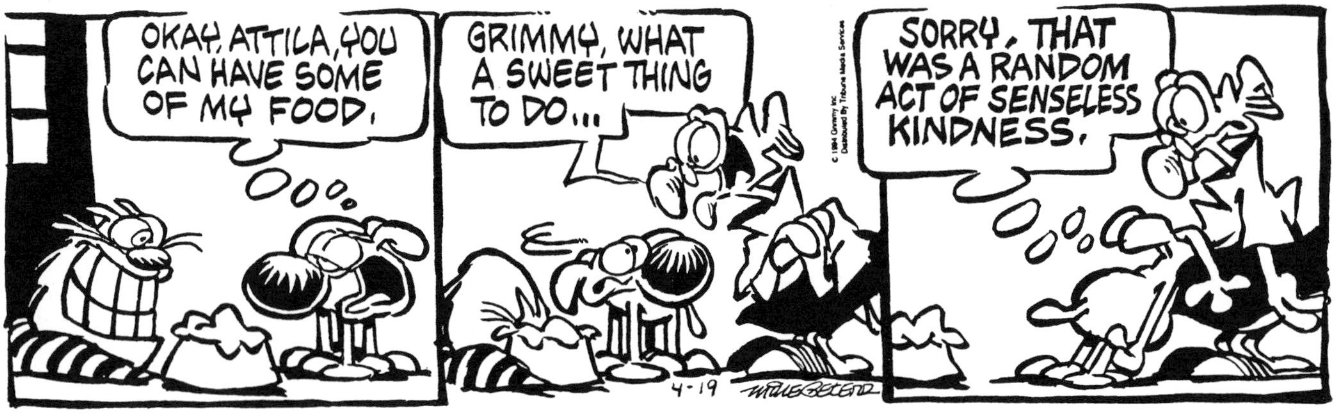
OKAY, ATTILA, YOU CAN HAVE SOME OF MY FOOD.
GRIMMY, WHAT A SWEET THING TO DO...
4-19
© 1984 Grimmy Inc. Distributed By Tribune Media Services
SORRY, THAT WAS A RANDOM ACT OF SENSELESS KINDNESS.

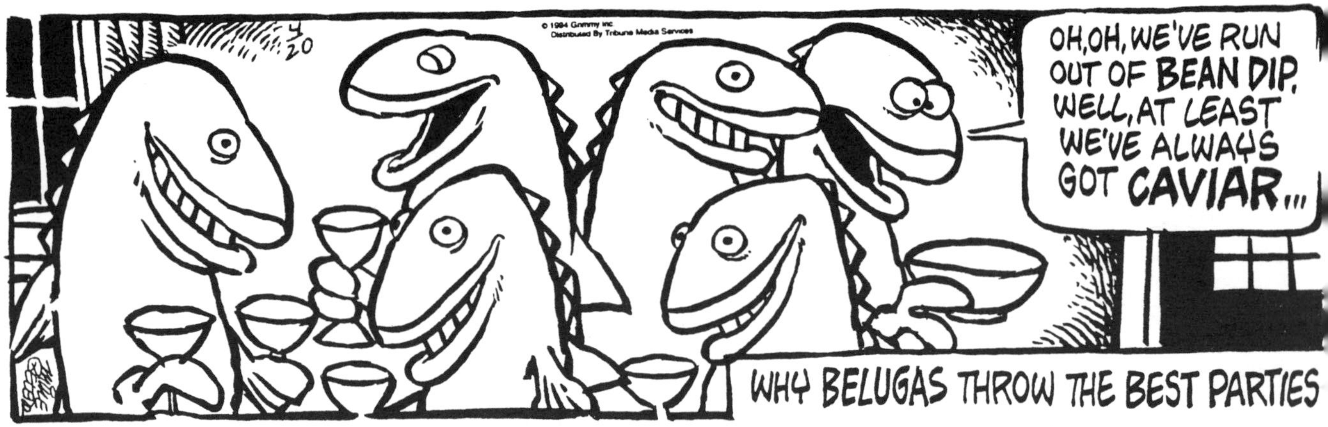
4 20
© 1984 Grimmy Inc. Distributed By Tribune Media Services
OH, OH, WE'VE RUN OUT OF BEAN DIP. WELL, AT LEAST WE'VE ALWAYS GOT CAVIAR...
WHY BELUGAS THROW THE BEST PARTIES

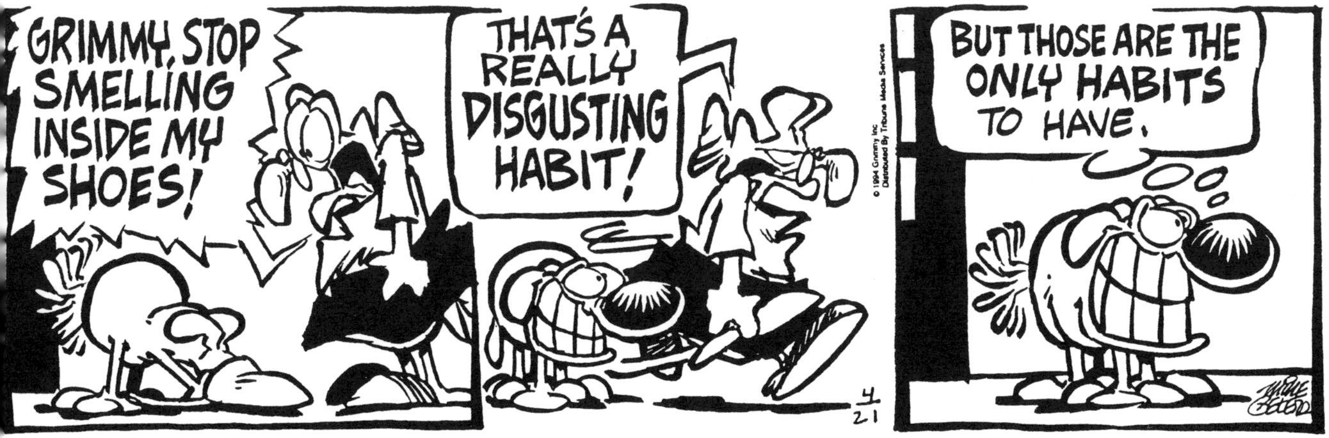
GRIMMY, STOP SMELLING INSIDE MY SHOES!
THAT'S A REALLY DISGUSTING HABIT!
© 1994 Grimmy Inc Distributed By Tribune Media Services
4/21
BUT THOSE ARE THE ONLY HABITS TO HAVE.

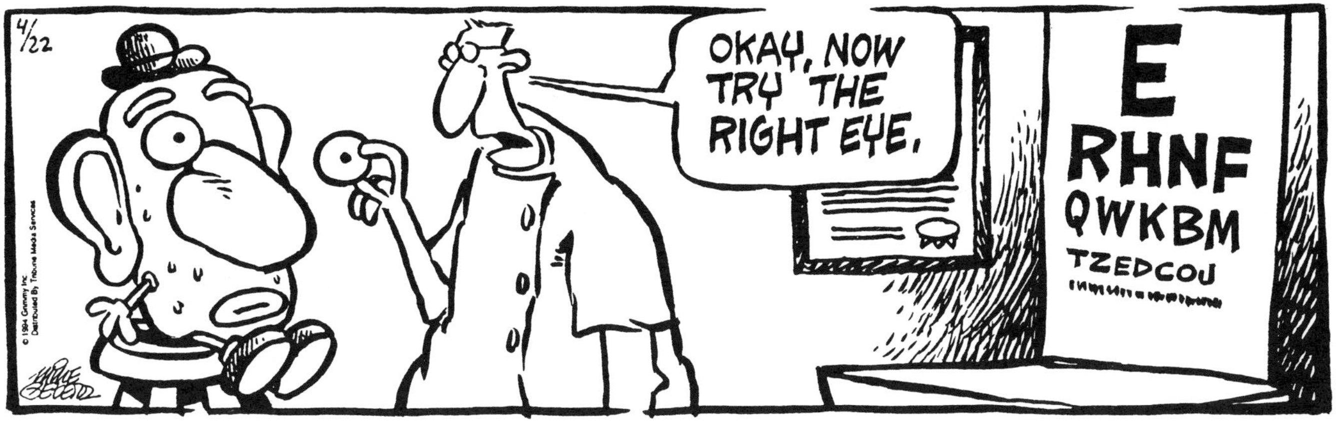
4/22
© 1994 Grimmy Inc Distributed By Tribune Media Services
OKAY, NOW TRY THE RIGHT EYE.
E
RHNF
QWKBM
TZEDCOU

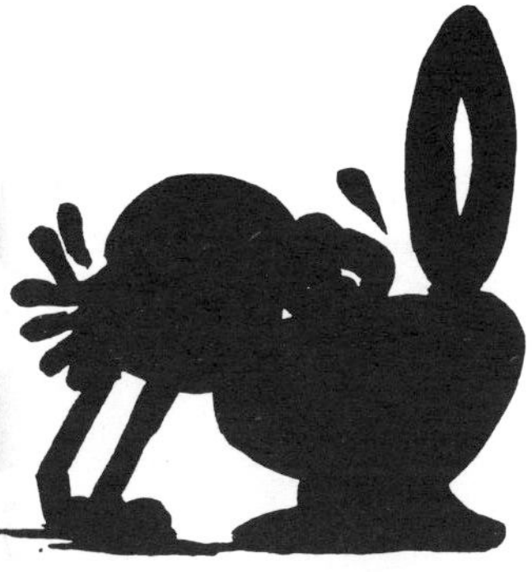

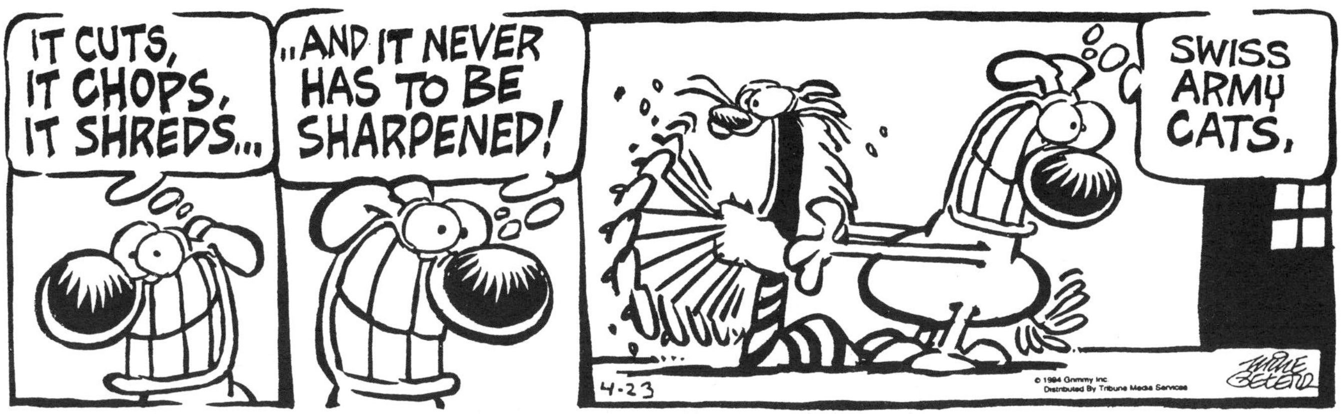
IT CUTS, IT CHOPS, IT SHREDS...
..AND IT NEVER HAS TO BE SHARPENED!
SWISS ARMY CATS.
4-23
© 1994 Grimmy Inc Distributed By Tribune Media Services

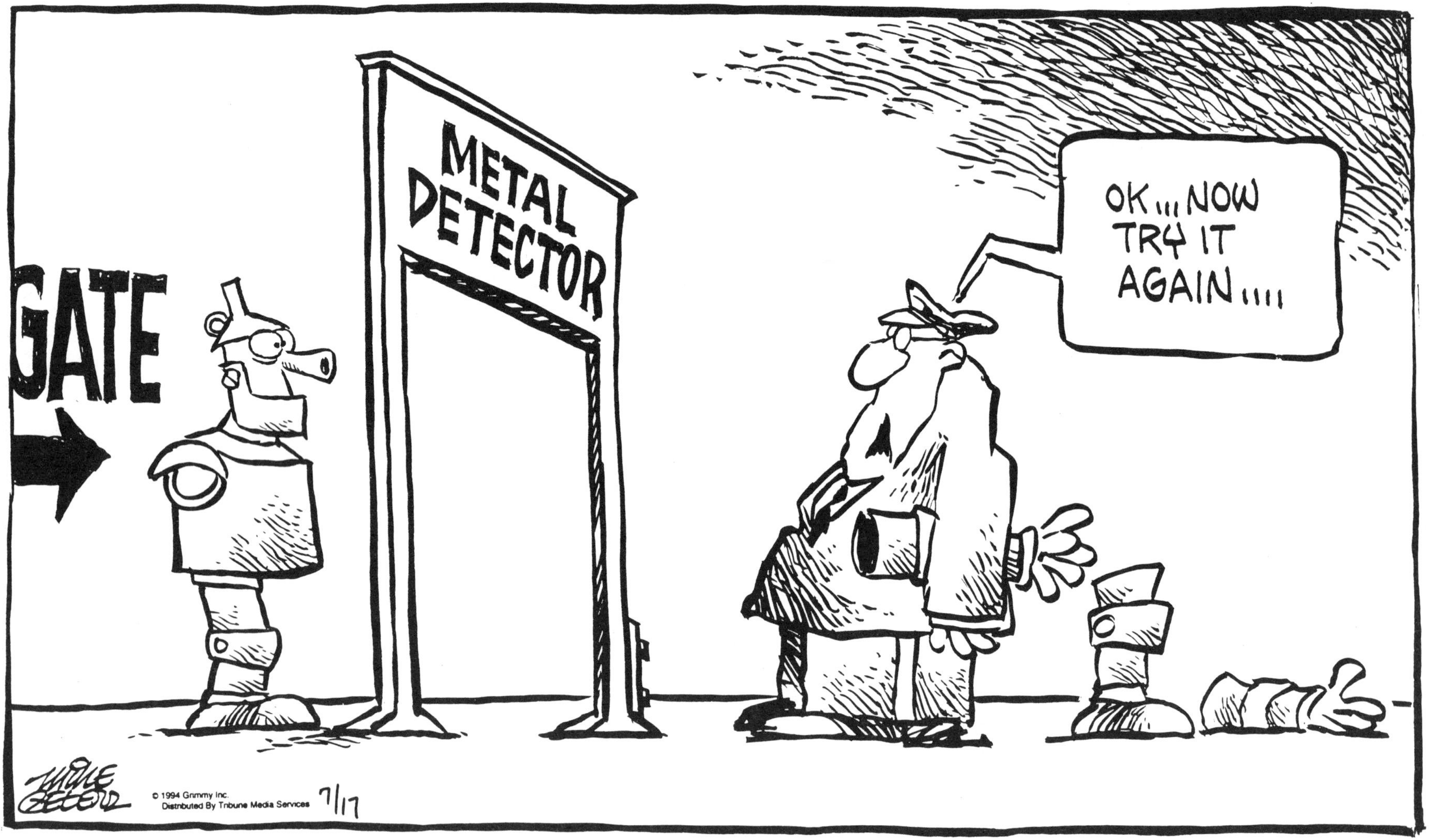
GATE
METAL DETECTOR
OK... NOW TRY IT AGAIN....
© 1994 Grimmy Inc.
Distributed By Tribune Media Services
7/17

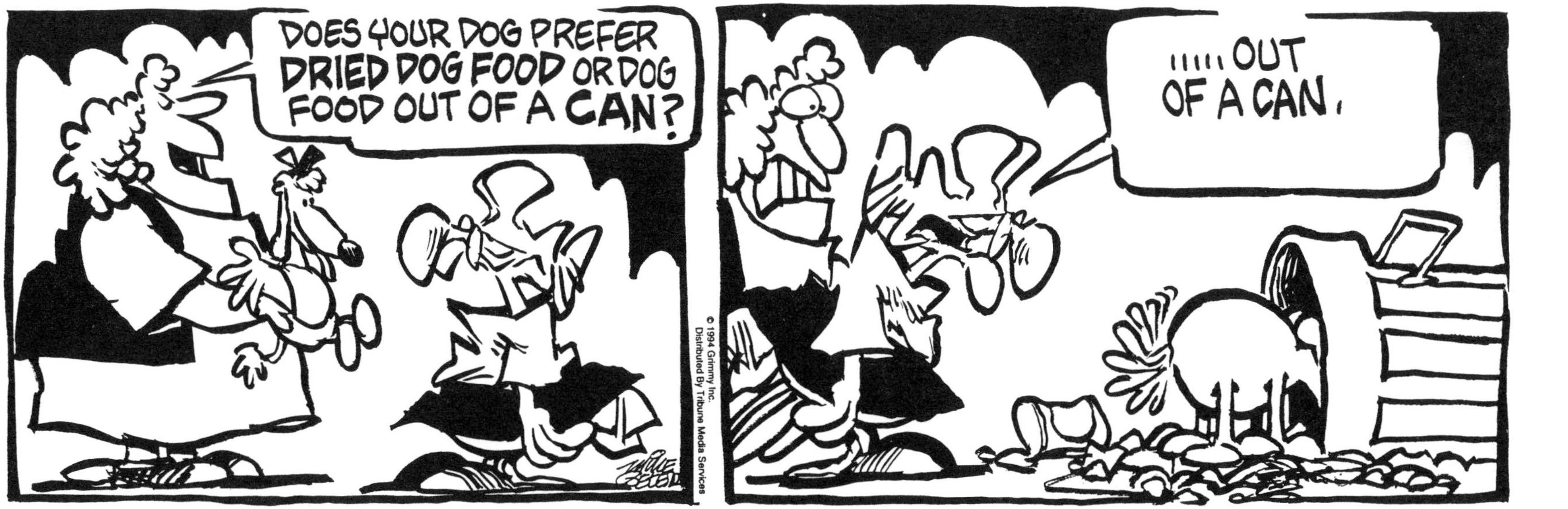
DOES YOUR DOG PREFER DRIED DOG FOOD OR DOG FOOD OUT OF A CAN?
© 1994 Grimmy Inc. Distributed By Tribune Media Services
,,,,, OUT OF A CAN,

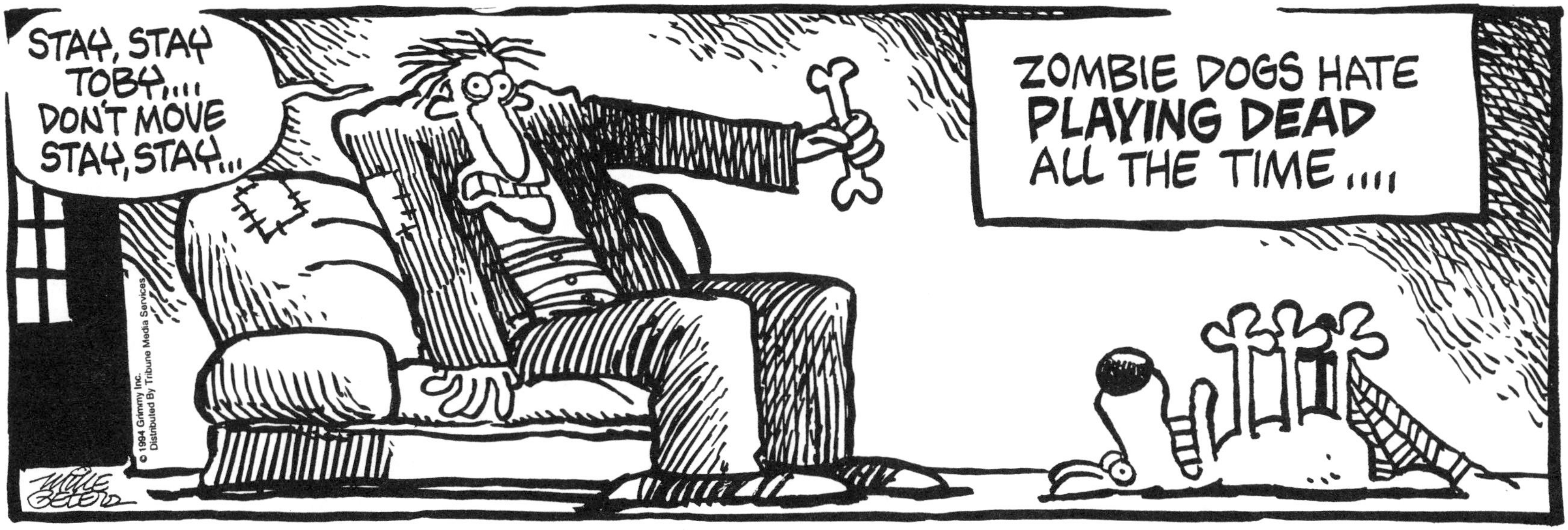
STAY, STAY TOBY,... DON'T MOVE STAY, STAY...
ZOMBIE DOGS HATE PLAYING DEAD ALL THE TIME ....
© 1994 Grimmy Inc. Distributed By Tribune Media Services

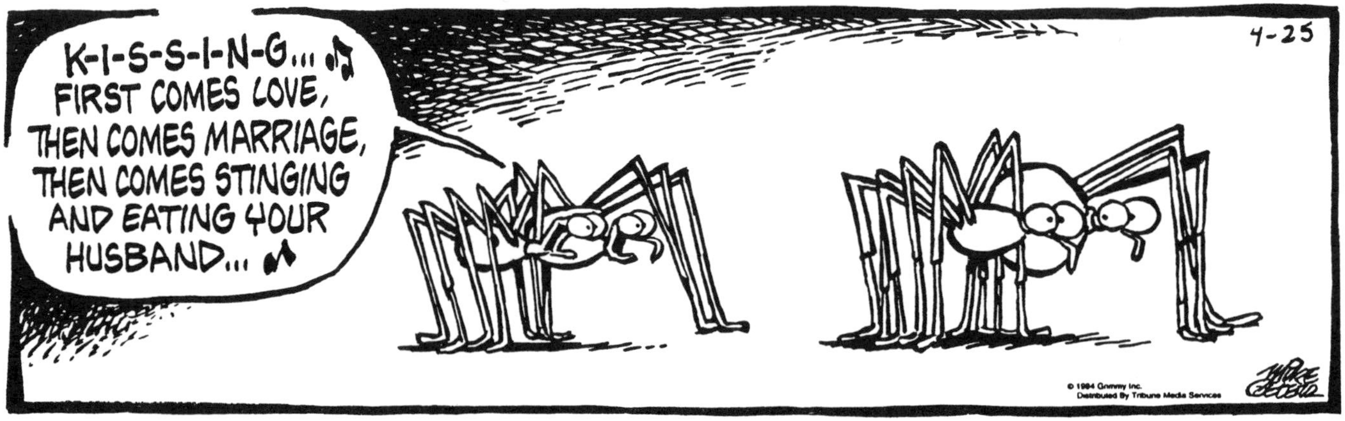
4-25
K-I-S-S-I-N-G... FIRST COMES LOVE, THEN COMES MARRIAGE, THEN COMES STINGING AND EATING YOUR HUSBAND...
© 1984 Grimmy Inc. Distributed By Tribune Media Services

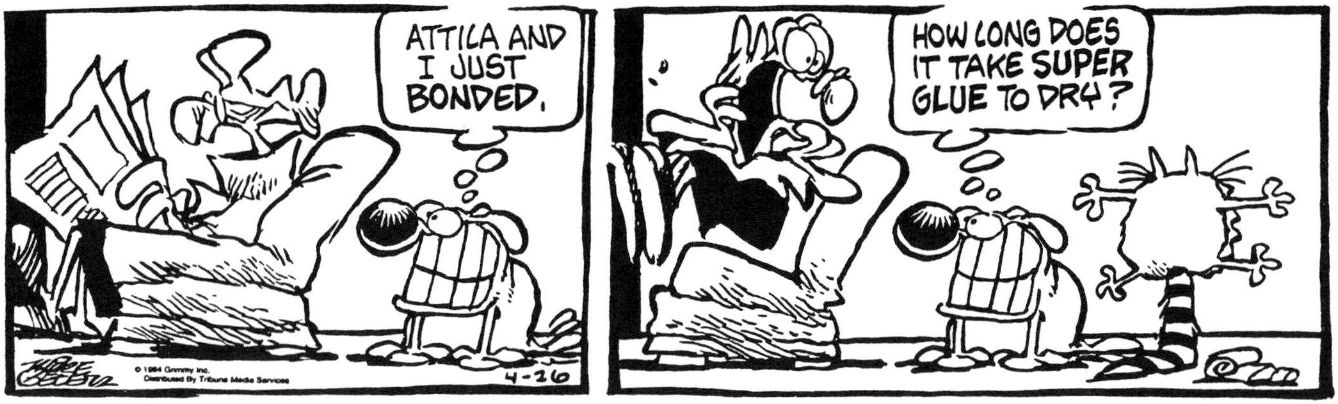
ATTILA AND I JUST BONDED.
© 1984 Grimmy Inc. Distributed By Tribune Media Services
4-26
HOW LONG DOES IT TAKE SUPER GLUE TO DRY?

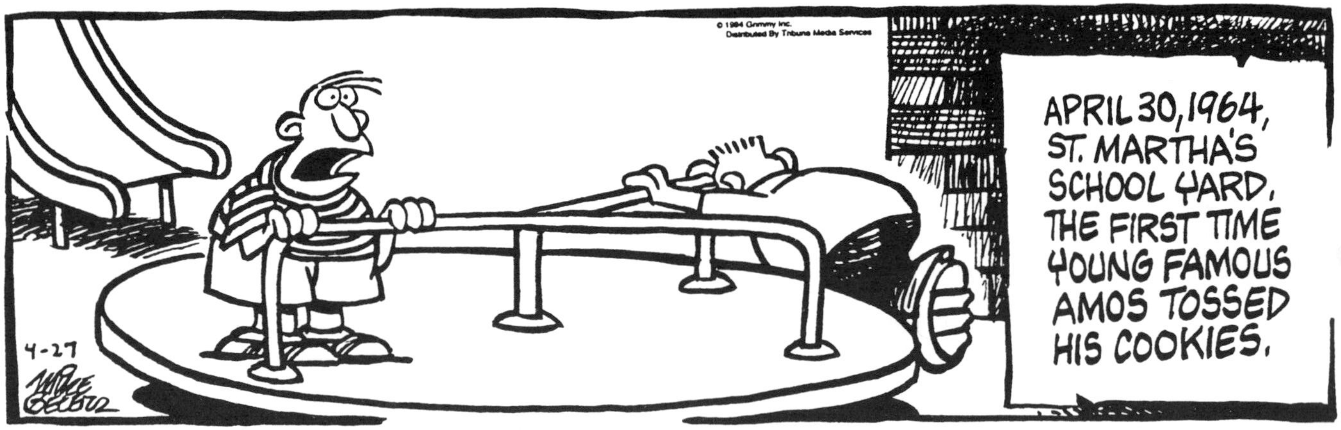
© 1984 Grimmy Inc. Distributed By Tribune Media Services
APRIL 30, 1964, ST. MARTHA'S SCHOOL YARD. THE FIRST TIME YOUNG FAMOUS AMOS TOSSED HIS COOKIES.
4-27

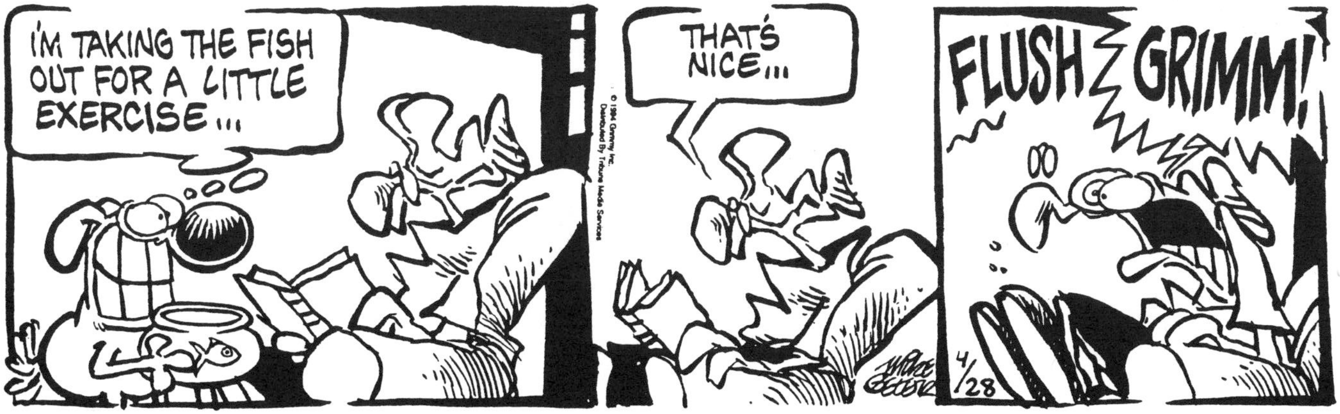
I'M TAKING THE FISH OUT FOR A LITTLE EXERCISE...
© 1994 Grimmy Inc. Distributed By Tribune Media Services
THAT'S NICE...
FLUSH
GRIMM!
4/28

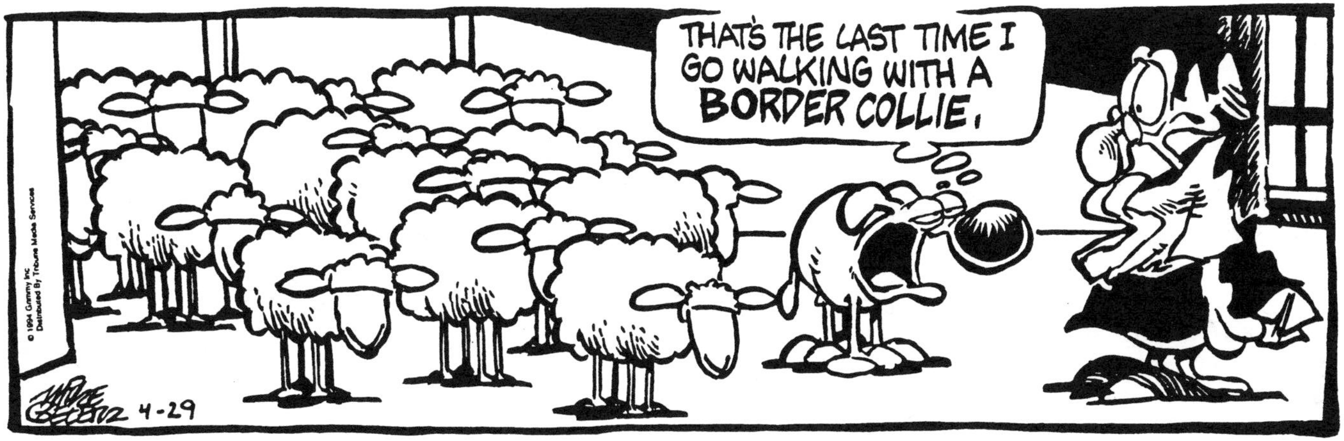
© 1994 Grimmy Inc. Distributed By Tribune Media Services
THAT'S THE LAST TIME I GO WALKING WITH A BORDER COLLIE.
4-29

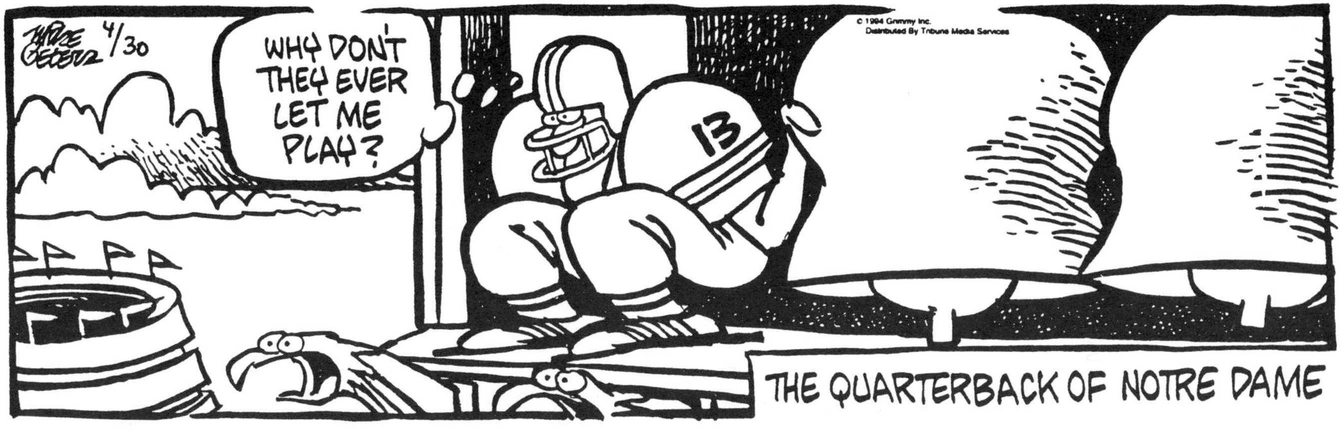
4/30
WHY DON'T THEY EVER LET ME PLAY?
© 1994 Grimmy Inc. Distributed By Tribune Media Services
13
THE QUARTERBACK OF NOTRE DAME

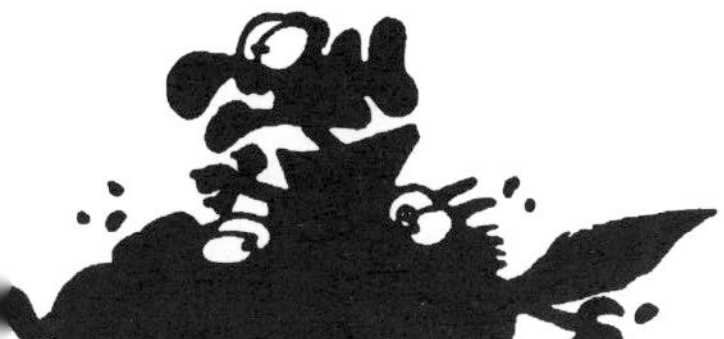

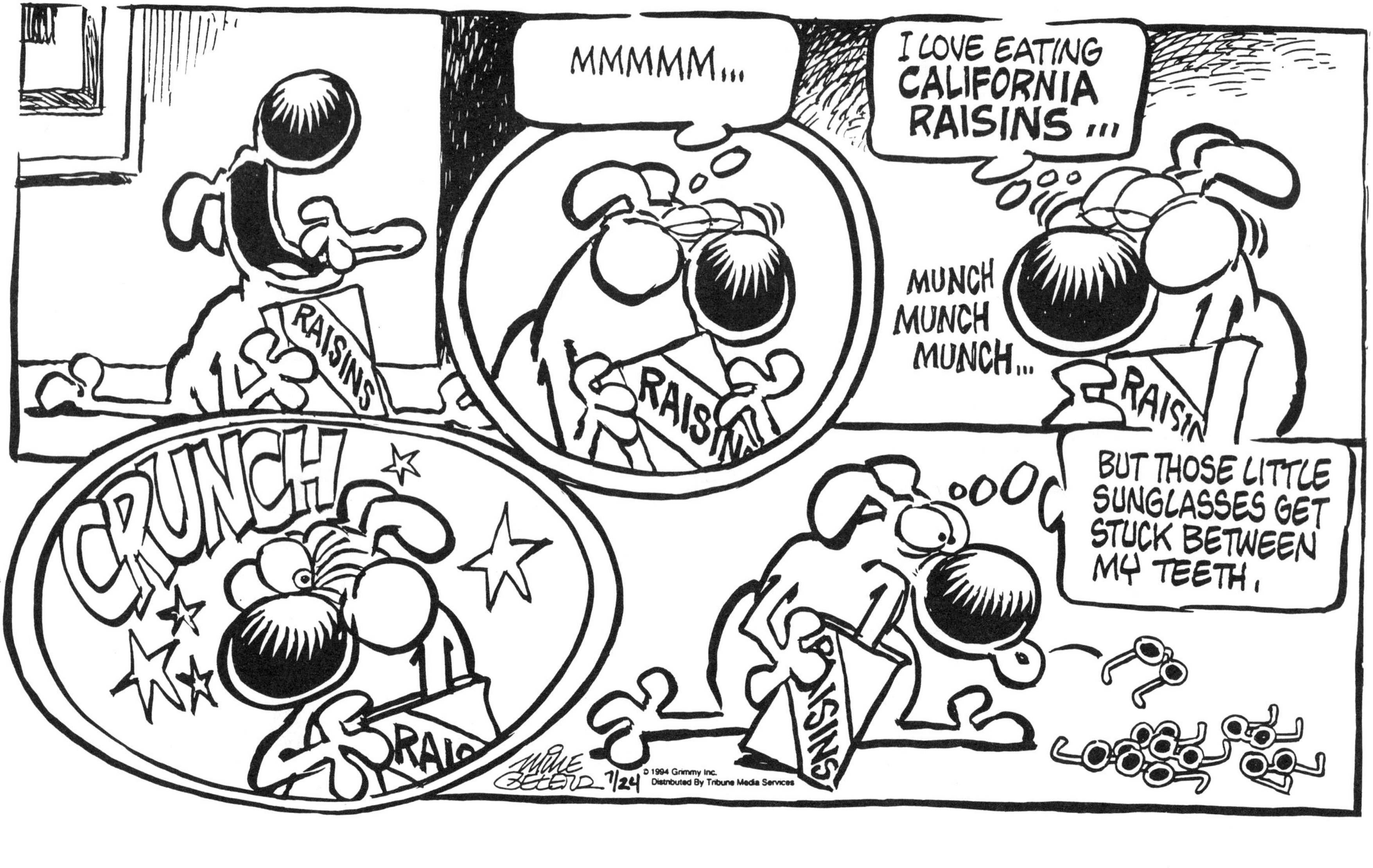
MMMMM...
I LOVE EATING CALIFORNIA RAISINS...
MUNCH MUNCH MUNCH...
CRUNCH
BUT THOSE LITTLE SUNGLASSES GET STUCK BETWEEN MY TEETH.
RAISINS
7/24
© 1994 Grimmy Inc.
Distributed By Tribune Media Services

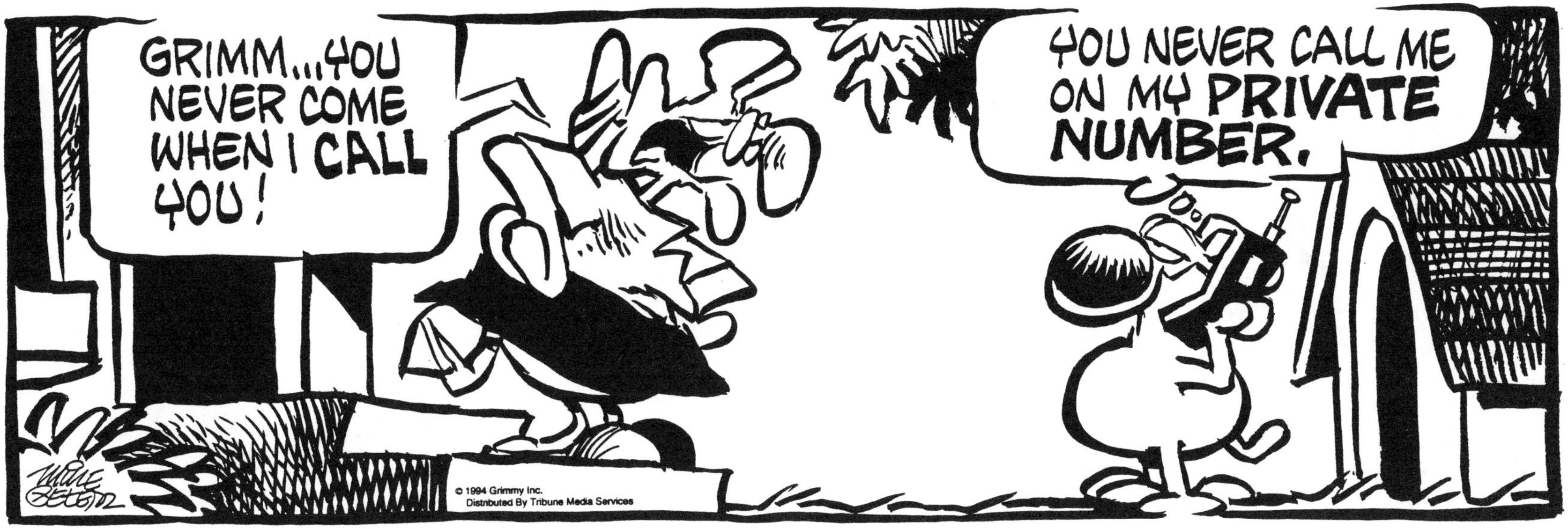
GRIMM...YOU NEVER COME WHEN I CALL YOU!
YOU NEVER CALL ME ON MY PRIVATE NUMBER.
© 1994 Grimmy Inc.
Distributed By Tribune Media Services

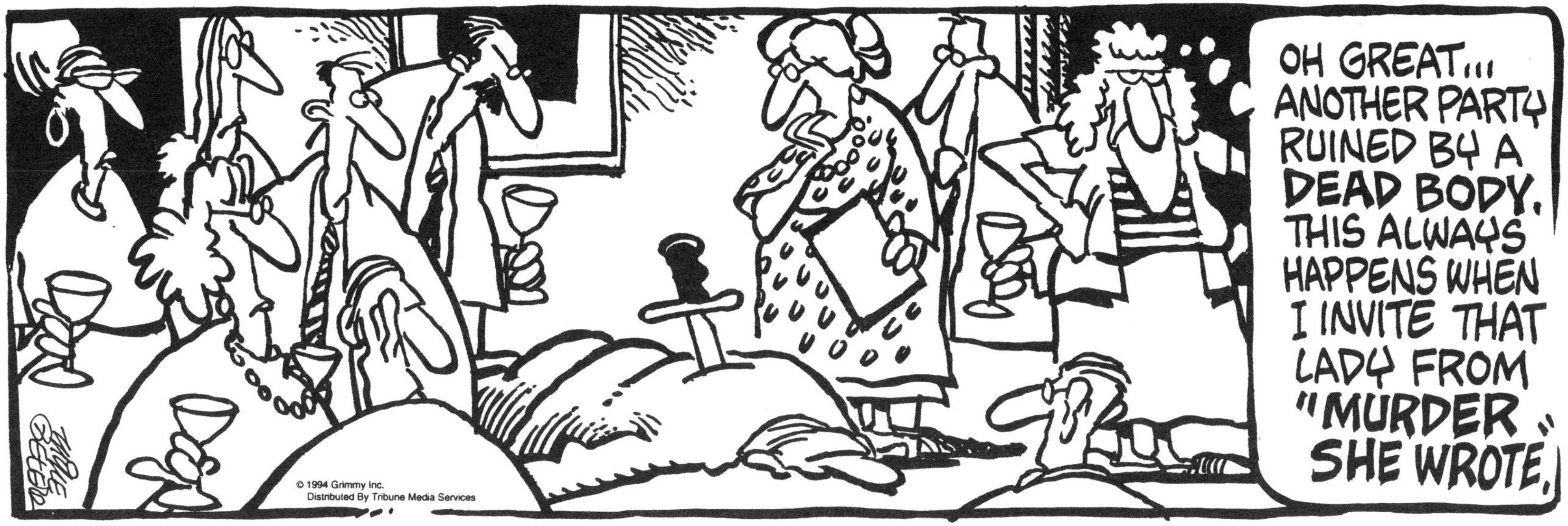
OH GREAT... ANOTHER PARTY RUINED BY A DEAD BODY. THIS ALWAYS HAPPENS WHEN I INVITE THAT LADY FROM "MURDER, SHE WROTE."
© 1994 Grimmy Inc.
Distributed By Tribune Media Services

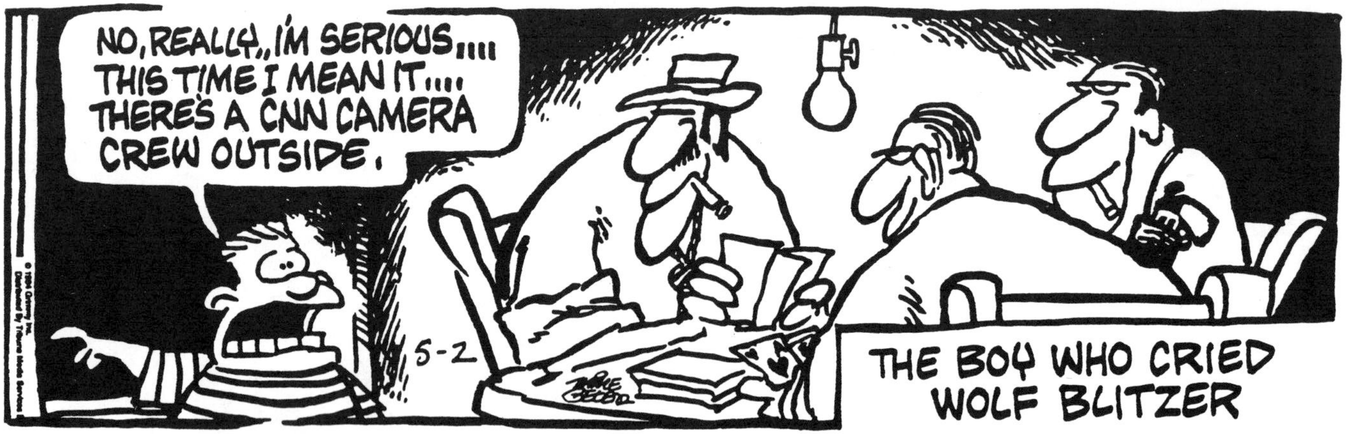
NO, REALLY,, I'M SERIOUS,,,, THIS TIME I MEAN IT.... THERE'S A CNN CAMERA CREW OUTSIDE.
5-2
THE BOY WHO CRIED WOLF BLITZER

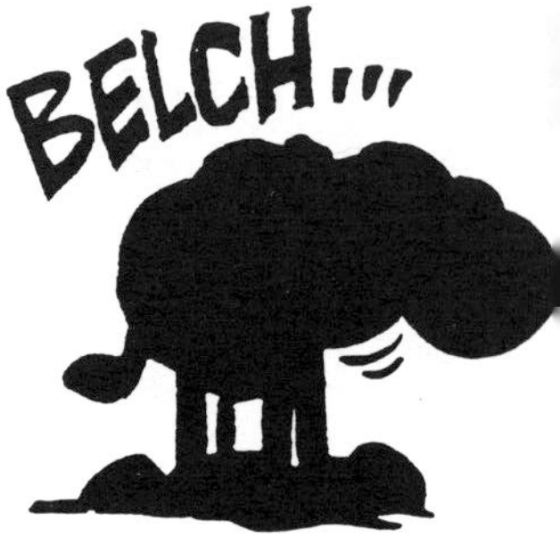
BELCH,,,

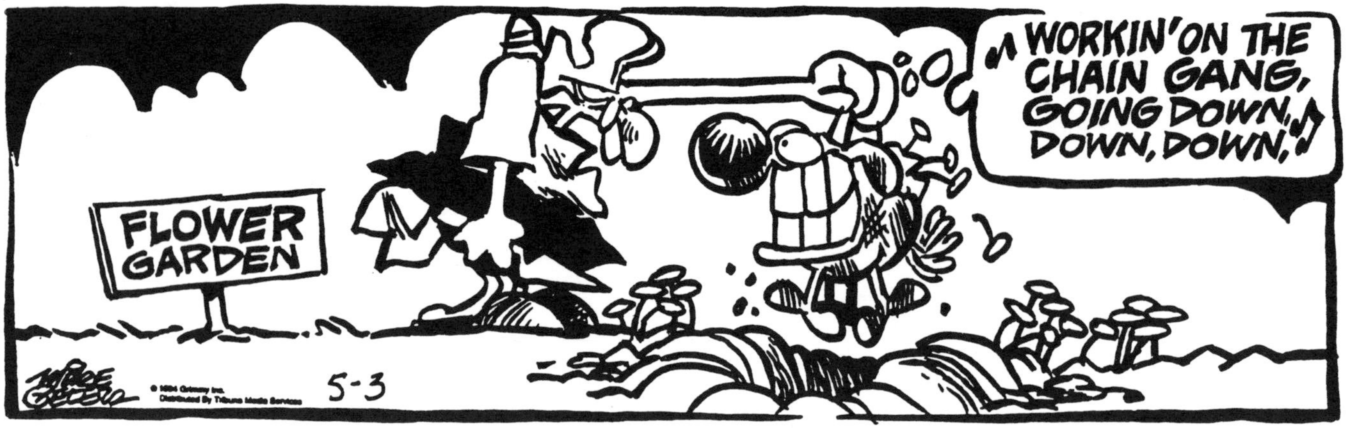
FLOWER GARDEN
WORKIN' ON THE CHAIN GANG, GOING DOWN, DOWN, DOWN,
5-3

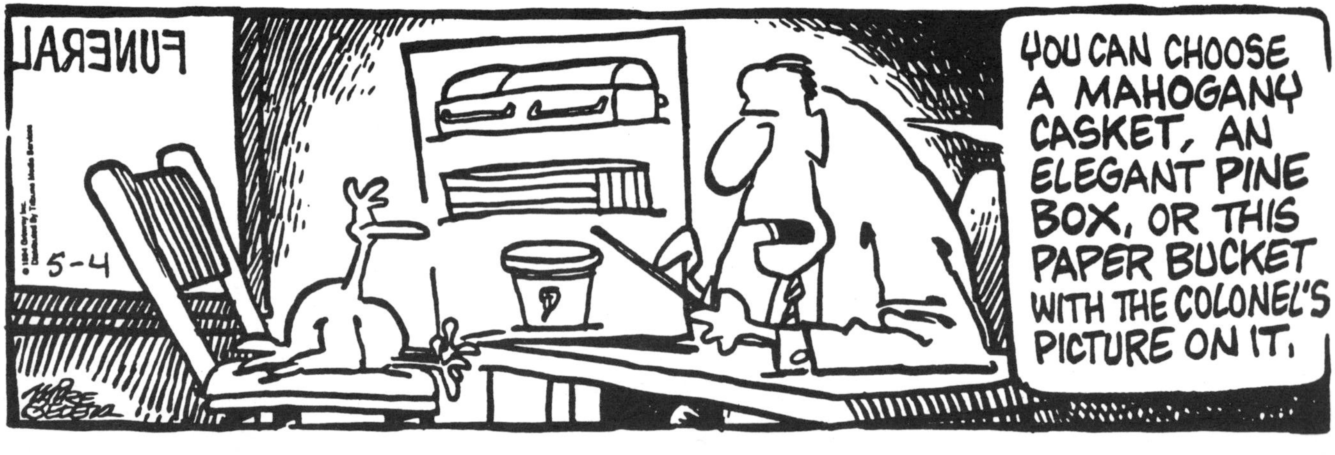
FUNERAL
5-4
YOU CAN CHOOSE A MAHOGANY CASKET, AN ELEGANT PINE BOX, OR THIS PAPER BUCKET WITH THE COLONEL'S PICTURE ON IT.

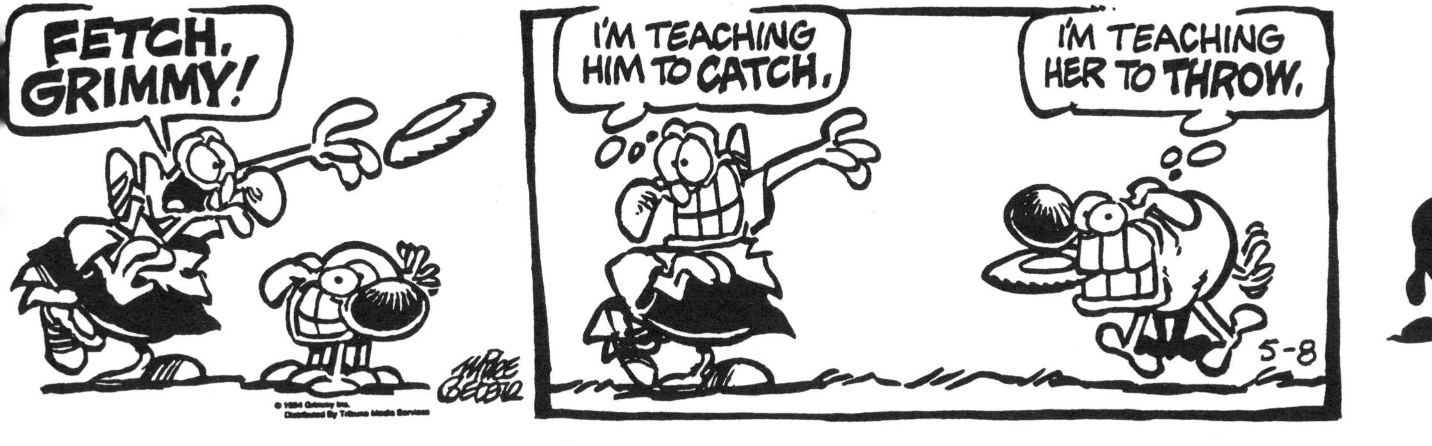
FETCH, GRIMMY!
I'M TEACHING HIM TO CATCH.
I'M TEACHING HER TO THROW.
WHEW!
5-8
MIKE PETERS
© 1994 Grimmy Inc. Distributed By Tribune Media Services

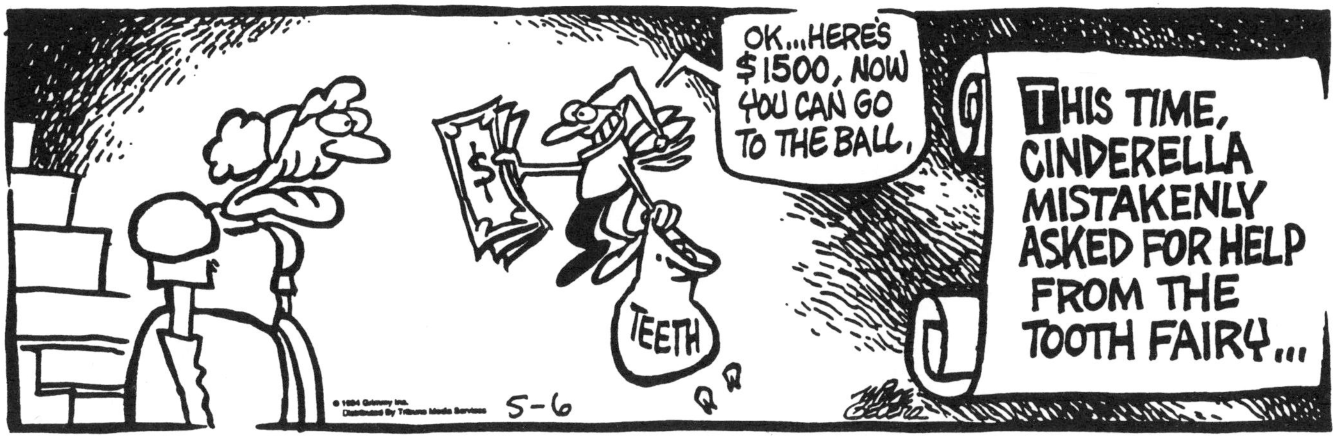
THIS TIME, CINDERELLA MISTAKENLY ASKED FOR HELP FROM THE TOOTH FAIRY...
OK...HERE'S $1500, NOW YOU CAN GO TO THE BALL.
TEETH
5-6
MIKE PETERS
© 1994 Grimmy Inc. Distributed By Tribune Media Services

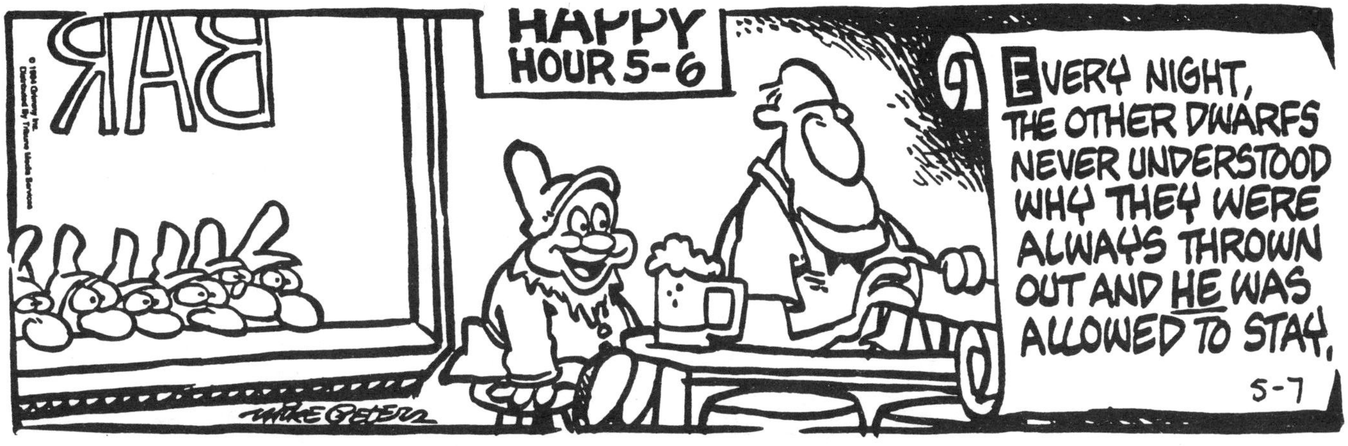
EVERY NIGHT, THE OTHER DWARFS NEVER UNDERSTOOD WHY THEY WERE ALWAYS THROWN OUT AND HE WAS ALLOWED TO STAY.
HAPPY HOUR 5-6
5-7
MIKE PETERS
© 1994 Grimmy Inc. Distributed By Tribune Media Services

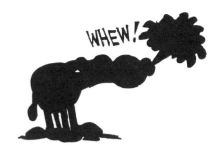

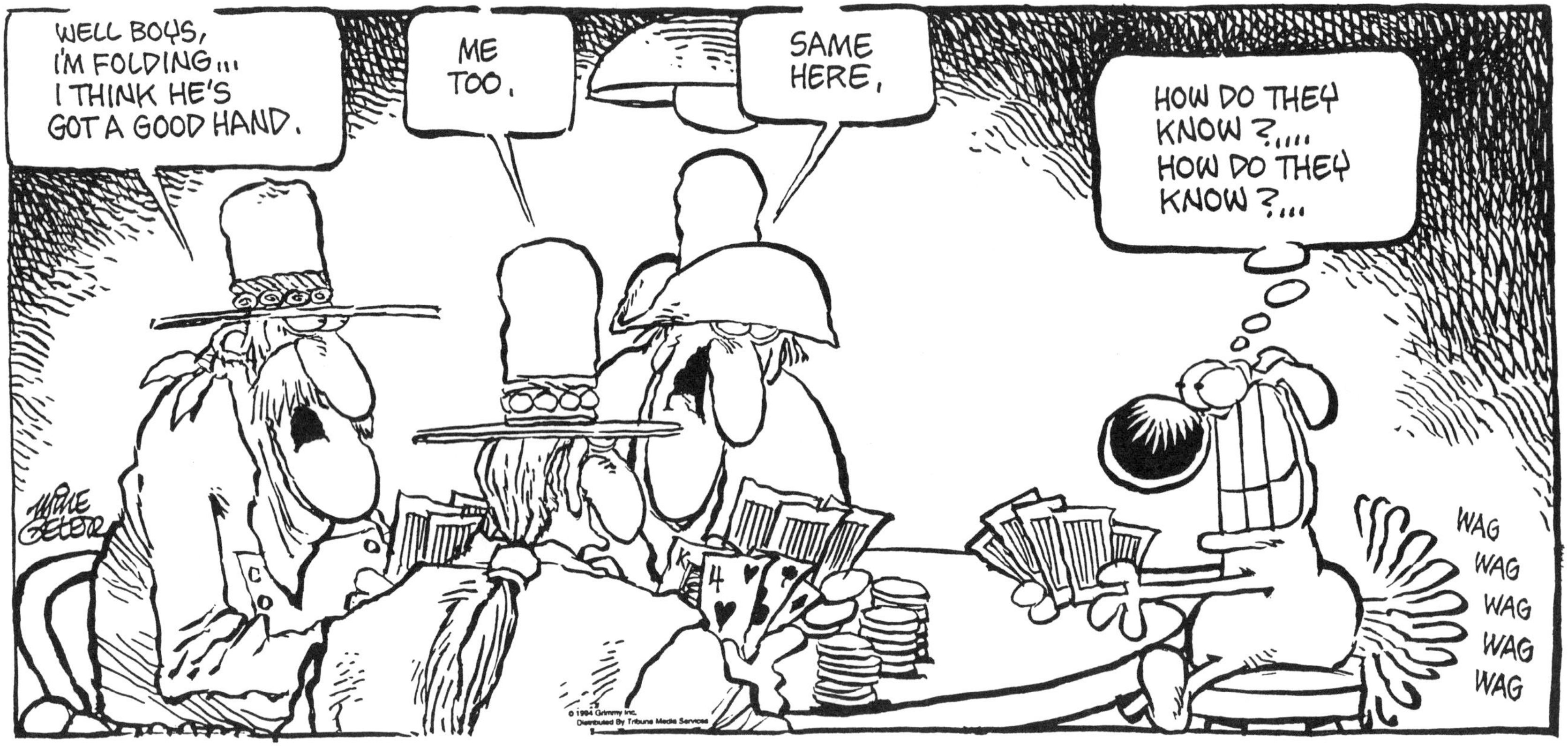

WELL BOYS, I'M FOLDING... I THINK HE'S GOT A GOOD HAND.
ME TOO.
SAME HERE.
HOW DO THEY KNOW?.... HOW DO THEY KNOW?...
WAG WAG WAG WAG WAG
© 1994 Grimmy Inc. Distributed By Tribune Media Services

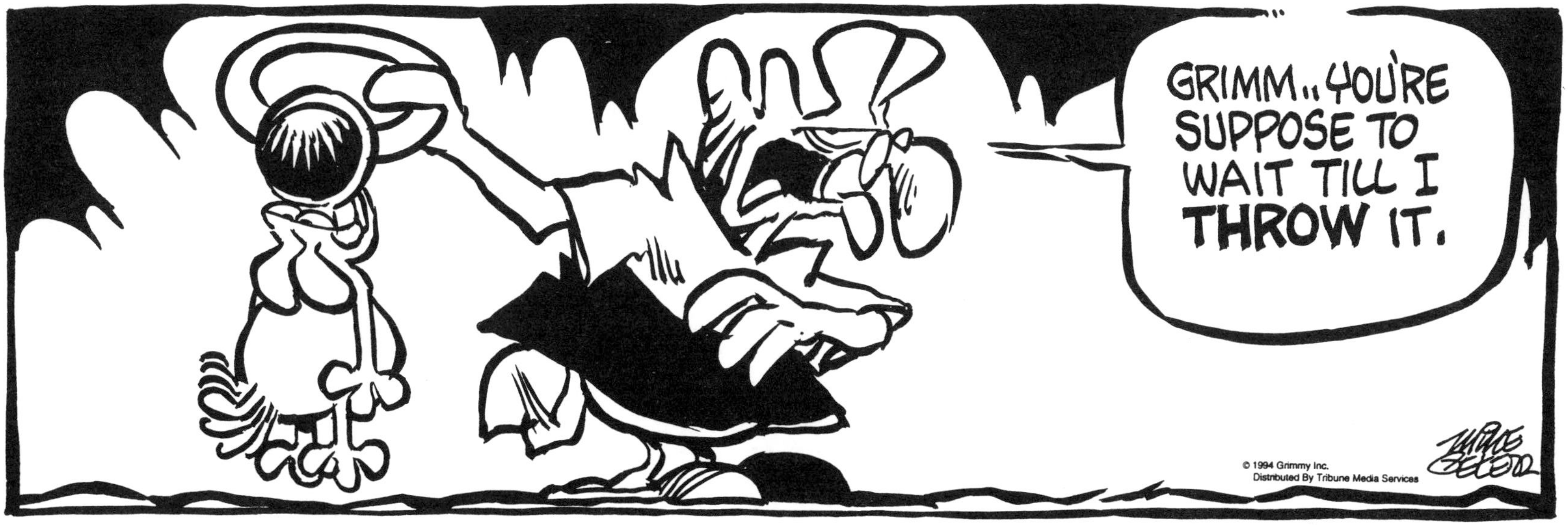
GRIMM.. YOU'RE SUPPOSE TO WAIT TILL I **THROW** IT.
© 1994 Grimmy Inc.
Distributed By Tribune Media Services

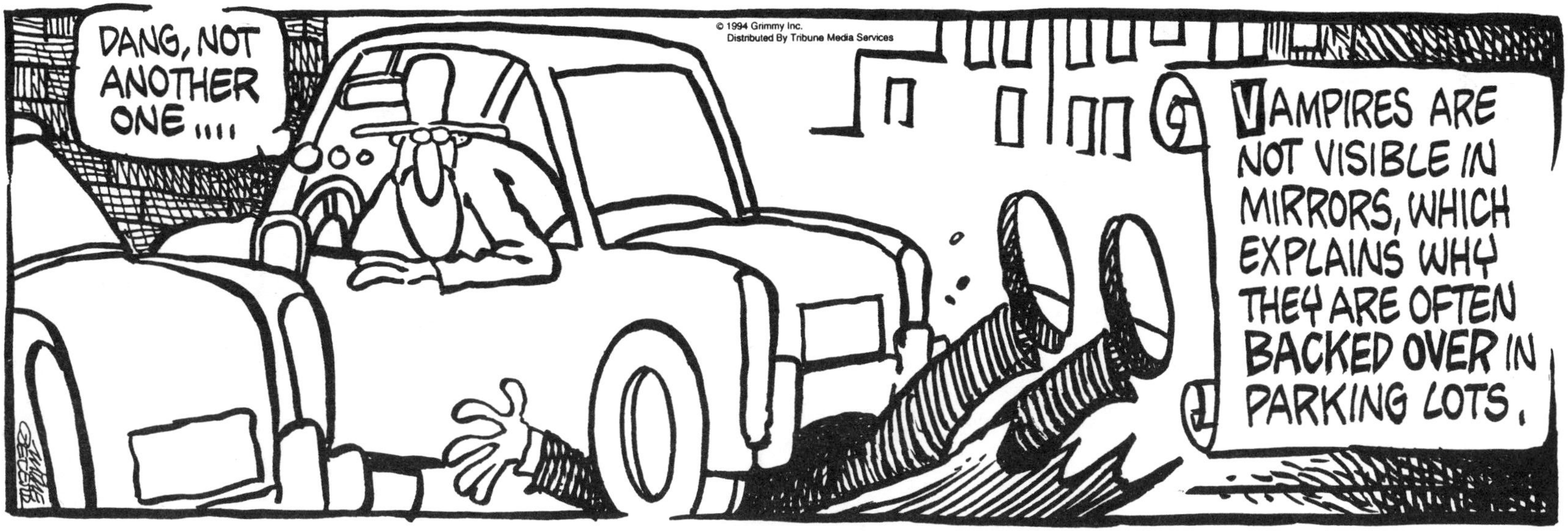
DANG, NOT ANOTHER ONE....
© 1994 Grimmy Inc.
Distributed By Tribune Media Services
VAMPIRES ARE NOT VISIBLE IN MIRRORS, WHICH EXPLAINS WHY THEY ARE OFTEN **BACKED OVER** IN PARKING LOTS.

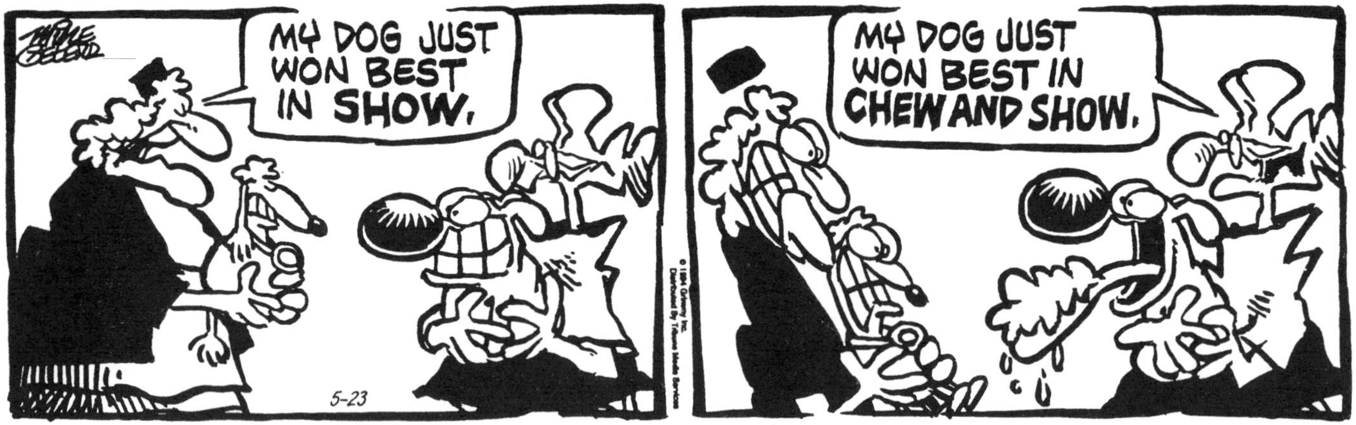
MY DOG JUST WON BEST IN SHOW.
MY DOG JUST WON BEST IN CHEW AND SHOW.
5-23
© 1994 Grimmy Inc. Distributed By Tribune Media Services

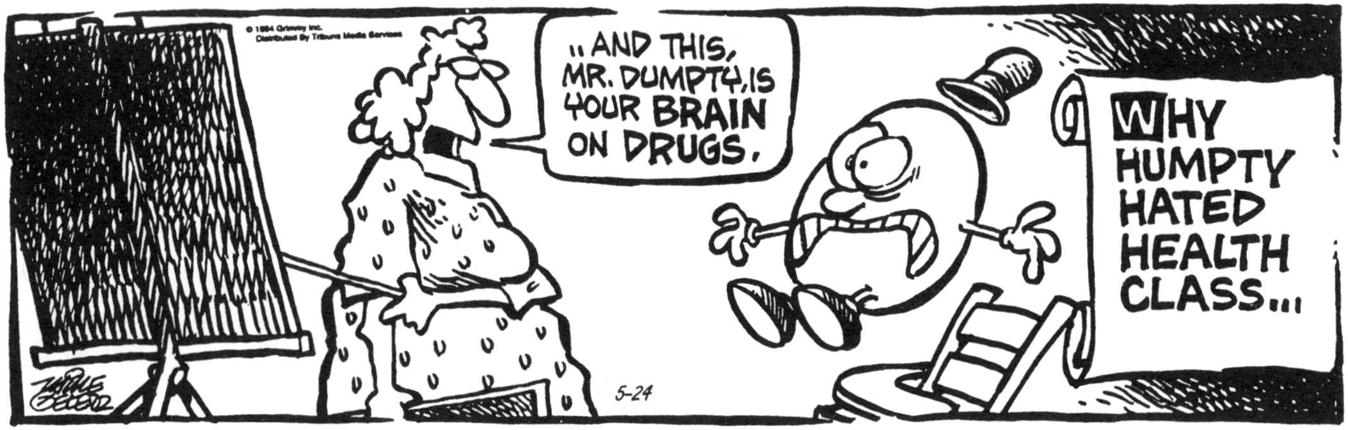
© 1994 Grimmy Inc. Distributed By Tribune Media Services
.. AND THIS, MR. DUMPTY, IS YOUR BRAIN ON DRUGS.
WHY HUMPTY HATED HEALTH CLASS...
5-24

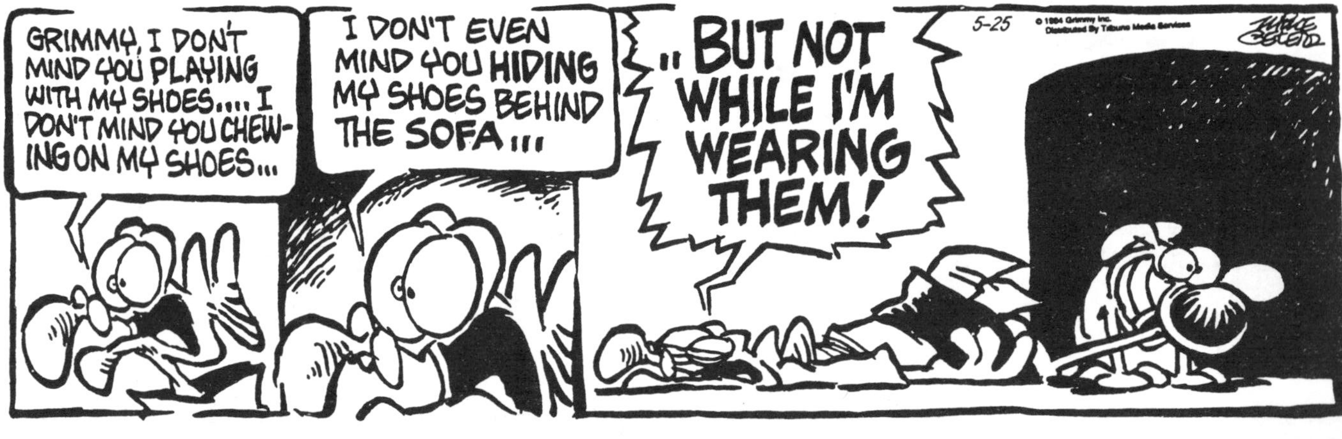
GRIMMY, I DON'T MIND YOU PLAYING WITH MY SHOES.... I DON'T MIND YOU CHEWING ON MY SHOES...
I DON'T EVEN MIND YOU HIDING MY SHOES BEHIND THE SOFA...
.. BUT NOT WHILE I'M WEARING THEM!
5-25
© 1994 Grimmy Inc. Distributed By Tribune Media Services

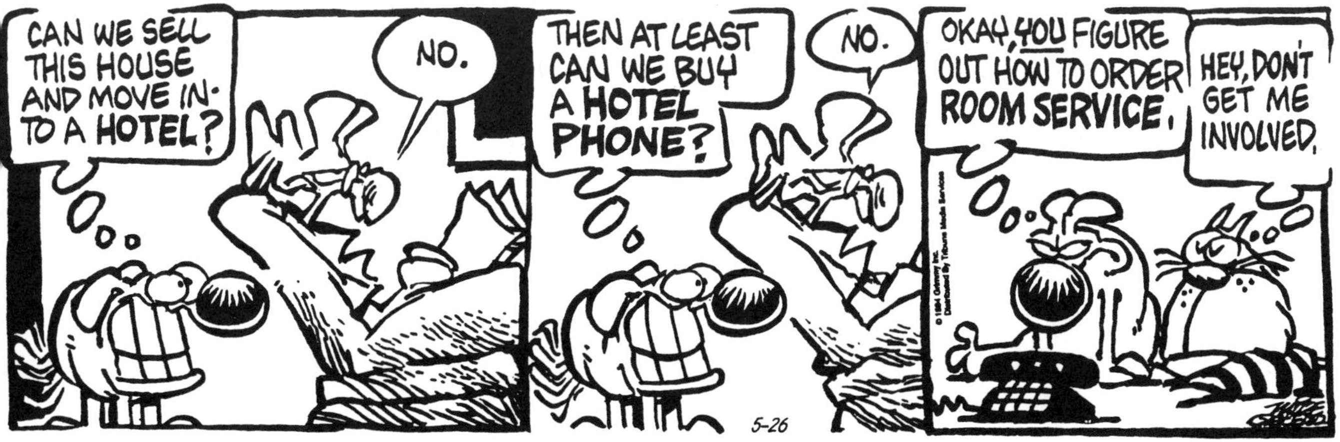
CAN WE SELL THIS HOUSE AND MOVE INTO A HOTEL?
NO.
THEN AT LEAST CAN WE BUY A HOTEL PHONE?
NO.
5-26
OKAY, YOU FIGURE OUT HOW TO ORDER ROOM SERVICE.
HEY, DON'T GET ME INVOLVED.
© 1994 Grimmy Inc. Distributed By Tribune Media Services

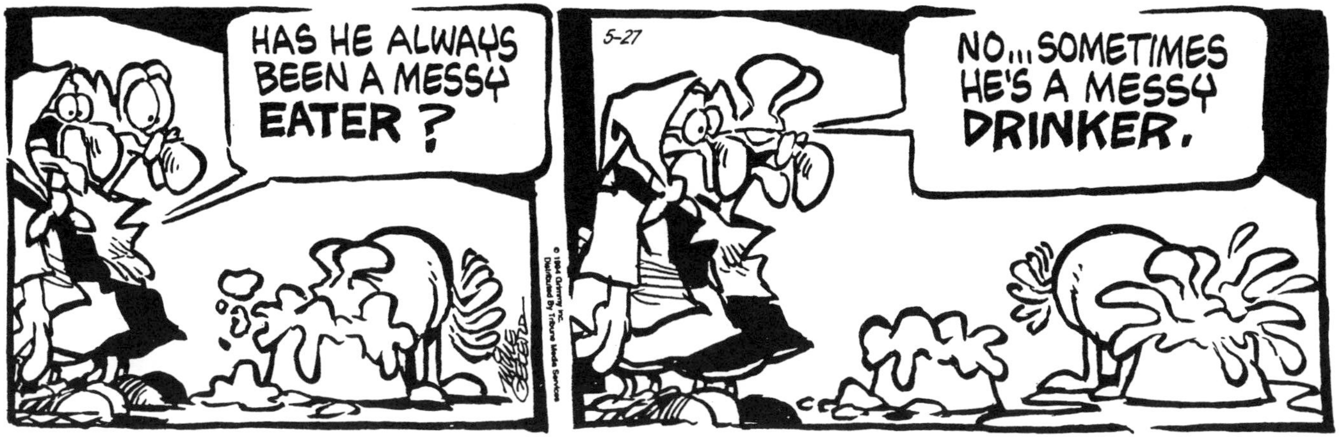
HAS HE ALWAYS BEEN A MESSY EATER?
© 1994 Grimmy Inc. Distributed By Tribune Media Services
5-27
NO... SOMETIMES HE'S A MESSY DRINKER.

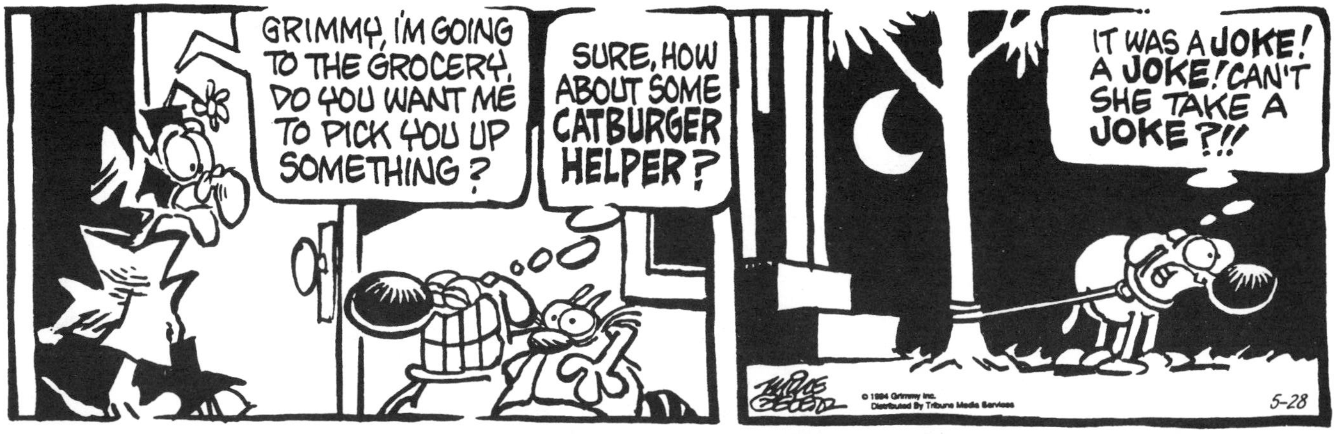
GRIMMY, I'M GOING TO THE GROCERY. DO YOU WANT ME TO PICK YOU UP SOMETHING?
SURE, HOW ABOUT SOME CATBURGER HELPER?
IT WAS A JOKE! A JOKE! CAN'T SHE TAKE A JOKE?!!
© 1994 Grimmy Inc. Distributed By Tribune Media Services
5-28

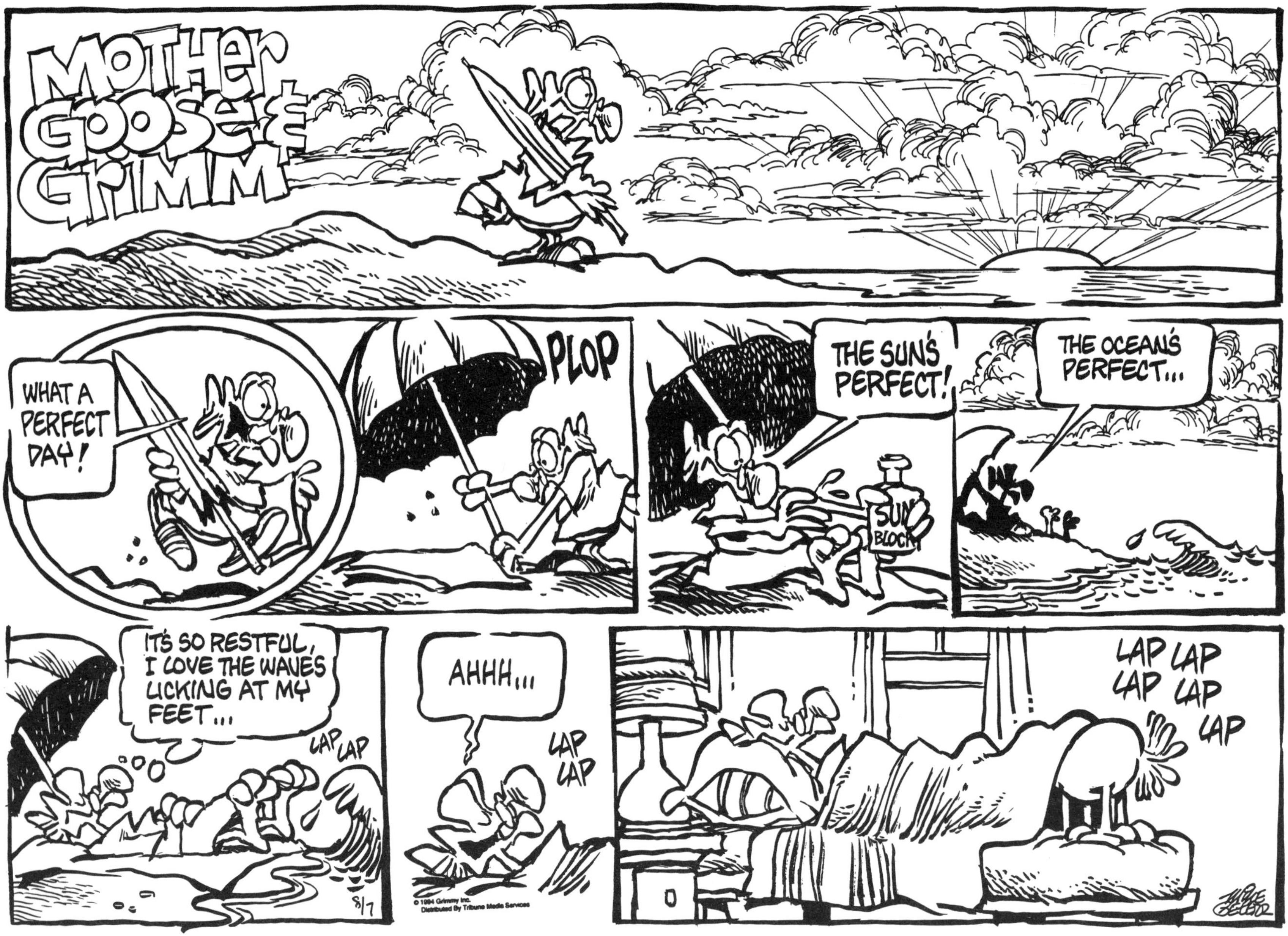
MOTHER GOOSE & GRIMM
WHAT A PERFECT DAY!
PLOP
THE SUN'S PERFECT!
SUN BLOCK
THE OCEAN'S PERFECT...
IT'S SO RESTFUL, I LOVE THE WAVES LICKING AT MY FEET...
LAP LAP
8/7
AHHH...
LAP LAP
LAP LAP
LAP LAP
LAP
© 1994 Grimmy Inc.
Distributed By Tribune Media Services

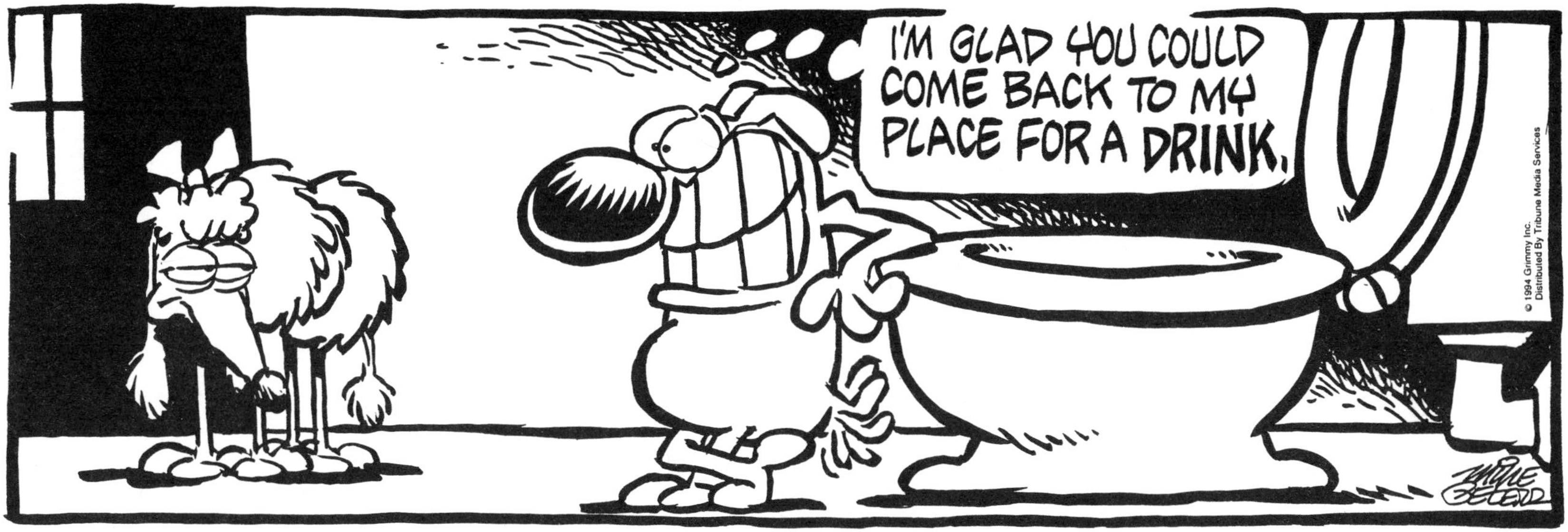
I'M GLAD YOU COULD COME BACK TO MY PLACE FOR A DRINK.
© 1994 Grimmy Inc.
Distributed By Tribune Media Services

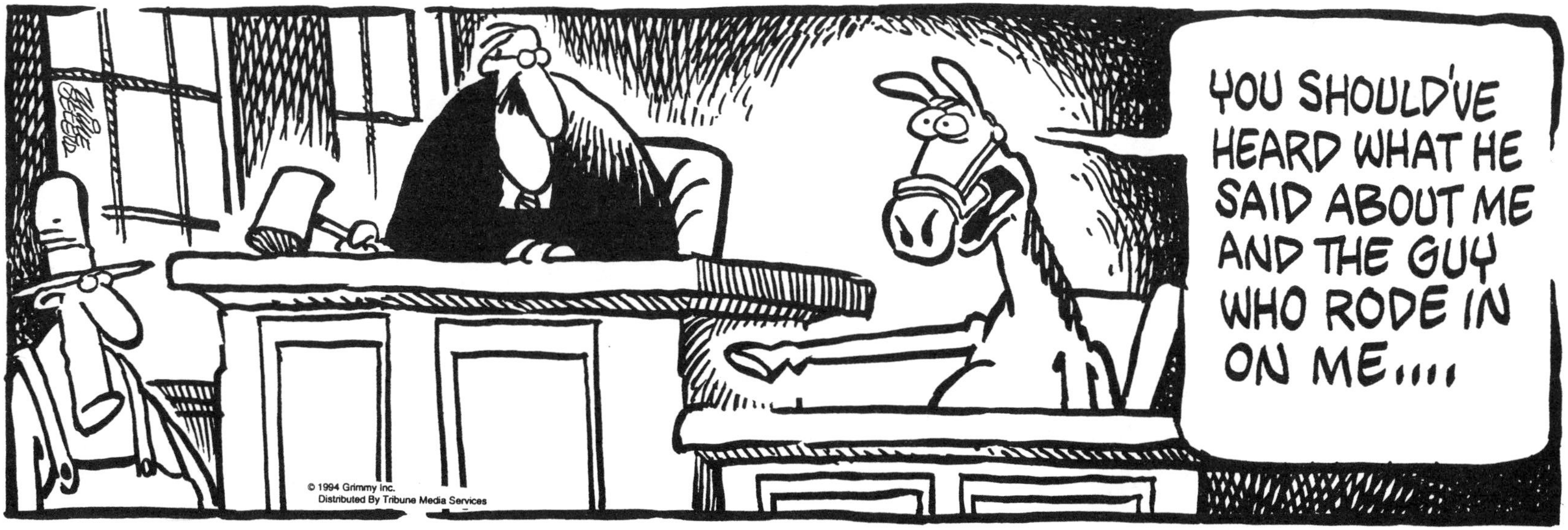
YOU SHOULD'VE HEARD WHAT HE SAID ABOUT ME AND THE GUY WHO RODE IN ON ME....
© 1994 Grimmy Inc.
Distributed By Tribune Media Services

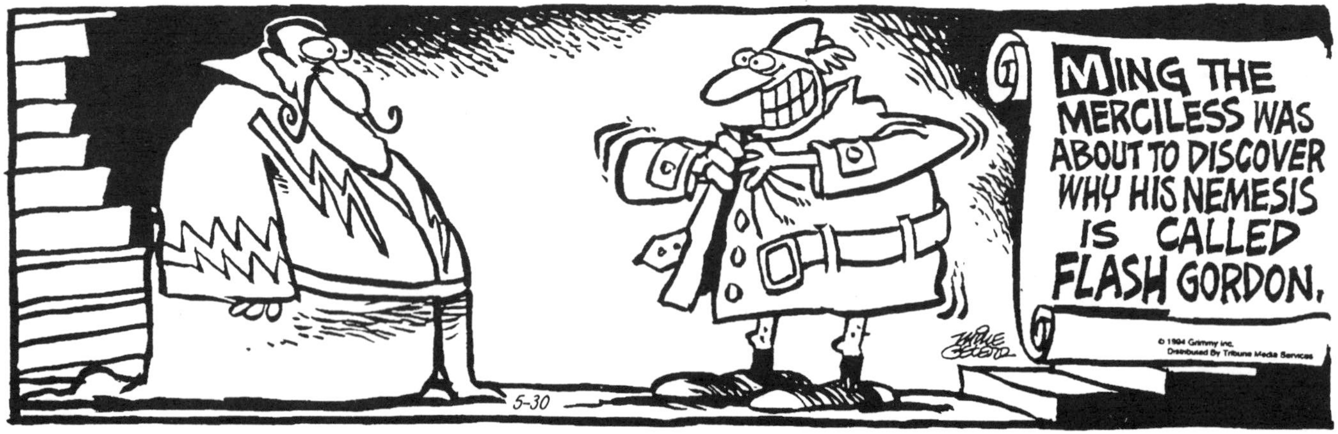
MING THE MERCILESS WAS ABOUT TO DISCOVER WHY HIS NEMESIS IS CALLED FLASH GORDON.
© 1994 Grimmy Inc. Distributed By Tribune Media Services
5-30

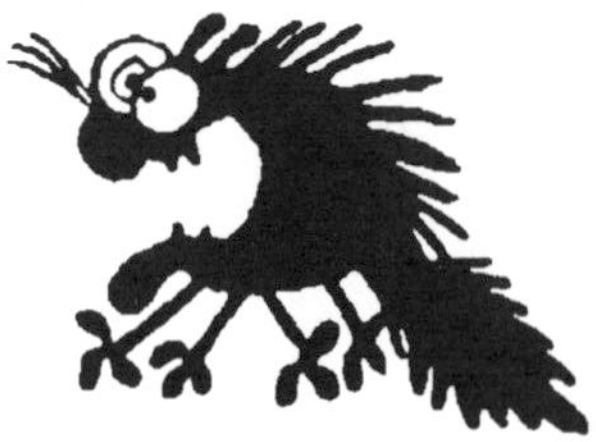

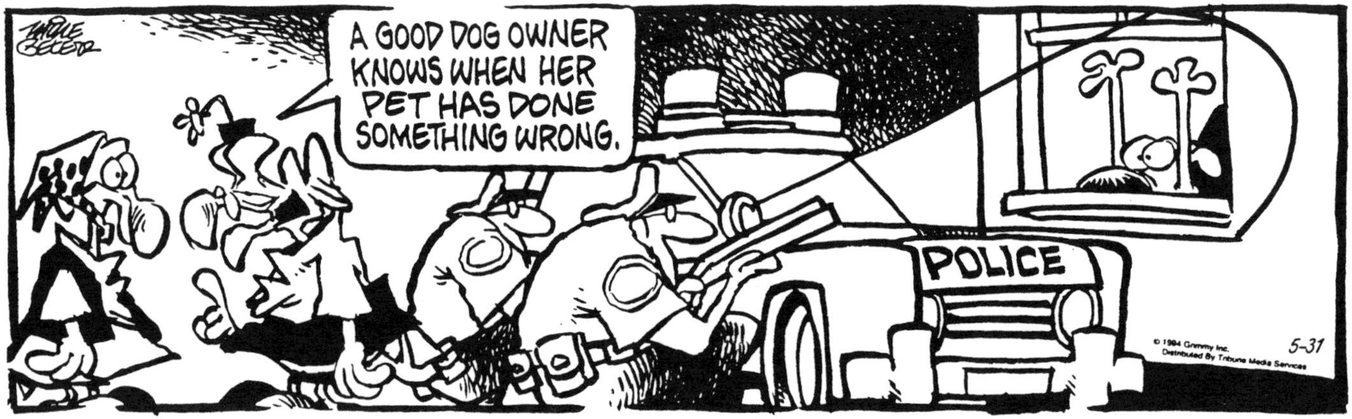
A GOOD DOG OWNER KNOWS WHEN HER PET HAS DONE SOMETHING WRONG.
POLICE
© 1994 Grimmy Inc. Distributed By Tribune Media Services
5-31

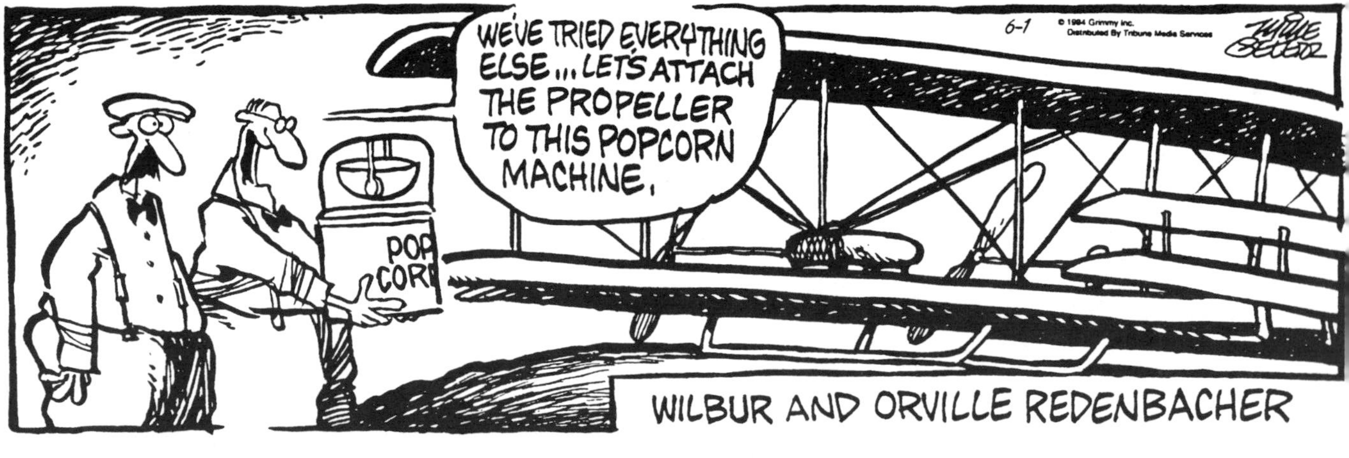
6-1
© 1994 Grimmy Inc. Distributed By Tribune Media Services
WE'VE TRIED EVERYTHING ELSE... LET'S ATTACH THE PROPELLER TO THIS POPCORN MACHINE.
WILBUR AND ORVILLE REDENBACHER

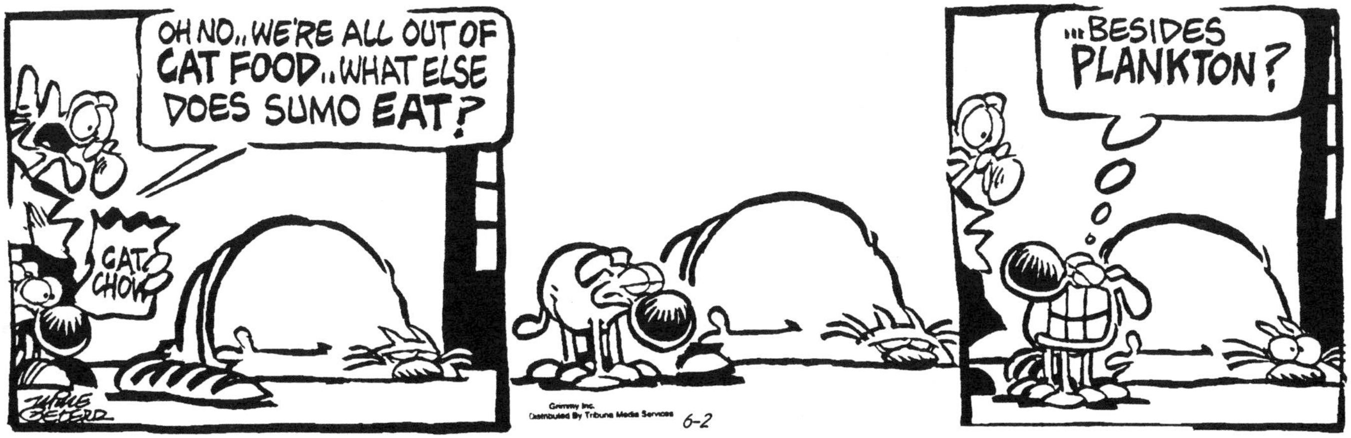
OH NO.. WE'RE ALL OUT OF CAT FOOD.. WHAT ELSE DOES SUMO EAT?
CAT CHOW
...BESIDES PLANKTON?
Grimmy Inc.
Distributed By Tribune Media Services
6-2

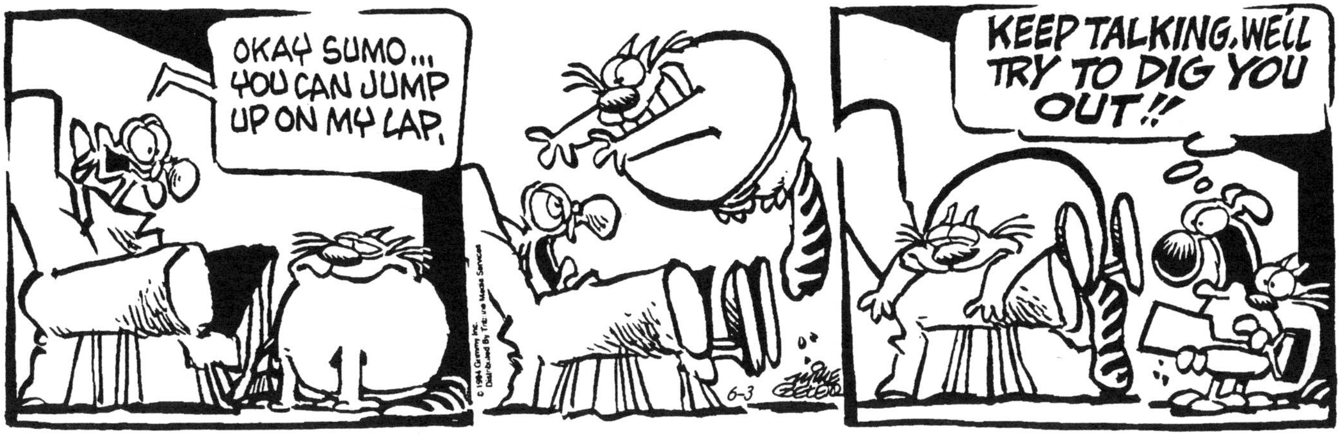
OKAY SUMO... YOU CAN JUMP UP ON MY LAP.
© 1994 Grimmy Inc.
6-3
KEEP TALKING. WE'LL TRY TO DIG YOU OUT!!

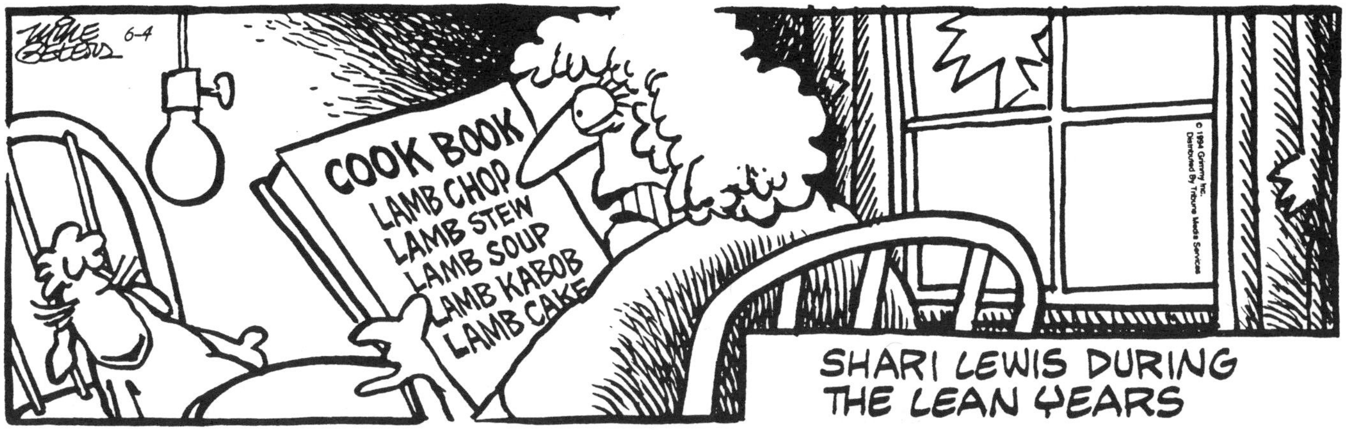
6-4
COOK BOOK
LAMB CHOP
LAMB STEW
LAMB SOUP
LAMB KABOB
LAMB CAKE
© 1994 Grimmy Inc.
Distributed By Tribune Media Services
SHARI LEWIS DURING THE LEAN YEARS

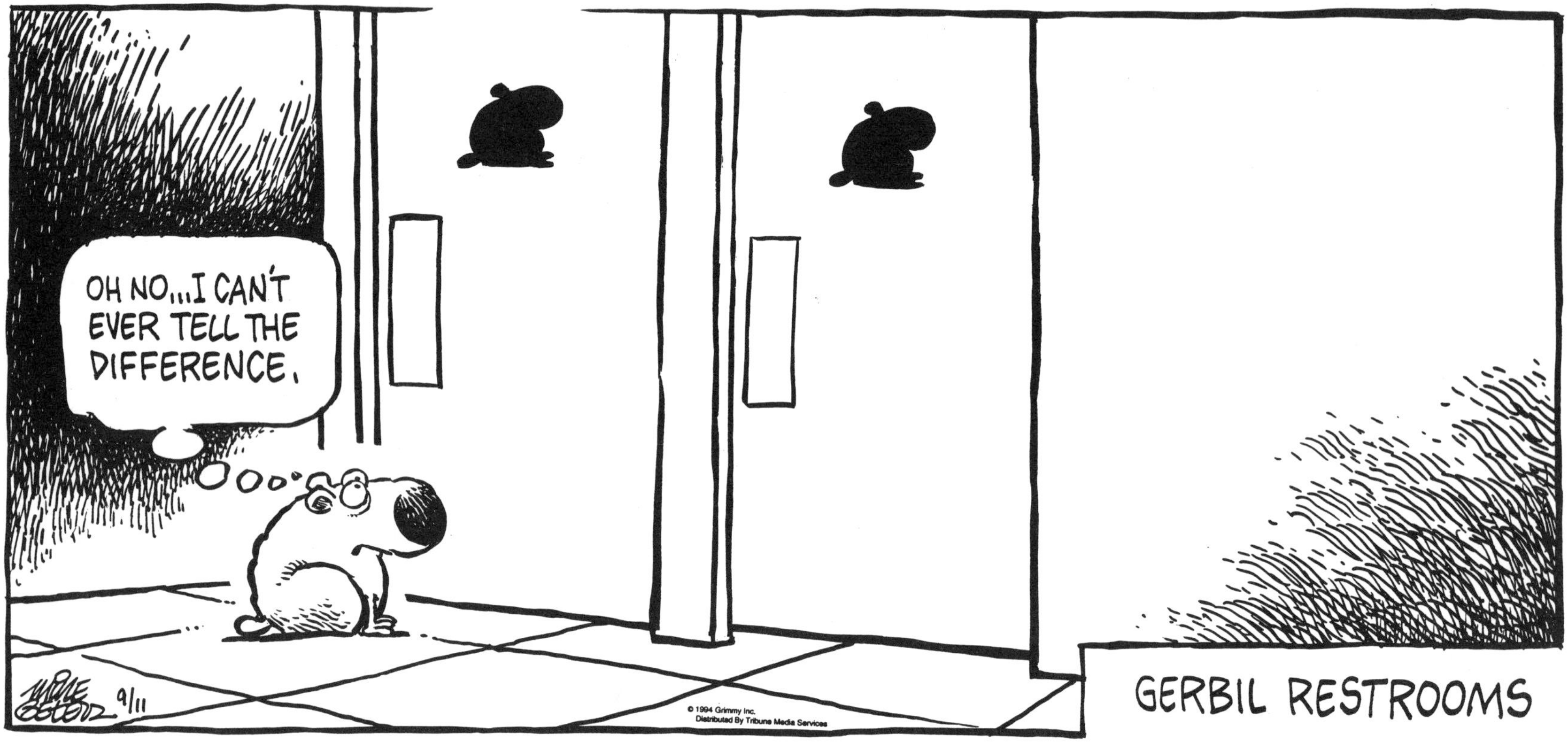
OH NO...I CAN'T EVER TELL THE DIFFERENCE.
9/11
© 1994 Grimmy Inc.
Distributed By Tribune Media Services

GERBIL RESTROOMS

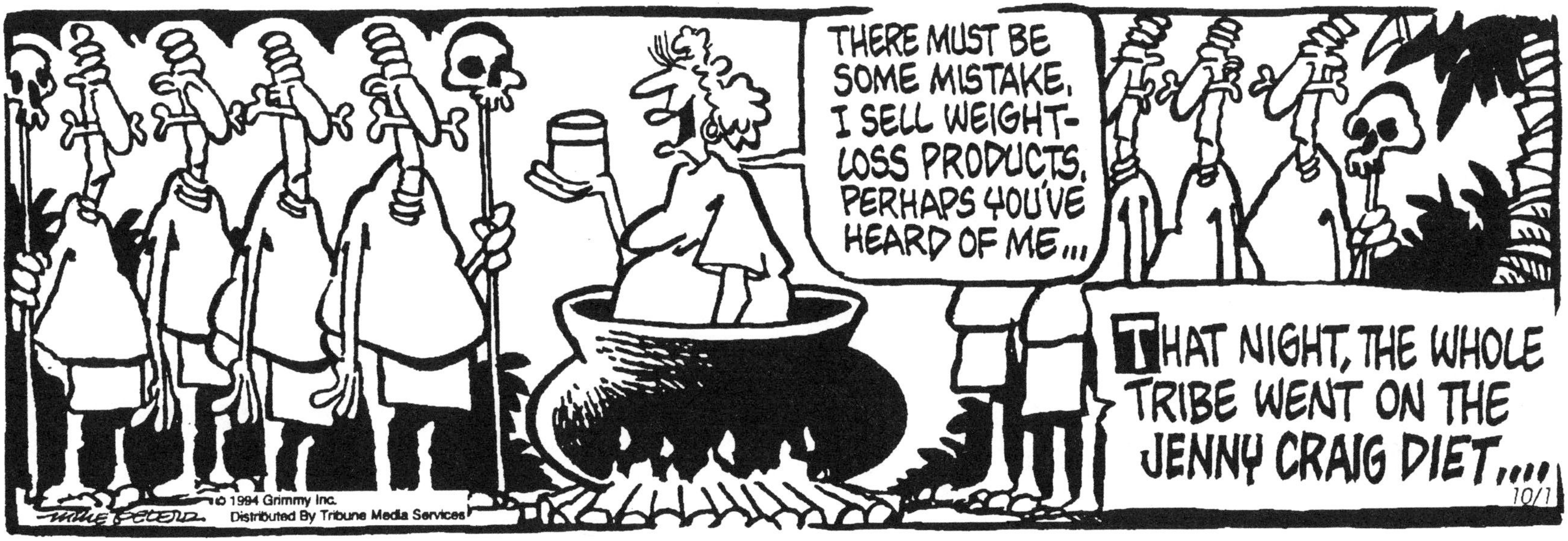
THERE MUST BE SOME MISTAKE, I SELL WEIGHT-LOSS PRODUCTS, PERHAPS YOU'VE HEARD OF ME...
THAT NIGHT, THE WHOLE TRIBE WENT ON THE JENNY CRAIG DIET....
© 1994 Grimmy Inc.
Distributed By Tribune Media Services
10/1

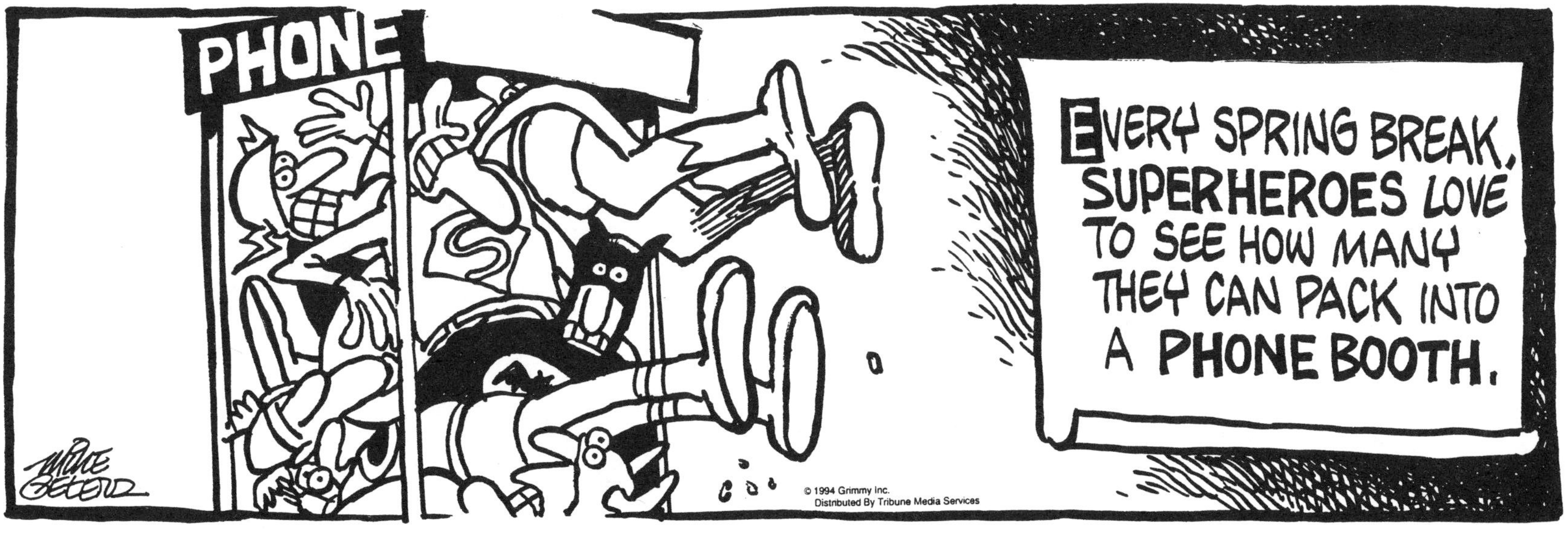
PHONE
EVERY SPRING BREAK, SUPERHEROES LOVE TO SEE HOW MANY THEY CAN PACK INTO A PHONE BOOTH.
© 1994 Grimmy Inc.
Distributed By Tribune Media Services

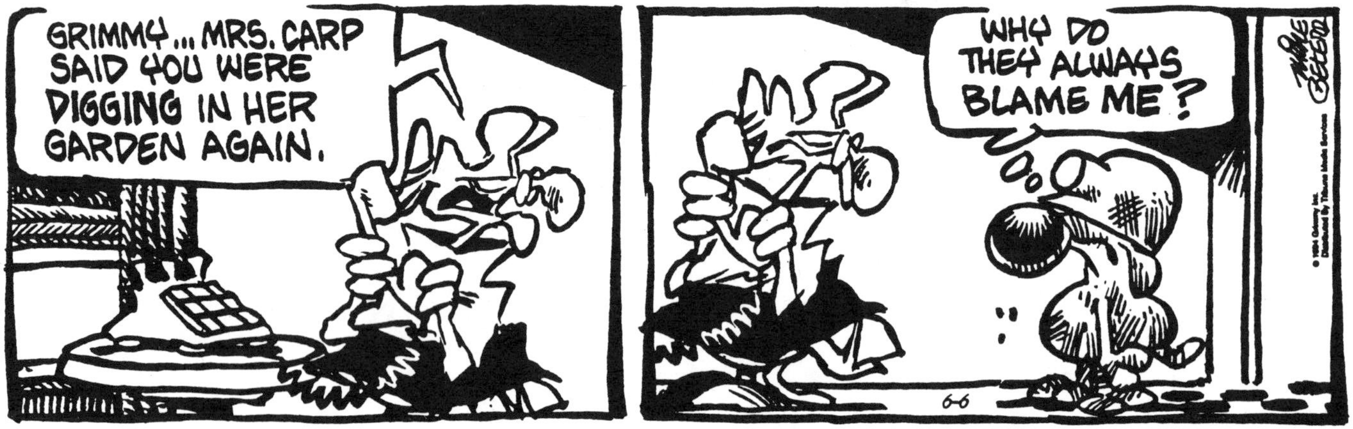
GRIMMY... MRS. CARP SAID YOU WERE DIGGING IN HER GARDEN AGAIN.
WHY DO THEY ALWAYS BLAME ME?
© 1994 Grimmy Inc. Distributed By Tribune Media Services
6-6

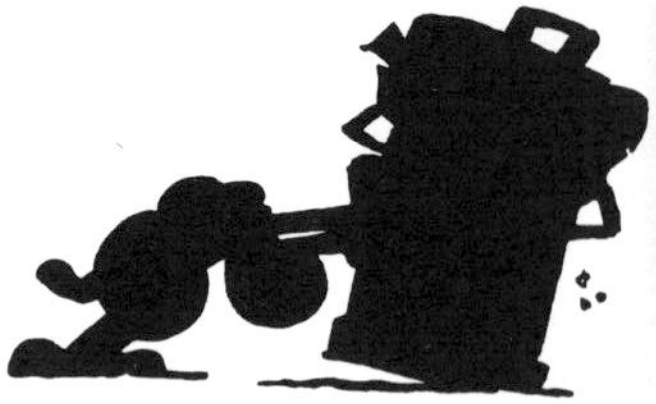

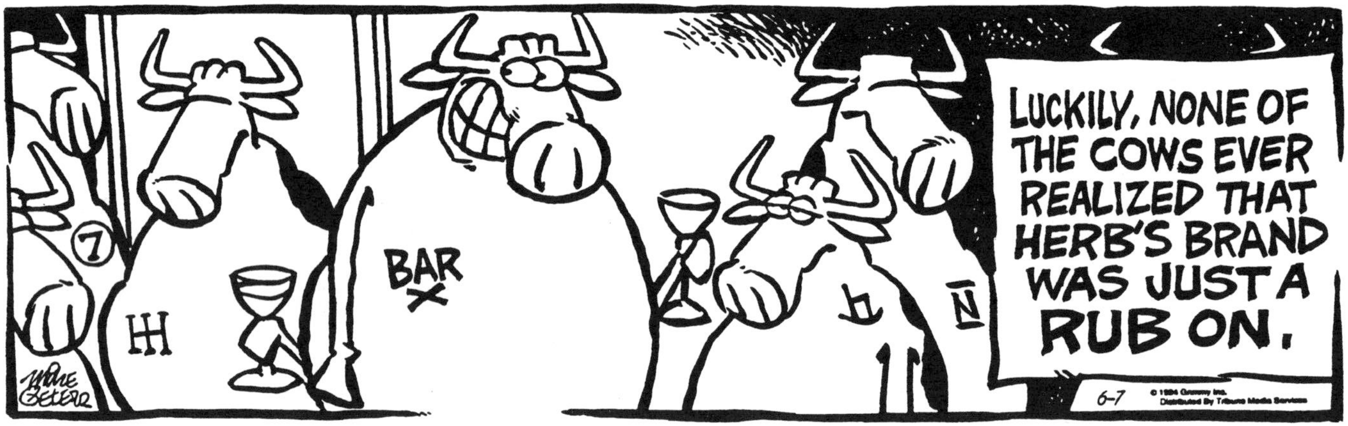
7
HH
BAR
LUCKILY, NONE OF THE COWS EVER REALIZED THAT HERB'S BRAND WAS JUST A RUB ON.
6-7
© 1994 Grimmy Inc. Distributed By Tribune Media Services

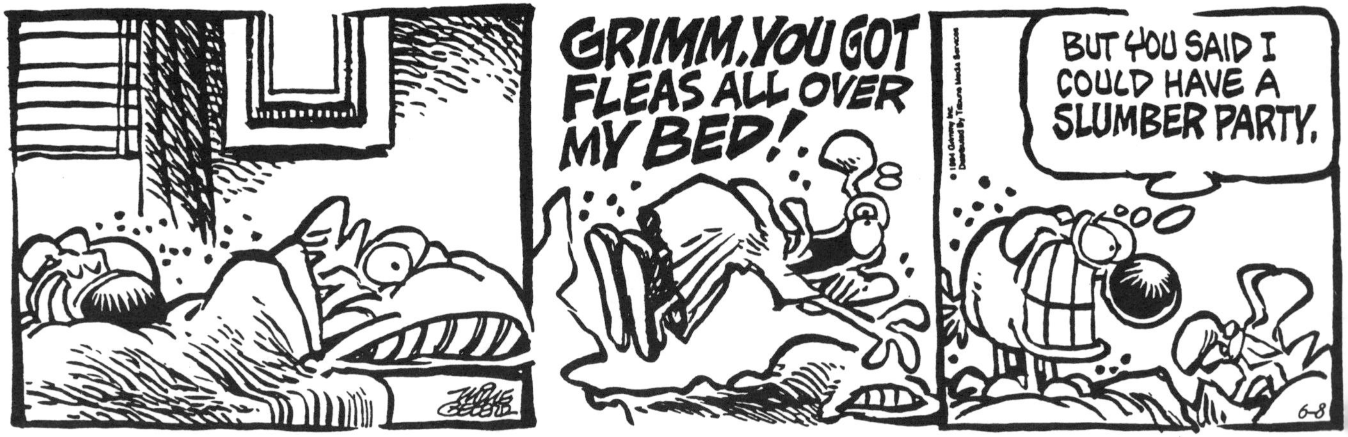
GRIMM, YOU GOT FLEAS ALL OVER MY BED!
© 1994 Grimmy Inc. Distributed By Tribune Media Services
BUT YOU SAID I COULD HAVE A SLUMBER PARTY.
6-8

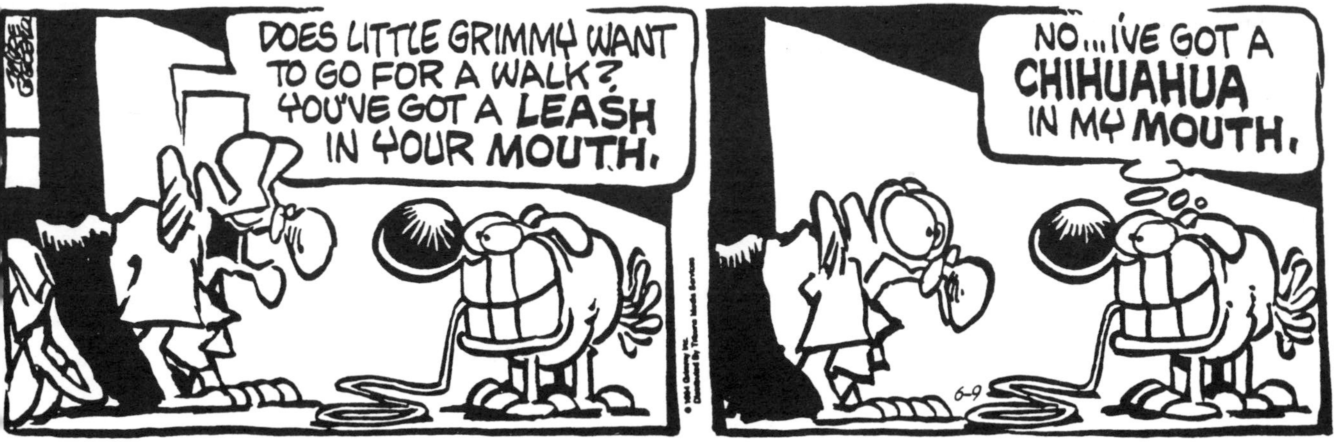
DOES LITTLE GRIMMY WANT TO GO FOR A WALK? YOU'VE GOT A **LEASH** IN YOUR **MOUTH**.
NO... I'VE GOT A **CHIHUAHUA** IN MY **MOUTH**.
6-9

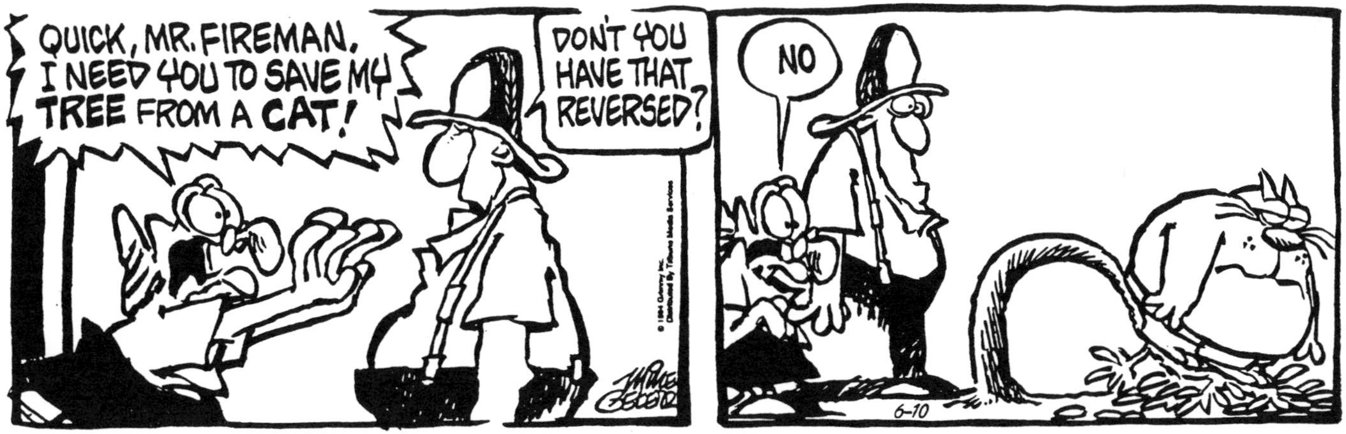
QUICK, MR. FIREMAN. I NEED YOU TO SAVE MY **TREE** FROM A **CAT**!
DON'T YOU HAVE THAT REVERSED?
NO
6-10

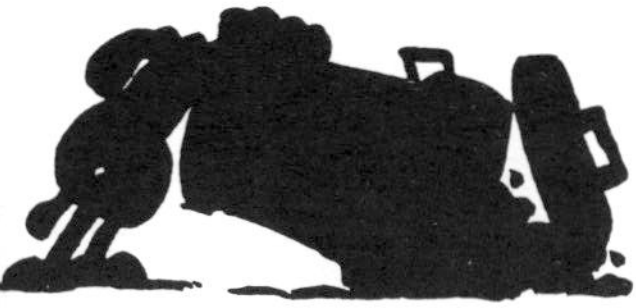

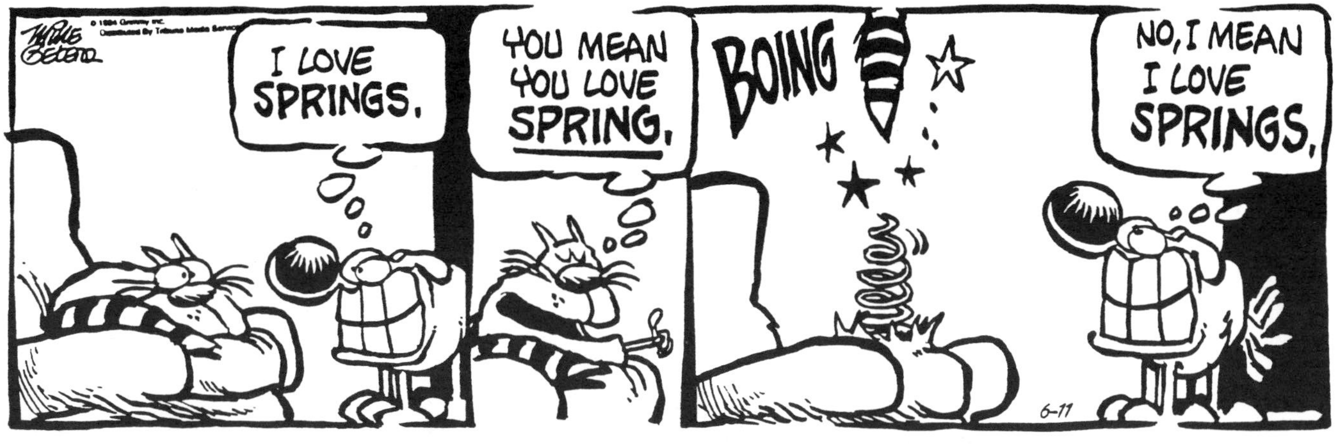
I LOVE **SPRINGS**.
YOU MEAN YOU LOVE **SPRING**.
BOING
NO, I MEAN I LOVE **SPRINGS**.
6-11

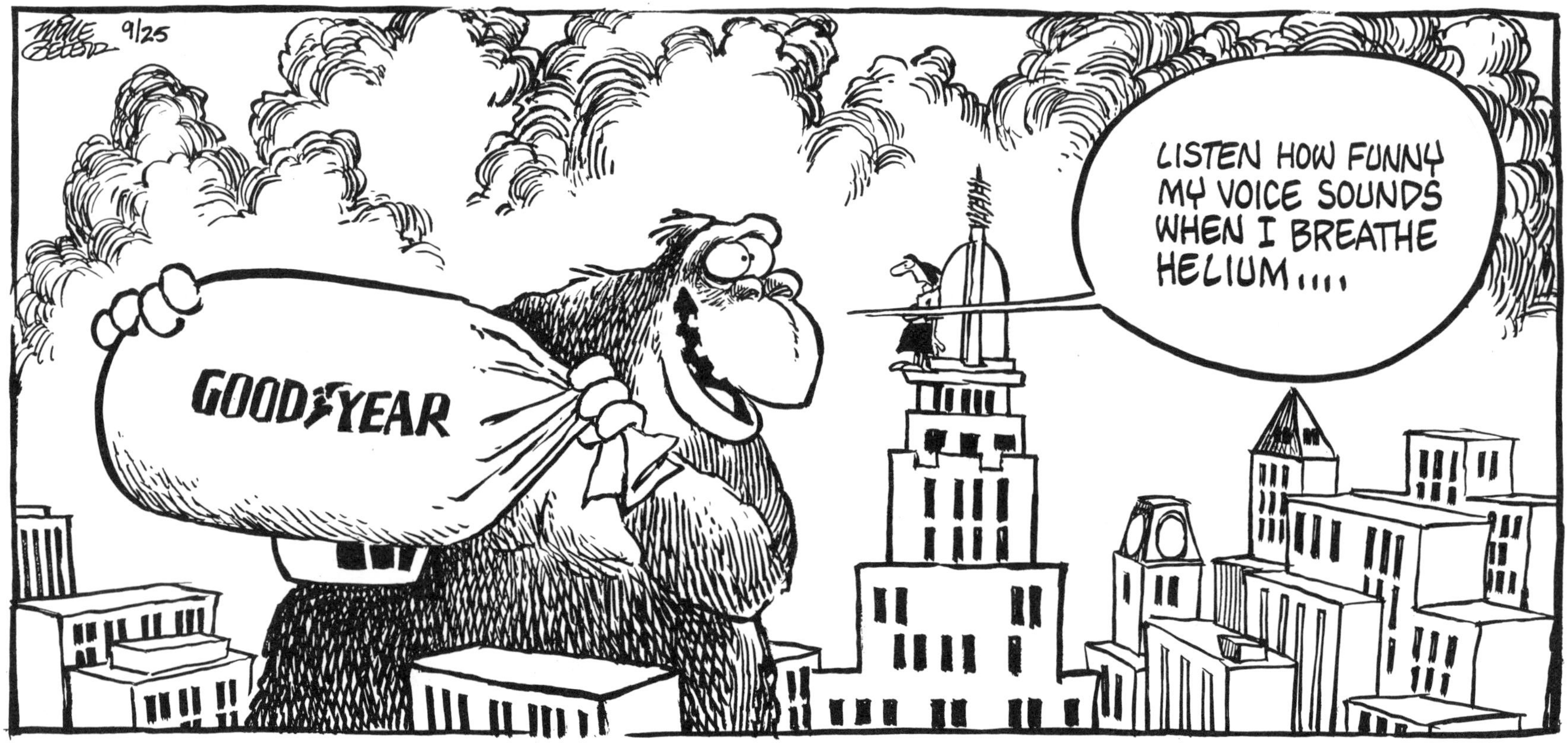
9/25
GOODYEAR
LISTEN HOW FUNNY MY VOICE SOUNDS WHEN I BREATHE HELIUM....

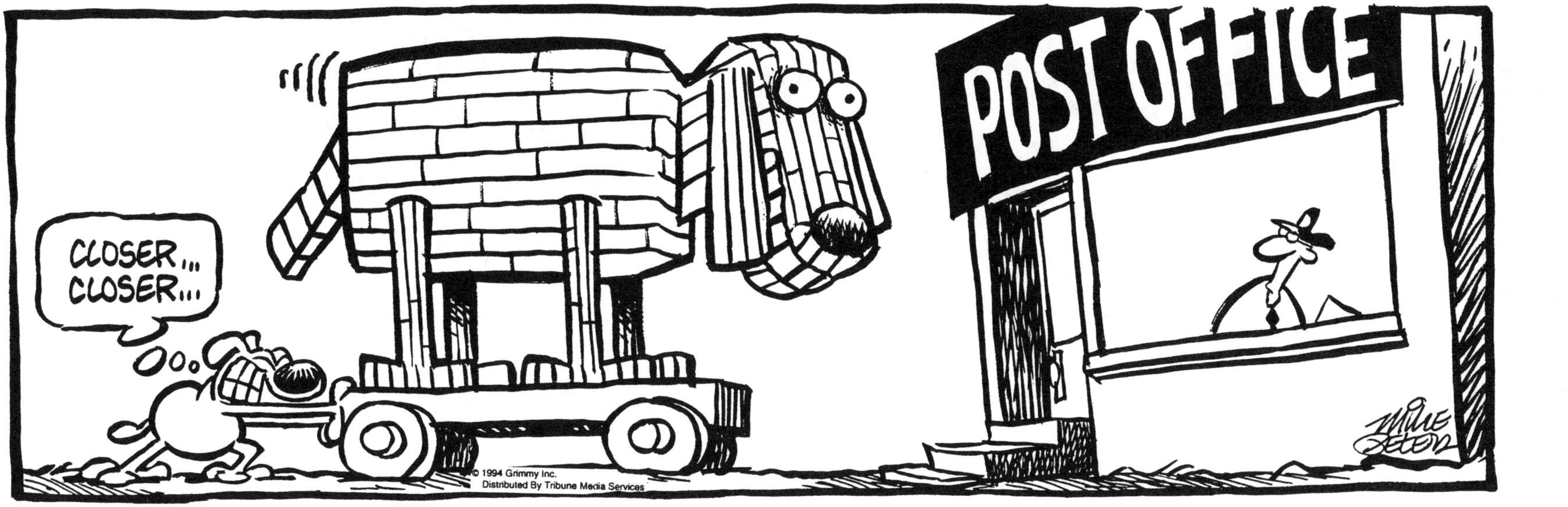
CLOSER... CLOSER...
POST OFFICE
© 1994 Grimmy Inc.
Distributed By Tribune Media Services

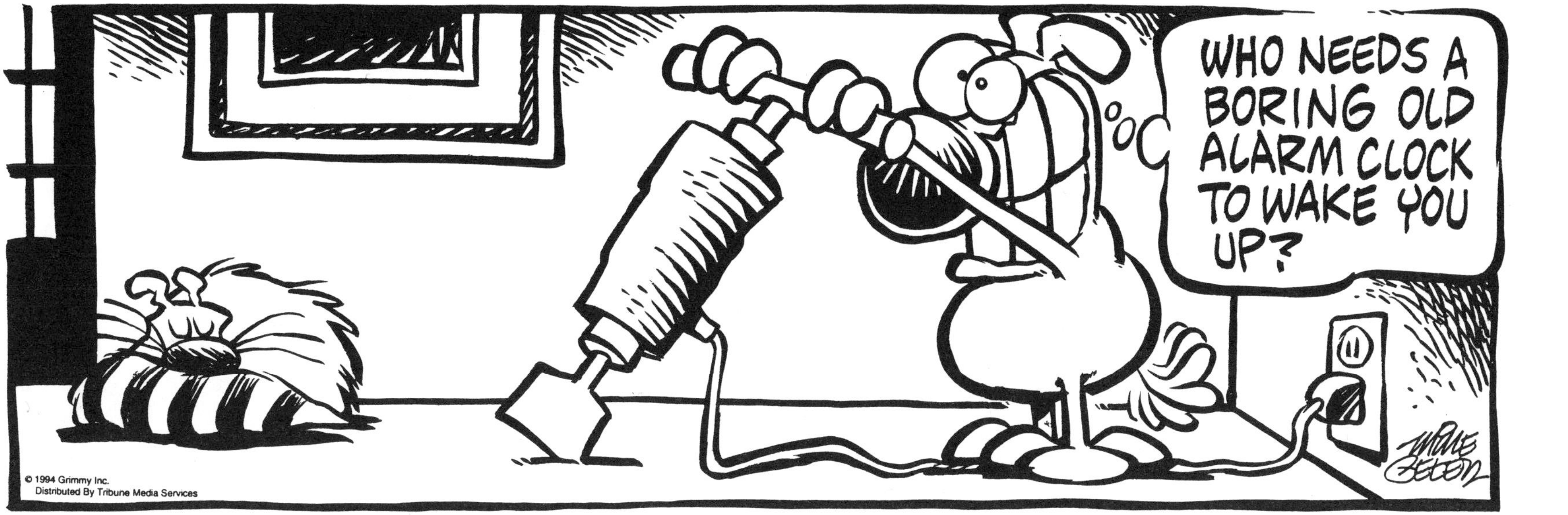
WHO NEEDS A BORING OLD ALARM CLOCK TO WAKE YOU UP?
© 1994 Grimmy Inc.
Distributed By Tribune Media Services

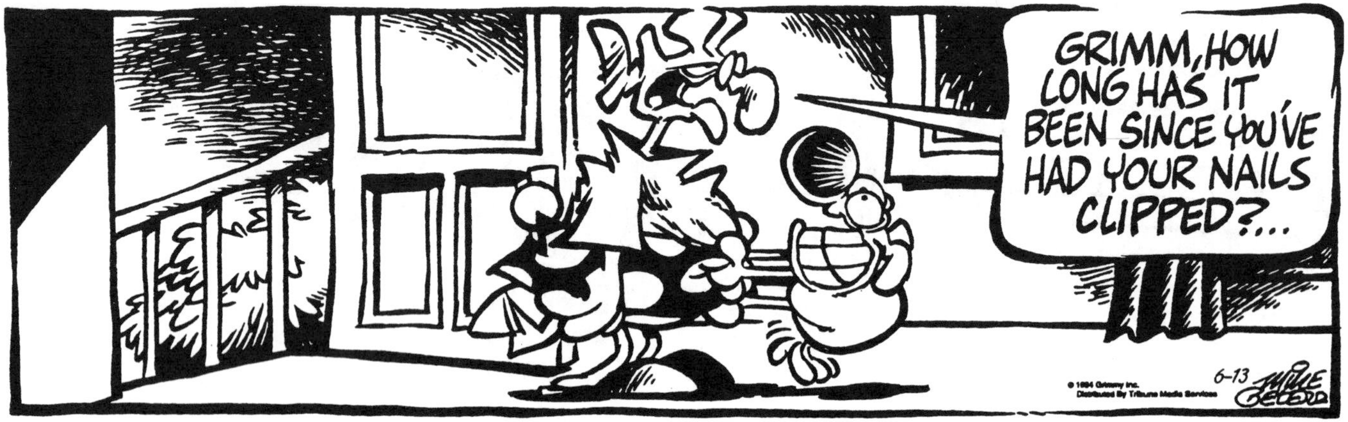
GRIMM, HOW LONG HAS IT BEEN SINCE YOU'VE HAD YOUR NAILS CLIPPED?...
© 1994 Grimmy Inc.
Distributed By Tribune Media Services
6-13

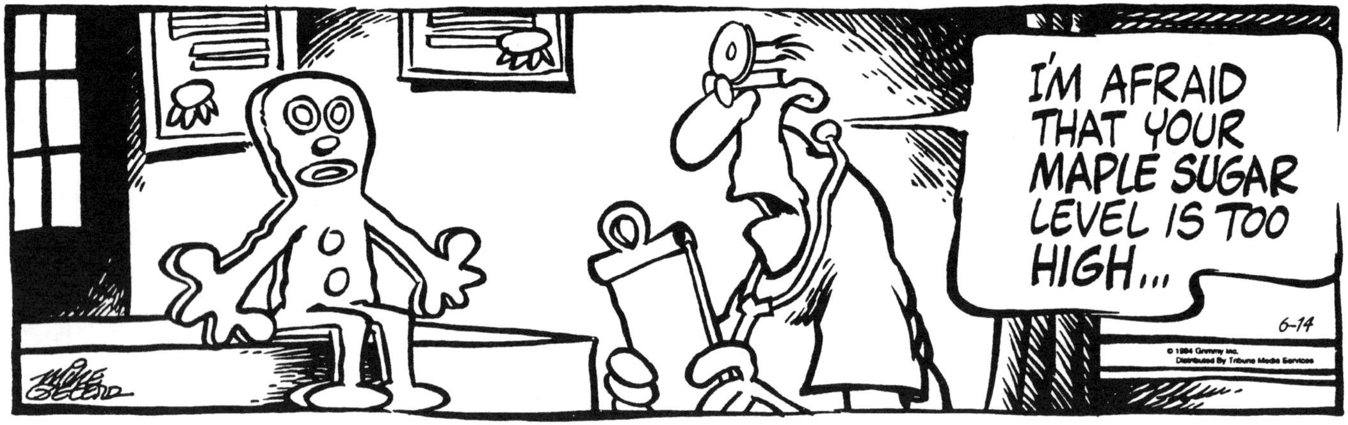
I'M AFRAID THAT YOUR MAPLE SUGAR LEVEL IS TOO HIGH...
6-14
© 1994 Grimmy Inc.
Distributed By Tribune Media Services

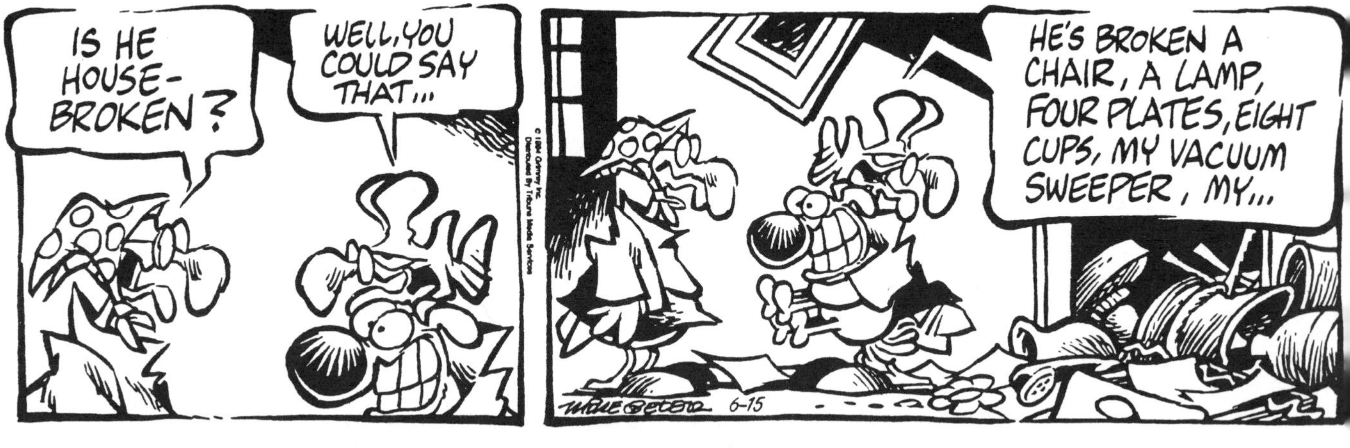
IS HE HOUSE-BROKEN?
WELL, YOU COULD SAY THAT...
© 1994 Grimmy Inc.
Distributed By Tribune Media Services
HE'S BROKEN A CHAIR, A LAMP, FOUR PLATES, EIGHT CUPS, MY VACUUM SWEEPER, MY...
6-15

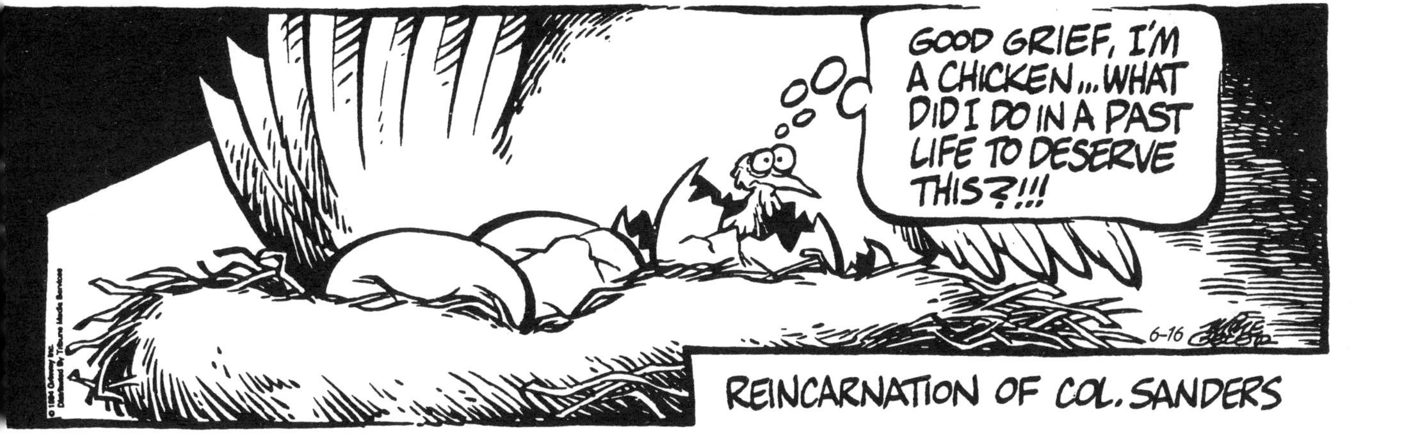
GOOD GRIEF, I'M A CHICKEN... WHAT DID I DO IN A PAST LIFE TO DESERVE THIS?!!!
6-16
© 1994 Grimmy Inc. Distributed By Tribune Media Services
REINCARNATION OF COL. SANDERS

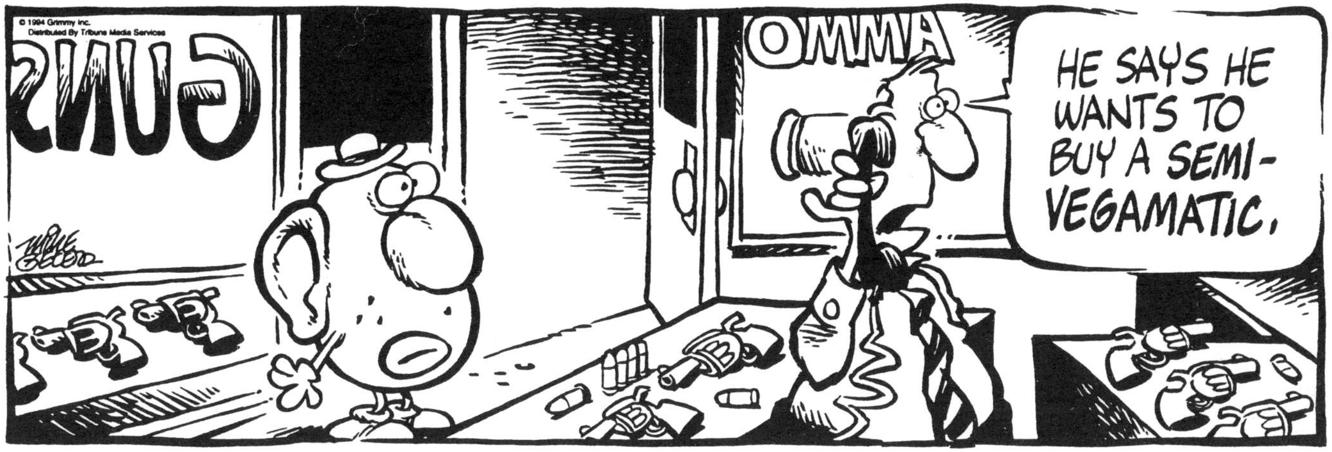
© 1994 Grimmy Inc. Distributed By Tribune Media Services
HE SAYS HE WANTS TO BUY A SEMI-VEGAMATIC.

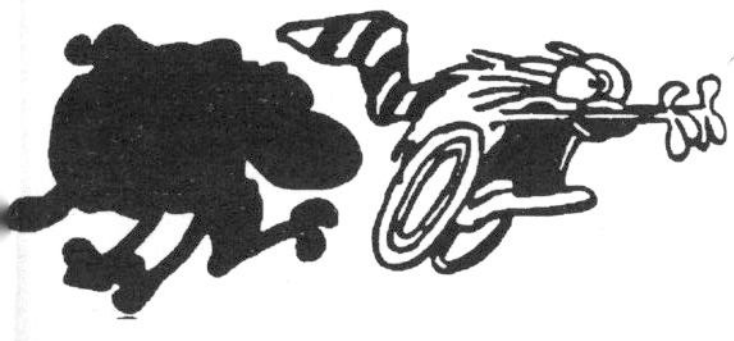

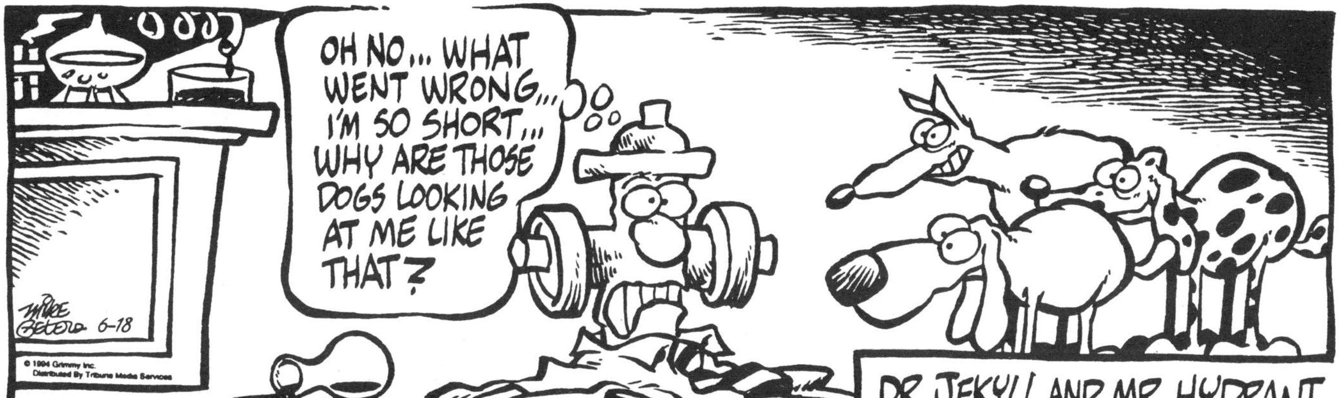
OH NO... WHAT WENT WRONG... I'M SO SHORT... WHY ARE THOSE DOGS LOOKING AT ME LIKE THAT?
6-18
© 1994 Grimmy Inc. Distributed By Tribune Media Services
DR. JEKYLL AND MR. HYDRANT

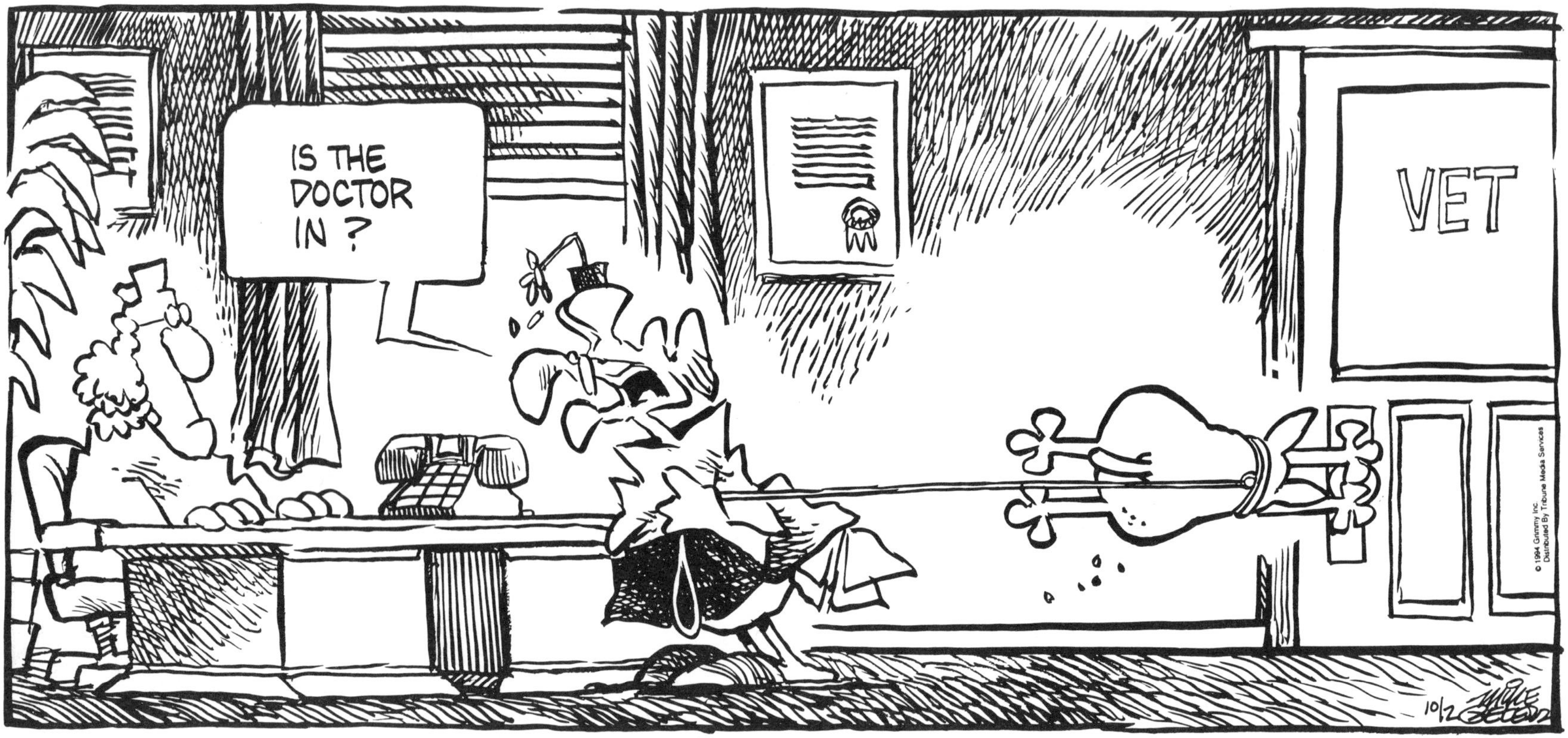
IS THE DOCTOR IN ?
VET
© 1994 Grimmy Inc.
Distributed By Tribune Media Services
10/2

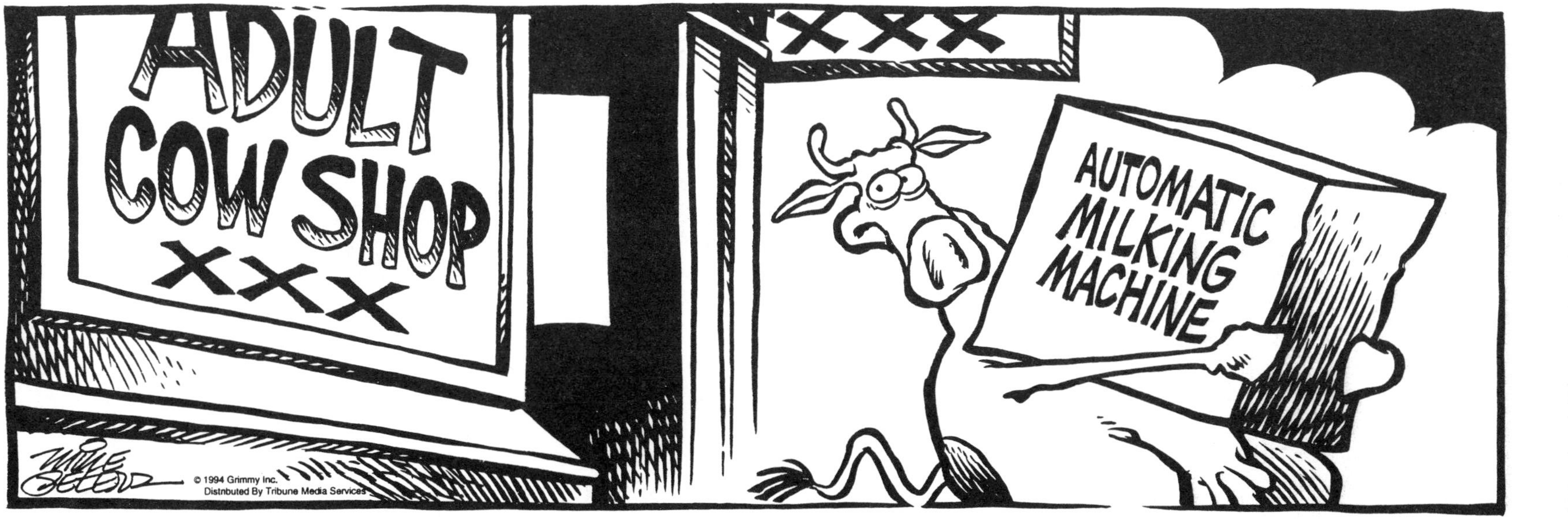
ADULT COW SHOP XXX
XXX
AUTOMATIC MILKING MACHINE
© 1994 Grimmy Inc.
Distributed By Tribune Media Services

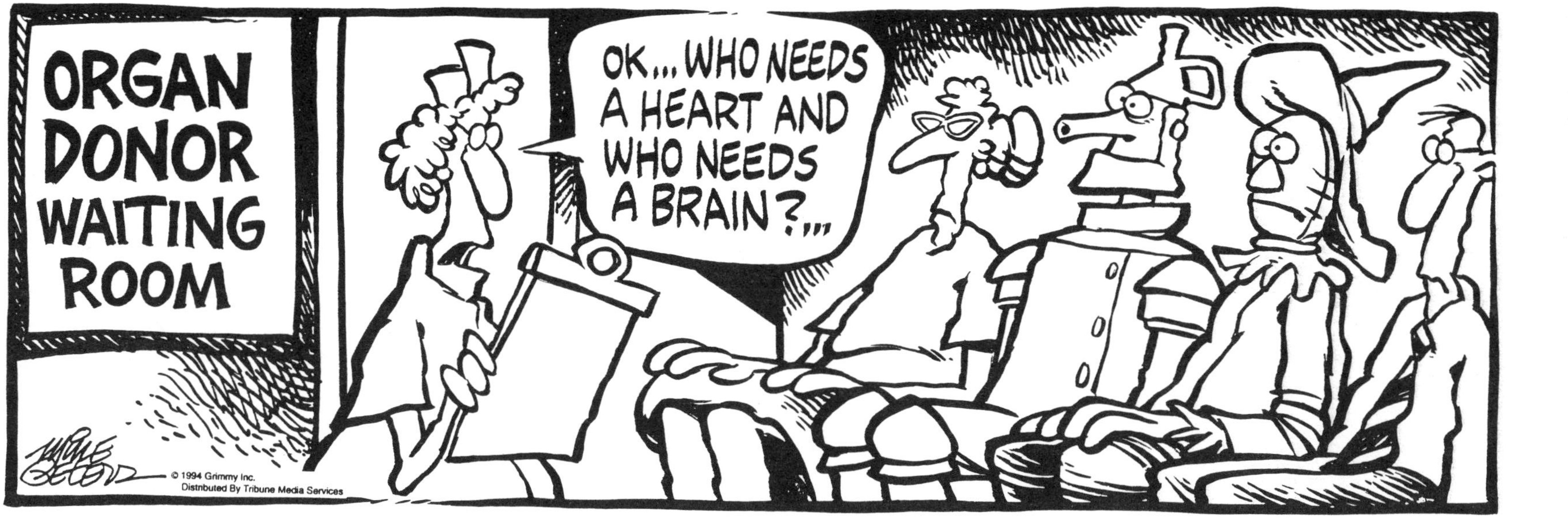
ORGAN DONOR WAITING ROOM
OK... WHO NEEDS A HEART AND WHO NEEDS A BRAIN?...
© 1994 Grimmy Inc.
Distributed By Tribune Media Services

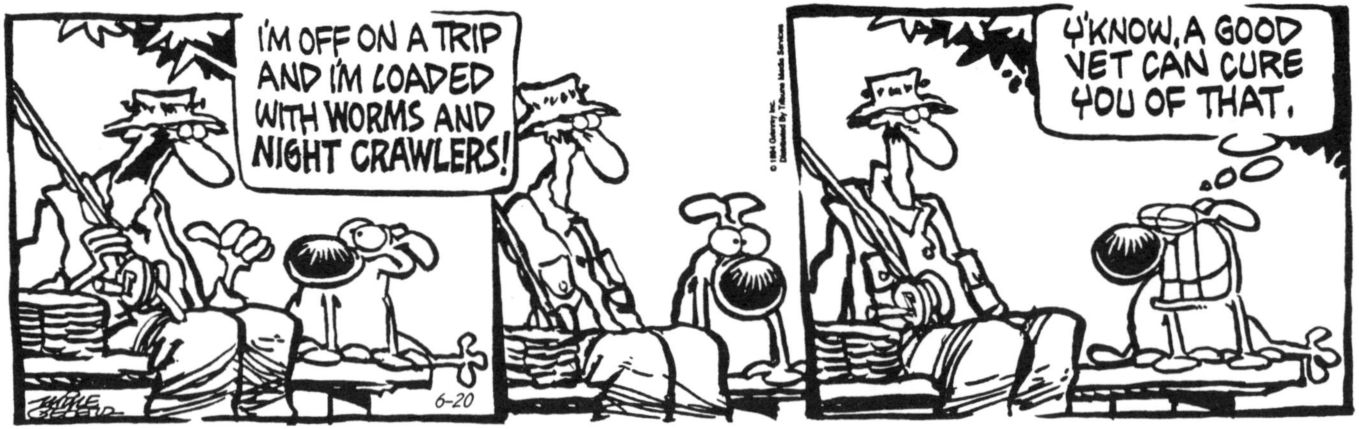
I'M OFF ON A TRIP AND I'M LOADED WITH WORMS AND NIGHT CRAWLERS!
Y'KNOW, A GOOD VET CAN CURE YOU OF THAT.
6-20

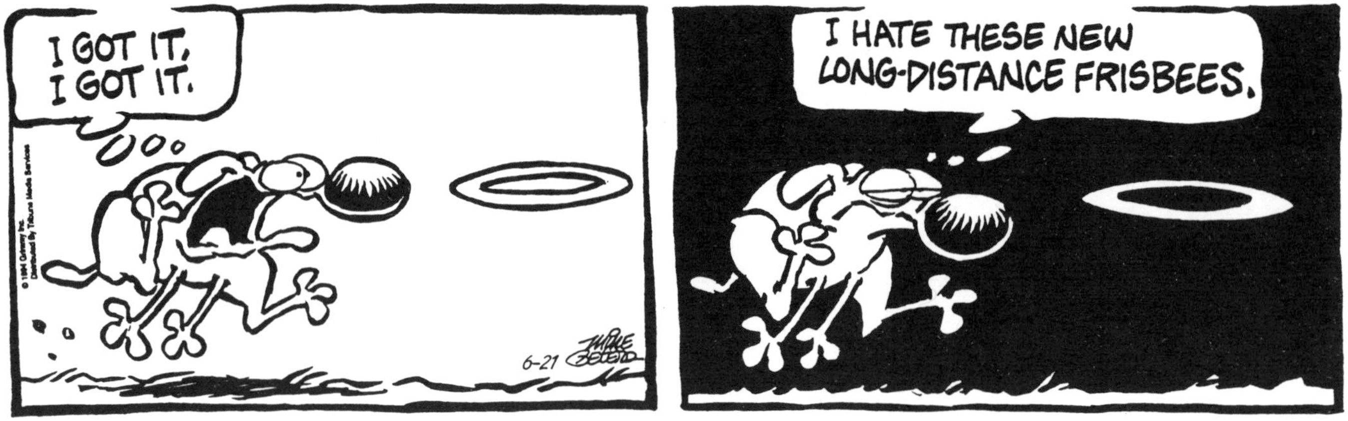
I GOT IT, I GOT IT.
6-21
I HATE THESE NEW LONG-DISTANCE FRISBEES.

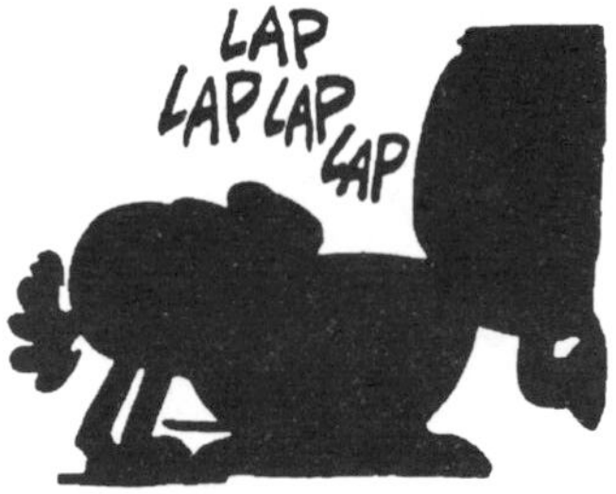
LAP
LAP LAP LAP

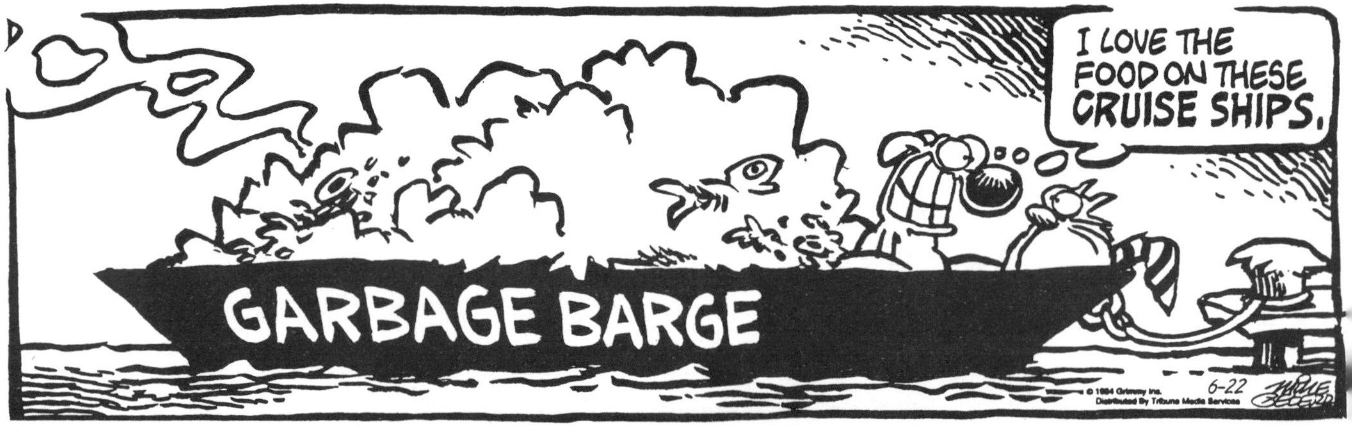
I LOVE THE FOOD ON THESE CRUISE SHIPS.
GARBAGE BARGE
© 1994 Grimmy Inc.
Distributed By Tribune Media Services
6-22

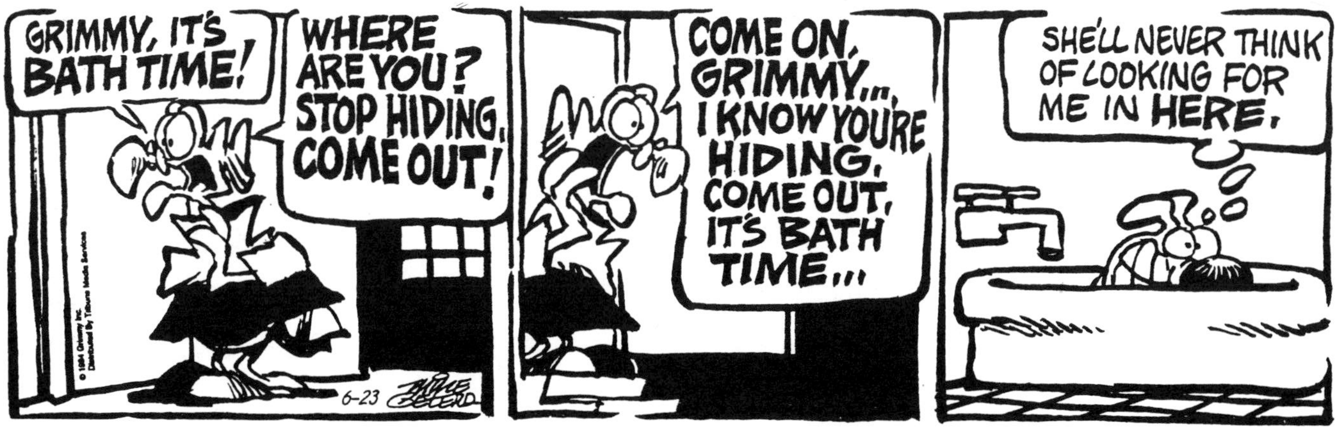
GRIMMY, IT'S BATH TIME!
WHERE ARE YOU? STOP HIDING. COME OUT!
COME ON, GRIMMY... I KNOW YOU'RE HIDING. COME OUT, IT'S BATH TIME...
SHE'LL NEVER THINK OF LOOKING FOR ME IN HERE.
6-23

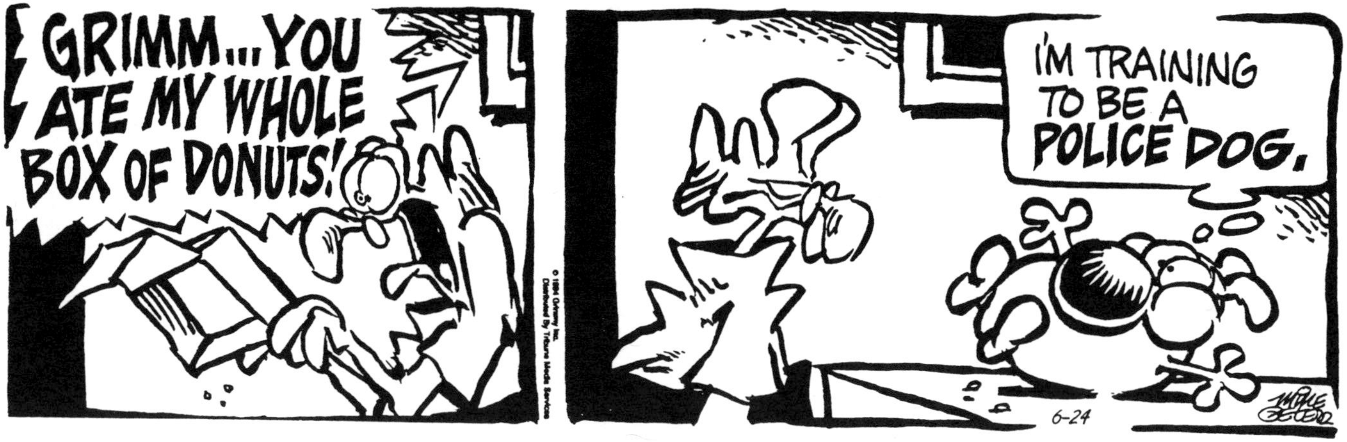
GRIMM... YOU ATE MY WHOLE BOX OF DONUTS!
I'M TRAINING TO BE A POLICE DOG.
6-24

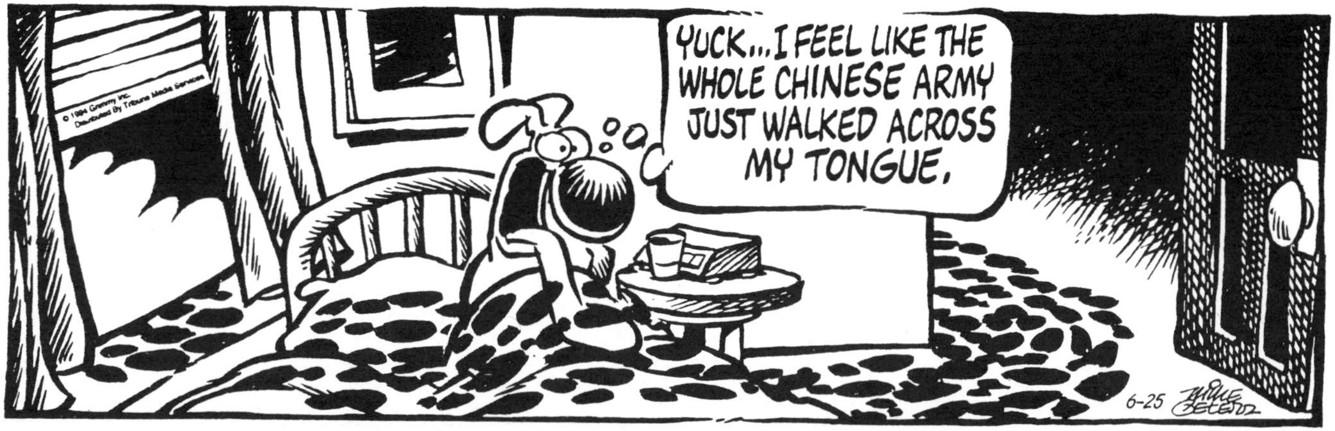
YUCK... I FEEL LIKE THE WHOLE CHINESE ARMY JUST WALKED ACROSS MY TONGUE.
6-25

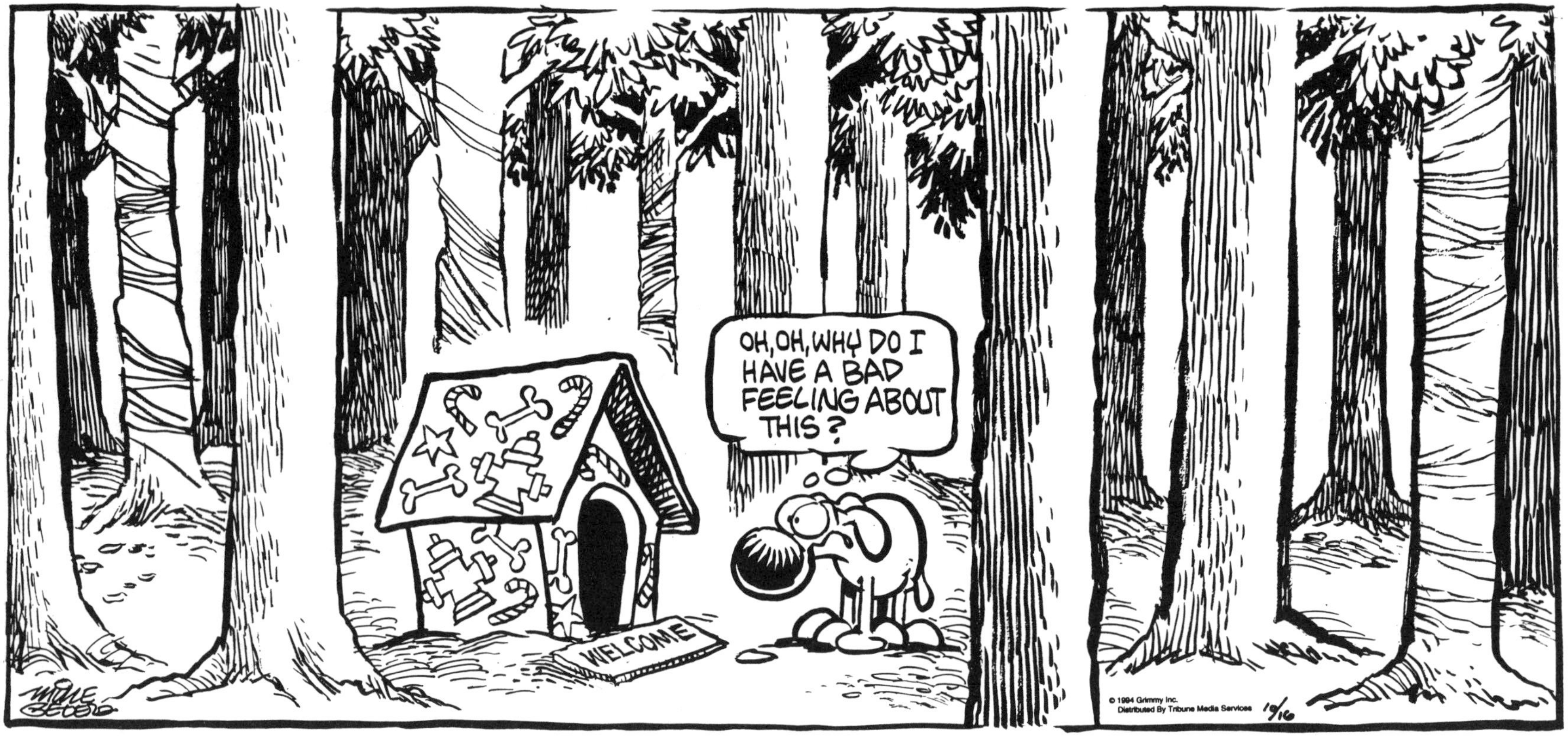

OH, OH, WHY DO I HAVE A BAD FEELING ABOUT THIS?
WELCOME
MIKE PETERS
© 1994 Grimmy Inc.
Distributed By Tribune Media Services
10/16

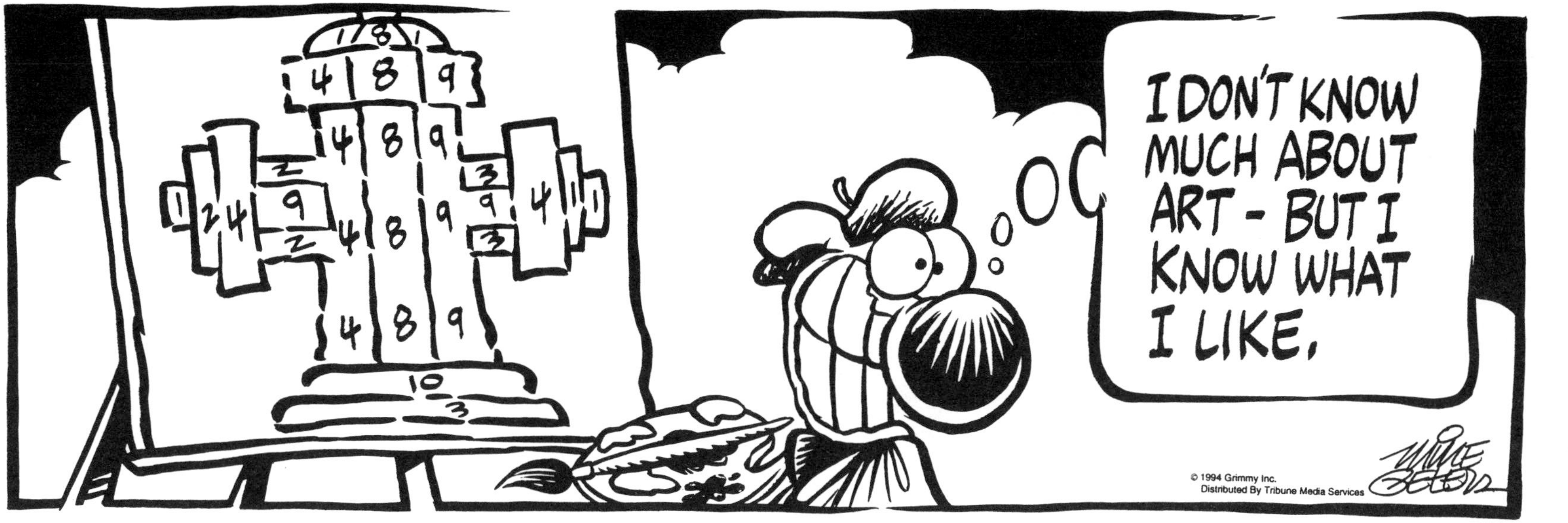
I DON'T KNOW MUCH ABOUT ART - BUT I KNOW WHAT I LIKE.
© 1994 Grimmy Inc.
Distributed By Tribune Media Services

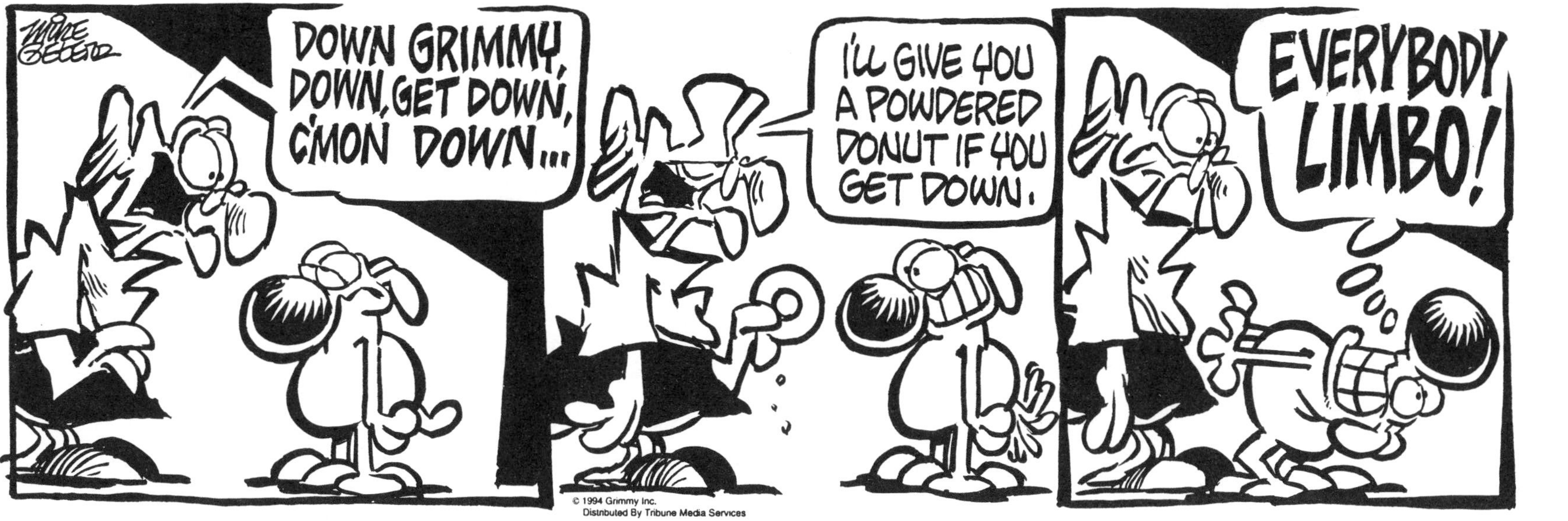
DOWN GRIMMY, DOWN, GET DOWN, C'MON DOWN...
I'LL GIVE YOU A POWDERED DONUT IF YOU GET DOWN.
EVERYBODY LIMBO!
© 1994 Grimmy Inc.
Distributed By Tribune Media Services

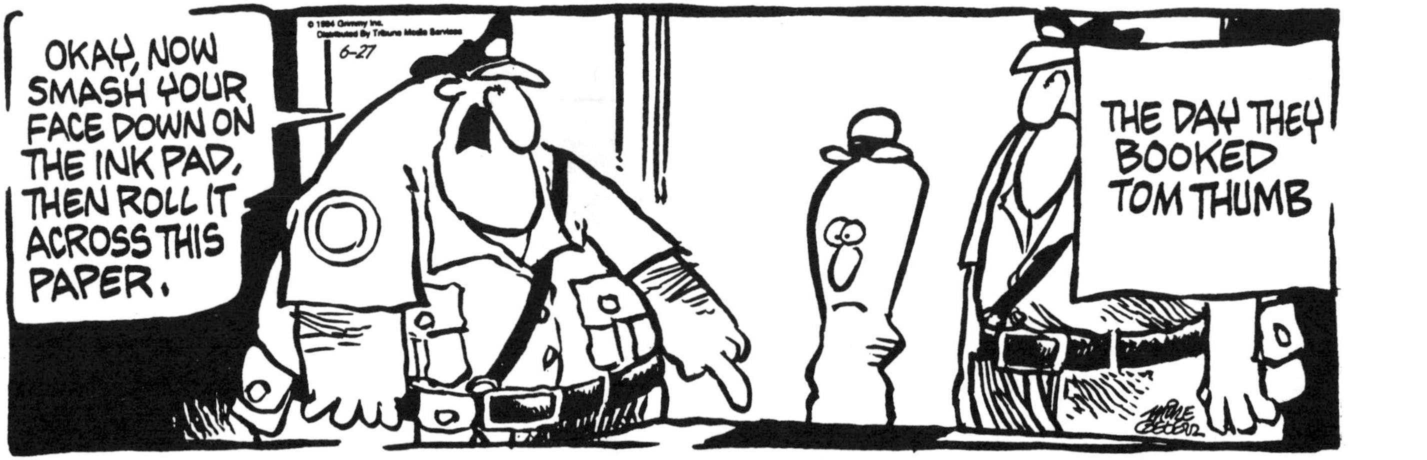
OKAY, NOW SMASH YOUR FACE DOWN ON THE INK PAD, THEN ROLL IT ACROSS THIS PAPER.
© 1994 Grimmy Inc. Distributed By Tribune Media Services
6-27
THE DAY THEY BOOKED TOM THUMB

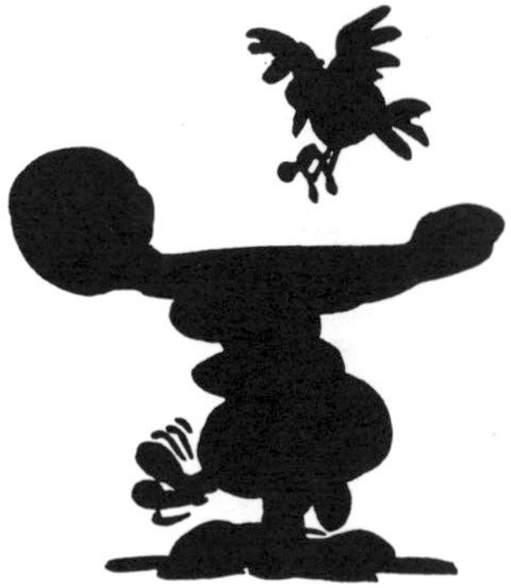

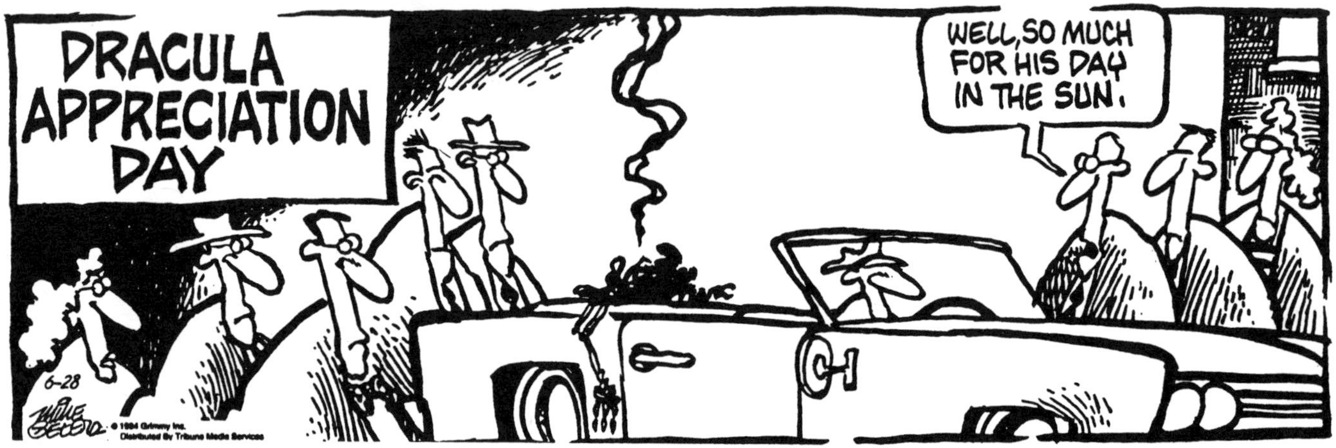
DRACULA APPRECIATION DAY
WELL, SO MUCH FOR HIS DAY IN THE SUN.
6-28
© 1994 Grimmy Inc. Distributed By Tribune Media Services

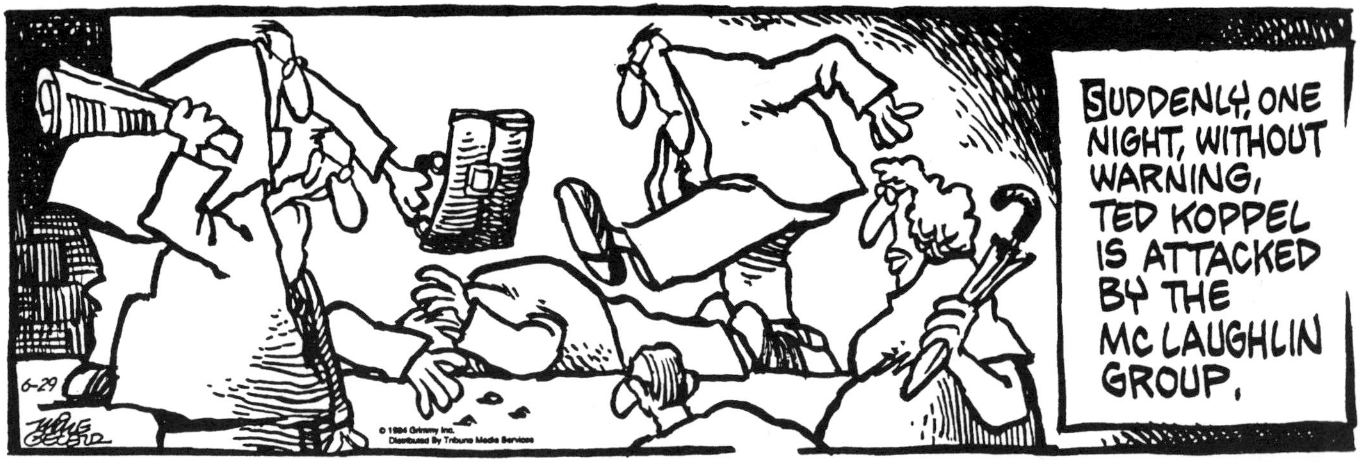
6-29
© 1994 Grimmy Inc. Distributed By Tribune Media Services
SUDDENLY, ONE NIGHT, WITHOUT WARNING, TED KOPPEL IS ATTACKED BY THE MC LAUGHLIN GROUP.

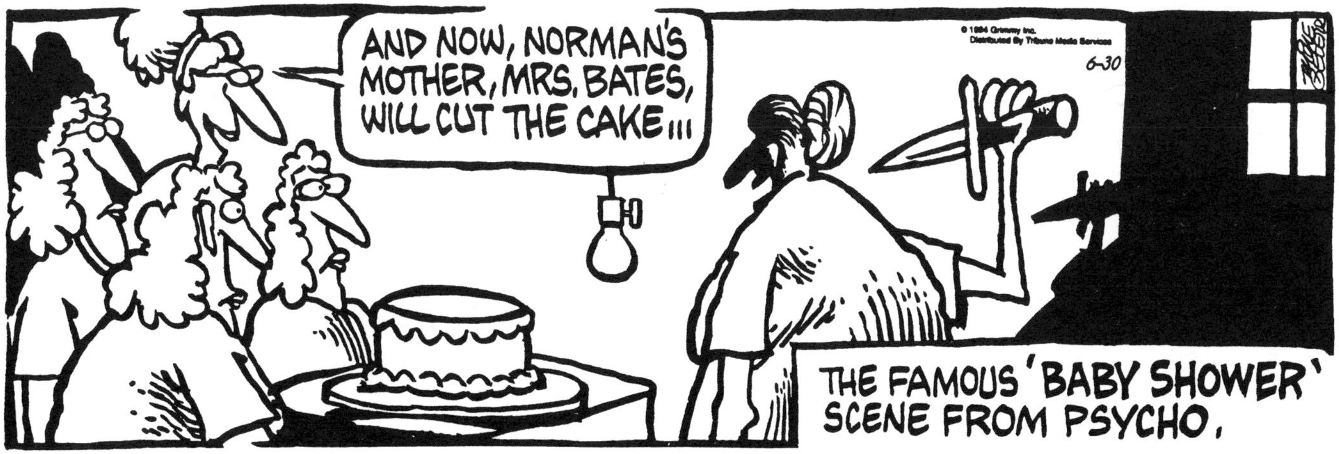
AND NOW, NORMAN'S MOTHER, MRS. BATES, WILL CUT THE CAKE...
© 1994 Grimmy Inc. Distributed By Tribune Media Services
6-30
THE FAMOUS 'BABY SHOWER' SCENE FROM PSYCHO.

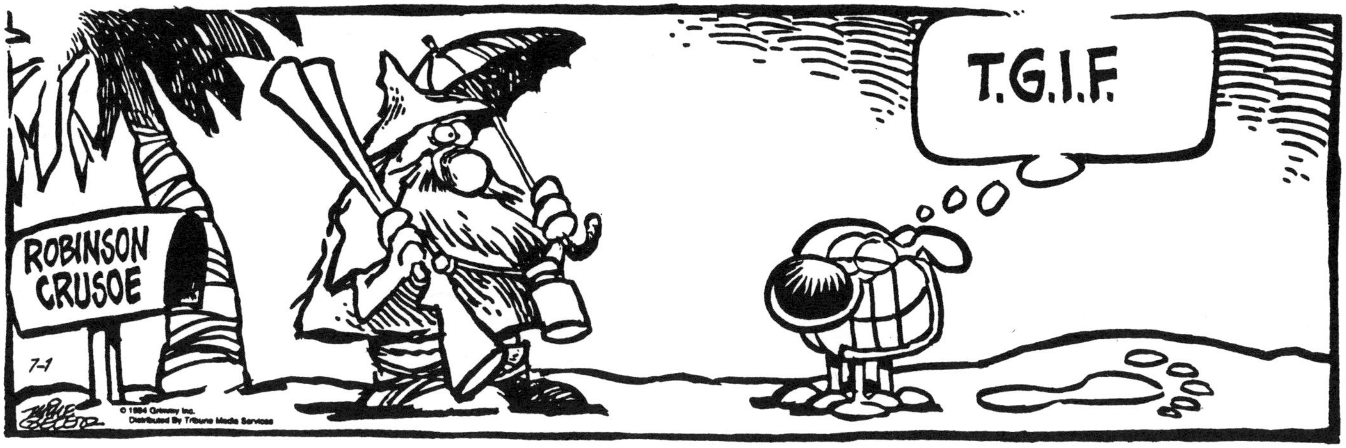
ROBINSON CRUSOE
T.G.I.F.
7-1
© 1994 Grimmy Inc. Distributed By Tribune Media Services

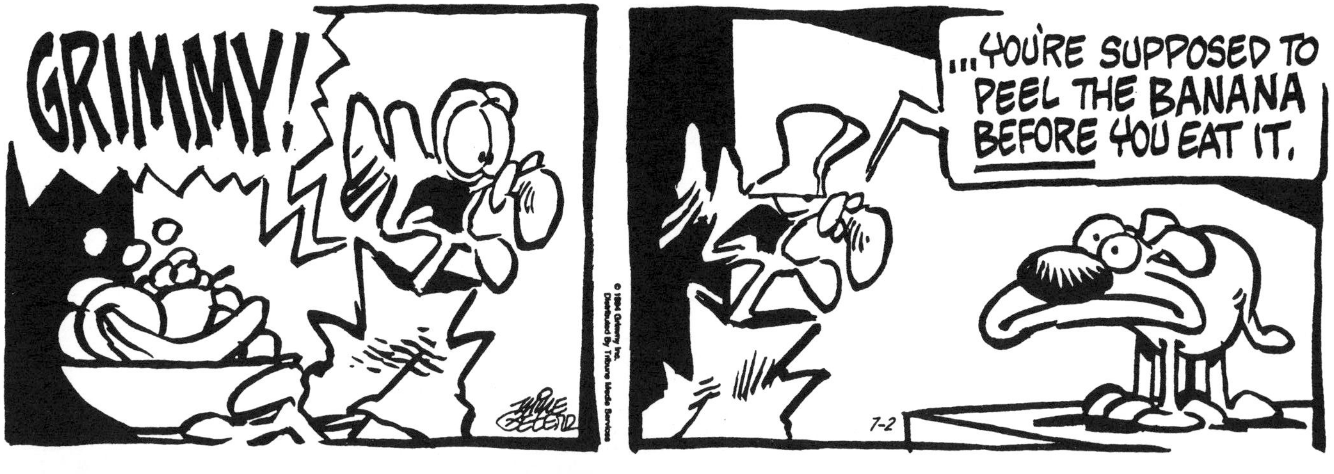
GRIMMY!
© 1994 Grimmy Inc. Distributed By Tribune Media Services
...YOU'RE SUPPOSED TO PEEL THE BANANA BEFORE YOU EAT IT.
7-2

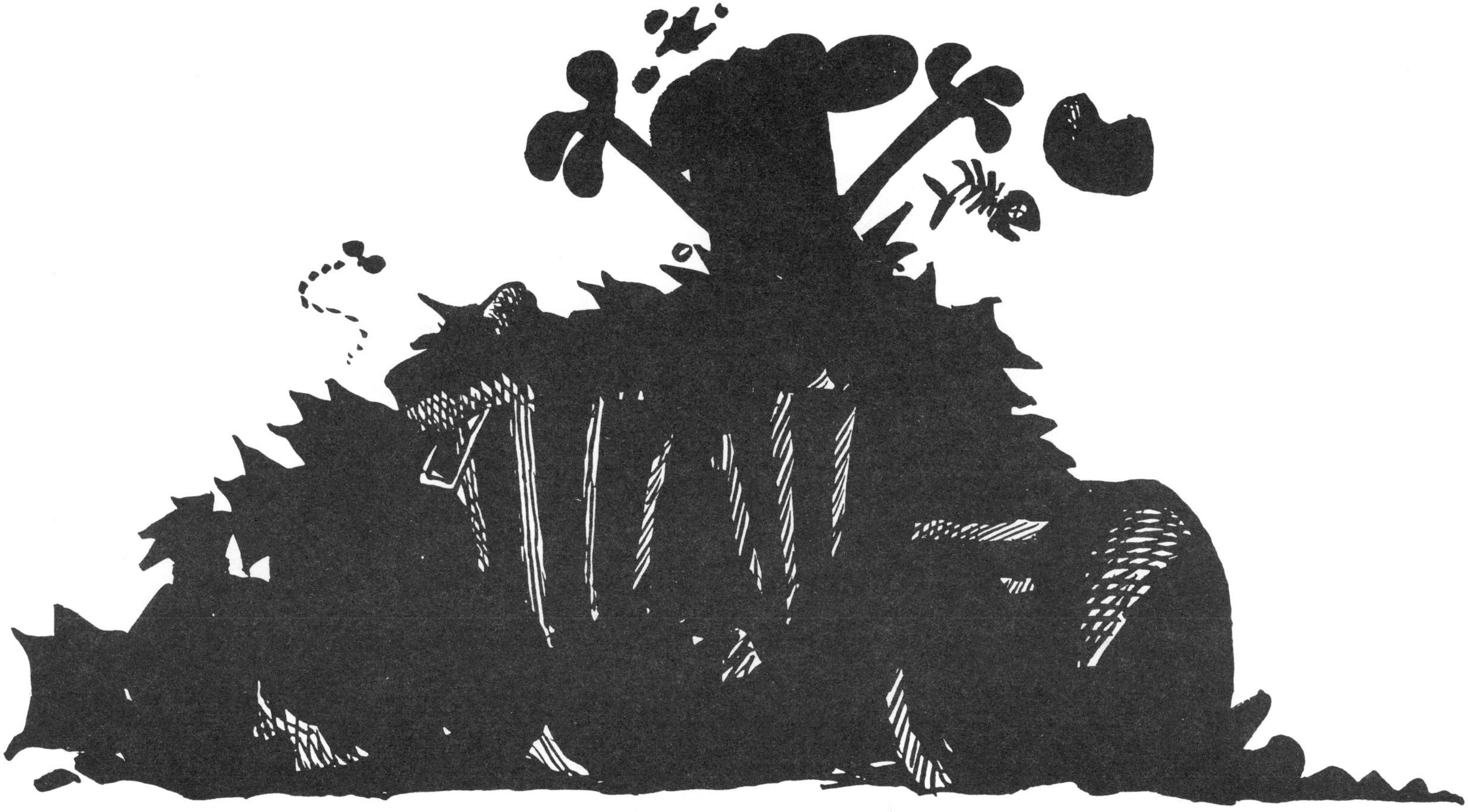

WHERE ARE THE GOODS?

MANY OF OUR READERS ASK HOW THEY CAN BUY GRIMMY MERCHANDISE.

HERE IS A LIST OF LICENSEES IN THE UNITED STATES THAT CARRY GREAT STUFF! GIVE THEM A CALL FOR YOUR LOCAL DISTRIBUTOR.

GRIMMY MERCHANDISE!!!

Antioch Publishing
888 Dayton St.
Yellow Springs, OH 45387

PH 513/767-7379
Bookmarks, Wallet Cards,
"Largely Literary" products:
T-Shirts, Mugs, Journals, Pens,
Notepads, Bookplates, Bookmarks

C.T.I.
22160 North Pepper Rd.
Barrington, IL 60010

PH 800/284-5605
Balloons, Coffee Mugs

Coastal Concepts
1200 Avenida Chelsea
Vista, CA 92083

PH 800/448-7844
T-Shirts

Gibson Greetings
2100 Section Rd.
Cincinnati, OH 45237

PH 800/345-6521
Greeting Cards, Party
Papers, Gift Wrap etc...

Linda Jones Enterprises
17771 Mitchell
Irvine, CA 92614

PH 714/660-7791
Cels

Second Nature Software
1325 Officers' Row
Vancouver, WA 98661

PH 360/737-4170
Screen Saver Program